Over The Next Hill

Over The Next Hill

An Ethnography of RVing Seniors in North America

SECOND EDITION

Dorothy Ayers Counts

David Reese Counts

broadview press

National Library of Canada Cataloguing in Publication Data

Counts, Dorothy Ayers
   Over the next hill : an ethnography of RVing seniors in North America

2nd ed.
Includes bibliographical references.
ISBN 1-55111-423-2

1. Recreational vehicle living — North America — Sociological aspects.
2. Aged — North America — Social life and customs.
3. Aged — Travel — North America.   I. Counts, David R.   II. Title.

TX1110.C68 2001   796.7'9   C2001-930384-X

Broadview Press Ltd., is an independent,
international publishing house, incorporated in 1985.

NORTH AMERICA	AUSTRALIA
P.O. Box 1243,	St. Clair Press,
Peterborough, Ontario,	P.O. Box 287, Rozelle, NSW 2039
Canada K9J 7H5	Tel: (02) 818-1942
	Fax: (02) 418-1923
3576 California Road,	
Orchard Park, NY	UNITED KINGDOM
USA 14127	Thomas Lyster Ltd
	Unit 9, Ormskirk Industrial Park
Tel: (705) 743-8990	Old Boundary Way, Burscough Road
Fax: (705) 743-8353	Ormskirk, Lancashire L39 2YW
	Tel: (01695) 575112
customerservice@broadviewpress.com	Fax: (01695) 570120
www.broadviewpress.com	books@tlyster.co.uk

Broadview Press gratefully acknowledges the financial support of the Ministry of Canadian Heritage through the Book Publishing Industry Development Program.

Cover and interior pages designed by
Zack Taylor   www.zacktaylor.com

PRINTED IN CANADA

To all our RVing friends

In memory of Kynon (1987-1994)
And to Goblin and Perdita
Friends who helped

Contents

Preface and Acknowledgements

We began the research embodied in this book out of pure curiosity and without a clue as to where it would lead. It has led us down a long road and over a great many hills. Along the way we have had the support of our universities, many colleagues, and countless generous and helpful RVers. There are far too many to list here, but some deserve special mention.

Many people did far more than merely talk with us or complete a questionnaire: they taught us what serious RVing is. Among those particularly helpful were Ron Allan and Grace Whitman, Joe and Jan Andrews, Phil and Doris Bedard, Phil and Mickey Burch, Janet Carter who generously shared insights with us, Dan and Adele Clifton, Judi and Norm Douglas, Irene and George English, Ralph and Marilyn Garneau, Karen Gault whose marvellous photograph of an eagle in flight epitomises the freedom RVers celebrate, Blanche Gollaher, Sylvia and John Golby, Jessie and Ralph Hartley, D.J. Jackson, Pat and Newell Kring, Marilyn and Bob Railey, Bob and Bessie Lider, John and Betty Mackesy, Gloria and Harold Michelson, Dell and Mary Roach, Lindsay Shafer, Ruth Stamper, and Kay Wenninger. George and Joan Murray and Vera and Doug Clark went beyond helping: they also became special friends. We owe particular thanks to Vera for giving us her copy of Betty Friedan's *The Fountain of Age*. Ideas from her book helped us to find the shape of this one.

To all of these and the many others not named here we offer what is said to be an Irish blessing: *May the road rise up to meet them and the wind be always at their backs.*

We also owe thanks to the following people:

Andrew Lyons, executive editor of *Anthropologica* granted permission for us to quote from our article "They're My Family Now" (*Anthropologica* 34(2):153-182). Sections from it appear throughout the book and make up a sizeable portion of Chapter Eight, which has the same name.

Amanda Valpy, librarian at the *Globe and Mail*, not only helped us to locate materials on the early history of Canadian trailering, she provided us with microfiche copies of much material published in the paper during the 1930s and 1940s.

Ron Lambert, chair of the Department of Sociology, University of Waterloo, read our manuscript and made helpful suggestions. Margaret Rodman and Matthew Cooper's book, *New Neigbours* was a model for us. Margaret's comments on our manuscript were also most helpful.

Richard Brymer, sociologist at McMaster, did his best to help us design a questionnaire that would generate useful information. Richard, now deceased, was responsible for any statistical merit our quantitative research might have.

Rebecca Counts suggested that because seniors are often said to be "over the hill" while RVers want to know what's over the next hill, *Over the Next Hill* would be the ideal name for this book.

Rebecca Counts and Tim Keenan were tireless in their effort to search and destroy stuffy academic jargon. For example, for those readers who care, the Gabra are *really* transhumant rather than nomadic. It is a significant difference, but not one that will be of interest to most of our readers. Rebecca and Tim were also our representatives from the grammatical correctness police. Any poor usage and incomprehensible jargon in this book survives in spite of their best efforts. Thank you, Tim and Rebecca.

Sherry Lepage read an early draft of the first chapters and suggested ways to make the book more accessible to non-academics, including the use of sidebars. Our thanks to her.

We are grateful to Heather MacAndrew and David Springbett of Asterisk Productions for their interest in our research. They put us into contact with Sherry Lepage, and they enabled us to participate in making a film that brings to life some of the people and the ideas in this book. In the fall of 1996 their crew filmed Roundup at two Escapees parks, Rainbow's End in Livingston, Texas and the Ranch in Lakewood, New Mexico. The result was a 26-minute documentary film, *On the Road*, one in the series *Ways We Live: Exploring Community*. The film is available free to college and university professors who order 50 or more copies of this book for their classes. To view or order the film, please contact Bullfrog Films at one of the following addresses:

P.O. Box 149 Oley, PA 19547
Phone (800) 543 3764 or (610) 779 8226
Fax (610) 370-1978
Email: *bullfrog@igc.org*
Website *www.bullfrogfilms.com*.

Thank you, Heather and David, for a new experience that was a lot of fun.

Permission to quote from and cite from Kristin Goff's "Snowbirds put on residency alert" published in *The Spectator* on April 14, 1994 was granted by *The Ottawa Citizen* where the story originated on April 14, 1992 under the title "Time out: Ontario 'Snowbirds' Fly Afoul of OHIP's Tougher Residency Rules."

Permission to cite and quote from the articles, "The Woman Motorist" (June 1930) and "Gypsying with a Caravan" (July 1930) was given courtesy *Chatelaine* magazine, copyright Rogers Publishing Ltd.

Permission to cite and quote from *The New Yorker Magazine* article, "Popular Chronicles: We Just Up and Left" (June 12, 1995), was given courtesy of the author, Susan Orlean.

Permission to quote the words from the song "Happy Trails," words and music by Dale Evans, Copyright 1951 and 1952 by Paramount-Roy Rogers Music Company, Inc. was given courtesy of Paramount-Roy Rogers Music Company, Inc. and Mr. Sidney Herman of Famous Music Corporation, Los Angeles, CA.

The RVIA graciously gave us permission to use "RV Categories." Bill Baker, the organization's Media Relations Manager, also updated our definition of RVs.

Material from *Galloping Bungalows: The Rise and Demise of the American House Trailer* by David A. Thornburg, copyright 1991 by David A. Thornburg (Hamden, Conn: Archon Books/The Shoe String Press, Inc.), is reprinted by permission.

Permission to cite and quote from *Wheel Estate: The Rise and Decline of Mobile Homes* by Allan D. Walls, published in 1991 by Oxford University Press, was granted by Oxford University Press, New York, NY.

The Good Sam Club granted us permission to reproduce their logo, the Good Samaritan.

The following articles were reprinted from *Trailer Life* magazine, with permission. TL Enterprises Inc., 2575 Visa Del Mar Drive, Ventura, CA 93001:

Courtney, Myrna. 1991. Great Escape Artists. *Trailer Life* 51 (6):76,78-79. Reprinted from the June 1991 issue of *Trailer Life* magazine.
Farris, Ken. 1995. A 'Cool' Custom Battery Box. *Trailer Life* 55(5):91-94. Reprinted from the May 1995 issue of *Trailer Life* magazine.

Lamarche, Robert, and Jacques Langlois. 1987. Earning Money. *Trailer Life* 47:60-61:144-154. Reprinted from the May 1995 issue of *Trailer Life* magazine.

Lusk, Norman M. 1991. Letter to Mail Box. *Trailer Life* 51 (6):19. Reprinted from the June 1991 issue of *Trailer Life* magazine.

Powell, Arden Giampaolo. 1993. Getting Started. *Trailer Life* 53(7):61-66. Reprinted from the July 1993 issue of *Trailer Life* magazine.

Trailer Life. 1988. The View From the Driver's Seat. *Trailer Life* 48(11):7, 165, 169. Reprinted from the November 1988 issue of *Trailer Life* magazine.

Trailer Life. 1991. Special Section. *Trailer Life* 51(7):27-71. Reprinted from the July 1991 issue of *Trailer Life* magazine.

Van Note, Robert. 1990. Letter to Mail Box: Whippersnappers' Complaint. *Trailer Life* 50(11):144. Reprinted from the November 1990 issue of *Trailer Life* magazine.

Ronald H. Epstein, Associate Publisher of *Highways* (The Good Sam Club, 2575 Vista Del Mar Drive, Ventura, CA 93001) graciously granted us permission to reproduce the Good Sam logo and to quote from and cite the following articles appearing in their magazine:

Anderson, William C. 1991. More Fun Than Plucking Ducks. *Highways* 25(10):32, 73, 77, 81.

Edwards, Beverly. 1991. It Was a Very Good Year. *Highways* 25 (4):14, 52-55.

Joens, Ray D. 1991. Good Samaritan Decal. *Highways* 25(4):4 (originally published June 1966 in *Trail-R-News*)

Highways. 1991. Mr. Good Sam: A Conversation With Art Rouse. *Highways* 25(4):18, 55+.

Phillips, Ray. 1992. Letter to Good Sam Grapevine. *Highways* 26(3):8.

Sullaway, John, ed. 1992. Newsline: Study Debunks Senior Driving Myth. *Highways* 26(10):16.

McMaster University's Arts Research Board awarded David Counts a grant of $5000 to do the pilot project in 1990. In 1993 Dorothy Counts received a grant of $5000 from the University of Waterloo small grants programme. David Counts received a similar award from the Arts Research Board of McMaster University. Funds for both of these programmes are provided by the Social Science and Humanities Research Council of Canada. Both of us acknowledge with gratitude the receipt of these awards.

Finally, we must acknowledge an enormous debt to Kay and Joe Peterson. They most generously allowed us to use the Escapees club logo and also granted us blanket permission to quote from letters, editorials, and articles published in the Escapees club magazine. Also, they welcomed us to their club in 1992 (though we didn't even own an RV then), smoothed our road, and gave generously of their time. This book would be very different without their help. We can think of no one with whom we had rather be locked in an office.

Introduction

We have all seen them: a grey-haired couple in a motor home or pulling a trailer with their pickup truck. We see them headed south in November, about the time when the furnace starts to come on at night. Their return, like the robins', is one of the sure signs of spring. Some of us have made uncomplimentary comments about their driving skills. "Come on, Grandpa. Drive it or park it!" They aren't in a hurry, even if we are. They just amble along, taking their time. Like they have all day. Or all week. And they can be almost impossible to pass, especially on a mountain road or a busy highway.

Almost all of us know some of them. Maybe they are our grandparents or parents, or crazy Uncle Jake and Aunt Em, or our mother's cousin Jane whose husband died two years ago. They just disappear for months at a time to go "on the road." What most of us do not know, and what we did not know before we began this study, is that there are literally millions of them. Nobody knows how many because there is no way to count them, but millions (two or three million seems to be a conservative estimate) do not just leave home to wander a few months a year. These folks *live* in those motor homes or trailers. They have no other home. Even if, as Canadians, they have a fictive permanent residence in order to keep their provincial health care, their rigs are their *real* homes. These are the folks with bumper stickers: *HOME IS WHERE I PARK IT*. You may have seen them.

It is remarkable, really, when you think about it. While young people have been spending their energy in sedentary pursuits, buying homes in the suburbs, working in factories and offices, and raising kids, a generation of elders have become nomads. They do not spend their days sitting on their porches in their rocking chairs or baking cookies in hope their grandchildren will drop by. Instead they are out roaming the blue highways, sleeping in truck stops, parking in the desert for months at a time. These old folks are not acting like old folks used to! What is going on here? What are these seniors telling us about the concept of aging in North America?

The notion of aging is changing. People are retiring earlier with pensions and an expectation they can live another twenty or thirty years in reasonably good health. Some are even retiring early *without* pensions thinking to keep their health. They spent their youth paying mortgages, raising kids and going to work and now those days are behind them. Not only do they *not* work — many have been told they *cannot* work any longer. What do they do with themselves for the last third of their lives? There are alternatives to the rocking chair in front of the TV set. They can sign up for Elderhostel programs. They can do volunteer work, or turn hobbies for which they never had much time into avocations or even part-time jobs. Or they can travel. If they are wealthy they can buy a yacht or take an around-the-world cruise. If they are wealthy, or even if they are not, they can buy an RV and set off to explore North America. And, as RVers, they can still do volunteer work, sign up for Elderhostel programs, develop avocations, and hold part-time jobs. They can even travel by RV in other parts of the world.[1]

Twenty or thirty years ago there were probably only a few of them, comparatively speaking. Some of them felt alone out there, without a network of like-minded souls with whom they could share experiences and brainstorm solutions to problems. That is one of the reasons Kay and Joe Peterson started Escapees, a club for serious and full-time RVers, in the 1970s. Now there are so many they make up a subculture. They have their own system of values, their own social networks, their own symbols and metaphors to explain who they are to themselves and to others. They have ways of identifying each other and ideas about how they should behave toward one another. They even have their own jargon — words and phrases exclusive to RVers or, even more specialized, to Escapees. So, we have included a glossary of terms commonly used by RVers and Skips[2] — members of Escapees — but probably not familiar to outsiders.

These elderly nomads, these RVers — especially those who are full-timers or serious enough about it to spend months each year on the road — are the focus of this book. It is an ethnographic account of them and their lives based on three stints of participant observation field work with them.

One thing we try to do in this book is to allow RVers to speak with their own voices. Much of the text that follows consists of quotes from RVers. We plead guilty, however, to the charge that we "do not exactly allow [our] informants to speak for themselves."[3] Throughout the volume we interpret their words for readers, suggesting they pay special attention to the way RVers use words like *family, home, gypsy.* And we draw conclusions using concepts, terms, and phrases they would probably never use to describe themselves or what they think and do: "zen affluence," "cognitive structure," "ritual greetings," "metaphors are reference points for identity." We plead guilty, but we do not apologize. Our interpretation is an essential part of the process of analysis. As Giltrow suggests, anthropologists make everyday things unfamiliar in order to emphasize their uniqueness and to turn them into appropriate subjects for study and critical appreciation. We hope that, in spite of the analytic process, the zest, excitement, frustrations, and good humor of RVers and their way of life remains.[4]

We were heartened by the reaction of RVers to the first edition of this book. Many of them told us that they recognized themselves in its pages and bought copies for members of their families, "so they'll know we aren't nuts." We also hope that our non-RVing readers finish this book with an understanding of why these seniors choose to live a life on wheels and thinking they would probably like most of the people in it — whether or not they ever think of trying the life for themselves. If they do, and if the RVers who helped and taught us continue to read it and recognize themselves and their way of life — both laughter and warts — then we will have been successful.

The nine chapters of this ethnography cover three broad topics. The first two chapters are about method and theory. Chapters Three, Four, and Five place RVing in context, while the final four chapters examine how RVing contributes to successful retirement.

Chapter One, "Lurking in the Laundromat," is about research method. In addition to explaining how we became interested in RVers and describing how we collected our data, we also discuss the pros and cons of using questionnaires in an anthropological study. Although their use is fraught with problems, if the conditions are right formal questionnaires can correct wrong impressions and provide guidance for effective follow-up interviews.

In Chapter Two, "Aging, Retirement, and RVing," we look at some of the literature describing post-retirement life and old age as a time of loss and dependence, a catalogue of insoluble problems and misery. This litany of despair gives way to a discussion of more upbeat findings that suggest all is not lost. Elderly people who keep their minds and bodies occupied, who have control of their lives, and who have a supportive network of friends and family can and do remain vital and independent until shortly before the inevitable decline into death. RVers say their lifestyle provides them with these. It gives them something challenging to look forward to, control of their lives, and people to care about. There are alternatives to the rocking chair, and one of them is the captain's chair in an RV.

Chapters Three, Four, and Five set the context for our study. In Chapter Three, "From Auto Camper to Escapees," we trace the historical roots of recreational vehicles and their use starting early in this century in North

America. Unfair though it may have been, the use of trailers during the Great Depression stigmatized both the vehicles and their users in ways that persist today in the pejorative terms "trailer trash" and "trailer park." Chapter Four, "Gypsies and Pioneers: Images of RVers," contrasts the stereotypes outsiders have of RVers with the way they see themselves and analyzes how both RVer and outsider use metaphors to categorize RVers and justify behavior toward them. Chapter Five, "If They Aren't Us, Who Are They?," investigates the kinds of people who become RVers and concludes that, indeed, they are us.

Non-RVers frequently ask "What do they [RVers] do all day?" Chapter Six seeks to answer that question by looking at their activities: the things RVers do on the road and when they are parked, whether on the desert or in an established campground.

RVers say they have interesting and challenging things to do: activities that promote the mental acuity and physical vitality necessary for successful retirement. Chapter Seven, "Home is Where I Park It," examines the meaning of home to people whose homes are not linked to any particular place, and the ways in which they turn their homes on wheels into extensions of their identities.

The RVing slogans, "Home is where I park it!" and "If I don't like it here, all I have to do is turn the key!" express their freedom and independence and their determination to have control over their lives. It is the quest for freedom and independence that lures elderly people into RVing life on the road, but, paradoxically, it is the communities they find and build there that keep them traveling for years. The communities populated by RVers, shifting and transient though they appear, provide their members with deep and lasting friendships and support when it is needed. Their communities permit them to establish the relationships they need to cope with the problems of being elderly and mobile.

Many North Americans believe that social change has resulted in the destruction of community. This concern is echoed by scholars who argue that, although Americans value mobility and privacy, these values deny us the opportunity to know each other well in casual, informal relationships. Our high regard for freedom and independence has robbed us of a sense of community, they tell us. If these scholars are right, RVers, who choose their lifestyle partially *for* its freedom, ought to be isolated, lonely people who have difficulty in establishing networks to help them cope with crises. This is not the case. Instead RVers have fashioned communities that give them the sense of belonging and mutual interdependence that many North Americans say is missing from modern life. They do this while building their lives on mobility and independence, values they equate with freedom. Throughout this book we examine how an apparently rootless life can give rise to communities of like-minded, caring friends. Although it might seem that a population of nomads would be loners, the friends they make and the communities they create become extremely important to them. Whether they are actively on the road or spending more time at a home base, RVers emphasize the sense of community their life style provides. In Chapter Eight, "They're My Family Now," we focus on how RVers create and maintain these communities and on a key value of the RV subculture — reciprocity — that is their foundation.

"Hanging Up the Keys," examines the options available to RVers who — because of failing health, disability or the death of a partner — are no longer able to travel. We focus on those alternatives that permit retired RVers to continue to share community with nomadic RVers and to participate in the RVing way of life.

Chapter endnotes are informative. We have placed there lists of references, information about the sources of some of our facts, statistical data supporting our assertions, and comments that would break the narrative flow of the chapters.

The appendices provide supplementary information for those who want to know more about a topic than we discuss in the chapter texts. Appendix One, "RV Living Survey," is the text of the questionnaire we used in our 1993-94 research and a breakdown of the answers to our questions. In Appendix Two, "Research Method," we discuss the strengths and weakness of questionnaire-based research in general and of our research in particular. Appendix Three, "Canadian Federal and Provincial Rules. . ." is of particular interest to Canadian RVers who wish to know provincial residence rules and how long they can be out of their home province in any twelve-month period without losing their provincial health care insurance. Appendix Four, "Glossary" defines some of the terms used by RVers that may be unfamiliar to non-RVers or that are used in an unusual way. Appendix Five, "What Now?," is new to this edition. It provides information and resources that may be helpful to readers who want to try serious or full-time RVing.

Notes

1. Those interested can receive a catalogue of Elderhostel programs and classes where there are facilities for RVers by writing:

> Elderhostel
> 75 Federal Street
> Boston, MA 02110-1941 USA
> Telephone 617-426-8056.

For an informative article about Elderhostel programs see Reed 1996.

The Escapees RV Club has an alliance between the club and the International Caravanning Association (ICA). The ICA provides information about people throughout the world who are willing to host RVers for a night or two and/or who have a spot where members may park an RV for a short time. See Peterson, J. 1995:56. The Escapees Club's *Parking Directory and Organizer* also has four pages of names and addresses of members in other countries who are willing to provide free parking and/or advice about RVing in their country to other club members (Escapees, Inc. 1994b:122-125).

2. The Escapees RV Club has adopted the Letters SKP as its acronym. SKP stands for a variety of claims, values, and goals espoused by the club's members: "Sharing, Karing People"; "Special Kind of People," *etc.* In everyday use among the members of the club, the acronym itself has been condensed to "Skip." To be a "real Skip" one should embrace the values and traditions of the organization. We discuss these more fully in later chapters.

3. The critique, including the quoted charge that we do not exactly allow our informants to speak for themselves, is from Giltrow 1995:50.

4. Unless we say otherwise, we have changed names and disguised the identities of the people who talked with us and filled out our questionnaires in order to preserve their privacy. We correctly identify only people who have given us permission to do so or whose words are a matter of public record.

Chapter One

Lurking in the Laundromat: Doing Research With RVers

"Why would you want to do a thing like that?"   "It sounds like a version of Hell to me!"
"When you finish this project, Counts, let's apply for a grant to study Club Med."
(Colleagues' reactions to our proposed RV research)

Getting Started

We are by inclination *field* anthropologists. Experiencing another culture directly, and coming to know it and the people of that culture well enough to explain it to others, has been heady stuff for us. From our first research in Papua New Guinea in the mid-1960s, our five periods of fieldwork there have been the highlights of our careers. We eagerly looked forward to each research trip.

Our colleagues and friends accepted our trips to the field in Papua New Guinea as serious research. After all, one had to be a "real" scholar (or crazy) to go for a year to a place far from any roads or airstrips. Malaria was endemic there, the monsoon rains awful and, lacking electricity, you could not even have a cold beer! In contrast, their reactions in 1990 to our proposed RV research ranged from "Ugh! Why would you want to do that?" to lightly veiled (and sometimes explicit) suggestions that we were not doing research at all. We had, some of them thought, fashioned a clever scam to spend part of a Canadian winter in warm places. Although our colleagues' reaction to our project surprised us, we had our own doubts. Could we tolerate spending months in a cramped RV associating with people who thought they were camping? We realize now that we and our colleagues were affected by some of the negative images plaguing RVers. We discuss these images and their sources in Chapters Three and Four.

Our interest in doing research on RVing as a retirement alternative grew out of our earlier cross-cultural research on aging and death in the South

Pacific. Our study in Papua New Guinea examined the way in which the people of Kaliai, West New Britain understood the processes of aging and dying. We were especially interested in the strategies elderly Kaliai used to maintain their place in society as they grew older. Elderly Kaliai struggled to be independent, to meet their own daily needs, and to play an important role in social events for as long as possible. Those who achieved these goals were respected and had authority. People ignored old people who were dependent and did not participate in the complicated economic exchanges and ceremonial life that enrich Kaliai culture. In some cases, such people were socially dead — they no longer mattered to the living. Retirement was not an option for an active Kaliai senior, and it was not a desirable alternative for anyone. In twenty-five years of research, we knew only a few healthy elderly people who chose to withdraw from active life and sit by their fires while others provided them with wood, water and food. They were invariably the subject of contemptuous gossip by their peers whose attitude (toward both physical strength and social influence) was "use it or lose it." It was against this background that we met our first full-time RVers.[1]

We have been avid campers for over thirty years. Although we briefly owned a "pop-up" tent trailer, most of our camping has been primitive tent camping and backpacking. For decades, the only thing we knew about RVers was that we were annoyed when a behemoth pulled in near us in a quiet campground and broke the stillness with its generator. Our favorite story about RVers was of a little girl who left her parents' shiny Airstream trailer with its television set and colored lanterns to visit our campsite and say wistfully, "I wish *we* could have a campfire."

In 1978 we first became aware of the possibility that large numbers of North American seniors might give up their homes, families, and communities to become rootless nomads living in their RVs. That summer eight of us went on a two-month camping trip in the US southwest. We visited several National Parks there, with an elderly couple in a motor home following us from one park to another. They would greet us and inquire where we intended to go next. They would be there when we arrived, find a campsite near ours, set up their chairs, and watch as we, with our tents, sleeping bags, and packs, spilled out of our two short-wheel-based Land Rovers and set up camp. Watching us was almost as much fun as watching a circus act, they said. They were full-time RVers. They actually *lived* in that motor home. They amazed us almost as much as we entertained them.

Our second meeting with serious RVers occurred in 1982. We had spent eight months of a year's research leave living in Victoria, BC where we worked on a book on aging in the South Pacific. On June 1 we started home to Ontario, camping as we went. Canadian schools are still in session in early June, and so the forest campgrounds were nearly deserted. The other occupants were mostly older people, friendly retired folks. Because the campgrounds were almost empty, we struck up an acquaintance with several of them as we shared a pot of coffee or an evening campfire. Some of them explained that they had sold their homes and were living as nomads, traveling around the continent in their RVs. They said that not only were they having the time of their lives, but, furthermore, there were thousands of others like them out there on the road. Bemused, we began to wonder if these people were right. Were there really thousands of them, or had we just run into a few eccentrics? We wondered why people would choose to retire in this way. Wouldn't they miss their families and the friends and communities where they had spent their working lives? How would they solve the problems facing all elderly people — the loss of partners and friends, declining health and physical agility? Wouldn't these difficulties be complicated by the challenges of a nomadic life style? How would they stay in touch with family (if they did)? Wouldn't they get lonely and bored? How would they receive mail, pay bills, get money? How would they renew their driver's licenses and register to vote? How, being among strangers, would they find a competent and honest mechanic or physician when either they or their vehicle had something go wrong? The question of why people would choose this as a retirement alternative, and how they created an interesting life for themselves in the process, might be an interesting research project someday, we thought. We labelled a file "Airstream Nomads," dropped in some newspaper clippings and a sheet of paper containing those questions, and put it in our filing cabinet under "possible research projects." Then we returned to our New Guinea research.

In 1990, twelve years after our first chance meeting with full-timers, we each had six months research leave. Because of the unstable situation in Papua New Guinea, we were uncomfortable about returning there. For the first time since 1966 we were without a compelling research plan or a field site. So we dug out our "nomads" file and began a literature search to find out what other academics — anthropologists, gerontologists, sociologists — had written about elderly RVers. We were surprised to find only brief mentions of RVing as a retirement alternative and to discover that little research had been done on RVers as a group. The notable exception was a doctoral dissertation done in 1941 by the sociologist Donald Cowgill. Cowgill based his research on a combination of questionnaires and participant observation. The other studies were primarily survey research. Anthropological-type research on modern RV retirement seemed possible.

It might be worthwhile to investigate further to see if there were enough people out there to study.[2]

We applied for and received a small grant for a pilot project. When we began, we had little but questions. We had no demographic profile. We were not even sure where to *find* RVers, although we knew there were many retired people in the southern mainland of British Columbia. We went to Vancouver and arranged to rent an old trailer for two and a half months. Then we pulled it to a nearby KOA park and started knocking on doors to find out where people went and when they left. The typical response was, "Well, when it starts to rain and the furnace comes on at night, it's time to head south."

As in 1966 when we first went to Papua New Guinea, we had a field research project, but we had no idea where it was going to lead us. We were lacking in technical know-how: poling a dugout canoe and backing a trailer into a narrow space both require a lot of skill. In both situations, the only way to learn is to do it. When it started raining, we headed for "the field."

When we began the research, we decided to sample as wide a variety of methods and styles of RVing as possible, and we learned about the options as we went. Although we did not exhaust the possibilities, we did try those people told us about most often, from destination boondocking in truck stops to staying in resort-type parks mostly occupied by snowbirds.

As it turned out, our first field research among senior RVers was more exotic and fascinating than we could have imagined. We lost count of the RV parks lining the highway between the eastern outskirts of Phoenix and Apache Junction. We pulled off the road and stared — speechless — down into the desert at the RVs "as far as the eye could see" when we topped the hill above Quartzsite, Arizona in November. People told us we should go to Slab City in California. We would not believe it, they said. They were right. We wouldn't have. When the residents invited us to participate in wedding festivities within minutes of our arrival at a primitive camping area in the southern California desert, we almost felt as though we were in a New Guinea village. Villagers immediately include newcomers, even strangers, in celebrations there, too. During our 1990 research we conducted 50 interviews with retired RVers, almost half with Canadians.[3] Wherever we were we found RVers to talk to. Because the sight of people traveling in a 25-foot trailer with a 130-pound Great Pyrenees dog is incongruous, when we walked the dog people stopped us to ask, "Where's his hitch?" We interviewed them. Doing the laundry was the occasion for so many interviews that we came to call that chore "lurking in the laundromat." Sometimes, when things were slow, we even washed clean clothes.

Where's his hitch?

We followed an interview guide and asked everyone the same questions, although not necessarily in the same order. We did not tape our conversations, which were informal and were intended to encourage people to talk in a relaxed context about what was important to them. Some of our informants were curious about us and our project and asked us as many questions as we asked them. Others seemed delighted to find an audience interested in RVing and talked with enthusiasm about their experiences. Some of the interviews were brief, lasting only an hour or so. Others lasted for hours over several days. Most people were extremely cooperative and helpful. Many spoke of a need for the general population to know more about RVing, and some hoped wider exposure would dispel a lingering stereotype of RVers as "trailer trash." Others labelled themselves as trailer trash or "trailerites" with irony and a fierce pride as if daring the world to despise them. A number of people said they had thought about writing a book on RVing themselves. Some brought us magazine articles they thought would be helpful to our research. Others introduced us to people whose stories they thought we should hear. And some sought us out to discuss the advantages of RV retirement. One couple even led us to a park 45 miles from where we and they were camped to show us where we could find Canadian boondockers, people who park free or for minimal cost in places where there are no amenities.

At the end of our initial research we had answered many of our early questions, but others arose during analysis of our data. In particular, we became interested in the ways RVers deal with the apparent contradiction between freedom and community, both of which seemed to be ideals basic to the lifestyle. We wondered how dedicated RVers cope with withdrawal from the lifestyle when age or infirmity force them to "hang up their keys." When it was time to return our trailer to Vancouver in December and go back to our jobs, it was difficult to put aside what had become absorbing field research.

Although we could not stay in the field, we could continue to make contact with RVers. We wrote letters to *Trailer Life* and *Motor Home* identifying ourselves and asking those willing to help with our research to write to us. We received a couple of dozen letters in response. Some were brief. Others were pages long. Some people even included us in their list of family and friends who received newsletters describing their adventures. If we were serious about studying full-time RVers, several correspondents suggested, we should join the Escapees club. They sent us applications for membership. We haunted RV trade shows and evaluated "rigs" on the basis of whether they had room for a computer, a printer, and a dog. We were hooked.

In April, 1992 we were invited to appear on a TVOntario network program to discuss our RV research. It, too, produced letters offering information. It also generated a spate of letters from people who thought we were experts on RVing, asking our advice on how to do it! Both our bemusement and our determination to finish the project were unabated. We planned to resume the research during full year research leaves in 1993-94, and to that end we prepared a research grant application for submission to a major granting agency. While the project was well-reviewed and approved by the granting committee, there were no funds for it. In the end, our universities gave us small grants to cover some incidental travel cost. The remainder of the research expense we bore ourselves, using our own tow vehicle and a 30-foot travel trailer we purchased used. While most of the information in the book comes from our research in 1990 and 1993-94, our commitment to the people we met and our interest in the complexities and possibilities of their lifestyle continues to intrigue us. In 1996 we exchanged our travel trailer for a 20-foot fifth-wheel trailer because we could park it in places that were inaccessible to the longer rig.[4] Then we returned to "the field." We spent three months — February through April 1998 — doing additional research with working RVers, both people who work because they need the money to stay on the road and people who work as volunteers. Some of that material is included in this edition.

Doing the Research

For nearly a century anthropologists have been unique in the way they do research, using a method called *participant observation*. Participant observation involves living with the people one is studying and doing what they do, while at the same time trying to maintain objectivity. It is considered bad form for anthropologists to become *too* emotionally involved with the people they study, and especially to "go native" — to become all participant and no observer. A perfect balance is difficult — probably impossible — to achieve, but most of us try hard and succeed fairly well. As a result, anthropologists come to understand why the people they study do the things they do because they participate in, and understand well enough to survive in, the world as the people experience it. One of our New Guinea friends pointed this out to us after we had spent the night trying to find the shell money and pigs needed to complete the ceremony incorporating our first-born child into village society. "For years you've written this down and you knew it intellectually," he said. "Now you *feel* it."

RVers are not New Guinea villagers. There are a lot more RVers than there are residents in a village, they do not stay in one place, and we and they mostly share the same culture. When anthropologists do research in North America they often borrow from the methodological tool kit of sociology and pass out questionnaires to large numbers of people whom they do not know well. They usually also do participant observation. In the next few pages we will briefly discuss our experience doing research with North American RVers. Readers wanting to know more will find a detailed discussion in Appendix 2: Research Method.

In 1990 we were uneasy about using questionnaires. We thought that research heavily dependent on questionnaires distributed in RV parks would miss RVers who avoid private resorts because they prefer to boondock in the desert. We also feared that asking RVers to complete questionnaires would jeopardize our rapport with them. In 1990 we were right. Many RVers were hostile to questionnaires and either refused to answer them or left blank personal questions on topics such as education and income. "I forget," we were told. While this attitude was especially strong among boondockers, we found it among RVers in private parks too. People ignored the questionnaires we deposited in club houses. Some were direct in their reasons for refusing to take one. For instance, one couple commented that they did not mind answering questions in conversation because this made us all equal, and they could ask *us* questions too. They would, however, respond to a formal questionnaire either by throwing it away or by lying. A man, when asked by Dorothy to fill out a questionnaire, inquired "Are you going to ask me if I eat dog food?" In his experience, he said, this was the sort of thing asked by people who use questionnaires.

Part of the problem with questionnaires is that they set up a one-sided relationship. Informants have no part in the construction of the instrument. Their needs, priorities, and interests may not be addressed. There is no mechanism allowing *them* to ask the researcher questions. There is, in short, no provision for the give-and-take between equals so important to RVers. The absence of this balance is, we think, one reason why our attempts in 1990 to use the questionnaire-based research method failed. People who willingly engaged in a reciprocal exchange of information rejected a relationship they saw as one-way and therefore demeaning to them. It does not matter whether any survey researcher ever asked a question about the consumption of dog food. Our informant's protest was not really about dog food, but about his perception that he would be the inferior party in an unequal relationship. The requirement of reciprocity may be particularly strong with RVers because it is so central a value in the sub-culture. We discuss this further in Chapter Eight.

Although we abandoned the use of questionnaires in 1990, we returned to them in 1993. We decided to use them, despite reservations, because we thought they could provide us with data otherwise unavailable to us. Obviously it was impossible for us to interview the people who responded to our appearance on television or to the letters in *Trailer Life* and *Motor Home*. We had to rely on correspondence, and we needed a way to collect the same kind of information from each correspondent. So in 1991 we sent each person who replied to our letter a form to complete and return (one recipient commented it was a cross between a short-answer and a multiple-choice exam). In early versions we included a request for correspondents' suggestions about questions we *should* have asked but didn't. As we analyzed responses, we also revised, omitting some questions, expanding others, changing some to multiple-choice, and adding new ones.

By the time we went back into the field in 1993, this process had produced a lengthy questionnaire that we revised that December when Dr. Richard Brymer, an old friend and a sociologist, visited us in the field. He read our questionnaire and held his head. "You can't do that!" he told us. We revised again, incorporating his many suggestions into the version we used in 1994 and which we have subjected to computer analysis. Any merit an authority on survey research might see in our questionnaire is largely due to Richard's efforts. He is not responsible for the rest of it.

Once we figured out how to use questionnaires we found them useful. One of their advantages was that they allowed us to correct our erroneous ideas about the RVing population. For example, we thought most of the

RVers we talked to had retired at the "normal" age. In fact, only a little over one-third of "our RVers" were past age 65. Many of them were in what gerontologists call the "young-old" category, and most of them had retired early, before the age of 65.

In one case, however, we are inclined to trust what we learned during interviews and informal discussions more than our questionnaire results. Both in 1990 and in 1993-94 we asked people if they were carrying weapons, particularly guns. In 1990, 80 per cent of the Americans we asked said they did have a gun or several guns on board. Some were reluctant to answer the question. Dorothy particularly remembers one woman who hesitated and looked around carefully to see if anyone might overhear her answer (they were alone in a laundromat). Then she whispered that although she was opposed to it, and she hoped they never had to use it, her husband insisted they keep a handgun in their rig. In contrast, in the 1993-94 questionnaire only a little over half the Americans said they carried weapons; 92 per cent of these weapons were guns of some sort.[5] When people are asked a sensitive question they are, we think, more likely to reply truthfully during a face-to-face interview than on a questionnaire. This is particularly true if the interview is a conversation and the question is asked near the end.

Following our correspondents' suggestion that we join the Escapees RV Club, we wrote to the founders of the organization, Joe and Kay Peterson, describing our project and asking permission to work with their members. We received a warm response from Joe, who sent us copies of their books on RVing, welcomed us as Skips (members of Escapees), offered us any assistance they could give, and invited us to come to Rainbow's End Retreat Park, the national headquarters for the club. Partly because of their cooperation, and partly because the organization is run for and by full-time RVers (the group on which we wanted to focus), we concentrated our 1993-1994 research on the Escapees club.

The history of Escapees, including its efforts to build non-commercial parks for their members and the joys and frustrations of park living, exemplify the history of the modern RV movement. Articles and letters in the club's *Newsletter* articulate the values, and problems shared by most full-timers. In this study we draw extensively on material from the *Newsletter*.

Once we began our research we discovered another advantage to working with Escapees. The club provides a friendly atmosphere for both participant observation and survey research. In most Escapees parks, newcomers are introduced and welcomed at "happy hour" held at 4 o'clock each afternoon in the club house. Whenever we arrived at a park and were introduced, we briefly described our project, pointed out the box of questionnaires placed in a conspicuous spot in a main room of the club house, and asked people to share their experiences with us. Skips responded enthusiastically. Not only did they complete our questionnaires, they critiqued them and volunteered to expand their answers to the questions that piqued their interest. Most of the respondents to our 1994 questionnaires were Skips. They were willing to help with our research because of their pride in their life style and their club. Most of those we met wanted to share it with others. Although it was not a questionnaire item, most of the Skips we interviewed said that they had learned about the organization from other Escapees.[6] Some of them heard about Escapees from friends. Others met Skips who could not stop talking about it. When we described our project, people usually responded it was "about time" someone outside the RV community took an interest in their lives. Others hoped our work would get people out of their rocking chairs and into RVs where they would probably live longer and stay out of nursing homes. The enthusiasm of Escapees for our study was reflected in their readiness to complete our questionnaire. Indeed, people came asking us for copies when the supply in the clubhouse dwindled. Escapees cooperated with us so readily in part because we were talking with them about something that interested *them*, not just us as researchers. Also, they did not see us as outsiders poking into their lives. Instead, we were fellow Skips who needed their help. The Escapees ethos of sharing and caring — generalized reciprocity — was strong enough to override the one-way communication problems of questionnaires. Many talked with us about the form and content of the questionnaires and made suggestions for improvement. We often took their advice. Others told us they hoped we would return their help by writing a book that would "tell it like it is" and dispel the negative stereotypes many outsiders have of RVers. Many asked how they could see a copy of the book when it was finished. We sent copies to each of the SKP (Escapees) parks where we did our research.

"Telling it like it is" does not mean restricting our telling exclusively to the good things about RVers and RVing as a way of life. A portrayal of RVing culture without problems and tensions would be a fiction that neither people in mainstream society nor RVers would find either believable or understandable. Rather, the telling involves depicting RVers and RVing from a balanced perspective that enables others to see them as experiencing lives that reasonable, intelligent people — people like themselves — might choose and live with pleasure, most of the time.

While the response to our research was overwhelmingly positive, some RVers expressed reservations about it. One person — a dedicated and extremely knowledgeable desert boondocker — declined to complete a questionnaire and refused an interview. He was worried a favorable book about RVing would attract more people who would invade the isolated places he enjoys and where there are already too many people for his liking. He hoped we would emphasize that the desert is either too hot or too cold, that poisonous insects and reptiles abound, that dirt and sand get into everything, and that it is miles to water or other amenities (all true!). Another man said he had decided not to fill out the questionnaire because he feared that exposure of the lifestyle in general (and of Escapees co-op parks specifically) would alert developers. They, in turn, would influence politicians to tax non-commercial organizations and parks out of existence. Several other people worried that public exposure of Escapees would bring in more members to strain already crowded facilities. They reminded us that some Escapees parks in Arizona are already so full in peak season it is often difficult to get in for more than a night, if at all. Still others were concerned publicity might attract the "wrong kind of people" or people who would join for the "wrong reasons."

Concerns about the "wrong reasons" and the "wrong kind of people" are mostly fears that people will join the club only because SKP parks are inexpensive places to park and the purchase price of lots in them is usually low. Many Skips fear these opportunists will not understand the SKP ethos of sharing and caring. They fear a sizeable influx of such people will destroy the special nature of the organization.[7]

Because we were in face-to-face contact with our potential respondents, we had to counter these doubts about the advisability of our research. We answered some objections by noting that the Petersons think club growth is necessary and argue that the "wrong kind of people" will either become "Special Kind of People" or leave. Other objections to our research were more difficult to answer. In some cases we simply have to recognize that not everyone is delighted we are doing it.

This book draws on the material we collected in 1990, 1993-94, and to a lesser extent 1998. Our different periods of field research contrast in at least two ways. First, in 1990 our research was a sampler. We tried a bit of everything: boondocking, public parks, private parks geared to overnighters, failed membership parks, and snowbird parks where most of the renters spend the entire winter. Nine days was the longest time we spent at any one location. The later work was much more focused, largely as a result of our having affiliated with Escapees. Except for a one-month return visit to a desert boondocking area where we had spent a week in 1990, we conducted almost all our research in 1993-94 and 1998 with Escapees. We met them in their parks, at their rallies, and on the road. The shortest time spent at any park was ten days. The longest time was a month spent at each of two parks.

Line-dancing: can you spot the anthropologist?

In the tradition of anthropological field research, these stays are woefully short. However, they are consistent with the way Escapees and other RVers live. The movement and short stays were characteristic of the subculture we were studying. Without planning, our stays in Escapees parks and at rallies overlapped with one couple four different times, with another on three occasions, and more than once with dozens of other Skips. In 1998 we twice met a couple who were retired Canadian anthropologists. They had read the first edition of this book and, intrigued, decided to try RVing themselves.

Second, in 1990 we were primarily *observing*. Our goal was to find out where to go, who was there, and what they did. In our later research that kind of exploration was behind us, and our emphasis shifted to more active *participation*. As SKPs, we not only had the opportunity to participate but, if we were to be "real" Skips, we *had* to participate. The parks have no paid staff to clean the clubhouses, rest rooms, and showers, to organize the dinners, or to schedule games in the evening. Members do this as volunteers. Not only do they perform the day-to-day maintenance, they *build* the parks using volunteer labor. So, by becoming Skips we became part of a migratory society with activities (both ritual and instrumental) in which we participated. We cleaned floors, served food, prepared potluck dishes, "emceed" social hours, gave slide shows on our field work in Papua New Guinea and seminars on our research on RVing, learned to line-dance, played games, helped our neighbors park their rigs, made friends, gave and received hugs, and in 1998 volunteered at the CARE center.

One of the goals of ethnography is to present an insider's view of the culture being studied. The aim is to share an analytically achieved

David emceeing.

but *accurate* view of what it is like to be a member of the exotic society. When the anthropologist is reporting the truly exotic, as with our research with the Lusi-Kaliai, this goal can never fully be realized. In Papua New Guinea, we learned to speak Tok Pisin and Lusi, we lived in a thatched house and we poled our canoe upriver to wash our clothing on rocks. We even participated in sponsoring ceremonies affiliating two of our children into village kin groups giving them — and us — relatives there. But we can never *become* Lusi. Nor can we ever be sure we speak for them with perfect accuracy. Field anthropologists recognize this paradox. As a result, they try to let the people speak for themselves and to be more forthcoming about their own place in the societies they study.

The necessity to allow people to speak for themselves — to elicit the "native point of view" — is critical, whether the "natives" are Melanesians or North American RVers.[8] The natives in this study are an articulate lot. In the chapters that follow they discuss how they see themselves, who they think they are, their strategies for coping with problems, how they create community, what their lifestyle means to them, and their plans for the future. Their voices come from conversations and interviews, from their comments on questionnaires and in letters to us, and from articles and correspondence published in RVing magazines and newsletters. One concern RVers raise is their frustration in trying to alter an old and increasingly inappropriate public image of "trailerites." Our work offered them the possibility of access to the public in a new way.

RVing and the Popular Imagination

Occasionally anthropological research catches the public imagination. In a recent series of three short articles in the *Anthropology Newsletter*, Maria Lepowsky recounts and analyses her experience in dealing with media interest following publication of her book *Fruit of the Motherland*. Lepowsky's articles emphasize the need for anthropologists to make their research accessible to non-specialists. At the same time she urges caution in dealing with the media, both print and broadcast.[9]

Our experience with this research project has led us, too, to consider both the opportunities presented by and the difficulties inherent in attracting the attention of mass communication media. Following our 1990 pilot project, a small editorial in a university-based gerontology newsletter led to an interview on Ontario public television. It generated newspaper articles, radio interviews, and other television appearances. One newspaper article by a syndicated travel writer appeared in some 200 papers. Following wide distribution of that article, we were approached by representatives of the Recreation Vehicle Industry Association (RVIA). This organization represents RV manufacturers and plans their marketing strategy. They proposed we become media spokespersons for them, touring in our RV and meeting with reporters to discuss our research. RVIA would set up the tour, determine the itinerary, and do the advance publicity to interest reporters in talking to us about the project.

Between 1995 and 1998 we did three tours sponsored by the RVIA. The first one, in May 1995 as "media spokespersons," involved our waiting in campgrounds to be interviewed by media representatives who were notified of our presence by the RVIA. While radio and newspaper interviews were desirable, the RVIA was most interested in our receiving television coverage. This first tour was both worthwhile and a learning experience. It allowed us to reach an audience otherwise unavailable to us. It was fun, and it put us on a steep learning curve. Academics are seldom trained to communicate their findings other than as scholarly publications. The preparation of learned articles and books bears little resemblance to trying to encapsulate research in a 45-second "sound byte" for some network affiliate's six o'clock evening news program. We found, following our first experience with a television news crew where we tried to be carefully academic in explaining what we were doing, that we must prepare several loosely-scripted, short, pithy responses to expected questions. Rumination was not in order. Once we realised we could not follow the professorial adage "When in doubt, mumble!" things went better.

While our 1995 media tour was a novel experience for us, we felt that we were wasting our time and the RVIA's money sitting around campgrounds waiting for media people to come and interview us. We were especially frustrated when those campgrounds were near university towns where we had acquaintances who might welcome our giving a talk on our research to a class or a student organization. We urged the RVIA to combine our professional experience as university lecturers with their media tour. They were persuaded when they saw the media response to our research. Following our delivery of a paper at the American Anthropological Association (AAA) meetings in 1995 in Washington, DC, the local Fox network affiliate filmed their morning news program from a motorhome provided to us by the RVIA. After we gave a paper on RVing at AAA meetings in San Francisco in 1996, our interview with a reporter was featured on the front page of the *San Francisco Chronicle*.[10] In September 1996 the Canadian Broadcasting Company's Sunday Report aired a brief coverage of our research, and in October 1996 the Canadian television network CTV did an eight-minute report on our research entitled "The Winnebago Tribe." In November 1996, acting as consultants for Asterisk Productions, we participated in filming a 26-minute documentary on RVing communities. This documentary, called "On the Road," was part of the series entitled "The Ways We Live," which was aired by Vision TV in April 1997. It is available on video from Bullfrog Films.

As noted above, in 1997 and 1998 we did two further tours which incorporated lectures at universities in the eastern and southern states of the US, sponsored by the RVIA. Our lectures at various places involved meeting with colloquia of faculty and graduate students, addressing classes and seminars, and giving evening lectures open to the general public. In addition, as on the earlier tour, at each stop along the way we were expected to be available for interviews by the local media. The exchange of ideas with colleagues and students was refreshing and challenging for us. Working with the public relations firm of a multi-billion dollar industry also continued to be educational and challenging.

We quickly realized that our perception of the dissemination of information and ideas was at odds with that of the RVIA and their public relations firm, Barton-Gilanelli. Nevertheless, we were still intrigued by the opportunity to do something completely different, and we thought that by doing the tours we could meet our commitment to RVers by publishing our research findings. We use the word "publish" in the broadest sense of making our results widely known so that the general public will better understand the lives of full-timers. That was the information we intended to disseminate. The RVIA and Barton Gilanelli's mandate sets for them a goal in which we have no stake at all. Their job is to make the public want to buy recreational vehicles. To this end the RVIA initially wanted us to address the advantages of RVing for young families, one of the industry's major target markets. We declined: our research did not focus on that population. Their goal of motivating North Americans to purchase RVs meant that they wanted our research and our lectures to receive the widest possible media audience — especially the television audience. On several occasions we were bemused when Barton Gilanelli rejected our suggestion of lectures at highly rated universities with excellent anthropology departments or programs in the study of American culture because the towns where the universities were located did not have television stations that might cover our presence there. A more serious problem, from our perspective, was their efforts to control our words. These efforts took two forms. First, they were literally concerned with the *words* we used. We were not to use the word "small" in connection with RVs, and "cramped" was right out. We should never suggest that RVing might not be for everyone, we were to deflect questions about the gas mileage of large RVs, and there should be no suggestion that the appliances and facilities found in an RV were not exactly like those in a modern home. Second, we disagreed with what they thought our research demonstrated. We do not define "evidence" in the same way as the RVIA and Barton Gilanelli. During our 1998 tour, for example, Barton Gilanelli interpreted our research findings as "showing evidence" that senior RVers "are more vital, and are more physically active and mentally alert" than are seniors who live in stationary homes. We were appalled to find that they sent out press releases making this claim, and for a time the RVIA posted the same information on their website. They appear to define evidence in the popular sense as "that which serves to indicate or suggest" while we consider evidence to have the more scientific meaning: "The data on which a judgment or conclusion may be based, or by which proof of probability may be established."[11] We have not done the longitudinal research required to produce "evidence" to substantiate the industry's claim made for our research, and we know of no other study that does. There are doubtless many ways to enjoy a happy, healthy, and productive retirement. Many of the RVers we interviewed do believe that they are healthier and happier and live longer than do the friends and family they left at home, but their belief does not constitute evidence.

Working with print and broadcast journalists who are looking for topical content is more comfortable for academics than producing "sound bytes" for local TV news shows. The interviews are more relaxed. Also, if journalist and interviewee have the right mix of skills, scholars can communicate their message to audiences who will never read an academic book or paper. Even here, though, there are cautions. Though they may have been provided with advance information about the research and the researchers, sometimes reporters are woefully unprepared. In 1995 a TV crew came to our campground expecting to find hundreds of people at an all-day seminar on RVing for families. They looked at us — two aging professors and their dog — and asked "Where is everybody?" During that same tour, one reporter showed up expecting to interview us about our study of RVs as *vehicles*: he was the auto editor for his paper. Another actually began her interview with the question, "What am I doing here?" Some reporters were sceptical of our association with the RVIA. One — a journalism student who, we suspect, was not cowed by her professors — asked directly whether we were being paid to give academic credibility to the RVIA's marketing strategy. "Are you being paid to tout RVs?" was the way she put it. While we had a straightforward negative answer to her question, it was disconcerting to have to field it.

Finally, one of the dangers noted by nearly everyone who deals with the media arises from the scholar's lack of control over the material that is finally printed or broadcast. Lepowsky calls it "the timeless cry of the media interview subject, 'That's not what I said!'" One article about our research quoted David as referring to RVers as grey-haired hippies and as being the easy riders of the 1990s. An inset box suggested that he thought RVing was a weird way to live. He had said neither thing: fortunately *that* article was not widely syndicated!

When we began this project we were not sure there was anything out there to study, but by the time we had been on the road for a month in 1990 we asked ourselves each morning "What's going to astonish us today?" From then, up to our flirtation with show-biz as RVIA spokespersons, our research with RVers has been an adventure. In part the adventure and our astonishment came from our discovery that a subculture in our own society, one composed primarily of older people, is so exotic.

Doing field work in one's own society entails a different set of problems for an ethnographer than does field research in an exotic place. It is not breaking down the distance that is hard, it is maintaining enough distance to permit analysis. In a piece Dorothy wrote for an Escapees sub-group (Birds of a Feather or BOF) newsletter, she jokingly said that an anthropologist working with Skips was in danger of "going native." It is sometimes hard for us to place ourselves accurately in the society of RVers — to tell the difference between "us" and "them." For example, David spent two years as a member of the Escapees Club's Advisory Council, and both of us are on the organization's Speaker's Bureau. The lines between observation and participation have become blurred during our field research.

Notes

1. See Counts and Counts 1992a for discussion of the concept of social death in Kaliai.

2. References to earlier studies include Born 1976; Cowgill 1941; Guinn 1980; Hartwigsen and Null 1989; Hartwigsen and Null 1990; Hogan 1987; Hoyt 1954. We discovered the reference to Cowgill's work in 1993.

3. Thirty-four of our 50 interviews were with full-timers and 16 were with part-timers; 25 were with Americans, 24 with Canadians and one was with a British couple. Sixteen of the 24 Canadians and 18 of the 25 Americans were full-timers. We were able to ascertain the ages of 81 of our informants; 2 of these (both women married to older men) were in their 40s; 13 were in their 50s; 45 in their 60s; 19 in their 70s, and two in their 80s. Our youngest informant was 46; the oldest 86.

4. And for other reasons. See end note 8, Chapter Four for a discussion of one of our neighbor's concerns about what the presence of our trailer on our lot would do to his property value.

5. Of Americans responding to this question, 51 per cent said they carry weapons. Of these, 6 per cent said they carry a gun (generic); 28 per cent carry guns (plural); 39 per cent carry a hand gun; 13 per cent carry a shotgun; 2 per cent carry a rifle; 4 per cent carry a gun and some other weapon. The remaining 8 per cent of weapons include mace, clubs, and other such as crowbars, ice picks, and a fire extinguisher.

6. In the January / February 1994 Escapees Newsletter, Joe Peterson says "over 93% of our new members still come from referrals" (Peterson, J. 1994:8).

7. These concerns are discussed at length by Gibb and Gibb (1987:31) and Hazzard and Hazzard (1987:22).

8. For a discussion of this point see Marcus and Fischer 1986:25. Readers who are interested in the similarities in doing ethnographic research in Papua New Guinea and among RVers are invited to read Dorothy's paper, "Where Are the Bones in Their Noses?," located in the section of papers on our West New Britain website: *http://arts.uwaterloo.ca/ANTHRO/WNB/WestNewBritain.html*

9. Lepowsky 1994a, 1994b, 1994c, 1995.

10. Petit 1996.

11. Morris 1982:455.

Chapter Two

Aging, Retirement, and RVing

D.J. is a full-time RVer, a long time member of Loners on Wheels (LoWs) as well as the Escapees RV Club. Widowed in her late 40s, she raised five children and made a career in social work. At age 63 she retired and began traveling in a recreational vehicle. Seventeen years later, she is still single, still in her motor home. For 12 of those years she often traveled with Jim, whom she met through LoWs. They never married or shared an RV, but his death a year ago left her more lonely than when she was widowed 30 years ago.

Welcoming visitors, she apologizes for the clutter in her 30-foot motor home. "It's not as clean as I'd like it to be," she says, "but at my age I have to make choices between cleaning this thing and going for the hikes I enjoy — and I have my priorities straight." Just inside the door of D.J.'s home is a pegboard wall hung with her well-used set of tools. Looking at the tools, she chuckles, "I'm the third owner of this motor home and I'm beginning to find out why!" D.J. worries she might soon have to stop RVing because she is beginning to slow down. She has trouble closing her holding tank valves at dump stations. The last time she changed her oil, it took her nearly half a day.

Images of the Elderly

In the past century the United States and Canada have assumed a demographic shape new to human history. A greater proportion of their populations is elderly and living longer in reasonably good health than ever before. Gerontologists estimate that by the second decade of the twenty-first century, 15 per cent of the US population and 22 per cent of Canadians will be 65 years of age or older. Most seniors say they are in good or excellent health, and describe themselves as being happy and satisfied with their jobs, their close personal relationships, and their living accommodations. Only 14 per cent of Canadians over age 75 live in a nursing home or other institution.[1]

The greying of North America has captured the attention of both industry and academia. Recognition of the growing proportion of elders has generated an industry of the old. Academic societies and bureaucratic institutions focus on seniors. Magazines target them as an audience, special interest groups lobby government on their behalf, and businesses identify them as their primary clientele. Most of these institutions, according to one disgruntled senior, are peopled by decision makers who regard older people "first as a tax burden and second as a market."[2]

One organization focussing on seniors as a market is the Recreational Vehicle Industry Association (RVIA). The reason for RVIA's interest is easy to discern. In 1992, 40 per cent of the members of the American Association of Retired Persons (AARP) who responded to a questionnaire were owners of recreational vehicles. RVIA also noted that seniors control vast sums of money and that their ownership of RVs is growing rapidly.[3]

While business and industry woo the growing senior population as consumers, those with an academic interest in the elderly associate them with problems. Some see the increasing number of elderly persons in our society as a problem in itself. Many economists, for instance, worry about the implications of a population pyramid turned on its head. Not only are there more old people, they are living longer! Who, they wonder, will contribute the funds required to pay pensions to, and provide the health care needed by, all those old people? The editor of the journal *Canadian Social Trends*, for instance, notes that the provision of health care, housing, and well-being in general will be a major issue for the future because more elderly people are being supported by a shrinking work force. Others echo the same concern.[4]

Worry about the shape of the population pyramid and the implications for retirement are not just the concern of the "dismal science." The popular press is also sounding the alarm. For instance, in the June 1995 issue of the influential monthly *Saturday Night*, P.S. Taylor forecast the demise of the entire retirement system in modern society. According to Taylor, too many people are retiring early and living too long. Seniors are not only burdening the pension system, he says, they are doing so unfairly because their pensions are paid by the taxes of young working people. This pyramid-like scheme must soon collapse, leaving young workers overtaxed and without hope of their own retirement. The situation, Taylor says, is ripe for tax revolt.[5]

Bureaucrats, economists, and popular writers view the existence of the elderly as a potential problem. Academics often see the elderly as a group whose lives are characterized by *their* problems: isolation, depression, poverty, dislocation, dependence, frailty, senility, failing health, loss, and decline into childishness. University degree programs in gerontology often focus their training on the problems of aging and the "plight" of the aged.

If students gained their understanding of old age only by reading the contents of gerontological journals, they would assume it is a bleak and hopeless time of life. For example, the December 1993 issue of *The Gerontologist* (selected at random), contains 13 articles covering the following topics: one deals with measuring urinary incontinence; six articles consider problems of demented patients, including the institutional management of acute agitated behavior in elderly demented patients, Alzheimer's disease, "sundown syndrome,"[6] and problems in medication of the elderly. Two articles focus on problems in organizations devoted to maintaining social health among the elderly. One discusses "ageist" images in Victorian art. Only two articles portray seniors as healthy (an article on exercise and health in adults aged 50 to 65) or care-giving (an article on grandparents who become surrogate parents for their grandchildren). Furthermore, the "care-*giving*" article concentrates on the obstacles faced by community intervention and social service programs designed to aid the grandparents.

Such a litany of dismal particulars suggests the need for an army of professionals — gerontologists, geriatricians, social workers, health-care workers, psychiatrists — to help the hapless elderly who become their clients.

Bleak stereotypes of the elderly as either incapacitated or regressing into second childhood also dominate the way many non-academic North Americans see them. Although 95 per cent of the aged are neither helpless nor dependent, the stereotype of the old person as sick, helpless, and undesirable persists. It is expressed in epithets such as "crone," "geezer," "crock," "hag," and "old goat." These are malignant and damaging, and suggest old persons have no value. Time and resources spent on them are, therefore, wasted. Other epithets may seem benign and be expressed as denial that a person is actually getting old. Children's literature, contemporary fiction and poetry, films, jokes, and advertising communicate this stereotype. In *The Fountain of Age*, Betty Friedan catalogues many examples from films, advertisements, and other mass communication media representations that reduce elderly people to child-like status. Her examples range from "kiddies' menus" for "kids under 10 and over 65" to Dr. Seuss's *You're Only Old Once!* for "obsolete children."[7] Just after we read Friedan's chapter on "denial and the problem of age," we were appalled to hear a voice on a national Canadian radio program discussing a new course teaching people to identify birds. The discussant extolled the first stages of the program as being ideal for "children of five and seniors."[8]

One source of this pervasive stereotype is the widespread use of technology to maintain life artificially. Use of medical technology to extend life in old age may lead to an ordeal of decline into death, lending credence to the stereotype of old age as a period of infirmity, senility, and worthlessness. The notion that to be old is to deteriorate into dependency contributes in turn to the fear of aging. This fear is so pervasive in our culture that scholars have given it its own name: "gerontophobia."[9] Some of the consequences of gerontophobia are negative stereotyping, rejection, avoidance, and the withdrawal of elderly people from social interaction. Whether rejection causes elderly people to retreat, or their withdrawal results in rejection, the pattern of negative interaction often becomes a downward spiral leading to dependency, loss of control, and debilitation.[10] One of the greatest fears associated with gerontophobia is of loss of mental ability. The idea that old age brings with it a decline into senility and irresponsible behavior is genuinely frightening. It is so horrifying that it is a source of black comedy. Ruth Gordon's senile Mama in the film *Where's Papa?* is a good example. She is both a harmless child as she eats her breakfast of Lucky Charms with Pepsi and an intolerable burden on her frustrated son who has murder on his mind. The good news is that this stereotype is wrong. The brain does not have to decline with old age. In studies of both humans and rats, the brains of aging individuals who are healthy, have supportive social relations, and engage in regular, challenging activity function well and are active until just before death![11]

So, as life expectancy is extended, many people can enjoy good physical and mental health for most of their later years. It is important, therefore, for people to have interesting and rewarding things to do during the decades of their retirement. What are the alternatives for these years, and how do people take advantage of them?

What are the Alternatives?

"My job was my life! It was my identity, my value, my worth. And, most of all, it was something I used to keep so occupied that I never had time to look at myself." (Full-time RVer reflecting on the "rage and self-pity" he felt when he was forced into early retirement.)

Most North American retirees have the potential to be vital, relatively healthy, and independent. They may live meaningful lives for 20 or even 30 years, until they are well into their 70s or 80s. Some, however, may not realize their potential because retirement can bring stress instead of relaxation and pleasure. Retirement may result in a reduced income, an altered daily routine, and a diminished social life including fewer contacts with friends from work. Retirees may feel worthless if their notion of who they are is too closely tied to their jobs. Such people suffer a loss of self-esteem and self-respect and, for those unprepared to cope with these changes, life in retirement can be empty and meaningless. If these changes combine with physical decline or the death of a spouse or friends, the stress level can be devastating. The result is isolation, loneliness, a sense of helplessness, depression, vulnerability to illness, and premature death — including suicide.[12]

Some of what is at issue here is that retirement is a new social form. Few human societies — and those only in the last century — have expected older people to withdraw from productive life. Savishinsky regards this as "the invention of ... a new stage of life" and points out that we quite literally have almost no traditions to guide people through it. Small wonder it is a potentially troublesome stage of life.[13]

There are some curious contradictions in studies of retirement. On the one hand some authorities say the suicide rate among seniors in both the USA and Canada is much higher than it should be. On the other hand, the vast majority of seniors in the same two countries report themselves happy with their lives in retirement. Possibly it is not age that leads to depression, isolation, and suicide, but the stress of *retirement* itself. Or perhaps the *reason* why people retire is critical. McDonald and Wanner conclude retirement is a crisis for *some* people, but not for everyone, depending on the circumstances surrounding it. Relevant circumstances include whether retirement was voluntary or involuntary, the reasons for retirement (such as poor health, recession, and the health or retirement of a spouse), and whether the retiree had control over the circumstances of retirement.[14] The issue of *control* seems to be an especially important one, and one to which we return later in this chapter.

David, who is under the age of 40, said on his questionnaire that he quit his job and became a full-timer following the "Sickness and death of parent after 'saving' to retire for 42 years. Father died, mother sick, no retirement."

Whatever is at issue, the notion that death follows soon after "normal retirement" has become a widely held belief among many retirees. One version is that people who work to normal retirement age live to enjoy their retirement for only a short time. Some RVers said they decided to retire early because they had "seen figures that Company X paid pensions for only a few months." They retired early, "took the money and ran," lest death cheat them if they waited until age 65. Another version is that retirees die or become incapacitated by strokes or heart attacks soon after retirement because their lives are purposeless and boring. RVers told us of friends who had died or had suffered a stroke or some other debilitating medical problem forcing them to enter a nursing home shortly after retirement. They asserted that RV retirement, which they saw as neither boring nor without purpose, had enabled them to escape the fate of their friends.

Although much research portrays retirement as bleak, there are also those that see promise. The decades of retirement need not be tedious, lonely, and dreary; they do not have to be a living death. Some gerontologists even see the elderly as pioneers. Consider, for example, the following comment in a pamphlet commissioned by the Department of the Secretary of the State of Canada: "Contemporary elders in Canada are pioneers of a new but uncertain society; they will shape and define societal roles for those who are elders tomorrow." Other far-sighted experts recognize that retirement does not necessarily result in disengagement from purposeful life and society. They see retirement as a time of potential productivity, and the willingness of seniors to undertake volunteer work a particularly valuable contribution.[15]

This approach suggests that seniors with adequate income and reasonably good health can enjoy successful retirement if they plan a future enabling them to do the following:

1. engage in organized, purposeful, complex behavior;
2. exercise control over their own lives and environment;
3. participate in meaningful social relationships with persons for whom they care and who care for them.

Organized, purposeful, complex behavior

> D.J. has taken care of her own needs for years. On one occasion she drove her motor home for over 1000 miles needing an oil change because she could not find a place that would do it. Consequently, she decided she needed to be more self-sufficient. When her son offered to change her oil for her, she refused. "I can't come back here every time I need to change my oil," she said. He taught her how, and she's been doing it for herself ever since.

"Use it or lose it" applies to both our bodies and our brains. A challenging environment and purposeful activity are necessary for an active mind and a vital and alert old age. In the 1950s the US National Institute of Mental Health conducted a long term study of factors that might contribute to a person's survival to age 81. The researchers reported that "a largely optimistic picture of old age" emerged from their study of men who improved their level of mental performance and reported "an exhilarating new sense of success starting in old age." This study found that a key factor allowing survival into old age was a complex and organized life. When the project began in 1956, some men were more sociable, more active, had a more satisfied outlook, and also had more complex lives than the others. They were the ones who survived until 1967.[16]

In the same vein, Ellen Langer and her associates sought to determine whether physical and mental decline is inevitable in old age. Their alternative hypothesis was that decline might be what people expect of old age and, therefore, under the control of the "willful mind." During their research, they changed the environment of groups of institutionalized elders, requiring them to make decisions, deal with a challenging and cognitively demanding milieu, and otherwise engage in mindful activities. Langer and her associates report a marked improvement in the members of the experimental group relative to comparison groups. These elders "became more alert, more active, happier, and healthier." Their long- and short-term memories, general alertness, and adjustment improved, and fewer of them died within the time frame of the study. Furthermore they found that much of the debility normally associated with old age was subject to improvement if the elderly persons voluntarily engaged in creative mental activities—and the improvements were both physical *and* psychological. The researchers conclude, "We feel there is enough evidence to suggest that the 'inevitable' decay of the aging human body may, in fact, be reversed through psychological intervention." They argue the seemingly natural and irreversible process of decline in old age may occur, or occur sooner, because people see no alternative. These studies strongly suggest that seniors who see alternatives, who find a way to spend retirement in demanding, purposeful activities requiring complex planning may successfully delay decline and improve their quality of life in old age.[17]

There is a *caveat*: another study emphasizes that people should begin before retirement to do the things they plan to do afterwards. Evidence suggests that people seldom develop new leisure patterns after retirement, and few increase the number and frequency of their activities. Examining the evidence for factors contributing to a satisfying retirement, the authors conclude that the cultivation of leisure interests and activities early in life is vital.[18]

In summary, if seniors make new friends, expand their social horizons, and awaken each day with something interesting to do, they may extend their years of vitality and growth.

Exercising control over one's life and environment

D.J. came to Rainbow's End to check out the CARE program. She first decided she was not ready for CARE. She did, however, choose to stay at Rainbow's End in the regular campground for $5.00 a day and pay for the services she needed. At 80, she was short of breath, her energy level was low, and she had trouble closing the holding tank valves when she dumped her sewage. She traveled for a week between dumps, going from the house of one child to another, or to a friend who would help her. But she needed the help. "I resent very much a physical thing that keeps me from doing what I want to do," she said. Realizing her situation, she had a set of directions posted on her wall in case she was found unconscious. She did not want resuscitation because she considered extreme efforts at her age "iffy." She had a lung problem that concerned her, but she planned to stay in east Texas if it did not get worse. If it did worsen, she planned to go to the desert. In November 1994 she decided to enter the CARE program.

If people are to have control over lives with purpose, they must have certain rights. They must be able to control their environment. They must have the right to decide how they spend their time, to choose whom they see, when they see them, and what they do with them. Above all, they must take responsibility for their own actions. This is true for everyone, but it is crucial for elderly people who are particularly at risk of losing control over their lives, especially if aging brings loss of income, decline in physical ability, withdrawal from social interaction, and mental inactivity. Elderly people who retain control are likely to age successfully. Schulz says, "to the extent that aged individuals are able to maintain a predictable and controllable environment, they should experience relatively less physical and psychological deterioration with increasing age."[19]

Elderly people should stay mentally active. Researchers say those who do are happier, healthier, better adjusted, and more intelligent than those who do not. Many people discontinue mental and physical activities they once enjoyed and become passive and reflective, an attitude thought to be appropriate for older people. At least one researcher wonders if such inactivity contributes to the decline of the immune system. Perhaps the pressure on an elder to be reflective, conservative, and wise accelerates aging? He concludes:

Faced with the choice between a reflective attitude ("wisdom") and social acceptance, on the one hand, and an action-oriented attitude and longevity on the other hand, most people might prefer the latter and avoid the costs of wisdom by staying active, innovative, and alive.[20]

Involvement in a network of meaningful social relationships

If my SKP family from the Ranch had not been there to help and comfort me [after the sudden death of her husband], I don't know if I'd have made it through.

They helped me at the scene, carried me to and from Artesia to make arrangements to get Ray home to Rhode Island, searched for his watch for hours, made untold phone calls to both east and west coasts, made plane reservations, purchased a proper outfit for me to wear, and cared for me through the night. There were so many offers to take my rig back to R.I. for me! Finally, they took me over 200 miles to Albuquerque and put me on the plane.

The flag at The Ranch was lowered to half staff and a memorial service was held that evening for Ray.

All of this and much more was done with love and understanding and great care to make it as easy for me as possible by people that I had either known for a very short while or had never met before.[21]

Informal networks of support among family members, friends, and neighbors are crucial for older people who depend on them both for emotional support and for help in maintaining independence. A large body of research shows the loss of such support is harmful to the health of the elderly. Social isolation increases vulnerability to illness and premature death. People with a supportive social network have improved chances for a longer, better life.[22]

A study commissioned by the Canadian Government's National Advisory Council on Aging examined strategies used by seniors to deal with problems making independent living difficult. The study found seniors rely heavily on friends, neighbors, and family members for help. It concluded that the presence of a circle of supportive friends and relatives is important to the elderly in a number of ways: it can improve feelings of worth and competence, help in gaining access to community services, and, in general, prevent problems from arising.[23]

Elderly people prefer to spend their time with friends. Indeed, friendship with peers may be more important in old age than at any other time because the elderly share experiences such as retirement, loss of partners and friends, declining health, and the nearness of death. They also find relationships with people their own age to be more stable than bonds with younger people and, while they inevitably lose friends to death, age is not a barrier to the establishment of new friendships. Some note that people who learned earlier in life to make friends will fare better during old age than those who did not.[24]

When people lose mates and friends, when they have no one to confide in, to share experiences with and to care for, they become depressed. Depression has serious consequences for a person's vitality, sense of well being, and longevity. There is, however, serious disagreement among scholars as to whether elderly people express these symptoms because they are depressed or are depressed (appropriately) because they have these disabilities.[25] One thing is clear: human beings are social animals. In one sense they are bundles of relationships. As the number of ties a person has to others declines, so does the person. Too few relationships can be dangerous for one's health. We do not fare well as isolates.

These studies send a message to people planning their post-working years. Those who spend their retirement doing enjoyable, challenging things, who expand their network of friends, and who have control over and responsibility for their lives live longer and age successfully. The goal is a retirement that expands horizons and affirms life, not one that withdraws from it.

RV Retirement

> We woke up one morning and said "What are we doing here? Our lives are almost over and if we are going to do anything we'd better do it now!" (Response to question, "Why did you start full-timing?")

There are no accurate figures on the number of serious and full-time retired RVers. Nomadic retirees do not form a category for census takers. For one thing, there is no clear answer to the question "What is a full-time RVer?"[26] The narrow definition is someone who has all their possessions in a recreational vehicle. They have no home base, not even a storage shed. However, many RVers who refer to themselves as full-timers do have a home base. It may be a storage shed in an RV park or on a relative's property. It may be a parking place on land belonging to family members. It may be a cottage, a room in a relative's home, or a house on a lot associated with an RV park. Although our definition does not help count them, we define full-timers as those who consider themselves to be *living* in the recreational vehicles they take on the road. We do not focus on vacationers or on "snowbirds" who keep residences in the north and south and travel between them seasonally. While various estimates exist, all we are sure of is that there are hundreds of thousands of serious RVers. There may be millions.

Most serious RVers are retired and many are in their 60s or 70s or even older. Many, like D.J., continue to be nomads well into the later years of their lives. They have discovered that life after retirement need not be a time of decline. Instead it is a time of growth and involvement, a time to grasp opportunities and expand their lives. They say RVing permits them to realize this. This is not a new phenomenon. Thornburg notes trailerists have rejected the old patterns of retirement virtually since the movement began. He says:

> For generations, old age and retirement had meant a contracting of activity, an acceptance of mental and physical decline. When you got too old to plow, you handed the reins to your kids and retired to the rocking chair to exude wisdom and tobacco smoke and await the grim reaper. That's what your parents had done, and their parents before them. That's simply what old people did.
>
> But this new creation, the house trailer, offered the 1930s retiree another alternative: instead of settling back to die, he could set out to see the world — cheaply, and at pretty much his own speed.... Retire to adventure.[27]

Donald Cowgill who, in the late 1930s, conducted the first fieldwork among trailer dwellers, makes a similar observation:

> In one large group of trailerites, namely retired couples, we find the cares of the world largely eliminated and at the same time life is still interesting and dynamic for them. If the trailer at any point justifies its existence, it is in this group of trailer folk. We have in recent years come to realize the necessity for providing economic security for our old folks, but we lag far behind in recognition of the necessity of another value, namely that life shall maintain its interesting and dynamic qualities or in simpler terms that these people shall have something interesting to keep them occupied. The trailer, in at once providing the possibility of travel and comfort at a small expense for these people, supplies that added value.[28]

The people whose lifestyle we describe here challenge the stereotype of old age as a time of decline into senility, poverty, and illness. Their descriptions of their experiences, and their depictions of themselves and their fellow RVers defy the myths about elderly North Americans. They do not think of themselves as suffering the "plight" of the elderly. The stereotype of seniors being lonely, isolated, ill, dependent, and suffering from the trauma of the "empty nest" or meaningless retirement does not apply to them. They see themselves and their peers as adventurous, self-reliant, flexible, friendly, and "gutsy." Many say they have more friends than ever before. At the same time they treasure their self-sufficiency and independence.

One of our correspondents, Tonia Thornson, describes the difference between RVing seniors and those living in a home for the elderly. She left RVing in 1993 at the age of 81 because, she says, of the "bunch of crooks" who repair RVs. She now regrets her decision. In her letters written in 1994 and 1995 she says:

> I was on the road 15 years. When my husband passed away I joined Loners on Wheels and SKPs.... I loved RVing and had many good years. Crossed US 5 times and Canada and Mexico.
>
> I am living in a Senior complex.... Very lively here with tourists, but the seniors are not the same as "traveling seniors." Aches and pains and TV all day!! Very depressing. We used to say people were "playing organ music" when they continually talked bad health, and there was very little of it in LoWs or SKPs. I traveled with crutches and wheel chair for two and a half years and it really didn't slow me down at all. Also oxygen which I never mentioned. People stay young on the road and I wish I was back in my MH.... I have a friend Evelyn Wilson (a Loner) living in Canada. She is about 85 and travels to Alaska and Mexico. Went thru Alaska last year alone. Also uses cane to get around. Age doesn't seem to stop them!

In *The Fountain of Age* Friedan challenges the stereotype of the later years that focuses on pathology and problem and cites examples of seniors who have expanded their lives and their social vitality. Many of her examples are exceptional people: a Jungian analyst, a television producer, a New York lawyer, a Harvard professor. The RVers with whom we have worked provide a more accessible model, for these are *ordinary* people. The occupational backgrounds of our RVers range from truck driver to teacher to bank president. They were farmers, housewives, social workers, mechanics, accountants, store clerks, and engineers. Most of them were not outstanding in their youth and middle age. They represent the full spectrum of North American life. Their very ordinariness assures us it is not necessary to be brilliant, talented, privileged, or rich to have an enriched retirement as a serious RVer. Anyone can do it.

Although anyone *can* do it, not everyone should. Most RVers are quick to acknowledge that RV retirement is not for everyone. Some try it and hate it. Other retirees will never try RV living. They shudder at the thought of the confined space and loss of privacy RVing may entail. Still others remind us there are many ways to achieve a worthwhile retirement. Some retirees experience growth and fulfilment while living in one place and have no desire to pull up roots and go on the road. We asked experienced RVers about the downside of RV retirement. What would they warn people about? What kinds of people would not enjoy it? They said the following:

1) Both partners in a couple must be enthusiastic about it, or at least willing to try it with an open mind. If one partner enters the life style unwillingly, RVers told us, the result is usually a disaster. We discuss this further in Chapter Five.

> It [serious RVing] can become a "total commitment" so both husband and wife had better agree to that commitment and know what they are getting into.
> (From a letter from a full-timer)

2) People must be able to find satisfaction and purpose in a nomadic life style. Building a meaningful life is a challenge for almost all retired people. However, those whose lives are given significance by the treasures they have collected, their non-portable hobbies, or their close relationships with nearby family members may find RVing life to be meaningless and unsatisfactory. In contrast, for some RVers the ability to travel taking their home with them enables them to enjoy lengthy visits with far-flung family members and friends they would otherwise seldom see. These people say RVing brings their families and friends together. If, however, it separates people from loved ones whom they miss and without whom they are lonely, serious RVing is probably not for them.

> We urge people considering full-timing to consider the following: What do you do when you are home? Can these activities be pursued in an RV? Do you golf? garden? play cards? make crafts? read? talk to the neighbors? baby sit? volunteer? do club work? music?.... What would it take for you and your spouse to live in small close quarters?
> (From a letter by Ruth Dalgleish)

3) People who cannot live in a small space will probably have trouble retiring to an RV. Some people find room in their RVs for amazing things — a katchina doll collection, geological specimens, a piano, a train set. Others pride themselves on their ability not to be possessed by possessions. But those who are attached to collections, antiques, or treasures they do not want to live without would likely be unhappy full-timers.

4) Folks devoted to serious hobbies — such as gardening or woodworking — that require their continuous presence or tools that take up a lot of space probably would be frustrated by life in an RV. Although we did meet one former engineer who had transformed the back of his motorhome into a machine shop, and several people who carried their gardens with them as pots of flowers or tomatoes, many hobbyists said the thing they missed most from their former lives was their garden, their shop, or their garage.

In Chapter Five we discuss in more detail the qualities experienced RVers say are required for successful RVing.

Although RV retirement is by no means the universal solution to retirement problems, most of the RVers with whom we have lived and traveled seem to find happiness in their retirement choice. The remainder of this book explores the nomadic RV subculture created by Canadian and American retirees, with a focus on the Escapees club. Skips proclaim that their retirement alternative offers them new and challenging experiences, the freedom to control their circumstances, and a system of social networks that allows them to create and participate in community whenever they wish. As one Escapee commented, "To be happy you need just three things: someone to love, something interesting to do, and control over your life. RVing has two out of three built in, and that's not bad." During a seminar when we were explaining our research to a group of RVers, we quoted this comment and someone responded from the audience, "If you're a *real* Skip you've got all three." As we move into an era in which older people become a powerful force in our society, there should be guideposts to point them to richer, expanded lives. Our research has convinced us that the older people who have cut themselves loose, who have "escaped" to follow the byways of North America, have found a way to do just that. While those who concern themselves with the problems (or the problem) of the elderly were not paying attention, hundreds of thousands of RVers have been busy. They have been creating a subculture they feel enables them to celebrate their freedom, participate in community, and enhance their social and physical vitality and at the same time allows them to learn and grow through new experience.

Notes

1. In the United States, the number of people over the age of 65 grew from 3 million in 1900 to 28 million in 1984, and researchers estimate by 2030 their numbers will reach 50 million (Berezin, Liptzin and Salzman 1988: 665). The elderly were 4 per cent of the US population in 1900. In 1988 they were 12 per cent, and expectations are they will be 15 per cent of the population by the year 2030 (Berezin, Liptzin and Salzman 1988:665). Most of these elderly live with family members (70 per cent) or alone or with persons who are not family (25 per cent). Only 5 per cent of the elderly live in institutions such as nursing homes. Furthermore, 71 per cent of those aged 65 and older said they were highly satisfied with their standard of living (Berezin, Liptzin and Salzman 1988:666).

In Canada, the median age of the population increased from 23.9 years in 1921 to 33.8 years in 1992. It is projected by 2036 the median age will be between 41 and 49.9 years. The proportion of the population aged 65 and over grew from 8 per cent in 1961 to 12 per cent in 1991 (McKie 1993:3-5), while 4.7 per cent of Canadians were 75 years or older in 1991, compared with 3.1 per cent in 1971 (Statistics Canada 1993b). In 2036, according to Statistics Canada projections, 24 per cent of the population will be older people of working age (45-64), while 22 per cent will be over 65 (McKie 1993:3-5). Chappell reports the Census of Canada projects that by 2031 45.1 per cent of the Canadians over the age of 65 will be 75+, 26.1 per cent will be between the ages of 70 and 74, and 28.8 per cent will be between 65 and 69 years of age (Chappell 1990).

In 1985 and 1990, two-thirds to three-quarters of Canadian seniors reported they were in good or excellent health. In both years 90 per cent of Canadians aged 55 and over described themselves as being happy or very happy. The same proportion said they were satisfied with their jobs or other activities, their relationships with their family and friends, and their current accommodations (Keith and Landry 1992). In 1991, 35 per cent of Canadian seniors aged 75 and older lived in a home they maintained, 31 per cent lived alone, 11 per cent lived with others (such as their children) in a household they did not maintain.

The reference for the number of Canadians found in nursing homes is Priest (1993:25).

2. Gifford 1990:2.

3. The RVIA reports, "Currently the 64 million Americans over 50 represent more than 25 per cent of the total adult population. They have combined incomes of more than $800 billion, control 51 per cent of the nation's discretionary income and account for 40 per cent of consumer demand." Since 1980 RV ownership increased 50 per cent among householders age 55 and up.

4. Consider, for instance, the following comment:

The well-being of seniors will be a central issue in years to come because, it is forecast, those age 65 and over will be supported by a shrinking labor force (if the labor force is still comprised mainly of individuals aged 15-64). Thus, health, pensions, housing and other services for seniors will certainly continue to be topics of concern. (Editor, Canadian Social Trends 1992:16).

Similar concerns are echoed by a Statistics Canada researcher. He predicts the expected increase in the percentage of seniors will have a profound effect on Canadian economy and society. He says:

The needs and priorities of the dominant age group will likely shift the focus of public policy, alter the composition of the labor force, and change the nature of privately and publicly provided goods and services... Pension plans will likely be more stressed in the future because a large number of baby boomers will reach retirement age at about the same time. By 2010, the oldest baby boomers will have reached age 65, the conventional age of retirement. (McKie 1993:6).

McKie observes that many of the women of the baby boom generation have careers and will, therefore, put pressure on pension plans. Young workers' contributions pay the pensions of current retirees and do not build a retirement account for the contributor. Consequently, as the number of workers paying into the plan declines and the baby boomers retire, the problem will be exacerbated. He also predicts there may be a shortage of labor in some essential services — such as police, fire, construction workers — requiring strength and agility, qualities found in young workers. Furthermore, if large numbers of retirees continue to move to favorite places, such as the west coast or the sun belt, the concentrations of older persons will put pressure on those areas' public and private sectors for additional services. To make matters worse, small families may not be able to care for elderly relatives, and finding caregivers may be a problem.

Today's small families may find their capacity to provide care for elderly relatives severely limited, both because of family size and the geographic dispersion of family members. Thus, additional institutional facilities, as well as new approaches to care for seniors may be required in the future.

5. Taylor 1995:20.

6. Sundown syndrome is an increase in agitation and delirium occurring after sunset in patients with dementia.

7. Information on stereotypes of the elderly in literature are in Butler (1980:9) and Rodin and Langer (1980:13). The example of Dr. Seuss is found in Friedan (1993:56-58).

8. Another, much different, interpretation of this phenomenon is offered by Faith Popcorn in the *Popcorn Report*. Popcorn says (1991:57,59):

> This refusal to be bound by traditional age limitations is the trend we are calling Down-Aging: redefining *down* what appropriate age-behavior is for your age.... The first aspect of Down-Aging has to do with redefining-down the idea of age: 40 now is what used to be 30, 50 is now what used to be 40, 65 now is the beginning of the second half of life, not the beginning of the end.... Down-Aging is how you explain Dr. Seuss on the best-seller list, *three* movies in one season in which a kid and an adult switch bodies ... and all that advertising that tell you how Snickers and Oreos and Frosted Flakes and Kool-Aid connect you back to the kid you have inside.... We are turning, as often as we can, into big goofy kids. And oh, the release it affords us.

9. Berezin 1978:542.

10. Rodin and Langer 1980.

11. One aspect of this stereotype of the aging process most people find particularly frightening is the possibility of deterioration of the brain, resulting in senility and mental incapacity. Recent research, though, suggests mental decline is not an inescapable part of growing old. The brain is capable of *either* growth or decay, even in old age. Other research indicates that whether an older person's brain deteriorates or grows is not age but the way the person uses it. In a comprehensive review of brain research, Diamond reports geriatric rats (animals equivalent in age to 75- to 90-year-old humans) placed in stimulating environments experienced increases in both brain size and activity. Even though Diamond's research is with rats, its implications for humans are profound. Her

research challenges the myth of inevitable mental deterioration in old age. If, even in extreme age, a healthy brain exposed to a stimulating environment is capable of growth and increased activity, there is no need for the aged to deteriorate into senility. Diamond reports that even rats given extra attention and "Tender Loving Care" lived longer than those who were not.

Some researchers think mental decline is not a characteristic of old age but rather an indication of impending death (Diamond 1988).

Chappell, Strain and Blandford report senile dementia is rare in early old age. It is not until they are over 80 that as many as 20 per cent of elderly people suffer from dementia (Chappell, Strain and Blandford 1986: 43). As a result of this research, the traditional model of gradual decline in mental powers in old age is being replaced. The new model is of a "vigorous adult life span followed by a brief and precipitous senescence" (Labouvie-Vief 1985:507).

In his 1992 Kleemeier Award Lecture to the 45th Annual Scientific Meeting of The Gerontological Society of America, Paul Baltes argued the aging mind has potential for wisdom, self-development, and self-management that traditional studies of aging often fail to recognize. It is no longer appropriate for gerontology to use a simple model of the aging mind (Baltes 1993:592). As Rowe and Kahn note:

> Research in aging has emphasized average age-related losses and neglected the substantial heterogeneity of older persons. The effects of the aging process itself have been exaggerated, and the modifying effects of diet, exercise, personal habits, and psychosocial factors underestimated (Rowe and Kahn 1987:143).

The medical view of successful aging is also changing. Some medical researchers now direct their geriatric research to the "compression of morbidity thesis." According to James Fries of the Stanford Medical Center (Fries 1990:35):

> Rather than assuming that disease is a fixed part of life and the life span indefinitely extensible, the compression of morbidity thesis states that the species' life span is finite and the onset of chronic disease is relatively easily delayed. Thus, the period from onset of chronic infirmity to death may be shortened, with benefit to both individuals and society.

12. Minkler says "retirement marks the beginning of the roleless role, older persons being forced to create their own roles in the absence of socially defined ones" (Minkler 1981:119; Berezin, Liptzin and Salzman 1988).

In Canada, the rate of suicide for people aged 62 and older — 6.2 per 100,000 — is high when compared to that for the total population — 14.3 per 100,000 (Health and Welfare Canada 1982: 11-18, cited in McDonald and Wanner 1990:82). Although people aged 65 and older made up only 12 per cent of the population of the United States in 1988, they account for 20.9 per cent of reported suicides; in 1988 the rate of suicide was almost 50 per cent higher for elderly Americans than for the population as a whole, with a rise in male suicide rates occurring around retirement (McIntosh 1992:17-18).

In the United States, suicide is among the top twelve leading causes of death among seniors, and is the leading cause of preventable death among them. According to the US Institute of Medicine, "Elderly depressed persons are at even higher risk than younger ones: 20 per cent of all suicides occur in persons over the age of 65, and the rates are strikingly higher for elderly white men than for other groups."

13. The quote is from Savishinsky 1995:243.

14. McDonald and Wanner 1990:72-73.

15. The quote starting "Contemporary elders in Canada..." is from Chappell 1990:31.

In 1993 an official with Statistics Canada wrote as follows:

Realizing the threat of becoming rapidly and insidiously isolated, many elderly are already involved in cultural group activities. With ever-improved mental capacities, the future elderly will use retirement to start or complete certain studies, promote political views and organize social activities which are too time-consuming for those fully involved in adult life activities. For governments ... the elderly represent a cooperative and benevolent workforce which could be an unsuspected source of productivity.

Thanks to these various types of activities, society will no longer associate retirement with idleness, uselessness, sterile consumption and other negative, pejorative or belittling ideas. Retirement as lived nowadays did not exist in ancient societies. As an institution it results from the eighteenth and nineteenth century concept of man-machine. Based on the model of after-work rest enlarged to the entire life, retirement represented the final inactive stage, a model that will appear less and less justifiable in the context of a human existence that has changed pace. The cohorts now involved in the labor market already know that they will have to retrain several times to take on the roles which are constantly created as a result of progress. For this reason, after retirement the elderly will be better prepared to play new roles ... and thus to live actively for as long as they can (Statistics Canada 1993a:106).

16. In this 11-year study by NIMH researchers, all the subjects were male, most between the ages of 65 and 75. Of the fifteen variables studied, two — highly organized and complex daily behavior and cigarette smoking — were as good for predicting survival as all the others taken together. The more organized and complex a man's behavior, the better his chance of survival. Some of the subjects were mentally active and "maintained a high degree of involvement in living." According to the researchers, "Life for a majority of the men was characterized by vitality, interest, and enjoyment during most of old age. Their lives typically did not gradually deteriorate over a long period."

About half the participants in the study did not experience this sense of success. The researchers suggested these men "could have had even more successful lives after retirement if they had been prepared to take up a substantial part of their new free time with some special interest." Some of the men agreed. They wished they had planned activities that demanded more of them.

17. They defined "mindfulness" as "the type of cognitive activity that occurs when an individual actively deals with a novel environment or deals with an old environment in new ways" (Langer *et al.* 1990:117).

18. McDonald and Wanner (1990), see especially pages 92 and 93.

19. The risk of loss of control is particularly high for the institutionalized elderly. For them it may result in feelings of helplessness, depression, withdrawal, and early death (Schulz 1976:563-64). Research conducted with nursing home patients demonstrates that people who control their environment may enjoy an old age marked by vitality instead of decline. Those elderly who relinquish or lose control more frequently decline into helplessness. See also Kuhl 1986 and Rodin and Langer 1977:902.

20. (Kuhl 1986:28). By having control over intellectual functioning, researchers mean elderly people should, for example, think they are capable of using a map to find their way in a strange place, or express responsibility for keeping their own mental faculties from deteriorating.

21. Browning 1988:20.

22. Youmans and Yarrow 1971:102; Rowe and Kahn 1987; Pilisuk and Minkler 1980.

23. NACA 1990:11.

24. See Chappell 1990:27; Chappell, Strain, and Blandford 1986:70, 71.

25. The experts do not agree on whether clinical depression is a problem for elderly people. Berezin, Liptzin and Salzman say it is difficult to diagnose depression in an older person because the clinician may confuse it with loneliness and sadness. Older people who have lost friends, spouse, income, and feelings of personal worth have reason to feel sad and lonely. Berezin and his colleagues think affective disorders in general and depression specifically "are probably less common among the elderly" than they are in younger people (Berezin, Liptzin and Salzman 1988:672). Other researchers contend that the major "risk factors" for depression in seniors are circumstances associated with isolation (Institute of Medicine 1990). When there is an absence of detectable disease, all physical symptoms in older people, including those of Alzheimer's, may indicate "masked depression" (Institute of Medicine 1990:202). Depression has a disabling effect on daily activities such as bathing, walking, visiting with friends, or working. These effects were "comparable to those of a serious heart condition and greater than most … other medical conditions. Only arthritis was judged to be more painful, and only serious heart conditions resulted in more days in bed" (Institute of Medicine 1990:212).

26. Even if there were an agreed-on definition of full-time RVer, no census of them would be accurate. Many have no permanent home base. They use the address of a friend or relative to license their vehicles and get driver's licenses, register to vote, and pay their taxes. "Full-time RVer" does not appear on Canadian or US census forms. Full-timers are, in effect, an invisible population, and many of them prefer it that way. Many have no interest in being enumerated. They fear that if "the government" finds out about them it will tax them or otherwise destroy their lifestyle and their freedom.

Estimates of the numbers of full-time and serious RVers vary widely. In 1992 the Recreational Vehicle Industry Association claimed people over age 55 owned almost half of the 8.5 million RVs on the road in the United States. It expects this number to increase significantly as America's largest population group reaches "the prime RV buying years" (RVIA 1992:1). Another source estimates that of the 30 million Americans who own or rent RVs, between 350,000 and 700,000 people live in them full-time. Further, 90 per cent of full-timers are age 50 or older (Wolf 1992:C-1). Keating calculates 200,000 persons live for long periods as nomads in RVs, and that 1 in 5 Americans between the ages of 55 and 59 travel in RVs (Keating 1988:27). Finally, an official of the Good Sam Club who is in charge of insurance policies for full-timers estimates there are 3,000,000 full-timers in the United States. This official adds that nobody will ever know for sure because censuses do not identify them, and because nobody agrees on how full-timing is defined. The official based her approximation on data from 1990, but she thinks the number is growing rapidly because so many people are taking early retirement (J. Carter, personal communication, 1993).

27. Thornburg 1991:67.

28. Cowgill 1941:41.

Chapter Three

From Auto Campers To Escapees

I am in favor of the removal of all trailer camps from Toronto... I do not think they are desirable in Toronto.

* * *

Today the advocates of mobile living in Canada are organized. They're battling for their rights not only to our roads but as responsible citizens, who are willing to pay taxes, live quietly and decently among more settled folk.[1]

There is no one image of the RVer. Citizens living in communities where someone proposes to build a trailer park often take up the cry, "Not in *my* back yard." Some of them think of people who live on wheels as being poor, dirty "trailer trash." Others consider RVers to be rootless, immature people who have rejected community and who live meaningless lives while they travel in large, expensive, resource-guzzling machines. Some local governments see RVers as "cash cows" to milk whenever possible. Conversely, many RVers see themselves as heirs of the pioneers who crossed North America in covered wagons seeking freedom and a new life. It is noteworthy that one of the first commercially built travel trailers was named the Covered Wagon. It had a fixed canvas roof and looked a bit like a small Conestoga wagon on rubber tires. The resemblance between the covered wagon and early auto camping was not lost on a poet who published the following in 1937:

> Time has not dulled that urge.
> The wanderlust lives forever in the hearts of men.
> Trails have grown smooth and comfort goes along
> As covered wagons travel West again.[2]

Today many American RVers see themselves as the lineal descendants of those pioneers, the embodiment of the American dream of freedom and independence. They would identify with Mrs. Miriam Mathers who, in 1945 at the age of 62, loaded her four goats, three horses, and covered wagon on a ship to sail from Seattle to Seward, Alaska. Mrs. Mathers had been trying to cross into Canada by land since 1940, but "always the officials turned her away because, she said, they couldn't believe a woman could get safely through the Canadian wilderness to Alaska." When Mrs. Mathers occasionally ran out of money, she worked for a while for "a new grubstake." Mrs. Mathers said that she felt a "sorta restlessness" that "kept pushing her." She told reporters she thought "some of the restlessness will disappear when she gets to Seward, hitches her team to the wagon, and strikes inland to 'find me a home.'"[3]

Early Homes on Wheels

Ironically, the contrasting images of rootless gypsy and freedom-seeking pioneer both have their origins in the history of RVing. In this chapter we briefly outline this history of the RV movement and draw from it the sources of the contradictory images of contemporary RVers.[4]

After the settlement of the west, but long before vacation camping in cars became a craze in the 1920s, some North Americans lived in mobile dwellings. Families of migratory workers such as professional horse traders, circus and carnival people, and gypsies lived in wagons, often simple ones with straight-bed bodies and canvas roofs. Cowgill describes the horse traders of his childhood: "The families were usually rather large with somewhat dirty and ill-fed children.... The horse-traders usually had a few horses tied behind the wagon. These families had a bad reputation, deserved or undeserved, in respect to stealing."[5] The image of dirt and dishonesty attached to trailerites still haunts RVers.

The North American predecessors of the modern recreation vehicle were a mixed lot. In addition to the covered wagon and the horse-drawn caravans of traveling workers and gypsies, there were camping rigs such as the automobile camper and the tent- or cloth-top-trailer. Freight and livestock trailers were also RV ancestors. They provided the model for the modern fifth-wheel trailer. In his history of the American house trailer, David Thornburg credits the English with inventing the modern automobile trailer in 1906. British motor caravans, two-wheeled copies of the gypsy caravan, were camping toys for the rich. Although the British manufactured large numbers of motor caravans for vacation use after World War I, it apparently never occurred to them to use the caravans as homes.[6] In the United States, evangelists, traveling salesmen, and fishermen built their own boxes on wheels. At the same time, wealthy and powerful people began auto camping in an attempt to return to "first principles" while enjoying nature in comfort. In 1921, for instance, Henry Ford, Thomas Edison, and Harvey Firestone were guests on an auto camping trip hosted by President Warren Harding. Similarly, the president of Packard Motor Company went "camping" in a custom motorized van with built-in cupboards, folding tables, and berths to sleep six[7].

Auto campers in the 1920s and early 1930s slept in a variety of rigs. These ranged from simple lean-to tents supported by the side of the car to elaborate two- and four-wheel trailers with beds, kitchens, and even screened windows. The early popularity of auto camping is suggested by an article in the monthly column, "The Woman Motorist," in the Canadian woman's magazine *Chatelaine*. The article contains instructions on how to adapt the back seat of the family automobile to "use your car for a comfortable double bed." It also tells how to curtain the car "to make one's bedroom private," and points out that car camping enables the camper to avoid cold mornings and "extremely draughty" tents. If the camper's rig included a tent, the article suggested that on rainy days campers should use the tent for a dressing room and the car for a bedroom.[8]

The Curtiss Aerocar was the only commercially produced trailer in the 1920s. This elaborate and expensive rig derived from a trailer custom built by Glen Curtiss, the aircraft designer. The body of the trailer was rounded, with a forward section that fit over the trunk of the tow car. This design foreshadowed modern fifth-wheel trailers. The Aerocar had four berths, a galley, and a glass-roofed observation cockpit. The top-of-the-line model had clerestory windows near the cockpit at the front. These provided the passengers with a "panoramic view" from their lounge chairs in air-conditioned comfort.[9] Curtiss deliberately priced his "motorized Gypsy van," as he called the Aerocar, beyond the reach of the mobile poor and migratory workers who might have used it for a home. Curtiss feared his trailer's association with these people "would hurt the trailer's image with the well-to-do." He identified with the affluent and built his trailers for them.[10]

The elite and technologically advanced Aerocar enjoyed only modest sales but remained in production until the late 1930s. Most of the trailers on the road in the 1920s and 1930s were home made. There were few regulatory restrictions on trailers then, and many books with construction drawings were available for the do-it-yourself builder.[11]

Although most do-it-yourselfers were undoubtedly men, women also participated. An article in a 1930 issue of *Chatelaine* describes "How two women turned a motor truck into a modern covered wagon." In this article, which could have been written to describe modern RVing women, the author says of a mother and daughter team:

> A motor caravan would seem to be the ideal answer to the needs of wanderers who have the gypsy instinct ... at least it has been considered so by two Canadian women ... who, during the past few years have done most of their traveling by this means. They turned a one-and-a-half ton motor truck into a modern covered wagon (which is really a movable apartment well suited to fit all the needs of human life); and in it they were able to travel thousands of miles independent of trains, boats or hotels; to regulate speed by inclination, to get up or go to bed when so disposed, to follow the beaten track or to wander in highways and byways, to live en route in as great comfort as if at home, and to be untrammelled by time or place or people.

The older woman did most of the preparation of what would now be called a motor home. She "showed a good deal of architectural sense and a deftness with tools in arranging for cupboards and other clever fittings suggestive of the cabin of a ship." At a touch the interior became a kitchen, a sitting room, or a bedroom:

> The walls of the caravan are full of surprises. There is not an inch of wasted space. At a touch, an innocent-looking panel will slide down or back and disclose toilet articles fitted comfortably in place. Another touch brings down a hinged shelf behind which may be cutlery or dishes.
>
> These ardent caravaners claim that they enjoy the same comforts and most of the luxuries en route as they would at any hotel, with the advantage that no matter in what part of the country they are, they always feel at home.

Their motor home had benefits for these early RVers beyond allowing them to travel in home-like comfort. During a trip of 8,000 miles through western Canada and the United States it also opened opportunities to them that they would otherwise have missed. It also confounded customs officials. This was no mean feat, even 60 years ago.

> Their caravan has introduced them to a Canada that they would never have known by the usual travel route.... So great was the interest taken by the Customs officers at the border in

permitting a "house" to cross the border that they did not even look at the luggage of the travelers.

The article concludes:

> The only drawback — if it can be so described — to a trip of this kind is that it has a tendency to develop the gypsy spirit and to make one unwilling to settle down for any length of time.
> Certain it is that a caravan trip cures one of being too deep-rooted in one spot. Such travel is a teacher of the mind, a healer of the heart and the base of supplies for happy memories.[12]

Many modern RVers prefer to travel independently, following their own schedule. Others choose to spend at least some time traveling together or meeting periodically to see old friends and share experiences and information. Trailerites and others who are road struck have been doing this from the very first. In December 1919 a group of motor campers in Tampa, Florida, founded a club for auto campers east of the Mississippi River. The organization is referred to variously as the Tin Can Tourists of the World, Inc., the Tin Can Tourists of America or perhaps the Tin Can Tourists Association. Whatever their official name, they were generally known as the "Canners," the "Tin Canners" or by their initials, the TCT.[13] They held rallies twice a year, and their goal was to enhance the image of the automobile camper. The charter of the organization emphasized friendship, cleanliness, responsible use of campgrounds and property, and mutual assistance. The tin can stood for the canned food that auto campers characteristically ate and was their talisman. An empty soup can "badge" hanging from the automobile radiator cap identified members of the club and alerted other Tourists when a fellow was in distress.[14] In 1966 the Good Sam Club revived the idea of a logo used to signal membership and to encourage mutual help with its "Good Samaritan" sticker. The Escapees club emblem of the little house on wheels is another such insignia.

The official theme song of the TCT, "The More We Get Together," emphasized togetherness (*The more we get together, the happier we'll be*), friendship, and unity (*For your friends are my friends and my friends are your friends*). There were no dues and no fees: just fun and companionship. In 1936 2000 members attended a rally in Sandusky, Ohio. By the end of that decade the estimated membership of the TCT was nearly 100,000.[15]

The Tin Can Tourists embody the move from automobile camping to trailering. Although the club began as an organization of tenters and car campers, by the end of the 1930s it was primarily a trailering organization.[16] Other organizations of trailerites were formed in the 1930s: the Automobile Tourist Association, whose rally in the summer of 1935 was attended by 2,728 participants; the Eastern Campers Association; the New England Tourists; the National Travel Trailer Association; and the Wally Byam club, created exclusively for Airstream Trailer owners.[17]

The increasing number of trailerites and trailering organizations created a need for campgrounds. At first, when auto campers and trailerites were few, they commonly pulled off the road by a creek, in a farmer's field, anywhere they could find a spot to spend the night. (Boondocking RVers are their heirs as they continue the practice today.) As their numbers grew, and as all-weather roads suitable for automobiles pulling trailers linked towns and cities across the continent, many small towns dedicated a few acres as a park. There travelers often were allowed to park free, and sometimes parks generously supplied toilets, drinking water, electricity, showers, or even a kitchen shelter with stoves and tables. Wallis notes that between 1920 and 1924 there were 3000 to 6000 municipal parks in the United States. Travelers repaid their hosts' generosity by purchasing food, fuel, and other items from local merchants. The provision of free or inexpensive camping areas in small towns along North America's blue highways[18] continues. RVers find them through publications such as the *Guide to Free Campgrounds*[19] or the "Day's End" column in the *Escapees Magazine*.

Local merchants saw the campers as potential customers, and towns took pride in their parks and in a reputation as "a nice place to stay."[20] By the mid-1930s developers were also planning and building private parks with paved parking pads, toilets, and individual hookups. The quality of private parks varied widely at first. There were few codes to regulate trailer camps, and those that existed were seldom enforced, especially in small towns. Some camps, located on the land where the owners were resident, provided utilities and toilets. Others were little more than dirt roads on vacant land with facilities limited to an outhouse, a seep hole for waste water dumping, and a tangle of extension cords to an oversubscribed electric outlet.[21]

Because of the differences in the quality of trailer camps, magazines and guidebooks identifying the better ones soon appeared. The first was *Travel Trailer* magazine in 1936, followed by *Browns Trailer Park Directory* and *Woodall's Park Directory* in 1937. *Western Trailer Life* was first published in 1941 and became *Trailer Life* in 1949.[22] *Woodall's* and *Trailer Life*, among others, continue this service.

Trailering — now RVing — is a product of the twentieth century: an outgrowth of the spread and popularity of the automobile and of the system of paved highways built to facilitate automobile use. Its history reflects the significant social events of the period. During the prosperity following World War I, automobile ownership became a possibility for the multitudes. Mass ownership of cars and the construction of roads across the continent made automobile travel feasible. For the first time, it was possible for ordinary people to enjoy traveling vacations that took them into the countryside and to the scenic wonders of North America. During the 1920s and early 1930s, automobile camping and trailering became popular pastimes for the growing middle class as well as the wealthy few.

By the mid-1930s, however, much of the joy of auto and trailer camping was gone, a victim of the Great Depression. Itinerants replaced the short-term camper-as-customer. These trailerites, often indigent and unemployed, had no fixed address, and perhaps no hope of one. Driven by their need, these people stayed in — lived in — the free parks as long as possible. In response, municipalities began closing their campgrounds to avoid their being turned into "Hoovervilles" — shanty-town settlements of the homeless and unemployed who lived in battered old trailers, cars or tents. With their bedrolls on their running boards and their possessions strapped to their roofs, Hooverville residents looked very much like car campers. The threat of their presence changed the image of the trailerite.

While the economy was prosperous, travel trailers were toys for leisure use, and "respectable" users were accepted. In the Great Depression, people began using trailers as homes while they sought work. During economic difficulties:

> The RV tramp has it easier than his buddies who live in a more conventional style. Without deep roots and the commitments that house owners have, the tramp who lives in an RV home can take both his family and his home to wherever work is available.[23]

Kay Peterson, the author of this passage, meant to show the advantages of contemporary trailer living; however, during the Depression, to those in fixed houses who had made a commitment to their community, the term *tramp* was loaded with ugly and heavy baggage. To seem to have it "easier than his buddies" created enmity and mistrust of the "trailerite."

During the hard times of the 1930s, and despite the social disruption of World War II and the stigma of using a trailer as home, trailer use burgeoned. During the 1930s the number of serious users appears to have been large. It was as hard to pin down the exact number of people living full time in their trailers 60 years ago as it is today. Nevertheless, experts speculate that in the mid to late 1930s over a million people were on the road in as many as 400,000 trailers. Wallis estimates that 25 per cent of the trailers were full-time housing. The trailer industry, with its own image at stake, wanted to distance itself from full-time use, especially of home-made and presumably inferior trailers. It suggested that families living in such cramped conditions would soon be at each others' throats.[24] Cowgill, who did field research with trailerites in the late 1930s, argued that such worries were unfounded. He thought people could live in trailers for long periods of time because of a general North American trend toward smaller living space, especially in small apartments. He said, "The trailer in point of size is not a radical step from these small apartments and sleeping rooms. Because of its compactness and built-in features it is, as a matter of fact, often more liveable than are some apartments."[25]

When the population of trailerites changed, the attitudes of municipalities toward trailers and their occupants were transformed. Community leaders feared that massive numbers of trailerites would demand public services (such as education for their children) while providing little, if any, tax revenue. Municipalities responded to this fear in a variety of ways. In addition to closing their free parks, they enacted zoning bylaws against other trailer parks. They imposed new taxes and fees and required trailer dwellers to get parking permits. These permits limited the time trailerites could stay in one spot, thereby insuring their transience. For example, in the 1930s Detroit, Michigan, and Toledo, Ohio, passed ordinances limiting trailers to a 90-day stay, while Rochester, New York, limited parking to two days.[26] The image of the trailerite as unwelcome beggar or worse, persisted long after it ceased to be appropriate. In Canada, as in the United States, the negative view of trailerites lingered long after the country's entry into World War II. By that time most of those living in trailers were not the unemployed, but war industry workers unable to find other housing. For example, in 1941 municipal leaders in York Township (near Toronto), Ontario decided they would not allow "trailer colonies" under any circumstances. After the council turned down an application to establish a trailer camp in the township, an official commented, "People are renting them [trailers] to save both taxes and rent, and yet they expect to receive all the benefits that a taxpayer does in the way of education for their children, transportation, and so on." The official then smiled and suggested "Forest Hill is a much nicer spot — I suggest that they ask permission to go there. They'll have ever so many advantages there that York can't give them."[27]

Toronto was no more generous than Detroit or Toledo. Its municipal leaders spent seven years trying to expel trailerites from what had begun as an impromptu park in the downtown core. Officials justified their attempted expulsions by charging trailerites with several offenses. For example, they alleged that the occupants violated bylaws forbidding children of the opposite sex over the age of ten to sleep in the same room, and prohibiting food preparation and eating in the same room where people slept. As most trailers were legally defined as one-room dwellings, the residents were automatically in violation of these bylaws.[28] Frustrated in their efforts to remove the trailer dwellers in any other way, Toronto city council finally provided them with a new, serviced site outside the city center, called Ryding Park camp. There, although the new location had been purchased for the purpose of a trailer park, trailer dwellers remained unwelcome; residents were permitted to stay for no more than two years. Furthermore, largely to appease the protests of local residents, the rules prohibited newcomers from moving in when a space was vacated.[29]

Despite such opposition, during the 1950s both the number of trailer dwellers and the trailer industry grew dramatically. For example, by 1950 trailer sales in Canada alone amounted to almost a million dollars. By 1954, the trailer population of North America was estimated to be over two million. Had all these trailerites been concentrated in one spot, one observer suggested, they would have formed the sixth largest city on the continent.[30] Perhaps in recognition of the economic potential of this growing population, some members of the financial community began to acknowledge a refurbished — and positive — image for trailerites. For instance, Peter Newman, wrote in the business-oriented *Financial Times*:

> The free-wheeling homes — once mobile kennels for shifty itinerants — have now grown up.... The trailerites that inhabit these "20th Century Turtle shells" may be restless nomads, but trailer living is no longer a form of hoboism. The gypsy concept went out with World War II, when the housing shortage saw trailer settlements mushroom around military camps and defense plants. And today, the hastily built boxes of that era have evolved into respectable residences suitable for permanent living.[31]

Newman's article emphasized trailers as housing for workers — such as those in mining camps, oil fields, pipeline construction, hydroelectric and other power projects — who moved both frequently and to out-of-the-way places and wanted their families with them. He also emphasized the normality and stability of trailer family life:

What kind of people live in trailers?... Young married couples, military personnel, construction and hydro workers, and elderly retired couples make up almost 90% of Canada's trailer population — estimated at over 20,000. Only 1% of trailers belong to vacationists who like to ignore advance reservation worries by carting their summer cottage behind them. Most mobile homes are moved only once in 12 months.... About a third of present trailerites have been living on wheels for over five years. A C.M.H.A. [Central Mortgage and Housing Authority] survey shows that the income of trailer families ranges from $2,500 to $7,200, with the average running around $3,800.[32]

Despite the renewed respectability of trailerites and recognition of the growing market potential of trailers and their residents by the business community, many of the same problems continued to plague trailer dwellers. Communities did not welcome them and made it difficult for them to find a place to park. As one newspaper article noted, civic governments run by "men with memories long enough to recall slum-like 'trailer camps' of another era" continued to oppose trailer parks. To fight this negative stereotype, people with an interest in trailering began to organize. In 1953, for example, trailer manufacturers, park owners, and trailerites formed the Canadian Trailer Coach Association (CTCA) to take on the issue. As Gordon McCaffrey, the CTCA's General Manager announced, "We all know what our problem is ... Thousands of Canadians want to enjoy mobile living, but millions of Canadians are hostile or indifferent to mobile living. We must end that hostility and change the indifference to a friendly interest." McCaffrey's goal was "to make peace with communities which still regarded trailer inhabitants as 'squatters sending their children to school but not paying taxes.'" To achieve this, he urged all interested parties to join the CTCA, which would draw up a voluntary code of standards for trailer park owners. In addition, trailer dealers, park operators, and park residents should participate in local affairs, join community organizations, and pay taxes. "This is the only way we will erase the stigma of the 'trailer camp,'" said McCaffrey.[33]

McCaffrey's efforts were successful. By 1956 the hostility of Canadian officials toward trailerites was replaced with some tolerance. That year the Ontario legislature repealed a 1952 amendment to the Ontario Municipal Act prohibiting trailers from staying in any municipality for more than 60 days. It also passed legislation permitting local municipalities, which had been unable to collect property tax on trailers, to raise revenues through license fees. This eased local governments' concern that they would be forced to provide services to people who paid no taxes. In the same year the Canadian Department of National Defence recognized trailer living as a way of life. It permitted camp commanders to extend camp facilities such as garbage pickup and hydroelectric power to trailer parks. It even considered buying trailers to rent to those who preferred them to houses.[34]

In 1958, an article in *Maclean's Magazine* announced that 10,000 trailers had been sold in Canada in 1957. Furthermore, the population of trailerites in North America was almost 3,000,000 with 60,000 in Canada. More than half the Canadian trailer owners were itinerant workers. They were no longer automatically derided as parasitic and prolific nomads parked behind gas stations in home-made square boxes on wheels. Instead, trailer dwellers were acknowledged to be respectable, hard-working individuals who were financially stable. *Maclean's Magazine* reported, "Most trailer owners are under forty and, contrary to popular belief, there are rarely more than three people ... to each trailer." Because oil and construction workers had incomes "well over average," local businesses were no longer as fearful a trailer-owning debtor "might up stakes in the middle of the night and drive off into the dark blue."[35]

The manufacturers of mobile homes and of travel trailers shared their facilities and their market during the 1940s and 1950s. In February of 1960, for instance, the Canadian Mobile Home Association held its seventh annual all-Canadian mobile home and travel trailer show in Toronto.[36] Gradually, however, things were beginning to change. During the 1960s the diverging interests of those requiring sedentary manufactured housing and those wanting a vehicle for comfortable travel led to a split between the industries catering to these different needs. The units built for people wanting inexpensive, spacious, but not necessarily moveable trailer-type housing were unsuitable for personal towing, even if they did come on wheels. They were too long and too wide to meet highway regulations restricting travel trailers to a size of 8 feet wide by 12 feet high by no more than 45 feet long.[37] Manufacturers had to decide whether to specialize or to manufacture both travel trailers and mobile homes for different markets. The usual decision was to specialize. In 1963 manufacturers of homes delivered on wheels but not intended to move (called, ironically, *mobile* homes) and those who made rigs intended to travel — travel trailers, fifth-wheels, and motor homes — separated into independent industries in the United States. American travel trailer manufacturers identified themselves as the recreation vehicle (RV) industry and formed a lobby group, the Recreation Vehicle Association (RVA).[38] The two industries are now completely separate, as evidenced by their decision to hold their trade shows on the same day.[39] With a smaller market, the Canadian manufacturers of travel trailers did not make this separation until 1975. That year they split into the Canadian Recreation Vehicle Association for manufacturers of travel trailers and motor homes and the Canadian Manufactured Housing Association for those who made "mobile" homes.[40]

The separation of RVs from other types of moveable manufactured housing was not the only development of the 1960s. That period also saw the creation of a new organization for RVers. Mutual aid among people on wheels had been the custom since the formation of the Tin Can Tourists early in the century. However, as travelers came to perceive violence as a problem, they were increasingly reluctant to offer help to, or accept it from, strangers. A growing number of RVers felt they needed a way to know one another. The Good Sam Club began in the mid-1960s as a way to meet this need. The assumption was that if RVers of good will could somehow recognize each other they could safely offer assistance to (and accept it from) other club members.

In 1966 Ray Joens wrote a letter to the magazine *Trail-R-News* suggesting it give subscribers identifying decals for the bumpers of their trailers. Joens assumed the readers of the magazine would be "all in the same lot — they like the same things," and that this commonality would be sufficient for trust. The magazine editors agreed to furnish its readers a "Good Samaritan" decal if there was enough interest, speculating, "*It could be the start of something big!*"[41] In 1968 *Trail-R-News* merged with *Trailer Life*. That same year Art Rouse, publisher of *Trailer Life*, bought the Good Sam Club with its membership of 10,000 RVers. When he retired in the mid-1980s, the club had more than 400,000 members. By 1991 it had a membership of nearly 800,000. Rouse thought the organization was so successful because in the 1950s and 60s

> we were trailerists, and it was "low class," and people looked down on us. We were downtrodden. Back then what RVers needed was recognition, to belong, not to be kicked out ... We've finally overcome most of that, but there is still a lot of prejudice against our tin houses. Good Sam gave them a chance to belong to an organization that appreciated them.

Today the Good Sam Club is part of TL Enterprises, North America's largest commercial, profit-making operation catering to RVers.[42]

Banding together in clubs, a move starting with the Tin Can Tourists and reaching its pinnacle with Good Sam, is a hallmark of RVing and of RVers. People with special needs, specific interests, or a particular lifestyle organize their own RV clubs. There are, for instance, clubs for people who wish to associate with others who own the same name brand of RV. There are clubs for women, the disabled, African-Americans, full-time RVers, and veterans — even for veterans who served in submarines. Single RVers who own motor homes have their own club. There are clubs for people who like to camp in similar sorts of places, and there is at least one for singles who camp in the same spot year after year (Slab City Singles). The Recreation Vehicle Industry Association's pamphlet, "Camping and the RV Lifestyle," lists 12 "national" RV clubs and 32 clubs organized for owners of RVs of particular brand names.[43] Their listing only scratches the surface of the phenomenon. Most of these clubs are (at least in theory) non-commercial. Vehicle manufacturers sponsor some "brand-name" RV clubs, and, while they sponsor rallies and provide opportunity for communication and fellowship, their clubs are also transparent attempts to encourage customer loyalty. Many clubs not only provide for occasional get-togethers (Airstream Rallies, Good Samborees, Escapades, etc.), they also keep members in communication through newsletters. Some even provide parks for their membership. The non-commercial club that does all these things and has an open membership policy is the Escapees Club, with headquarters in Livingston, Texas.

Escapees

Joe and Kay Peterson started the largest noncommercial organization for serious and full-time RVers in the summer of 1978 as a way for full-time RVers to stay in touch with one another:[44]

> As we thought back to the fear of isolation we experienced when we left family and friends behind to start full-timing, we knew others coming into the RV lifestyle would feel the same sense of isolation. By banding together, we could encourage and support each other. So we set about to form a network, where help would be available from others who understood our needs.

The Petersons were themselves already full-timers. They lived in a travel trailer and were raising a family, supported by Joe Peterson's highly mobile skill as an electrician. It was a style of life they had chosen because of the opportunity for travel and adventure, not one they were forced into by economic necessity. By July 2000 their little club, started as an informal network linking a few friends who were all full-time RVers wanting to stay in touch, had become a corporation serving over 60,000 members.[45]

Escapees Inc., with over 100 full-time employees, supervises or directly administers the operation of 18 RV parks. It also provides voice mail and mail forwarding services to members and publishes a 60-page magazine six times each year. Furthermore, in June 1992 it opened the CARE center providing inexpensive day care for members who are unable to travel but want to live in their RVs and stay in touch with their friends in the club. We discuss the CARE center more fully in Chapter Nine.

Although the "little club" the Petersons envisioned has become a large business, it has remained determinedly noncommercial. The low cost and the multiple services provided account partly for Escapees' rapid growth. Another important factor is the absence of membership restrictions. Almost anyone can be, and can afford to be, an Escapee. Founded by and for full-timers, over the years the shape of the club's membership has changed. The organization, which began as a group of working youngish families who called their RVs home, now primarily serves people in the later years of their lives who may not be full-timers. The rapid growth in membership worries some members. It does not worry the Petersons. To them the boundaries of membership are inclusive. Paraphrasing Edwin Markham,[46] while discussing the issue at a social hour, Kay Peterson said: "He drew a circle that shut me out: I drew a larger circle that brought him in." Being a full-timer is not a membership requirement. Even if it were, in the Peterson's view, full-timers are people who choose to define themselves that way. It does not matter if everything they own is in their rig, or whether they live in it for only a few weeks each year.

The club began modestly. Kay Peterson, who wrote a monthly RV column for *Woodall's Travel Trailer Magazine*, offered in her June 1978 column to start a club for full-timers if enough people wanted it. By August, a four-page newsletter was ready to mail to 34 members of the nameless club. The Petersons asked members to suggest names for the new organization. Many names submitted contained references to being free, but the Petersons finally chose the name "Escapees," proposed by Harry and Peggy Lewis. The Lewises also suggested using the abbreviation S-K-P, as the initials could be an acronym for many things. Kay Peterson says: "There were many ideas about what S-K-P could stand for, but 'SKPs are a Special Kind of People Sharing Knowledge and Pleasure' best stated what we were all about." The club adopted the acronym, and SKPs began referring to themselves as "Skips." They set the dues for the club at $3.00 a year, thinking the sum would pay the cost of printing and mailing a four-page newsletter. By the time of the second newsletter, there were 100 families and the newsletter was 10 pages long. They made up the difference in cost from Joe Peterson's salary. In 2000 dues are $50.00 US a year.[47]

Not only did the club's membership grow faster than expected, its shape changed, as well. Forty of the first 100 members were under 50 years of age, while only five were over 65. By 1990, only 7 per cent of the membership was under 50, while two-thirds were over 60 years of age![48]

The rapid growth of the club surprised the Petersons. A cartoon published in a 1984 *Escapees Newsletter* shows Kay and Joe Peterson talking. Kay says "Do you think if we start a little RV club we'll have a hundred members someday?" The title of the cartoon was "August 1978."[49] Kay Peterson recalls the early growth of the club:

> Before the second newsletter we had almost tripled our membership. And new members have been coming ever since.... The dues in those early years didn't even pay all the newsletter expenses let alone buy the new equipment we constantly needed to keep pace with the new members who kept coming.... We realized we must raise the dues enough to pay all the club expenses which Joe had been subsidizing *and* allow us — for the first time — to receive some compensation for running the Club. We raised the dues, but new members kept coming.[50]

The organization has continued to grow, with a dramatic leap in membership between 1984 and 1986.[51] The club never retires membership numbers, which mostly refer to two members, so they do not tell us how many active participants there are in the organization. At the 1994 Spring Escapade a member of the Advisory Board estimated that each month the club gains over 200 members and loses about 100. At the time there were approximately 18,300 *active* membership numbers in Escapees. About 85 per cent of all membership numbers include two people, so the active club membership was then about 33,700 individuals.[52]

Escapees began as a way for a small group of people to share information and give one another encouragement and support. However, its rapid growth and entrance into the business of park ownership and management precluded its being a democratically run organization:

> We had grown into a mature organization in a world of law suits and big business takeovers. We needed to protect our club from both. So we formed a closed corporation to insure that even after our death, Escapees would continue under the ownership and management of Cathie and Jack who understood and believed in the SKP concepts.[53]

As the Petersons told us, they discovered to their sorrow that democracy-in-action is not the way to run a business. For several reasons they have decided to keep control in their hands and maintain authority over the club's direction.

The first — and perhaps most important — reason is their determination to preserve Escapees' noncommercial status. Second, they fear electing the organization's board of directors would lead to wrangling and perhaps to legal problems of the sort that plague some of the club's co-op parks. As they see it, co-op lease holders are tempted to elect board members because they are nice people, have lots of friends in the group, and are hard working. Too often, election to a board of directors is a way of honoring friends rather than a decision based on business experience and ability. According to the Petersons, many Skips do not think of a co-op as a business involving real estate. Consequently they fail to recognize that a bad decision by the board may cost members money and lead to trouble. When the situation is finally recognized, it is often too late.

Finally, they know the organization has to change as conditions do. It must grow if it is to continue to meet the needs of both traveling RVers and those who require a home base. The first SKP members all shared a dream of a small, intimate club in which everyone knew everyone else. Their dream was different from the kind of organization that Escapees has become and the Petersons are saddened that some of their oldest members now "feel like we've taken their club away from them."[54]

The growth of Escapees has mirrored the growth of RVing in North America. By 1991 there were more than 8,000,000 RVs registered in the US, each of them traveling an average of 5,900 miles per year.[55] Against this background, and the experience of the Escapees club, we read with wonder Thornburg's mournful description of the passing of the trailerists:

> They had a dream — a sentimental, Arcadian dream of sunshine and neighborliness and simple self-sufficiency. And despite a depression and a world war, a lot of them managed to live it.
>
> They're gone now, those five million indigenous American gypsies, and so is the way of life they created. Sometime during the 1950s, the narrow road they were traveling came abruptly to a fork. One branch led straight to the mobile home villa of today, with its chlorinated swimming pool, its nine-hole golf course, its security guard at the gate. The other branch led to a barren and overpriced campground beside some noisy interstate. The old-time trailerites, casual and cantankerous and fiercely independent souls, weren't comfortable or welcome in either

place, and so they simply ceased to be — sold their rigs and faded quietly back into the mainstream and were forgotten.[56]

He is wrong! Like the reports of Mark Twain's death, Thornburg's announcement of the death of the trailerite's way of life is premature.

Notes

1. First quote from the mayor of Toronto, *Globe and Mail* 1945b:4. Second quote from the *Financial Post* 1954:36.

2. Information from Cowgill 1941:1; poem is from C.E. Nash 1937:88, quoted in Wallis 1991:37.

3. *Toronto Globe and Mail* 1945a:3.

4. This is not intended to be a comprehensive history of the RV movement. We direct those who are interested in the topic to the following sources which should be available at most good libraries: David Thornburg's *Galloping Bungalows* is a study of the travel trailer movement until the 1950s. It is marred by his conclusion that the trailering way of life is "dead and gone" (190). Allan Wallis's *Wheel Estate* is a history of mobile homes detailing the split between RVs and mobile homes. *Trailer Life* 51:7 (July 1991) contains articles on the history of RVing, based on articles from 50 years of the magazine; a biography of Art Rouse who is the publisher; articles on Airstream and Shasta trailers, the only RVs that have been around for 50 years; and letters and pictures from people who were RVers in the early days. Kay Peterson discusses the history of the Escapees RV club in her column entitled "Looking Back," *Escapees Newsletter* 15:1 (1993):5; in her book *Home is Where You Park It* (1990); "Escapees history in brief," *Escapees Magazine* 1995a; and *History of the Escapees Club in Prose and Pictures* (Peterson and Paddock 1998).

5. Donald Cowgill's PhD thesis published in 1941 is the earliest study we know of full-time RVing. See Cowgill 1941:2.

6. Thornburg 1991:8.

7. The histories of trailering by Wallis and Thornburg both published in 1991 contain a wealth of rich historical data. See especially Wallis 1991:32.

8. Jury 1930 (5):52-53.

9. See Wallis 1991:32. The tradition of luxury for the wealthy continues. For example the 45-foot long Marathon Prevost motor home has granite flooring, full climate control, leather-covered seats, a bath with 6-foot mirrored doors, and a combination washer/dryer. It weighs 43,600 pounds with water and fuel tanks full, leaving 1400 pounds of reserve capacity for passengers and supplies out of its gross vehicle weight

rating of 45,000. This RV sells for $725,597 US, putting it "within the reach of the very fortunate few" (*Highways* 1994:18).

10. See Thornburg 1991:11.

11. An estimated three-quarters were home-made (Wallis 1991:39).

12. Pease 1930:12.

13. Authorities disagree on the name of this group: see Cowgill 1941:5; Thornburg 1991:23; Wallis 1991:43.

14. Thornburg 1991:23.

15. Wallis 1991:44; Thornburg 1991:24.

16. Cowgill 1941:4.

17. Wallis 1991:4.

18. Good secondary roads that are not major truck connections are marked on many road maps in blue ink. The term "blue highways" refers to this practice. The travel book bearing this name by William Least Heat Moon is probably the source of the wide use of the term among RVers and other travelers (Moon 1982).

19. Wright 1990.

20. Wallis 1991:39.

21. Wallis 1991:42-43.

22. See Wallis 1991:42-43; *Trailer Life* 1991:28.

23. Peterson, K. 1990:75.

24. Wallis 1991:68-70.

25. Citing figures from *Recent Social Trends* of 1931 and 1933, Cowgill reported that apartments shrank from 4.19 rooms in 1913 to 2.23 rooms in 1928. For his argument about trailers see Cowgill 1941:6-7.

26. Wallis 1991:71 and footnote, 26.

27. Toronto *Globe and Mail* 1941:25.

28. Toronto *Globe and Mail* 1940:4.

29. Toronto *Globe and Mail* 1947:5.

30. The 1950 figure is from the *Financial Post* 1954:36. The 1954 figure and the comment about the sixth largest city is from Newman 1954:13.

31. Newman 1954:13.

32. While the annual income figures cited by Newman in this article may seem appallingly low by the standards of the late twentieth century, in fact this demonstrated that the income of "trailerites" was slightly *above* the national average! (Newman 1954:13).

33. See *Financial Post* 1954:36, and Newman 1954:13.

34. Maclean 1956:31.

35. *Maclean's Magazine* 1958:11.

36. *Rod and Gun in Canada* 1960:14.

37. Newman 1954:13.

38. The RVA has been succeeded by the Recreation Vehicle Industry Association (RVIA) with headquarters in Reston, Virginia. Almost all Canadian Manufacturers of recreational vehicles belong to this organization as well as to the Canadian analogue. The RVIA claims about 97 percent of RV manufacturers in North America are members of its organization (G. Labella, Vice-president, RVIA, personal communication, February 1994).

39. Wallis 1991:132.

40. Donald Mockford, CRVA official, personal communication, December 12, 1994.

41. Joens 1991:4.

42. *Highways* 1991:56-67.

43. RVIA 1994:14.

44. In an article in the *Escapees Newsletter* explaining why parking fees at their parks will be kept to a minimum, the editor of the newsletter (probably Kay Peterson although the article is unsigned) explains that Escapees parks are and will remain non-commercial. The article says: "The only reason commercial and membership parks have to charge so much is that they want to make a profit. We don't." (*Escapees Newsletter* 1983:17)

45. In 1995 the club had issued 40,000 numbers (Peterson, K. 1995a:14). By the Fun Days rally held in late July, 2000 club officials announced that the membership numbers of the club had passed 60,000. Most of the numbers are held by couples.

46. In Evans 1978:107.

47. Peterson, K. 1984 :7; 1990:71, 1995a:14, and webpage *www.escapees.com/website/how.htm* July 28, 2000.

48. A survey of the first 100 members shows that the original membership of the Escapees club was relatively young. Of these members "10 were under 30; 9 were 30/40; 21 were 40/50; 37 were 50/60; 18 were 60/65 and 5 were over 65. Five children were traveling with their parents" (Rensen 1988:2). A comparison of Escapees membership in 1978 and 1993 clearly shows the changing profile of the organization as the percentage of members over the age of 50 went from 60 per cent in 1978 to 93 per cent in 1990 (K. Peterson 1993a:5):

Age	1978 survey	1990 survey
under 40	19%	1%
40 to 50	21%	6%
50 to 60	37%	27%
over 60	23%	66%

49. *Escapees Newsletter* 1984b:21.

50. Peterson, K. 1987b:24.

51. Growth figures released in 1986 show the following pattern (*Escapees Newsletter* 1986b:3):

Year	# of New Mem.	Mo. average	Daily average
1978	119 (6 mos)	19.8	0.6
1979	162	13.5	0.4
1980	178	14.8	0.5
1981	313	26.1	0.85
1982	676	56.3	1.85
1983	839	69.9	2.3
1984	801	66.75	2.2
1985	1740	145.0	4.7
1986	1809	200.7	6.6

52. Carr 1993b:7. By May 30, 1995 the club had issued 36,871 numbers (Peterson, K. 1995a:14).

53. Cathie is the Petersons' daughter, Jack was her first husband. She and her present husband Budd Carr are the co-owners and managers of the Escapees corporation.

54. Personal communication, 23 November 1993.

55. *Highways* 1991:55.

56. Thornburg 1991:3-4.

Chapter Four

Gypsies and Pioneers: Images of RVers

He [John Bunnell, the sheriff of Multnomah County] said that trailer parks are exactly where he would have gone looking for someone like Timothy McVeigh.... He never passes a trailer park without getting the creeps.[1]

* * *

Outsiders distrust RVers for the same reason that they distrust gypsies. They think, "They're not us. They are rootless. They might steal our silverware or our daughters." (Statement by an RVer, from our 1994 journal)

* * *

What I especially like about the LTVA is the friendly people and that we can take care of ourselves. We're not dependent on others for entertainment. The pioneer spirit. (From an interview of an LTVA resident, 1990.)

Outsiders often stereotype "people who live on wheels" as being like gypsies.[2] They think both are homeless, dishonest, untrustworthy, tax-avoiding "trailer trash" because they are nomadic and assumed to be poor. RVers, on the other hand, emphasize the freedom and independence of their way of life and think of themselves as being like the early pioneers. Both sedentary folk and RVers use the metaphors of gypsy and pioneer to create stereotypical images of RVers. The images emphasize different aspects of pioneer and gypsy and lead to dissimilar conclusions about RVers and their way of life. In this chapter we explore how RVers and outsiders manipulate words and other symbols in order to manage images and influence behavior.

Stereotypes are generally oversimplified images based on one or two exaggerated characteristics that come to describe the entire category (blondes are dumb; seniors are bad drivers). Although stereotypes are seldom accurate, people tend to behave toward the categorized group as though the images were true and real. Stereotypes are often constructed of symbols and metaphors that can be reference points for identity. Symbols and metaphors tell us something we did not know about someone, or direct our attention to a particular characteristic of a person or group.[3] Remember, for example, the perception we have of RVers from the metaphors used by columnist Peter Newman cited in Chapter Three:

> The free-wheeling homes — once mobile kennels for shifty itinerants — have now grown up.... The trailerites that inhabit these "20th Century Turtle shells" may be restless nomads, but trailer living is no longer a form of hoboism.[4]

Although Newman purportedly was making a positive statement about trailer living (it is now "grown up" or mature and by implication respectable and acceptable to polite society; it is no longer a form of hoboism), the reader is left with an image of "restless nomads" and "shifty itinerants" living, animal-like, in their kennels and shells. Would *you* want these (respectable, perhaps, but not quite respectable enough to live in a human dwelling) folks as your neighbors?

Gypsies, Trailer Trash, and Slightly Affluent Street People

"People think because you live in a trailer you're trash."[5]

The terms "gypsy" and "pioneer" resonate with conflicting metaphoric and symbolic meanings. Depending on the qualities to be emphasized, a nomad may have a heroic image — the courageous pioneer — or a disreputable one — the gypsy. One persistent image is that RVers are gypsies. If we say of an RVer "he is a gypsy," we have a different picture of him than if we say "he is a pioneer." Both gypsy and pioneer are in the domain of persons who live on wheels. Gypsies and pioneers are on the move, without settled homes, on the margins of mainstream settled society. However, gypsies are negatively stereotyped as being untrustworthy. They are portrayed as rootless, poor, dirty, dishonest transients who attempt to get something for nothing. Landlords are reportedly reluctant to rent to them because they fear rubbish, loud noise, and damage to property.[6] They have, in Sahlins's terms, a relationship with the rest of society characterized by negative reciprocity: "the attempt to get something for nothing with impunity" using strategies that include "'haggling' or 'barter,' 'gambling,' 'chicanery,' 'theft,' and other varieties of seizure."[7]

Outsiders often have the same image of people whose houses are on wheels, whether those homes are actually movable or not. Wallis quotes an individual whose objections to a mobile home owner becoming a neighbor are representative:

> People who live in mobile homes just don't take care of their property. You see trashed out cars, propped up on milk crates, sitting in the front yard for years at a time. What's that kind of thing going to do to our property values?[8]

A similar sentiment was expressed to us by a member of a bankrupt membership park, whose original clientele was limited to those able to pay a membership fee of several thousand dollars. When we met him in the failed park he told us that although he had always liked the park, he was wary about taking advantage of his opportunity to buy an undivided interest in it because he was uncomfortable about the possible quality of future campers. When park residents were restricted to those who were members of a nationwide membership organization, he felt secure in leaving his doors open and belongings out on the table while he was gone. He stopped doing that after the park opened its gates to casual travellers because of "the type of people we get in here. Anybody can come in now." He was referring specifically to "trailers with flat tires and people live in them anyway."

The idea that people on wheels were violating North American values became particularly strong in the 1930s when trailers were home for many families. Some became trailerites out of choice, some to follow possible work opportunities, and some because they could afford nothing else. These early full-timers were an independent lot who broke the rules of polite society, supposedly endangering family and community. Their behavior threatened the establishment and contributed to the legacy of negative images that still plagues people on wheels.[9]

One component of the gypsy metaphor that adheres to RVers is the notion that people who have no fixed address — whose home is not attached to a piece of ground somewhere — are nomadic and, therefore, irresponsible and untrustworthy. As a full-timer told us, the biggest problem with RVing is "the way 'normal' people see RVers as nomads and shiftless, when nothing is further from the truth." The Petersons explain the distrust of some outsiders as deriving from the mistaken notion that RVers are homeless: "Most of us are afraid of what we don't understand, and our society certainly does not seem to understand that an RV can also be a home. The general attitude seems to be that full-time RVing is a new social disease. They say, 'Responsible people don't live like gypsies.'"[10]

In part, outsiders place RVers in the same category as gypsies or the homeless because they do not know what else to do with them. Escapees recount with wry humor the results of their inclusion in the US census count in 1990 during the fall Escapade in Los Banos, California. After the Skips were enumerated, the story goes, officials were unsure where to put them because there is no census category for RVers whose only address is their rig. So they classified them as "homeless people." One official was overheard wondering if they shouldn't be termed "slightly affluent street people."[11] We were told that so many Escapees were enumerated that federal funding for the needy was increased in Los Banos.

Definitely Not Us: Negative Images of RVers

Like gypsies, "trailerists" are sometimes stereotyped as challenging the mainstream values of "rootedness," permanence, land-ownership, and community. As we saw in the previous chapter, local officials may allege that they enjoy public facilities without paying taxes to support them, that they are without a sense of community, and that they take no pride in their homes and surroundings. Furthermore, there is a belief that their environment is a haven for criminals. Consider the following description of a trailer park from the *New Yorker* magazine:

> John Bunnell, the sheriff of Multnomah County ... told me that trailer parks are populated with elderly folks and migrant workers and people with no money who need shelter, but that he mostly thought of trailer parks as places to go if you want to get lost, so they are the first places he heads when he's looking for a suspect. He said that because trailer parks are isolated and secluded, they harbor a lot of crime, like drug dealing and prostitution; law-enforcement people have nicknamed the worst parks "Felony Flats." ... He said that trailer parks are exactly where he would have gone looking for someone like Timothy McVeigh, someone who wanted to live in the margins, to be self-contained, to conduct business unnoticed. Then he added that he never passes a trailer park without getting the creeps, because the first crime scene he ever investigated was in a park near Portland: in the middle of the night, a drunk, half asleep in his trailer, had heard a noise, grabbed his gun, and fired. The bullet pierced the wall of the trailer as if it were cutting through a cracker; it struck a three-year-old boy, who was peeing outside, and killed him.[12]

These are powerful and frightening images. The sheriff in this piece alleges that in addition to being harbors for criminals — presumed terrorists, murderers of children — parks resonate with violence, filth, and sneakiness. Their residents are marginal people seeking to commit their acts in secret. Even the unfortunate child is killed while doing in public an act decent people do only in private: urinating.[13] These images give *us* the creeps, and we lived in "trailer parks" for over a year. We know better!

Although RV parks and trailer parks are technically different sorts of places, they are conflated in the public mind and can overlap in fact as well. The park in this *New Yorker* story was probably an RV park well along in its life cycle. In older parks, some residents, mostly elderly folks, live permanently in *immobile* homes or skirted-in RVs. (A rig is skirted in when its wheels are covered to prevent weather damage due to long immobility. See the Glossary for a more detailed explanation.). Others — itinerant workers or snowbirds — stay for months at a time. Still others are travellers parked overnight or for a week or two. Most RV parks eventually reach this stage. Whether you think of a park like this as an "RV park" or a "trailer park" depends on whether you focus on the skirts over the wheels or the "Overnighters Welcome" sign; on whether you see the colorful tourist's shirt, the torn T-shirt, or the stained work shirt. It is a matter of perspective.

Kay Peterson protests that it is inappropriate to label the RV way of life with frightening metaphors.

> The idea of "being rootless" actually scares some people. And some just can't get rid of the connotation given to gypsies of an earlier time period. The word "transient" echoes in their minds with contempt as they picture a "hippie" van on which all sorts of belongings are tied to the roof and the back bumper. Inside are people who are undependable, dishonest, and lazy.... It doesn't matter that the full-time RVer is none of those things. It doesn't matter that modern RVs are luxurious homes with every convenience. Tags and labels are part of the society we live in. To be wrongly labelled is intolerable.[14]

The images of RVers as gypsies and as pioneers have a common root: nostalgia for a mythological golden age of North American society existing some time back in the "Paleoterrific," a time when we were, in Stephanie Coontz's words, "the way we never were." The characteristics of this ideal society were mutually contradictory. As Coontz observes, the vision of the ideal traditional family is "an ahistorical amalgam of structures, values, and behaviors that never co-existed in the same time and place."[15] For instance, the model of family life was an extended family residence pattern with children settling near their parents to care for them as they aged. At the same time, young couples were urged to be independent and self-sufficient, and society idealized the heroic pioneers who pulled up roots to follow the call of the open road and adventure. This ideal society was law-abiding and respectful of a hierarchically imposed authority, while simultaneously enshrining the inviolability of individual liberty. People were expected to respect and obey authority while also being created equal to anyone and thus responsible for their own decisions and behavior. Their national identity depended on their having the courage to rebel against restrictions on their freedom. In this society women were cherished as modest, circumspect, and family-oriented. Like June Cleaver, they should submit to the needs of their husbands and families. But they should also be strong and independent. Their role models helped drive the Conestoga wagon west, worked long hours in the fields, made do with few comforts, and fought hardship, wild animals, and hostiles beside their men. It was a society of pioneers in which neighbors trusted, helped, and depended on one another. It was also a society where people were independent, self-reliant, and free to move on when the country became too crowded or when claims by others on one's time and resources became too demanding. Its people were home-loving, dependable and stable folks, with gypsy feet and the courage to seek adventure and freedom.[16] Inevitably, trailer dwellers could not live up to these contradictory role models. Some of them did not even try, and as they violated the rules of proper, middle-class society, they contributed to the opprobrious label of "trailer trash."

They ignored standards of dress and proper behavior

Middle-class dress codes of the 1930s demanded that women dress in calf-length skirts and men in ties and coats. Trailerites declined. In the "shirt-sleeve society" of trailer camps, women wore pants and men dressed in polo shirts. Some men were even seen outdoors in their undershirts. A casual attitude toward dress is also characteristic of contemporary RVers whose wardrobes seldom contain garb appropriate for even moderately formal occasions. We met only one full-timer who wore stylish and expensive-looking clothing and who changed outfits at least once a day. In her former life she had been a nun! This casual approach to appearance has fed the image of RVers as slobs, an image highlighted in 1988 by an advertisement in the national trade publication *Advertising Age*.

US magazine, in a promotional layout that appeared in the 23 May 1988 issue of *Advertising Age* contrasted its readership with people who might be described as "trailer trash." The ad consisted of a two-page spread dominated by a photograph of an RV campground peopled with aging, slovenly men and women sitting in disarray — some of the men in undershirts — around shabby RVs. The side bar text made no reference to the photograph, but noted the high median income, the active social life, and the generally upscale life style of *US* readers. The contrast was made explicit by the photo's caption: "Definitely Not *US!*" The advertisement was reprinted in *Trailer Life* and readers were asked to send letters to the publisher of *US Magazine* with copies to *Trailer Life*.[17]

As a typical RV person, I am 60, own a $75,000 home on a half-acre, have a $22,000 truck and a $30,000 fifth-wheel trailer. My retirement, completely disposable, is well over $31,000 a year (Response to *US Magazine* ad by Graydon Lewis).

* * *

You will often see me and my husband relaxing in camp, but usually after a day of hiking nature trails, bird watching, breathing fresh air, and just plain enjoying nature. My idea of relaxation is definitely not going to an expensive resort crawling with snobs showing off their clothes (Response to *US Magazine* ad by Marilyn Noon).

They rejected the consumer ethic

Collecting "things" had, by the 1920s, become a North American preoccupation. It is, however, impossible to fit many things into a covered wagon or a travel trailer. Like the pioneers before them, dedicated RVers must sell, pass on, or store non-essential articles. Even pets must be portable. One group of RVers who were organizing their own park included in a 1993 version of their bylaws a prohibition against pets more than 15 inches high! Another park is reputed to prohibit a total pet weight of more than 20 pounds.

Thornburg says the early trailerites "deliberately stepped out of the world wide, centuries-old cycle of inherited property." Their rejection of the importance of consumer goods threatened the economic establishment and violated "the American way." Rather than being praised for their frugality and their asceticism in living the simple life, they were castigated as being poor, shiftless, and untrustworthy.[18]

Today RVers who reject the consumer ethic and attempt to live frugally are perceived as trying to get something for nothing, as being "cheap," a criticism levelled particularly at boondockers since the early days of the auto gypsies who lived for months in free campgrounds.[19] Boondockers are regarded by others with considerable ambivalence. On the one hand, the way boondockers live epitomizes the values on which America was founded. They are independent of rules and regulations. They live simply with a minimum of luxury and expense. They embody the qualities of individualism and ingenuity. And they cooperate on their own terms for mutual security and to share resources. On the other hand, they are marginal to North American society. Many of them have no fixed address — not even a mail box in an RV park. Many, particularly those who are flea marketers, participate in an underground economy that avoids regulations and taxes — a fact that is not lost on officials of nearby towns. Most instructive and, we think, representative of the attitude of civic officials toward boondocking flea marketers, is a letter cited by Errington that expresses the resentment of a small town businessman toward transient vendors who pay no taxes and little rent and face none of the risks and costs endured by town retailers. "Let's tax 'em." he says, "Let's set up a licensing procedure that will discourage the money hounds."[20]

Boondockers are also marginal because of the kinds of places they park. They camp on the desert, often in the shade of a creosote bush or small thorn tree, without any amenities, recreation facilities, or external protection from ruffians who might harass or rob them.

A particularly fascinating area where boondockers gather to spend the winter months is known as Slab City or the Slabs. People who spend much time there are likely to be stereotyped as both cheap and marginal. The site of Slab City is an abandoned US military base near Niland California.

"SLABS
Population Unknown
Most Residents Live
Somewhere Else"
(Sign at the entrance
to Slab City)

It is named for the concrete slabs that served as floors for the temporary World War II buildings. RVers who approach the Slabs for the first time are soon aware that it is an unusual place. They are greeted by a sign informing them that the population of Slab City is unknown and that most residents live somewhere else. An empty guard kiosk, painted blue, announces: "Slab City. Welcome." To the right of the entrance is Salvation Mountain, a barren hill that one resident has spent over ten years decorating with painted birds and flowers and with messages celebrating God's love. To the east the US military has a bombing range in the Chocolate Mountains. During the Gulf War, Slab City residents enjoyed the nightly light show that was the result of the military's bombing and shelling practice.

Slab City is entered by a paved road and is criss-crossed by dirt roads leading to blocks of concrete slabs. Residents either park their rigs on the slabs or use them as a patio base. Some do both. While most of the residents of Slab City are seasonals who stay from November or December through early March, some live there permanently. Everyone lives there free.

We first heard of this site during our 1990 study. Several RVers told us that our study would be incomplete if we missed the Slabs. They usually added that we would not want to spend more than one night there. To them Slab City was a spectacle to behold rather than a place to stay. In describing

Residents either park their rigs on the slabs or use them as a patio base. Some do both.

it, they emphasized that people live there *permanently*, often in shabby or broken down rigs. The place has neither formal structure nor services for the people who live or winter there, they said. Consequently many residents dispose of their sewage by simply digging a hole in the desert, putting their drain pipe into it and covering it over. They could not, they said, understand how people could live like that.

The "trailer trash" image of boondockers in general and Slab City residents in particular is shared by some law enforcement officials. In February 1994 we talked with one such individual in El Centro, California, about his perceptions of local boondocking areas. In his opinion, boondock-ers — especially at the Slabs — are "people who don't have much money. If they did they'd go to RV parks or somewhere they'd have water and comforts." They are, he said, "the type of person that is less than you find in the population as a whole." It was his impression that most boondockers are people over the age of 60. According to this man, the sheriff's office has "many calls" about the Slabs. He also characterized Slab City as a gathering point for fugitives, people on welfare, and people on drugs, accusations reminiscent of the statements of Sheriff Bunnell. He went on to allege that the major problem with the Long Term Visitor Area located at the Hot Springs was pollution of the water from people defecating in it, adding that there had been drowning deaths of elderly people who had too much to drink and were put to sleep by the warm water.

Not all local officials in the El Centro area agreed with the man we spoke to or shared his negative image of boondockers. When we asked at the El Centro Chamber of Commerce if the problems detailed by this official were widespread, they were appalled by his comments and claimed to know of no such difficulties. Rangers at the Bureau of Land Management local office, too, denied knowledge of drownings in the hot springs for any reason.

The founders and many of the early members of Escapees were dedicated boondockers and, as we see later in this chapter, the club encourages members to boondock as a way of experiencing freedom. Bob, one of our Escapees informants, recalled that when he was a child his family lived in a trailer park for military personnel. "The park was the pits and we were treated like the dregs of society," he said. The image still haunts him. He thinks the emphasis Escapees place on boondocking contributes to the problems experienced by RVers. When people stay in the K-Mart parking lot for days rather than pay to go to a local park, Bob says, outsiders get a bad impression and apply it to all RVers. In a letter to the *Escapees Newsletter*, Judy Apple, both a businesswoman and an Escapee, details the objectionable behavior of some boondockers and argues that the unacceptable behavior of a few tarnishes the image of all. Her critique charges that boondockers ask a favor and then take advantage of the generosity of others, are filthy and contaminate the area where they park, are inconsiderate of others who are left to clean up after them, and have no respect for the rights or property of others. She argues that local residents are rightfully disgusted by this behavior which they assume is characteristic of all RVers. Therefore they stereotype all RVers as dirty, inconsiderate, and opportunistic, and treat them accordingly. She concludes, "Granted, not all RVers are this way; however, this is how we get a bad name and consequently have anger vented at us by locals in the area where we visit.... Camping areas are being closed daily because of the 'low-lifers' who call themselves 'RVers.'"[21]

There was — and still is — little privacy

Of necessity, much of life in an RV park is spent outdoors, and many activities are carried out in public view. Some RVers even hang their laundry — including their underwear — outside their rigs for everyone to see. For many people, in the 1930s and today as well, there is something vaguely immoral about people who eat, play, and live outdoors much of the year. By the 1930s, mainstream social life was becoming isolated and impersonal. Instead of sitting on their porches visiting, people stayed inside listening to radios, behavior foreshadowing the isolated, fenced-in back yards and television couch potatoes of the 1990s. In contrast, trailer society retained older, communal patterns of life. Today, as in the 1930s, RVers spend time together working and playing. In good weather, they sit outside under their awnings and visit. Or they play games, go for walks, or share tasks. At The Hot Spring they clean the spring and pool, they play horseshoes, or they glean harvested fields for free food. In Escapees parks they rake leaves, repair walking paths, or work on construction crews. In bad weather they gather in club houses to visit, play games, do crafts, share food, dance, and sing. They behave like people in a community.

They appeared to violate the work ethic

Although many trailerites worked, outsiders presumed that anyone who lived in a dwelling with wheels and a striped awning must be on permanent vacation. They were criticized for not being useful or improving themselves, for flagrantly wasting their lives and talents, and for being engaged in the "conspicuous pursuit of leisure." They were, in other words, behaving like stereotypical gypsies. A disgruntled member of the Good Sam Club specifically applies this aspect of the gypsy stereotype to today's RVers:

> When we joined Good Sam we thought we were joining a group of people who shared our enjoyment of the great outdoors. We didn't realize that Good Sam membership required investment in tremendously expensive and questionably useful RV machines. Nor can we visualize ourselves as full-time gypsy tourists, roaming aimlessly around the country with neither roots nor any object in life other than the desire to be somewhere else at any given time.... Instead of being a fountain of information useful to the broad range of campers, it [the Good Sam Club] panders to the impulse buyers of the recreational dinosaurs of the open road.[22]

They violated the stereotype of old age

The disgruntled Good Sam member's description of RVers as "gypsy tourists" points to a fundamental problem that mainstream North Americans have with people who live in homes on wheels. Unfortunately, it is not the only one. Retired RVers are doubly stigmatized because they occupy two categories of marginalized, devalued people: they are both elderly and RVers. The stereotype of older RVers as an undesirable category is insidious and pervasive. For example, in 1994 Louis Harris and Associates did a survey on public perceptions of RVs and RVers for the Recreation Vehicle

Industry Association. One of the perceptions of RV owners that Louis Harris considered to be negative was "RV owners tend to be elderly." This contrasted with the positive impression, "RV owners are successful well-to-do people.[23]

Retired RVers are also criticized because they challenge the stereotypes of the elderly as rocking-chair bound, cookie-baking Golden Agers and Perfect Grandparents. Retired RVers — from the 1930s to the 1990s — found an alternative to sitting back and waiting to die. They choose action, non-conformity, and life rather than "wisdom," social acceptance, and early death. This behavior makes some people uncomfortable, especially when seniors spend their savings rather than putting them aside for the next generation. They are seen to be using up scarce resources, an image that may be reinforced by their bumper stickers reading "I'm spending my children's inheritance." Their choice is also seen as one inappropriately separating them from children and grandchildren. At the time of their lives when they should be surrounded by their children and dandling their grandchildren on their knees, they are off partying in the desert.

Ironically, some local people resent retired RVers not because they are poor, but because they seem to be rich. For instance, in 1993 a resident of an Escapees park discussed with us her concern over local resentment of the "rich RVers" in the park. She had overheard grumbling about the "rich people in their big motor homes" while she was using the local "washateria." There is a lot of unemployment in the local community where most of the 5000 people subsist on minimum wage, she said. One man — toothless, dirty, and an unemployed electrician — told her he would like to take her home so she could see how *he* had to live.

There is no requirement that concurrently held stereotypes be consistent. While some portray RVers as cheap non-consumers, others depict them as being possession-crazy, selfish devourers of scarce resources. Recall Phillips' complaint that RVs are "the recreational dinosaurs of the open road." Another writer, exaggerating for humorous effect, lumps together RVers of all kinds and portrays them as driving

> massive, self-contained dwellings on wheels that took up three parking spaces and jutted out so far that cars coming in could only barely scrape past. These things, these RVs, are like life-support systems on wheels. Astronauts go to the moon with less backup. RV people are another breed — and a largely demented one at that. They become obsessed with trying to equip their vehicles with gadgets to deal with every possible contingency. Their lives become ruled by the dread thought that one day they

may find themselves in a situation in which they are not entirely self-sufficient.... You can see these people at campgrounds all over the country, standing around their vehicles comparing gadgets — methane-powered ice-cube makers, portable tennis courts, anti-insect flame throwers, inflatable lawns. They are strange and dangerous people and on no account should be approached.[24]

While this author plays on the image of RVer as avaricious over-consumer, the following letter combines the images of elderly RVers depleting scarce resources and grasping, self-indulgent seniors who are dependent on the taxes paid by those whose resources they greedily exploit:

> We are not retired, and during the majority of the year we have to work. We work a five-day week in order to enjoy the weekends for camping. Friday comes, and we head for our favorite parks that are not too far away.
>
> What do we find when we arrive? A park full of senior RVers.... They have come in the night before and totally taken over the park. They have not only taken the choice spots, but, in many cases, have taken every spot. We travel for an hour after getting off work, only to be turned away.... Why do senior groups wait until the weekend to get together? Why aren't they coming into the parks on Sunday, when the rest of us are on our way home?... Come on, you retired folks, leave the weekend for those of us still putting money into the Social Security system for people like you to live on![25]

This is, indeed, the image of elderly RVers who are spending their children's inheritance, a view that exists simultaneously with the stereotype of the dependent, incompetent elderly person. One example of this image is, ironically, enshrined on the mantelpiece of the club house at Escapees headquarters, one of the last places one would expect to find seniors who have retired to their rocking chairs to wait to die. In a framed letter, the Texas Alcoholic Beverage Commission gives the Escapees club permission to have bingo games "for the amusement and recreation of the patients."

In summary, a typical stereotype of RVers in general, and retired RVers in particular, is that they are gypsy-like. They are homeless and cheap; they violate the consumer ethic; they threaten community and "family values"; and they are trailer-trash and slobs. At the same time, they are seniors who do not act their age. They are selfish, immature, gadget-ridden consumers.

They pollute the atmosphere, spend their children's inheritance, and selfishly consume scarce resources. They are having fun instead of vegetating in their rocking chairs.

Playing With Images: Turning It Around

In "talking-point" guidelines for industry "spokespeople," the Recreation Vehicle Industry Association (RVIA) suggests spokespeople avoid using the term "RV lifestyle." The organization reasons as follows: "While this term has been widely used in the past, research has shown us that RV owners do not see RV ownership as a lifestyle in and of itself, but rather as a means of enhancing their enjoyment of the activities they choose to pursue."[26]

The RVIA is undoubtedly correct with respect to RVers who use their rigs primarily for vacations or snowbirds who only use them as fixed homes and drive from one to another. For many serious and full-time RVers, however, the complex of community and self-image they associate with RVing creates a distinctive way of life to which they are deeply committed. The gypsy image, which ironically embodies many of the negative stereotypes of RVers, is also an element of their identity. Kay Peterson conflates the image of gypsy and pioneer. She says: "The earliest camping pioneers called themselves auto gypsies. They were like the boondockers (dry campers) of today."[27] In styling themselves as gypsies, RVers focus on the qualities of travel — freedom and the adventurous spirit — positive components of the gypsy image. One respondent, in answer to the question "What do you think made you capable of going full-time?" replied "Willingness to try new things and places. A good measure of gypsy helps." Another told us during an interview, "I can hardly remember when I didn't think camping. I've always had terrible gypsy feet!"[28]

So, many RVers do not concede that the gypsy image is wholly undesirable. For them the idea of being gypsy-like, of having a gypsy spirit, is part of the definition of being an RVer. It is an aspect of the "RV lifestyle."

As Fernandez observes, people are creative and innovative in their use of metaphor. They play with images, emphasizing valued qualities (a jelly fish has a sting as well as being spineless) and putting a positive spin on a devalued metaphor.[29] The *Chatelaine* magazine reporter quoted in Chapter Three, who described the adventures of two women who converted a truck into the 1930s equivalent of a motor home, emphasized the appeal of being a gypsy. Although having a gypsy spirit prevents a person from settling down in one place for long, she says, it also "cures" a person of roots that are too deep. It leads one to travel, and travel is healing, educational, and a source of happy memories.[30] RVers would agree. They are her kind of gypsies!

By emphasizing the qualities of adventure and flexibility instead of transience and poverty, RVers may transform the image of gypsies so that they sound very much like pioneers. In her letter to us, retiree Peggy Bowhay of Georgetown, Ontario, nicely accomplishes this metamorphosis. In her discussion of why she enjoys RVing, she includes a return to old values of neighborliness and helpfulness; the opportunity to live near (but not with) scattered family; the qualities of adventure, flexibility, and freedom to decide spontaneously what to do and when and where to do it; the joys of travel; and the ability to leave things behind. All of these virtues are attributed to "gypsy blood" as in the following excerpt from her letter:

> By this method [RVing] we are finding again the old standards of neighborliness and helpfulness which, sadly, no longer seem to exist in "normal" day-to-day living, and because a lot of us no longer live (again sadly) close to our families, it is a way of seeing our children and living close by them, for a time, but not with them.... Another factor is, that we believe totally in trying to live in the moment, which again in the world as it is, is very hard to do, even when retired. However, we found it much easier in a motor home, where we could decide from moment to moment what to do and where and when.... I think you have to have a sense of adventure, and be ready to adapt to the situation at hand. Some people are not programmed to do that, and although I love my home life and my husband loves growing his organic veggies, we did find it easy to leave it all behind.... I must say it was satisfying to watch others mow lawns and tidy up camp grounds, whilst we walked, swam, lay and read or just plain idled!... Homo sapiens have obviously done a lot of roving down the centuries, and are still doing so. Possibly those of us in our motor homes are doing it in a more luxurious manner, but the "gypsy" blood is still flowing through our veins.

Although many RVers see themselves as gypsy-like, they also say that they are essentially like other North Americans. They challenge inappropriate labels which may have unfortunate consequences. For example, in the 1980s the town of Mariposa, California, blocked the efforts of a group of Escapees to locate a park there because they feared the residents would become welfare recipients. They saw SKPs building a "trailer park," not an "RV park."

The following letter to the *Sierra Star* is an effort by an Escapee to correct the misunderstanding. Marple argues that RVers are no different from their more sedentary fellow citizens:

> What are Escapees like? We are probably the most ordinary looking people you will ever see. Most frequently we are senior citizens, married couples, now retired from various backgrounds and occupations. Presently a group of about 28 SKPs are working on the premises south of Coarsegold. Among the people there are ex-teachers, businessmen, firemen, an accountant, contractors, mechanics, and [sic] optometrist, and a forest ranger. We are all there doing some preliminary work on the site of our "Park of the Sierras" Co-Op.... There are presently eight such Co-Op SKP parks across the US, another three are being built, and there is a retreat at the national headquarters in Livingston, Texas. All of these parks have been very popular in their communities and give a big boost to the local economies.
>
> You might see us patronizing your local stores, restaurants, churches, square dances, gas stations or banks, but it may be difficult to tell us from your local residents.
>
> So, there is no need to hide you [sic] children in the attic, lengthen the chain on your Pit bull or to lock up your chicken house, because we are people just like yourselves that happen to be retired and live an RV life Style.[31]

Adventurous souls and pioneers: How RVers see themselves

> Agatha is proud of her resourcefulness and her ability to manage on a small budget. She and Al like to boondock, she makes her own bread, and they glean food and share with others because they want to be independent, self-reliant, and self-sufficient. On her questionnaire, Agatha wrote that what she likes about the LTVA is "The friendly people. The fact that we can take care of ourselves, not being dependent on others for entertainment. The pioneer spirit."

In contrast to the gypsy, the pioneer is a cardinal symbol in North American culture, one with which RVers identify. RVers explicitly and self-consciously describe themselves as being the modern embodiment of the early pioneers. They see themselves as being, like pioneers, independent, sharing, caring, resourceful, self-sufficient, and free. They are driven by a yearning to know "what is over the next hill." In an article entitled "Pioneering Bloodlines" one RVer emphasizes the similarities between today's RVers and American pioneers. Both were required to be more self-sufficient and resourceful than their more sedentary contemporaries if they were to successfully meet the challenges they encountered. Also both had to deal with a dangerous society: "Our modern society is no less dangerous than that of the pioneers," she says.[32]

A full-timer is an adventurous soul, a saddle tramp who wants to go and see what is over the next hill. (Description of a full-timer by a full-time RVer. From our 1990 journal)

* * *

As Fernandez points out, metaphoric statements can be self-fulfilling.[33] Like Agatha, the RVer with a pioneer self-image may describe herself as independent and self-sufficient, a living representative of the "pioneer spirit." If she reinforces this image in her thoughts and words,

What kind of woman travels alone in an RV? She's the same kind who drove the Conestoga wagons and forded streams in her petticoats, discovering new frontiers (Powell 1993:61).

the metaphor may become a model for behavior, and she may come to reproduce in her own activities some of the definitive characteristics of pioneer life.

Boondocking provides many opportunities to reorganize the world into pioneer scenarios. When RVers boondock they are unconstrained by the requirements of water, sewage, and electrical lines necessary for hookups. This permits them to structure a social space reminiscent of pioneer life. They circle their wagons, front doors and awnings facing a central plaza. The modern wagon circle is designed not to keep "hostiles" out, but to draw friends together. There they gather around their campfire to sing, share a common meal, or play games. Indeed, this is often the physical setting in Long Term Visitor Areas (LTVAs) where many

One hundred years ago when the pioneers were loading their Conestoga wagons, they didn't have to worry about how they would carry their electrical power. But things do have a way of evening out; today we don't have to worry about the possibility of an Indian attack (Farris 1995:91).

boondockers spend the winter. Other RVers organize rallies where people dress in pioneer garb and "circle the wagons" to enclose themselves in a self-contained, independent community.[34] In a letter in October 1992, Lee Windheim, a member of the Good Sam Marin Amblers of California, describes just such a rally where the pioneer motif set the scene: "We dressed for our Sat. cook out in pioneer clothes and had a 'turkey shoot' and other games. Everyone has remarked what a great time they had. Why? It was 'back to our roots' of covered wagon days — without its stress and hardships."

Emphasizing independence and community, RVers also see themselves as pioneers creating a new internal frontier. In a letter to the *Escapees Newsletter*, Dave Weston compares the contemporary builders of Escapees co-op parks to early pioneers:

To me, we are the "pioneers" of our century — building new communities where none have been before, and creating brand new social structures at the same time. Of course there is friction. SKPs are independent types. But the original pioneers who settled this country must have been independent types, too. As I pulled into the Mariposa Fairgrounds I had a vision of ox-drawn covered wagons. Maybe, 200 years from now, people will talk about "the early SKPs who braved hostile county supervisors to settle Co-Ops in the wild sun belt."[35]

Even more important than the external manifestations — the dress and circled wagons — are the values that reveal themselves in pioneer life: freedom, independence, self-reliance, and community, including mutual assistance. The first of these is freedom.

Freedom

An essential element in the lifestyles of both gypsies and pioneers is the deeply held American value of freedom. The concept of freedom is a fundamental and inseparable component of the image of the pioneer, one that inspires in many a lump in the throat and nostalgia for the past.

Freedom means many things. One of its meanings is relief "as much as possible from the demands of conformity to family, friends, or community." Freedom may be incompatible with responsibility toward family and community. In this sense, the freedom to be left alone is really the freedom to *be* alone. It is difficult to reconcile this view of freedom with community, and it makes some people uneasy. As the authors of *Habits of the Heart* observe, there is in North America an anxiety about the individualist "who flees from home and family leaving the values of community and tradition behind." This unease is expressed in the charge that RVers have rejected community.[36]

Those who think of permanence and property as necessary elements of community assume that RVers *cannot* participate in community. They contend that RVers have opted out of society and repudiated community values — acts that threaten the very concept of community. This

Lana Brown's grandparents were full-timers when they were young, travelling from mine to mine where her grandfather was a blacksmith. Brown writes wistfully of her grandmother's memories of those days of freedom. "Their brood of five children spent much of their growing up time hanging on the running boards," and living in makeshift camps, she writes. "But most of all they had a canopy of stars that shined through the crystal clear desert sky." In talking about those days, Lana's grandmother Cassie "would whisper with a deep sigh in her voice, 'There was *freedom* out there then. Freedom to move, and freedom to decide to stay a while longer in a pretty place. Freedom to climb a mountain or freedom to sit by the campfire. I miss that more than anything else'" (Brown 1988:17).

assumption was voiced by a psychiatrist with whom we discussed our RV research. He informed us that retired people who leave their homes, friends, and children to take to the road are rejecting both community and responsibility. In his opinion, as a group they are selfish, immature, irresponsible, antisocial people. Wallis reports similar attitudes toward mobile home residents who perceive the potential mobility of the mobile home as a threat. "How, people ask, can people who live in houses on wheels honor a commitment to community?"[37]

As Thornburg observes, for some North Americans freedom is a necessity of life. The ideological heirs of the freedom-loving pioneers of a century ago were victims of the disease he calls "trailer fever." Trailer fever was probably an early variant of the affliction modern RVers call "hitch-itch."

> There is a certain type of American for whom freedom is more important than food. Always a minority, they reappear in every generation, right at the point where the social fabric is thinnest, right where the laws and mores and customs and taboos are just about to rupture and spill out into some new and temporarily looser mold: a new territory, a new social system, a new tomorrow.... They were the frontier folks, the sod-busting pioneers.... They're always on the road, and so they always have plenty of company.... In many ways they are quintessentially American.... They are a product of the system, but not quite a part of it. They're the observers, the outsiders, the misfits.... We can handle these misfits one at a time.... But what happens when ... a quarter million or more of them come out of the woodwork at once.... A quarter million self-sufficient individuals out there on the road, all marching in roughly the same direction, all following some hazy star of freedom and independence that's invisible to everybody else.... Does it excuse them to say that they're not really rebels, misfits, cranks — that they just have a bad case of a recently isolated disease called trailer fever?[38]

This individualist version of freedom emphasizes the difficulties inherent in a core value that separates us from our fellows. The authors of *Habits of the Heart* also observe the contradiction in simultaneously held values of freedom and individualism on the one hand and commitment to community on the other:

> Freedom is perhaps the most resonant, deeply held American value.... Yet freedom turns out to mean being left alone by

> others, not having other people's values, ideas, or styles of life
> forced upon one, being free of arbitrary authority in work, family,
> and political life.... And if the entire social world is made up of
> individuals, each endowed with the right to be free of others'
> demands, it becomes hard to forge bonds of attachment to, or
> cooperation with, other people, since such bonds would imply
> obligations that necessarily impinge on one's freedom.[39]

As these authors remind us, freedom may be incompatible with the North
American ideal of community. Indeed, perhaps "freedom and community
can be reconciled only in the nostalgic dream of an idealized past."[40]

This is why settled folk are uneasy with those who value freedom so
much they leave the responsibilities of home and community to strike out
into the wilderness. In the arena where self-sufficient individuals become
misfits, drifters, vagabonds, and migrants, the distinction between gypsy and
pioneer becomes hazy and the images merge.

For many RVers, their lifestyle *is* freedom and its companions, independence and adventure. In response to the question, "What do you like best
about RVing?," our respondents produced a chorus in praise of freedom,
independence, and adventure.

When asked what they would miss *most* if they had to give up RV living,
almost 20 per cent cited freedom or independence. When we asked who was
best suited to full-timing, over 50 per cent said such people needed to be
independent, self-confident, adaptable, and adventurous. Asked to identify
qualities that make for successful full-timing, one-third said independence
and love of adventure were most important. For example:

> A spirit of adventure, a love of the outdoors, an outgoing nature,
> an affinity for meeting people and making friends, a great sense
> of humor! An independent spirit.

> Wanting to find out what and who is on the other side of the hill
> and having the guts to do it.

> A sense of adventure, degrees of freedom not attainable, desire
> to see and do new places and things,... self-reliant, yet not
> bashful to ask assistance from others nor to admit others more
> knowledgeable and competent than himself in certain areas.

The spirit of adventure is a part of the pioneering image of RVers who feel
it links them to each other and to their pioneer forebears. As one RVer said,

"We modern pioneers have an indomitable spirit of adventure that links us one to the other as it does to all the pioneers who preceded us."[41] For some, like Karen and Scott Bonis, the freedom of RVing becomes their reality. The Bonises, who were aerospace engineers before they became full-timers, wrote in response to a friend who asked when they planned to give up RVing and return to the "real world":

> My reality involves, first, the freedom to do what we want with our time. Along with this is the ability to go where we choose, and to remain or leave as our whim dictates. In our complex and materialistic society, the reality of this lifestyle is one of the most important aspects of our lives.[42]

For others, the ideology of the Escapees club itself epitomizes freedom. In the following editorial Kay Peterson equates the Statue of Liberty with Escapees and, by extension, with both America and the RV lifestyle. As the Statue of Liberty represents America, Escapees represents independence. Skips should, like the Statue of Liberty, hold high their torch to guide those "yearning to be free":

> America — the land of opportunity and freedom. The opportunity to use one's own ingenuity and talent and sweat to climb as high as one is able to climb and the freedom to choose one's lifestyle.... We should be eternally grateful that our forefathers had the wisdom to come here. For had they chosen almost any other place on earth, it is highly unlikely that you and I would have the economic ability, or the freedom, to live the RV lifestyle.... We chose July 4th to be the official birthday of Escapees because just as the Statue of Liberty represents America, so does the Escapees Club represent the principle of independence.
>
> Individually, we are those with the courage to trade conventional homes for ones on wheels so we can have the freedom to move when we want, where we want. Collectively, Escapees Inc., is a proud experiment in banding together for the common good of all, for the sharing of knowledge and friendship, and for the dedication to the principle that one has the *right to be different*.... With freedom comes the responsibility to help others who wish to be free. We have an obligation to pass on what we have learned. Your membership in Escapees is a lighted torch. You can selfishly shield your torch so that only those closest

to you can see its glimmer, or like the Lady who symbolizes America, you can hold your torch so high it will be a beacon to guide all those "yearning to breathe free" through the darkness of doubt to the "golden door."[43]

Kay Peterson is not alone in associating Escapees with freedom. The following writer explicitly makes the same connection. Note that his notion of freedom includes freedom of movement, freedom of association, freedom to do what he wants to do when he wants to do it, and freedom from worry. All of this he attributes to being a member of Escapees and, by implication, a full-time RVer:

> While others dread change, SKPs look for new opportunities, the new, the exciting, the adventure that's all across this land of opportunity and the freedom to move without asking anyone's permission. I've worked in four states because I wanted to be there. I chose yesterday and I will choose tomorrow where I want to be. I don't have to be *here* unless I want to, because I'm an SKP. I don't have to live like everyone else. I don't have to live with worries. I can choose my friends anywhere and everywhere, all kinds of people wherever I roam. I'm not an SKP just for two or three weeks a year and hoping "someday they'll let me have 5 weeks if the Company doesn't fold." I don't have to wait for retirement to do what I want to do. I'm free to leave or stay because I'm an SKP without any limits except those I place on myself. I'm free, *really free,* because I'm an SKP.[44]

Some Escapees hold that the organization reconciles the contradiction between freedom and community and enables members to have both. Pat and Fred Kennedy, working RVers we met in 1994, say they especially value Escapees because the organization blends individualism and community. This combination tempers the danger that full-timers will become so self-indulgent they are unable to compromise or cooperate with others. Escapees gives RVers an opportunity to maintain their individualism and freedom and still be part of a community where they do things with and for others. "That's what life is about, as far as I'm concerned," Pat said.

Meanings of Freedom

Freedom has many meanings. When an RVer says, "I'm free," we must discover precisely what she means. Is it freedom *from* something or freedom *to do* something? There is no single, agreed-upon definition of freedom among RVers. To them freedom means many things. The following interpretations appeared repeatedly in our conversations with RVers and in their writings.

FREEDOM FROM

For some, it is freedom *from* others who would place limits on what they say or do or who have economic power over them. In response to the question, "What do you like most about RVing?," some RVers gave the following interpretation of freedom:

> The freedom, independence, and security. The fact I can travel, see many wonderful things and do it very comfortably, without great expense and not be tied down. Being free of the bonds (financial mostly) associated with home and property. To distance yourself if necessary from the abuses the business-govt/govt-business entity places upon you continuously.
>
> * * *
>
> We don't pay taxes. We're not bound to anybody, and if you don't like your neighbors you can be gone in 15 minutes.

When the freedom of RVers is threatened by imposed rules and regulations, they react fiercely and vote with their feet (or with their engines). The following example illustrates this response.

In the southern California desert, near the Chocolate Mountains, the Slabs, and the Imperial Valley, many boondockers annually gathered to spend the winter free of charge on land once used as an airport by the US military. In the mid-1980s an entrepreneurial RVer saw a way to profit from this practice and purchased a 99-year lease on the land. He then announced to his fellow RVers that henceforth they would follow rules he established for "his" property and pay a fee to park on "his" land. In response, one by one, during the following night and early morning, the RVers quietly moved their rigs to a nearby Long Term Visitor Area administered by the US Bureau of Land Management. They were also required to pay a small fee to park on this land and BLM rules apply there, but the boondockers so resented the "high-handed" and exploitive behavior of their former companion they refused to return, even when he offered to reduce the fee and forego the rules. One of the people who told us about this event chuckled as he commented that because the lessor had used his available capital to lease the land, he has had no choice but to continue to boondock there. Alone!

In response to a question "which [of a set of choices] is normally of greatest concern to you?," two respondents wrote in their own concerns instead:

> Loss of personal freedom due to oppressive laws and increase in federal police.
>
> * * *
>
> Our unresponsive-to-the-citizenry totalitarian, federal government. This leviathan is totally out-of-control. My fellow countrymen have no ideas re the obligations of citizenship and are very shallow in their understanding of our country's myriad political problems. Our country will undoubtedly take the same path as Hitler's Germany. I am very, very concerned about what will soon befall me, my family and friends.

FREEDOM = BOONDOCKING

For many RVers, freedom is equated with boondocking. Boondockers are free to go where they want when they want, and to leave on a moment's notice if they choose. While those who prefer formal parks may claim the same enjoyment of and commitment to freedom, many boondockers disagree. They maintain that a park-oriented RVing style requires advance planning, an inflexible schedule, and reservations for each night. They reject these restrictions and regard them as a form of imprisonment by fear, not freedom. The following discourse by phred [sic] Tinseth eloquently states the case for boondocking, noting that it gives the practitioner both freedom and self-sufficiency:

> The chief benefit of living in an RV is freedom. Using an RV as a means of going from place to place, then immediately connecting it to power, water, and sewer is a minimal use of that freedom. Using the RV's equipment efficiently, adding other equipment, and modifying the RV for self-sufficiency makes for *maximum* use of that freedom. Owners of an RV that is outfitted for long-term independent parking have maximum flexibility and maximum freedom — the freedom to pick and choose. Owners of a standard, off-the-shelf RV have no flexibility — and

pitifully few choices. They sit, attached to hoses and wires ... simply because they have no alternative.... When you park an RV in the boondocks, complete with toilet, refrigerator, and what not, you're not camping or boondocking — you are living in the boondocks with, what are to the primitive camper, "the amenities." Improving those amenities to the point where you can stay comfortably for extended period is "freedom." The more you improve your situation, the more you approach "self sufficiency."[45]

Boondocking also frees RVers from rules. Nobody tells them where to park or where they can walk their dog. Nobody limits the amount of time they can be visited by their grandchildren. The Petersons list the ways in which boondocking is freedom:

From Indian to pioneer to present day RVer, "boondocking" has been synonymous with "freedom."

Freedom to park where you want without worrying about security.

Freedom from hookups that tie most RVers to established campgrounds [see Glossary entry "established park" for definition]

Freedom from having to decide in the morning where you will spend that night because you must make a reservation.

Freedom from having to back into tight places and unhitch.

Freedom from having to leave because someone else has set your checkout time.[46]

Jackie, a boondocker at the Slabs stated the case for boondocking as freedom both eloquently and succinctly: "People think we're here because it's free. They're wrong. We're not here because *it's* free — we're here because *we're* free!"

FREEDOM FROM THINGS

"Do you own things or do they own you?" (Kay Peterson)

From the beginning, the need to adjust to limited space shaped the lives of RVers. By the 1930s, "thing gathering" had become the American norm, but collections of things just would not fit into a trailer. Whether they are poor or affluent, whether they prefer to boondock or stay in established parks, all serious RVers must face the common problem of limiting what they carry. Because space is limited in an RV, people who derive meaning from collecting things — especially bulky things such as antiques that cannot fit in a rig — are not good candidates for serious or full-time RVing. Neither are people whose passion is a hobby such as gardening or woodworking that requires being in one place for a long time or tools that take up room. Successful full-timers must be minimalists, choosing the important things and leaving the others behind. Lamarche and Langlois, who did a market study of full-timers, say the simple life is a characteristic of these folks:

> Full-timers are a different breed of retiree. In their approach to life, they are adventurous and curious, following the sun and enjoying the outdoors year-round.... "Life simplification" could be their motto: most sell their houses, keeping only a small fraction of the possessions they accumulated over their lifetime.... The respondents tended to be quite anti-materialistic. In order to "fit" in their RVs, most full-timers had divested themselves of many of their possessions. Some have storage facilities where they keep their clothing and other valued items, visiting them from time to time, for instance, to exchange clothing for different seasons. For the most part, however, they carried all of their possessions with them, not believing in the accumulation of "things" any longer.[47]

RVers celebrate minimalism, regarding rejection of the consumer ethic to be a virtue and a form of freedom. For them, getting rid of "things" becomes a rite of passage. Once accomplished it is a source of pride. RVers say the process requires them to have their priorities straight and to be efficient. They are no longer "possessed by their possessions." They know what is important in life, and it is not "things."

The need to be compact, to be creative in their use of space, to be neat, and to pare down belongings to essentials contributes to the image RVers have of themselves. After they make the decision to sell their home and strip themselves of unnecessary possessions, RVers must develop strategies for making the best use of the limited space in their rigs. Ideas on how to accomplish this are a favorite topic of conversation. Whenever they get together RVers share information on how to organize the interiors of their rigs most efficiently. They spend hours exchanging views on which kinds and models of RVs have the most space available, ways in which things can be made to do double duty (for example, cushion covers stuffed with jackets or extra bedding serve both as storage and as sofa pillows), and ideas on how to modify one's rig to make it "livable" nomadic space. Veteran full-timers invited us inside to demonstrate how they had solved the problems of limited storage. One couple pointed with pride to the retaining bars along the upper walls of their rig that held their entire collection of music recorded on cassette tapes, while another described an innovative RVer who had installed his model train track along the walls of his trailer.

Full-timers also share their memories of getting rid of their things. They talk of how they divided their things among their children, of how they told the kids, "Take what you want. We're going to sell the rest." Or they speak with irony of the thousands of dollars they spent storing for years things they did not think they could part with, only to find their treasures had mildewed or been eaten by mice or bugs. Or they could not remember what they had stored because those things no longer mattered. And they spoke at length about their sense of relief at being free of things.[48]

For some the freedom from things extends to their lack of dependence on amenities. Among boondockers the absence of amenities is a source of wry humor. In the Slabs, for instance, several people parked side-by-side had gone to elaborate trouble to fit out their rigs with fake hookups. Electric cords led from their RVs to metered posts, hoses led from water taps to water tank inlets, and sewage lines drained into concrete pipes apparently leading into septic tanks. The realistic-looking setup was a joke designed to fool the unwary newcomer, and when we asked our neighbors how hookups were possible our ignorance was met with guffaws of laughter.

Full-time RVers would likely identify themselves as enjoying what Marshall Sahlins terms "Zen affluence." Sahlins says that people may satisfy their wants "either by producing much or desiring little." The latter strategy is the "Zen road to affluence." It enables people to have "affluence without abundance" and to "enjoy an unparalleled material plenty — with a low standard of living." Indeed, for people who are on the move "wealth is a burden" and goods that have to be carried along become "grievously oppressive…. Mobility and property are in contradiction … wealth quickly becomes more of an encumbrance than a good thing." In a description of hunter-gatherers that might have been written about full-timers, Sahlins says limited material possessions relieve people of cares and permit them to enjoy life. People who enjoy Zen abundance use what they have when they have it, are satisfied with what they have, and feel no compulsion to

What one thing do you miss the most as a result of full-timing?

A big bathtub!! and a long soaking bath.

My piano, organ, and books.

Having a place to set up my sewing or craft supplies and leaving them.

The satisfaction of developing the old homestead. Landscaping, planting, small projects, etc.

Staying "home" [at a home base] long enough to get some serious drafting, painting, and sewing "in," but I wouldn't trade my freedom to roam and see new things and sights for staying home!

possess two or more of the same sort of thing. They are free of material pressures, and of the tyrants "ambition and avarice." They have an abundance of leisure time, and get plenty of sleep, more in fact than people in "any other condition of society." Sahlins says, "We are inclined to think of hunters and gatherers as *poor* because they don't have anything; perhaps better to think of them for that reason as *free.*"

Sahlins concludes that having few possessions is not the same as being poor. "Poverty is not a certain small amount of goods, nor is it just a relation between means and ends; above all it is a relation between people. Poverty is a social status."[49]

Although determined RVers fit an amazing variety of things in their rigs — pianos, tool shops, offices complete with filing cabinets — successful full-timing requires a philosophical bent toward Zen affluence. Most of the RVers we talked with do not think they live in poverty. Instead, they said they consider their lack of possessions to be liberating. Their freedom from *things* has enhanced their sense of self. Home ownership is a middle-class North American goal, and 94 per cent of our respondents said they owned their homes before becoming RVers. Many also said selling their houses had liberated them.[50] The Stehliks, full-timers, equate freedom with *unowner-ship* of property. They write, "Let the flags unfurl! Let the trumpets blare! The house is sold and we're in our cosy 25' Open Road towing a loaded down Honda car. Magically, there's a joyful kid-like freedom *unownership* brings."[51]

"When my house was finally sold and I pulled away from it for the last time, I had an undescribable feeling of freedom from temporal goods. I did not have to worry about whether it was broken into, whether my antiques were stolen. The feeling of freedom was one of the most intense experiences of my life" (comment on a questionnaire).

During our research in 1993, Dorothy was explaining to a full-timer our interest in understanding what enables some people to become full-timers. The woman replied "The intelligence not to be possessed by your possessions." Her biggest problem, she said, had been giving up a beautiful bedroom suite and a lovely desk that she treasured. She had planned to store them, but one evening a voice said to her, "I thought you said you didn't want any debt." After looking around because she thought someone was in the room with her, she replied, "I don't." The voice retorted, "What do you call storage fees?" She decided then and there to sell everything. After it was done she had a few nights when she wondered whether a friend would not have been willing to store the desk. Then she said to herself, "It's gone. Forget about it." Now she is free of it. A man sitting at the table listening to our conversation broke in saying, "Things don't mean a thing to me!"

RVers express the freedom they feel from having fewer things in their responses to the question "What do you think made you capable of going full-time?"

> Years ago I wanted to keep my parents' farm in our family because I felt my "roots" were there. I later learned that without them there, it didn't make me feel "secure." That's when I formed the opinion that my roots are between my ears, and I am not such a prisoner of "things." I am happier being comfortable doing without than in having "things" to do with.
>
> * * *
>
> A belief in one's self as a real being and not clinging to material things as "one's identity." Having a keen sense of adventure in seeing new places and meeting new people. If your only sense of worth is this season's latest "Dior original" — best forget RVing! RVers care about you — not what you have — not even what rig you own!
>
> * * *
>
> The ability to cut down on the amount of clothes you wear. We have a rule: if you want to purchase anything you have to know "Where are you going to put it?" or "Who are you going to give it to?" (Pat Kring)

"I can do what I want to do when I want to do it."

> We can go where we want, stay where we want, stop
> when we want, leave when we want, or stay a little longer.

For some RVers, freedom is the right to spend their time however they want and with whomever they please. It is a combination of freedom to travel and freedom of association. As we will see in the statements that follow, this notion of freedom provides an option that releases people from worry, stress, and unwanted responsibilities. The following are replies to the question, "What do you like most about RVing?"

> The complete freedom to do what you wish, when you wish. One night we were still wide awake at 3:30 a.m. so we got up, drove for a couple of hours, then stopped and slept for 4 or 5 hours and then drove on.
>
> * * *

FREEDOM! I don't have to be here at a certain time or there at a certain time. If I want to stay up until 2 o'clock in the morning I can, if I want to sleep until noon I can. If I don't like it here I can go somewhere else. When I get tired of being in one place, I go some place else. I have no worries, I save $700 a month over the expenses I used to have. It's money in the bank and I'm enjoying life. If I have food to eat and gas to travel, then I'm happy. If I spend a little too much one month, I spend a little less the next. If more people were doing it, there'd be fewer of them laying up in nursing homes.

* * *

If you don't like your neighbors you can pick up and leave.

* * *

I have no worries and no problems. I don't worry about rent or utilities. I've extended my life a long way.

In summary, then, although freedom has many meanings for RVers, it is an important component of their self-image as pioneers.

Can Pioneers Be Good Neighbors?

"If it weren't for the people at the [North Ranch Escapees] park we couldn't keep this place open. We get more support from them than from our own people" (Manager of the senior center, Congress, Arizona).

A strong recurring theme in our conversations with RVers and the managers of RV parks was their belief that people were isolated in the neighborhoods where they lived before they became RVers. Many told us there had been no sense of community there, and several claimed they knew their RV neighbors of a few weeks better than they had known the people who lived next door for 20 years in the suburbs. To our surprise, what seemed to be a characteristic of RVers — they had felt isolated and alienated when they lived in suburbia — was contradicted by our questionnaire results. Almost 70 per cent of those who completed our questionnaire said that some of their former neighbors had been friends whom they knew well or very well. Despite complaints about the isolation and anonymity of suburban life, over 75 per cent of them said they were involved in community life in their former homes.[52] Had we not used questionnaires we would not have discovered this fascinating discrepancy, which may be a contradiction between impression and fact. People who were friendly with their neighbors and involved in community organizations and volunteer work were not inclined to compare unfavorably their present life with life in their former communities. In contrast, people who were isolated were more likely to talk with eloquence and feeling because the contrast between their former lives and their RVing experience was so sharp. Or perhaps the shared values in RVing life provide more basis for community than is necessarily found in a sedentary neighborhood. Whatever the explanation, our impression was of an RVing population more isolated in their former communities than our survey indicates is the case. This contradiction in impression and fact once again emphasizes the advantage of using questionnaires to supplement interviews and participant observation.

The high level of community citizenship RVers report in their sedentary communities seems to continue when people become serious RVers. Indeed, they seem to be the sort of citizens who are committed to a variety of communities and who fulfil their individualism in community. This is the view of RVers that Kay Peterson promotes in response to the belief that they have turned their backs on community.

> A great many full-timers *do* participate in "community service" but it is in a community that changes as they move. Some of them help build houses for the homeless, or they may hitch up and head for a disaster area after hearing on the news that a town has been flattened by a tornado. Many of them belong to ... groups that move about North America, building and repairing churches and church schools.
>
> Others help to "build" SKP Co-Ops which are a small community within the larger community. Countless SKPs, who have no vested interest in that Co-Op, will stop by for a week or longer to help clear land, lay pipe, or pound nails knowing that it helps that "community" — even if it isn't "their" community.[53]

Although all RVers may not build houses for the homeless, many do, Peterson says, and these are people who participate in community. So, dissonance between freedom-seeking individualists and the notion of community is not inevitable. Bellah suggests that forms of individualism "that see the individual in relation to a larger whole, a community and a tradition" may best sustain genuine individuality and nurture both public and private life. This form of individuality is practiced by RVers who "define themselves through their commitment to a variety of communities rather than through the pursuit of radical autonomy." They practice "a form of individualism that is fulfilled in community rather than against it."[54]

Joe Peterson maintains that senior RVers are good citizens and that local communities should welcome them as a boost to, not a burden on, the local economy. As consumers they bring revenue into a area while their demands for public services are minimal. Speaking with animation, Joe ticked off on his fingers the reasons why a local community should be happy to see RVers, especially SKPs, move there:

- They don't compete for jobs.
- They don't have children so the county doesn't have the expense of providing schools for them.
- They have incomes and bring money into the community rather than going on welfare.
- They don't create trouble; the county doesn't have to hire additional police because they are here.

In 1993 Kay and Joe Peterson received the Polk County Chamber of Commerce's Economic Development Award. According to the Chamber:

> One of the most stabilizing factors in the local economy is the large number of retirees. They provide a financial input into the local economy from such outside sources as pensions, social security checks and private savings, which are dependable and consistent.[55]

The Polk County and Holtville Chambers of Commerce agree with Joe Peterson that RVing pioneers are good neighbors. "I see them as the most wonderful, lovable people in the world," said Liz Daker, president of the Holtville, California, Chamber of Commerce, talking about the RVers boondocking at the nearby Hot Springs Long Term Visitor Area (LTVA). The boondockers are a boon to the local economy. In the early 1990s a local businesswoman asked the Hot Springs residents to save their receipts from local purchases. Over the winter they collected $25,000 in receipts — mostly for groceries and hardware — not counting gas or restaurant meals. When we talked to her in 1994 Ms. Daker said that LTVA boondockers are essential for the survival of the town. She planned to go to the Hot Springs and ask the residents what they want. "Anything I thought they'd want, I'd bend over backwards to help them," she said. She also put together a list of the winter's activities for each month and circulated it to the LTVA residents because "I would like them to feel at home here."

Conclusion

A contradiction exists between the value placed on freedom by RVers and the commitment to community that society demands. The vehicles that are the homes of RVers explicitly notify others of their transience and cause them to be stigmatized as nomads. Thus census takers may identify them as being among the homeless, as being "slightly affluent street people." Kay Peterson speaks to this contradiction and places RVers in a more desirable place on the continuum between freedom and community when she says, "RV Snowbirds are not 'homeless' people. They are, in fact, the *ultimate homemakers* who make every place they go home."[56]

In a profound sense, the people of the RV subculture have discovered and claimed for themselves a new frontier. Instead of a line moving steadily westward, the RV frontier is an interstitial one, composed of areas not yet encroached upon by urban culture. Like the great frontier of the eighteenth and nineteenth centuries that so shaped the North American mentality, this one calls those who find encroaching civilization too much to bear to move on to a new and unregulated land. There, as nearly as possible, they live by rules of their own making, in communities that are consensual. Indeed, just about the only resistance we found to our study of RVing was expressed as a genuine fear that, should we publish about flea marketing RVers, "the government" would find a way to regulate them. It seems to us that in the mind of every full-timer and serious part-timer there is a ghostly image. It is a covered wagon, and the road stretches ahead.

Notes

1. Orlean 1995:50, 63.

2. Although the Romany people formerly called gypsies are usually called Travellers in contemporary ethnographies, we use the term "gypsy" here because it is a stereotypical label. The content of this label may bear little resemblance to the life and behavior of real Travellers.

3. For a discussion of the use of metaphor by anthropologists see Fernandez 1971:43-44.

4. Newman 1954:13.

5. Trailer resident quoted in Wallis 1991:19.

6. Sutherland 1975:59. Gypsies or Travellers in fact have strong family and community ties, but not to the mainstream community. Ethnographies of Traveller

sub-cultures report that while they explicitly reject sedentary non-Traveller culture, they form tight-knit communities of their own (Gropper 1975; Sutherland 1975; Sway 1988).

7. See Drury 1972:28 for a discussion of the negative stereotypes of Gypsies. The notion of negative reciprocity is from Sahlins 1972a:195.

8. The quote is from Wallis 1991. Such complaints are not the stuff of yesteryear. We can speak to this from our own experience. After the completion of our RV research, we extended the driveway of our suburban home and installed a parking and storage place for our travel trailer. The "pad" was poured concrete, designed to be landscaped. The trailer we intended to put there was a top-of-the-line, mint condition, aerodynamically designed unit. Before the construction was complete, word came to us that one of our neighbors expected to file a complaint against us with the local government authorities for by-law violation. Our trailer was 30 feet in length. By-law provisions permit storage of no trailer or boat in excess of 21.3 feet. Local authorities told us the by-law was not enforced unless there was a complaint, but should there be one we would have to make other arrangements. Our neighbors did not respond to our attempts to discuss the matter with them. Other neighbors told us their complaint was that the presence of our rig would make the neighborhood "look like a trailer park." Furthermore, its presence would decrease their property value. Thus prodded, we traded our 30-foot travel trailer for a 20-foot fifth-wheel trailer — well within the bylaw provisions. We also gave thought to putting a sign in front of it reading "Counts Trailer Park. Escapees welcome!"

9. Thornburg 1991:62-69.

10. Peterson and Peterson 1991:11.

11. Skips have (jokingly, we think) recommended that this be the title, or at least the subtitle, of this book.

12. Orlean 1995:48-51, 63-65. Timothy McVeigh was convicted of the 1994 bombing of the federal building in Oklahoma City.

13. This image calls to mind the charges of "filth" levelled against boondockers and Slab City residents who dump their waste in glory holes. We discuss these charges later in this chapter.

14. Peterson, K. 1987a:16-17.

15. Coontz 1992:9.

16. The reference to Coontz is to her 1992 work. June Cleaver was Beaver Cleaver's mother in the TV show, Leave it to Beaver.

17. The response of RVers to this ad is found in "The View from the Driver's Seat" (Trailer Life 1988:165, 169). The responses cited here are by Graydon Lewis and Marilyn Noon.

18. Thornburg 1991:65.

19. See Peterson, K. 1995b:8.

20. Errington 1990:642.

21. Apple 1987:19.

22. The comment about the conspicuous pursuit of leisure is from Thornburg 1991:68. The letter by the disgruntled Good Sam Club member is found in Phillips 1992:8.

23. Harris 1994:78-79.

24. Bryson 1989:93-95.

25. Van Note 1990:144.

26. RVIA n.d.a:13.

27. Peterson, K. 1995b:8.

28. For example, over 11 per cent of the people who answered our question, "What do you think makes a person capable of going full-time?" responded "a love of travel," some adding that they had "always been a gypsy." Almost 6 per cent said that the kind of people best suited to full-timing are those "who want to travel," "have itchy feet," are "gypsies."

29. Fernandez 1971:44.

30. Pease 1930:53.

31. Information about the actions of Mariposa is from Reimer 1992:3. Also see Marple 1990.

32. Just 1995:20.

33. Fernandez 1971:54.

34. In 1990 we watched while a member chapter of the Wally Byam club for Airstream owners acted out their pioneer fantasy in a casino parking lot in Laughlin, Nevada.

35. Weston 1986:13.

36. The quotes are from Bellah *et al.* 1985:23 and 148.

37. Wallis 1991:21.

38. Thornburg 1991:71-7.

39. Bellah *et al.* 1985:23, 144, 148.

40. Bellah *et al.* 1985:25. Also see page 148.

41. Just 1995:20.

42. Bonis and Bonis 1993:22.

43 Peterson, K. 1986b:2.

44. Muncy 1987:28.

45. Tinseth 1984:6.

46. Peterson and Peterson 1991:18-19.

47. Lamarche and Langlois 1987:144.

48. Sometimes the choices are difficult ones. Nineteen per cent of respondents to our questionnaire said that the hardest thing about making the decision to go full-time was getting rid of things. Another 3 per cent said that adjusting to the lack of space was most difficult.

49. Sahlins 1972b:1-2, 11-14, 37.

50. Almost 75 per cent of our respondents said they have either sold their home or have listed it for sale.

51. Stehlik and Stehlik 1984:29.

52. In response to questions about level of activity in community organizations, 50 per cent had been involved in at least one or two organizations. Twenty-five per cent were involved in one community organization or club, most likely to be volunteer oriented, while another 25 per cent were active in two, the second most likely to be church. Almost 29 per cent were involved in three or more community organizations or clubs. Only 21 per cent of respondents said they had been active in no community organizations at all. See questions 19 to 24 in Appendix One.

53. Peterson, K. 1989:3.

54. Quotes from Bellah *et al.* 1985:143 and 162.

55. Polk County Chamber of Commerce n.d.:13.

56. Peterson, K. 1989:3.

Chapter Five

If They Aren't Us, Who Are They?

As for providing you with a mosaic of the average SKP, I have discovered that is an impossible chore. There is no such thing. And, I guess that is what makes this gang of ours so great. Warts and all. (Norm Clinton reporting on the results of a questionnaire at Park Of the Sierra Escapees Co-op.)[1]

Full-time and serious RVers firmly insist they are definitely not the indolent slobs portrayed in the advertisement for *US Magazine*. Who, then, are they? They are couples, and they are singles. They are Canadians who keep one eye on the calendar, concerned lest they lose their provincial health care. They are full-timers who live in their rigs. They are retired people and they are "Boomers" who either dropped out or were pushed out of the mainstream economy. They are compulsive planners, and they are nomads who never know whether they will turn right or left when they reach an intersection. We will meet some of these people in this chapter.

RVers warned us it is impossible to generalize about the "average RVer" because each of them is unique. Indeed, like Clinton, many RVers see their resistance to classification as a virtue and treasure their differences. Although they insist there is no single RV lifestyle and that there is no "typical" full-timer or serious RVer, it is possible to make some general statements about them.[2] If you walk through the Slabs or sit drinking coffee in the club house of an Escapees co-op, most of the people you see will be between the ages of 60 and 65, of European extraction. You will see men and women in roughly even numbers. When you talk to them you may be surprised to learn that they are well educated, probably with at least some college or university training, and that two out of three of them have computers in their rigs. You will also discover that while the occupational backgrounds of serious RVers are diverse, they are as likely to be retired white collar workers, teachers, or health professionals as mechanics, bus drivers, or farmers.

We were surprised to find that before retirement most RVers did not hold jobs that required them to travel frequently. Over 38 per cent of the respondents to our survey had held jobs that never required them to travel.[3]

It seems to me that we are finding a much wider range of backgrounds in SKP areas than we did in the boondock areas and parks in 1990. Not only are there a lot of retired military, including officer types, but we have now found two college-level instructors (mechanical engineer and geologist), a psychologist, a couple of retired/disabled ministers, a former IBM executive, and a chemist with post-graduate education who had his own successful business. (From our 1994 journal)

It is nearly impossible to generalize about the income levels of RVers other than to observe that some are comfortably well off, some are living on the margins, and most are in the middle. For instance, about one in five of the respondents to our questionnaire had incomes of more than $25,000 per person, while almost 4 per cent said they lived on less than $5,000 each. The rest were in between.[4] In Chapter Seven we look at whether RVers consider theirs to be an inexpensive way of life, and discuss strategies used by RVers on limited incomes to make ends meet.

Singles On Wheels

"When you greet a couple and make them feel welcome it's wonderful. But when you do that for a single person it's ten times as wonderful." (Ellen, a single RVer, saying goodbye during the parting ritual at The Ranch.)

Between 15 and 18 per cent of RVers are single. The majority of these are widowed or divorced, and most are women.[5] About half of the people who write to the Escapees magazine reporting the death of their partners say they plan to quit full-timing. The other half continue to travel. Some try to quit and change their minds. To find out how people who quit RVing after the death of a spouse coped with returning to sedentary life, we wrote to people who had announced in the Escapees magazine that they were hanging up their keys. All of the people who responded said that they had missed traveling and their RVing friends so much they had gone back on the road.

When one loses one's lifetime mate, one has to give up so much. A wise, widowed friend advised me not to give up anything I didn't really have to, and this encouraged me to "keep on truckin'." (Letter from a LoW member.)

Some new singles intend to spend most of their time traveling. Others plan to stay in their rigs on their lot in a park where they will be among friends. Pauline Randolph is typical of those who make this decision. She writes, "I'm secure in the Saguaro SKP Co-Op with the loving kindness of my SKP family."[6] Some make the decision to continue RVing because they think the travel and the support of friends enables them to survive. Orrill Darby eloquently expresses this sentiment:

I can't begin to express what it means to me to be able to be out "here" changing my residence when I choose, meeting all sorts of interesting people — and re-meeting them along the way.

I think about my mother and other people — their friends gradually passed on and weren't replaced by others. Here, on the road, there are always new friends. I have met some truly remarkable people. So many stories of tragedy and yet they keep courageously on living with kindness and compassion for others and a sense of humor that makes things more bearable. What we have in SKPs and LoWs are "support" groups! Not just support in our way of living, but support in living itself.[7]

Singles say they have problems not experienced by RVing couples. They are lonely, they feel more vulnerable when they are ill because they have no one to help them, and they feel excluded by RVing couples who — they think — often see them as threatening. These concerns were addressed by a single full-time RVer who wrote on his questionnaire that the thing he misses most is a "constant source of friends. Being single, I find traveling increases and deepens sense of *loneliness and alone-ness*, when I'm in such moods." He wrote that he has "often" had serious medical crises while RVing, and that the prospect of a medical crisis "is [the] major drawback [to] being *single* and *full-time*. Risk is increased." When he is ill, he said, he must get help with his chores from RVing neighbors and friends or stop traveling.

Several single RVers told us they thought we should address the "loneliness issue" in our research because it is the most common and serious problem of single RVers. Perhaps the most poignant example of single loneliness was Barney. We met him at the short term parking area, behind vendor's row, in Quartzsite in 1990 while we were both exercising our dogs. Barney's dog was an ancient basset hound named BJ who dribbled urine as he walked. Barney commented that he and BJ were both getting old, but he didn't have the heart to put him down. We saw a lot of Barney and BJ in the next few days. He has a history of being suspicious of doctors, threatening them and being threatened by them, he said. His wife was ill with a brain tumor and had extensive treatment at Johns Hopkins over his vigorous protests. Because of his attitude toward her medical care, he had been estranged from her and their children since 1988. He frequently commented that he had not seen his family in almost three years, and he didn't care. He refused to answer his daughter's letters or to write to any of them telling them his whereabouts. "I was married for over 40 years and never did anything right; now I live alone and never do anything wrong," he said. During our first interview he commented twice that we were lucky to have each other to talk to. After years of having his wife to talk to it was difficult to be alone with just his dog, he said. He observed that he used a lot of electricity because he had difficulty sleeping. After taking BJ and himself out at about midnight he could not go back to sleep, so he had the radio on for company. "I have to have the radio," he said. When we asked where he was going from Quartzsite he responded, "I don't know. I've got no place to go and nothing to do when I get there."

Other RVing singles feel excluded by couples. The issue was addressed by recently widowed Norm Clinton who wrote that his "apprenticeship in the 'Single World' has been an eye opener."

> For some undefinable reason we [he and his wife Carol] always felt a little awkward around the occasional single person who parked next to us. We were always cordial but we never did develop a close relationship with a single in the manner that we so frequently did with couples.... Whatever awkwardness we felt was fleeting at most and we were off to better and bigger things.
>
> Now that I find myself on the other side of the fence, I sense that same awkwardness in many couples I meet. I have coined the phrase, "The Leper Syndrome." Be cordial, be friendly but don't get too close.[8]

Singles clubs and community

> DJ showed us her copy of the LoW newsletter and pointed out that an organized person can follow LoW rallies from one end of the country to another. She has never quite gone coast to coast doing that, but she has come close. Although they don't advertise it as much, there is more sharing and caring within LoWs than there is in Escapees. In LoW parks and other places where they get together, such as the Slabs or on LTVA land north of Blythe, there is much camaraderie. People take care of each other and help one another because each of them is alone "and there are so many jobs that require three hands. In Escapees they usually have four." (From our 1993 journal)

Many singles find a "third hand" by joining a singles' organization. Members support and help one another, provide relief from loneliness, and sometimes become like family to each other. One club, Wandering Individuals Network (WIN), is unique in having a membership that is mostly male and in permitting men and women to travel together and to marry. "Members who

Slab city singles have their own social center and welcome sign

arrive at gatherings with members of the opposite sex are not censured and members who marry don't have to leave the club."[9] The membership of most other organizations for singles is predominately female. Some clubs are exclusively for women.

The oldest and probably best-known singles organization is Loners on Wheels (LoW). This club has been in existence since 1971 and has chapters throughout the US and Canada. Although the members of singles organizations are mostly seniors, LoW Members emphasize that their club is "not a dating service, or a swingers' club." It is neither "a lonely hearts club nor a matchmaking service. Those of the opposite sex are not permitted to attend club sponsored events in the same vehicle. Members must conduct themselves as unattached singles."[10] This pronouncement is not mere rhetoric, as the experience of Ruth and Henry demonstrates. They met while spending the winter in the LoW encampment at the Slabs. Once they began traveling together and established themselves as a couple, the organization terminated their membership. They still winter at the Slabs and continue to be friends with members of LoW, but they must park in a different section, and they are not included in the club's social events. Slab City also has its own singles group, Slab City Singles, with its own social center and welcome sign.

Those who find LoW's rules too limiting may join Loners of America (LOA). According to our informants, LOA was formed by LoW members who left the parent organization because of the strict rules requiring separation of the sexes. LOA stresses that the organization is not a matchmaking service:

LONERS OF AMERICA is *not* a singles club to help members find a mate, or a matchmaking service. The club not only frowns on "hanky-panky" behavior, but will suspend an offender's membership. This is not to say that friendships and companionships are not encouraged. These situations must not "get out of control" to the detriment of other members and the club's reputation.[11]

Instead LOA is "a not-for-profit, member owned and operated organization." Its purpose is to provide single RVers with both companionship and privacy, and with the security of having someone to travel with.

Circumstances throughout life often result in a serious change in one's future. Loss of a mate — for whatever reason — can be a traumatic event that may find the survivor trying to "pick up the pieces — and get on with living." That is the heart of what LONERS OF AMERICA is about. LOA is an RV club that helps with being alone and attempting to fill a void through companionship, while still maintaining one's individual privacy.

Single Escapees say that joining a singles' club provides them with an enriched source of family-like relationships, an advantage emphasized by Lea Carter, who was both a Skip and the Secretary of LoW.

It seems to me that those of us who belong to both organizations can experience the best of both worlds — the single world in which we move most of the time through LoW *plus* the couple/family oriented world of SKPs because SKPs seems to be more receptive to the lone RVer and place less strain on the "loner" than many of the other couple/family groups do.

One reason for that may be that we know that the odds are one member of a partnership will live longer than the other. We know, when that time comes, that we won't want to isolate ourselves from the RV friends we have made just because we no longer have a partner.

Or perhaps the reason is simply that all of us who travel the open road for extended periods feel a kinship that is not limited by color, religion, politics, income, sexual preference, marital status, or any of the other "labels" that try to fragment us, making us less complete than we should be. We are all "family" in the larger sense of the word and like a true family we can have many interests and enjoy many organizations.[12]

Carter's emphasis on the feeling of "family" points to a feature of membership in RVing organizations such as Escapees and LoWs that is especially important for single RVers. Marjorie LeDrew, an active member in the Ontario chapter of LoWs, wrote "Joining Loners On Wheels was the best thing I did for myself when I was left on my own. The members, both in Canada and the United States, have become my extended family."[13]

For Kay, whose story is told below, fellow members of Singles International and the Family Motor Coach Association are her family now.

Kay

In November 1990 Kay was the host at an Arizona state park. When she learned about our research project she came to talk to us because she once was a nurse geriatrician and "gerontologists don't know a damned thing." Kay received her RN when she was a mature woman with grown children. She worked in New York and Montana as a nurse until she took early retirement at the age of 60. She supplements her pension and Social Security income by working as a park host in Arizona and Montana where she gets free parking space plus some hookups. She spends her day doing host chores: emptying garbage and cleaning out fire grates, checking for ground fires, and talking to campers.

Kay began full-timing when she retired in February 1988. She retired in order to RV because she was fed up with the working conditions for nurses in Missoula, and because "I saw so many others doing it." She also started full-timing "because I was looking for something." Although she tried a number of organizations after the end of her stormy and sometimes violent marriage, nothing provided what she wanted. One of her biggest problems was loneliness: "If you're alone for your birthday, it's not so nice." Physical contact with other human beings is what single people miss the most, Kay says. Then she discovered the Family Motor Coach Association (FMCA) and its Singles International (SI) group. Her membership in SI and her job as host eases her loneliness and isolation. When there is a problem, other RVers gather around and help out. They bake cakes for birthdays and give each other hugs when they meet and hugs when they leave. Last Christmas she invited all the campers in the park to bring their dinner to her site and share. "Full-timers help each other," she said. "They're my family now." Although she has five children, she seldom hears from them and doesn't think they know where she is because she forgot to send them her address.

Canadians

> Although we are full-timers we do have a condo in Ottawa in the event we were forced to stop traveling; as the Ontario government requires we have a residency address we would appreciate if it was never known to them that we only have a mailing address at the moment. (Letter from a Canadian full-timer)

During the winter months, Canadian RVers are a distinct minority in the American sun belt. Canadian RVers tend to seek each other out. They cluster in established parks that have the reputation of being friendly to Canadians and in specific Long Term Visitor Areas — such as "BC Flats" — in the southwestern desert. When they arrive in a new place, especially in a boondocking area that allows them to control where they park, Canadians often drive around looking for a maple leaf flag. If they find one they park nearby. In parks or boondocking areas where they gather, Canadians may make up almost half the population.[14]

It is more difficult for Canadians to become full-time RVers than it is for their American counterparts. The issue of residency is the source of most of the problem. Canadian RVers wishing to spend several months of the year in the US must satisfy American immigration requirements for Canadian residency which, ironically, are more stringent than are those of the Canadian federal or provincial governments. Consequently, each time Canadian RVers cross into the US they face the possibility of being turned back by American immigration officials. This issue is discussed by Jim and Joyce Johnson, Canadians who ran afoul of US Immigration:

> Immigration interprets "residency" as a *residence* in Canada and requires that such residence be permanently attached to the ground. They have made it clear they will not accept a movable or mobile RV under any circumstances whether on a lot to which you hold title or on a lot you own in an RV park. They do not accept an address which shows a box number only, but must have a street address. They also do not accept residency with a relative unless you have rental and utility receipts. They will accept a mobile home on your own lot or in a mobile home park provided it is permanently attached.

When asked for proof of residency, the Canadian must be able to produce rental receipts and utility bills satisfactory to the inspector. Failure to do so will result in refusal to enter the US. This has happened to only a few Canadians so far because only a few have been asked for proof of residency. If it were asked of all Canadian snowbirds, a substantial percentage would be turned back.... The bottom line is that at the present time it is not possible to be a full-time Canadian RVer if you wish to spend any time in the U.S. (almost a must with our cold winters) and be honest with the US Immigration inspectors.... Many Canadians are now full-timers and spend time illegally in the US. More would like to be full-timers, but cannot if they must approach the US border with the stress of dishonesty and the possibility of being turned away.[15]

As the Johnsons point out, a restrictive American definition of Canadian residency has not prevented most Canadian RVers from wintering in the US: at least not yet. A more compelling problem exists for Canadians who are or who want to be full-time RVers. Provincial legislation requires residents to be physically present in their home province in order to qualify for medical care coverage.

There are two problems.

First, Canadians worry about the cost of uninsured illness, especially in the US. When we talked with Americans about their worries, many of them expressed concern about random violence. Most of them carry weapons against the possibility of being robbed or attacked by the "crazies out there." We discuss these concerns more fully in Chapter Seven. In contrast, when Canadian RVers tell each other horror stories they talk about American hospitals charging Canadians thousands or tens of thousands of dollars for treatment of minor problems. The most extreme case we heard was of a man who received a bill for $2100 for the removal of a splinter from his finger in a hospital emergency room.

Second, RVers are characteristically on the move. Many full-timers have no home other than their rig, and those who spend over six months in an RV park may be declared non-resident because the park is not open year around. Canadian magazines and newspapers warn of the problems serious Canadian RVers face.

Trying to comply with last year's revisions in OHIP [Ontario Health Insurance Plan] has really put a crimp into our travels. We're proud to be Canadians ... willingly?? pay all taxes. Nevertheless staying six months in the province is almost impossible. Most campgrounds are only open five and a half months. The modification stating we need a permanent residence carries even more of an adverse impact. (Comment from a Canadian full-timer)

In April 1992, the Hamilton *Spectator* ran a story warning Canadian snowbirds that they could lose their Ontario Health Insurance Plan (OHIP) coverage. The story described an Ontario couple who were informed that their OHIP was canceled and were told to return their insurance cards even though they had made no medical claim. The couple had been spending six months in a mobile home in Florida and six months in Ontario in a trailer in a seasonal campground that is open only five-and-one-half months each year. Officials questioned whether the couple were not really residents of Florida and asked if their Ontario residence was "habitable and accessible on a year-round basis, or is it a summer home for vacation purposes?" The article reports that Ontario residency, for purposes of OHIP, requires "you must have a home in Ontario that is available to you on a year-round basis." It concludes:

> Just being in Ontario for six months or more isn't enough. For OHIP eligibility, people must also be able to show that Ontario is their permanent and primary home.
>
> The issue of a permanent home could also affect seniors who live with friends or relatives for six months of the year.
>
> Staying in a guest room isn't enough. Someone who claims their residency is in another person's home must have a room "reserved for your sole use" that they occupy for most of the year.... Because of the mobile lifestyle often associated with people in campgrounds and trailer parks ... campgrounds and trailer parks are viewed as suspicious addresses.

When interviewed about the situation, a spokesman for the Health Ministry said, "People who live in trailer parks and campgrounds that aren't open year-round may not necessarily lose OHIP coverage.... What would happen in that case would be an individual review of their situation. If OHIP was satisfied that Ontario was still their primary and permanent residence, they still could maintain their coverage."[16]

"Our Ontario government doesn't want us out of Ontario. If we go south for six months then we can't travel within our own country in summer. Because of weather, summer is the only time we can travel in Canada." (Comment from a Canadian full-timer)

A similar warning was published by Robert Chatfield, editor of an Ontario-based magazine for RVers. Chatfield cautioned that retired people who are out of province for more than six months, even if they are traveling in Canada, will lose their OHIP coverage. He also warns that RVers without a permanent residence are at risk of losing their OHIP coverage. Furthermore, he says, "It appears that one cannot use their children's address unless they have a portion of that address that is strictly theirs. Even if you are in the Province and living in a travel trailer moving from park to park you are apparently not eligible for coverage."[17]

The concerns expressed in these articles were repeated by Canadians with whom we discussed the problems of going full-time. In June 1995 we attended a rally of Ontario Escapees, many of whom were full-timers. During a discussion of our research project we asked how a Canadian could be a full-timer *and* obey the law. The response was laughter. Later people told us in confidence of an assortment of strategies, all designed to fool government bureaucrats into thinking they were physically present in the province when they were actually traveling somewhere else. After the rally we wrote to the ministries of health of the various provinces explaining the problem for RVers. We outlined several hypothetical situations in which it would be uncertain whether RVers would qualify for provincial medical insurance, and then asked for clarification of provincial rules. The results, as well as a summary of Canadian federal and provincial definitions of residency, are found in Appendix 3.

Although the length of time a person is required to be physically present in a province varies from four months (in Newfoundland) to six months plus a day (in most of the other provinces), no province permits people to claim residency for the purpose of health care eligibility solely because they pay income and property taxes and vehicle registration. One province responded that a person would not be denied residency status because they did not live in a permanent building. Ontario did not give this assurance. Negotiations between the federal and provincial governments may eventually create a category of Canadian resident who is eligible for health care without being physically present in any one province for a specified length of time.

Meanwhile, Canadian full-timers cope in various ways with the possibility of losing their health care coverage. Coping strategies vary. One, practiced by Jean and Pierre French who began full-timing in 1989, is to drop out of the system. The Frenches, who are in their early 50s, have no home base other than the address of a son in Alberta where they register and license their motor home, renew driver's licenses, and pay taxes. They are not in Alberta long enough to be covered by provincial health care, and Jean said with pride, "We have no health insurance at all. We don't intend to get sick." According to them, buying life insurance is buying into death, and purchasing health insurance is "buying into illness." Jean thinks a combination of vegetarian diet and positive thinking will keep her healthy. Pierre says that he does not have time to be sick. His religion, Ramtha, helps him to channel his energy and will, he believes, enable him to keep his body well.

Most serious and full-time Canadian RVers neither drop out nor skate on the margins of the law: most work within the system. The Kents are examples of Canadians who play by the rules. They retired early because they thought their stressful jobs were killing them. They plan their retirement budgets carefully, boondock, and spend their winters in the southwestern US. They are frustrated by government rules that restrict their freedom to spend their time where they please if they wish to keep their Canadian provincial health insurance coverage. The Kents' frustrations are echoed by many other Canadian would-be full-timers.

The Kents

"Where we like to go, we leave no tracks."

Both George and Sarah are in their early 60s. George is a Canadian, while Sarah has dual Canadian and American citizenship. Before they retired in May 1993 they spent 12 years managing hotels in several western Canadian and American cities. They drove the rounds of these hotels once a month while living in an eight-foot truck camper. Their pattern was to finish one job at six or seven in the evening, drive toward the next town until George was too tired to drive, and then pull over and sleep.

They finally realized that their life style — working 10 to 12 hours a day, seven days a week, with no time for vacation — was killing them. They had known several people, including two union representatives with whom they worked closely in their business, who died of heart attacks, and they had known many other people who worked until age 65 and then died shortly thereafter. George says they decided "It is better to live a long time on a little money than a short time on a lot!"

At first they were hesitant about early retirement because they feared they would not have enough money, but they set about systematically researching the economics of retirement. They asked retired friends how much it cost them to live. Then they listed all their assets, the estimated rental income from their properties, and the value of their pensions from US Social Security and Canada Pension. George put all this information on a spreadsheet, and they concluded that it would be to their advantage to take everything coming to them as soon as they could. Then they established their priorities. What do we want? What are we willing to trade off? What is the minimum we can live on and do the things we want to do? They bought a second-hand membership in a membership park for $1000,[18] figuring that if they stayed at membership parks (for a minimum fee) and boondocked — which they enjoy and would do as a matter of principle — they could afford to become full-time RVers. They spend $400 per week without touching either their investments or the income from them, which they keep for an emergency.

They bought their motor home in the same systematic way. They decided they wanted their rig to be self-contained and both spacious and short enough so they could go anywhere. The motor home they finally chose cost nearly $100,000 Canadian, almost one-third of which was duties, exchange, and taxes. It was worth the expense, they say, because it is their home now, and they are even more satisfied with it than they thought they would be.

They are frustrated by government restrictions making full-timing almost impossible for Canadians. They resent restrictions on their eligibility for provincial health care that limits when and where they can go and how much time they can spend doing it. They think their civil rights as seniors are violated by rules requiring them to be physically present in British Columbia for a specified time and to keep enough of their possessions at a BC home base to demonstrate that it is their residence. They are considering purchasing private medical insurance in lieu of provincial health insurance. Tax concerns also restrict their movements. Because Sarah is a dual American-Canadian citizen and they own property in Washington state, if they stay in the US for a total of six months in any 12-month period they can be declared US residents and required to pay taxes — including tax on their personal property — in Washington. Although they spend much of their time boondocking, a lifestyle that "leaves no tracks," they are careful to follow the law. To avoid tax and residence complications they conscientiously count the days they spend in the US, always leaving a safety margin of two weeks to allow them to visit Sarah's American children without jeopardizing their Canadian residency.

When we last saw them they were parked on a hill overlooking a small lake outside Merritt, BC, watching a family of loons and treasuring their solitude. In spite of the complications of residency requirements, they credit their survival to their decision to become full-timers. Says George, "If we weren't doing this, we'd be dead by now."

Serious Canadian RVers have problems that derive from inconsistent, confusing — and in the opinion of many RVers unfair — residency require-ments. Otherwise they are similar to their American counterparts.[19] In both countries, people too young to retire may drop out of mainstream economic life to become serious RVers. Some of these people call themselves Boomers.

Boomers

About 13 per cent of serious and full-time RVers are age 55 or younger. These are mostly people without pensions, who either dropped out or were forced out of the work place. Although they may have become full-timers out of desperation or economic necessity, many of them now work so they can continue to RV.

Boomers see themselves and their needs as being different from those of the "normally retired" seniors who make up the majority of serious RVers. Those who are members of Escapees have formed a Birds Of a Feather (BOF) group called Boomers. This group is intended for RVers born since 1940, although others who are "young in heart and mind" are welcome. In 1994 Dorothy attended an impromptu meeting of a group of Boomers in an Escapees co-op (such get-togethers are called mini-rangs as opposed to boomerangs which are larger meetings publicly announced at least a few days ahead of time). They discussed the ways Boomers differ from retirees:

> They started with a critique of most retired RVers whom they describe as being insured to the hilt, talk about nothing but health insurance (US or Canadian), and live in fear. None of the people at the table has health insurance and all are convinced that a decent diet and sufficient exercise will keep them healthy and without the need of a doctor. They wouldn't have insurance on their vehicles either if they weren't required to by law.
>
> They are amused and disgusted at the health practices of most of the seniors, many of whom are allegedly at least 50 pounds overweight. This is because their diets consist mostly of the "four food groups: salt, sugar, fat and caffeine," and because most of them ride their golf carts from their rigs to the club house rather than walk.
>
> The Norths, who are lot owners in Oregon, said they are out of favor (with their neighbors at their home base park) because they are never there. They have also heard their neighbors here "ripping little steaks" off the owner of the lot the Norths are renting because "they came here for the lot draw, and we haven't seen them since." All the Boomers combine work and travel and don't consider the people who buy lots and just sit on them to be real RVers. "People buy RVs in order to travel, not to sit on their lots," Judith observed. These Boomers do not stay any one place for long and think the name of the game is travel. Ted commented that one day they might all be like the residents

here. The others hooted at his comment, and all agreed that it would not happen to them: "We're different because we're doing this *now*." Quitting full-time secure jobs to go full-time traveling distinguishes them in their minds from the RVers who wait until they retire to do it. All of them say they left a well-paying job doing something that made them say "shit" when they woke up in the morning.

Pat noted that when Joe and Kay started SKPs they were in their 40s and had the interests and needs that today's Boomers have. She thinks Boomers are often discriminated against and that retired SKPs resent that they aren't working and paying into Social Security. Boomers have in common that they are active, have fewer health problems and fewer concerns about security, and most of them are still working RVers, she said.

As time has gone by the needs and interests of Joe, Kay, and their cohort have changed. Now they are interested in park model trailers (even the Petersons had one), health care (thus the focus on CARE), and senior citizens' clubs and activities. The club has turned its attention to those needs and does not meet the needs of Boomers any more.

They say that, even as they age, today's Boomers will always be different from other retirees because they share a history and a time: they see themselves as a subculture. They share social history (when they were young), musical tastes (one member defined a Boomer as someone who would turn off Lawrence Welk but who listens to the Beatles), and attitudes. You can always tell you are at a Boomerang, they said, because when Boomers get together the talk invariably turns to (1) who can live on the least money; (2) who gets the best gas mileage; (3) who can go longest before emptying their black-water tanks.

The Boomers organization loses as many members as it gains every year. People cannot live on the money they make as working RVers and have to leave the road. Pat and Fred had to do this for two years and felt isolated. She fears they'll have to work for a couple of years again, maybe starting next year, and she dreads it.

There is a current generation of new RVers in their 20s and 30s whose interests are different from those of the Boomers. Pat says, "They will have to form their own club. They are too young for us. They have their own needs and interests." (From our 1994 journal)

Although Boomers perceive themselves as forming an RVing subculture, their reasons for adopting the lifestyle vary. Some, like Rick and Sharon Chaffee, say that down-sizing and stress forced them into a simpler life: they are practitioners of Zen affluence. In the May 1994 issue of the Escapees magazine we published an article exploring some of the reasons for the growing RV movement.[20] The Chaffees wrote to us in response that while many people retired early to get enhanced benefits, there were others who retired rather than let their jobs kill them. Eighteen years after Rick began working for his former employer, and four years after the first threats of down-sizing, the branch where he worked was closed, and he was transferred. The pressure in the new place was unbearable. Several who transferred with him could not take it. Some died and others had serious health problems. After two and half years — before his fiftieth birthday — Rick Chaffee quit. He feels that there are many others like him, driven out of the work world by the stress and pressures put on those who are *not* laid off in the down-sizing process. He says,

My wife (who is a registered nurse) put it to me in simple terms. She said, "It really makes a lot of sense to ruin your health to get health insurance." She was right. (Rick Chaffee)

> Mine is not an isolated case. I just talked to a couple last week who have been full-timing for six years and took early retirement from [company Y] after his best friend and camping partner died of a heart attack. He suddenly realized he could not afford not to leave.
>
> With increased downsizing in corporations the stress on those that remain in the workplace will be enormous. I heard this again and again in my last few working years: "If you will just produce a little more, work a little harder they can't shut this place down." I hope you will research this facet of early retirement. Stress is forcing more of us to a simpler life.

Stress, down-sizing, and restructuring push some Boomers from the mainstream economy and into serious RVing as a strategy for survival, but others like the Kennedys jump voluntarily. Although it was their decision to opt out of the eight-to-five grind, their reasons for making that decision are similar to those given by others for choosing the RV life: avoidance of stress, desire for travel and adventure, and the realization of mortality. Like their senior companions they ask "Is this all there is?"

Pat and Fred Kennedy

Pat and Fred are working RVers in their early 50s who have been full-timing since 1986. We met them in the spring of 1994. Pat, a lively, outgoing woman, sought us out after we introduced ourselves at a co-op's happy hour and encouraged us to get to know Boomers because "we are weird and wonderful people or we wouldn't be doing this."

Fred and Pat started full-timing after separate crises. Fred said his crisis was "my wife threatened to go on the road with or without me." Pat's was a multi-dimensional "mid-life crisis." She worked for a large corporation in New York state for 20 years, and every morning when she got up she said, "Oh Shit!" Pat could tick off her reasons one by one. She was 45 years old and faced another 20 years of saying "Oh Shit!" every morning. And this was only one element of her crisis. Second, she worked days and Fred worked nights so they seldom saw each other. Third, their house owned them instead of their owning it. Fourth, her son announced she would soon be a grandmother. Fifth, she hated the weather in New York. Sixth, the head of the local crime syndicate, their next-door neighbor, was shot outside their bedroom window. Seventh, they both knew people who never made it to retirement. One friend died of a stroke brought on by stress. Another worked double shifts so he'd have enough money for retirement. He was hit in the head by a baseball during a company game and died of the injury. He left a rich widow. They had another acquaintance who developed emphysema and died shortly before retirement. Eighth, Pat's mother died of cancer, so she feared she would not live long enough to retire. Ninth, she worked with a 62-year-old who was terrified of being laid off. Tenth, Congress had already changed the Social Security rules. Pat and Fred figured that they might have to work until their late 60s or early 70s before getting Social Security pensions. Pat says she thought "*There has to be something better than this!*" and asked herself why, if they hated their jobs, they were living in a place they detested? They went to see the movie *Lost In America* about a couple who lose their jobs and take off across the US in an RV. She came out of the movie saying, "God, wouldn't it be wonderful to do that!" Fred had a basement full of books, and every time she expressed interest in something he said, "I've got a book you can read on that!" The book he gave her was Kay Peterson's *Home is Where You Park It*. After she read it she knew it was what she wanted to do.

Pat says she had always been a nervous, security-conscious person who needed to have a schedule to feel comfortable. So, Fred didn't take her seriously. It was if she suddenly was saying "Let's jump off the end of the world." He thought she'd quit after two weeks, but she figured if they didn't like it they could go to Atlanta where her son lives, the weather is nicer, and jobs might be easy to find. So they sold their house and bought an RV. Because they had always worked different shifts, they had seldom spent even 24 hours together, and they'd never traveled or camped. That was eight years ago and they have never looked back.

The Kennedys, the Frenches, the Chaffees, and the Kents have different stories, but all retired to become full-timers to escape stressful or unfulfilling jobs and all thought there must be a better answer to the question, "Is this all there is?" Most of the Boomers we talked with must work in order to continue living as RVers. Pat says the one thing she would change is the necessity to work much more than they travel. Nevertheless, none of them said they regretted their decision or wished they could go back to their well-paying, killer jobs. As one put it, "On your death bed, do you think you'll wish you'd spent more time in the office?"

RVing Styles

There is a continuum of types of RVers and styles of RVing. Neither our categories of RVers nor our examples are definitive or exhaustive. Categories overlap and shift. Full-timing Boomer Canadians may spend much of one year working and the next boondocking or caravanning to Mexico. The single full-timer who moved every two weeks last year may this year purchase a lot in a park and spend most of the time developing it as a home base. Although RVing is characterized by the flexibility and flow of the choices available, some alternative styles are touchstones of identity for RVers. For example, many RVers define their identity in terms of their choice to be full-timers.

Full-timers

> What do think made you capable of going full-time? Anticipation of new places, experiences, and people. A "joy of life" approach to problems and willingness to accept that not all experiences are perfect, fun, interesting, or successful.
>
> * * *
>
> A sense of adventure. "Rolling with the punches." Being "at home" where ever you are. Finding enjoyment in new places and people.

Over two-thirds of the people with whom we did research called themselves full-time RVers. As we discussed in Chapter Four, the experiences flowing from their decision to live full-time in their rigs makes theirs a unique life style. Some people love it. Others try it and do not like it. Still others would not even consider going full-time. Is there a type of person who is most likely to be a successful full-timer? When we asked full-timers this question they said such a person had to be flexible, adaptable, self-confident, adventurous, sociable, and independent. These are the qualities that full-timers think describe themselves. Examples of the responses to our questions, "What do think made you capable of going full-time?" and "What kind of people are best suited to full-timing?" illustrate what full-timers think they are like.

> *What kind of people are best suited to full-timing?*
>
> Adaptable, gregarious (and maybe a bit nutty?).
>
> * * *
>
> Someone who wants to get away from the drudgery and routine of an everyday typical lifestyle and has got the guts to try something dramatically different.

> Mutual desire to travel and see the country. We did not want to ever say "Oh if only we had done this or that." We prefer to see over the next hill and around the next corner.
>
> * * *
>
> Not being attached to things and not living for your family, i.e. "I don't know how they'll manage without us or me." You have to be able to love your family, but you've graduated from taking care of them. Now live your life your way.
>
> * * *
>
> Most I have talked to feel *they* control their life and activities. Followers are not capable of being full-timers. That's the key.
>
> * * *
>
> You can't be suspicious and afraid of the unknown. You have to be independent and confident. A strong dislike for mowing grass, painting houses, and pulling weeds helps!
>
> * * *
>
> You must realize you are only equal to everyone else. Retired generals and admirals have a hard time adjusting to this type of life. They still like to give orders.

The last response focusing on equality expresses a sentiment held by many full-timers. It does not matter who you were, what you did in your former life, or how much money you have. Full-timers characteristically insist "We're all the same here." Equality is the thrust of the Eberhard's letter to the *Escapees Newsletter*:

> How glad I am that we are members of this great fraternity of travelers that live in a classless society. We have friends

whose income tax obligation almost equals our income each year. Yet we are equals as we have dinner under the trees of some campground, all comfortable and happy, dressed in jeans and hiking shoes.

We have met people traveling in rigs costing well up into six figures, and others traveling in beat-up campers. But we are all in the same class — no one envious of the other's wealth or position. I am thankful every day that we have found a way of life in which I envy no one, but even pity those who are so dazzled by the pomp and wealth and circumstance that they can't find the beauty of the real world and real friendships.[21]

Not all serious RVers stress an egalitarian ideology. Some seek out those places — resort or membership parks — where they can find "a better class of people." Others bitterly resent the snobbery of fellow RVers who claim — usually of boondocking areas — "I couldn't live like that!" In our first published work on RVing, written after our 1990 research, we thought the dichotomy between membership park residents and boondockers represented a serious split among RVers. During our 1993-94 research, a number of RVers read that paper and quickly set us straight. We had it wrong. Most RVers try a variety of styles, boondocking some of the time and staying in membership parks part of the time. They are egalitarian. The RVers who see distinctions between economic classes are those who try to follow one RVing style exclusively. They boondock out of principle if they can, or they always stay in parks if possible. Because they do not experience the other way, they perceive those others as being unlike themselves.

Why do they start?

After two years of retirement they wondered, "Is this all there is?" While they were camping at a nearby provincial park they met an old man who was living in a dilapidated fifth-wheel. "He didn't have a pot to piss in but he was completely happy," said John. They asked one another, "Why don't we sell the house, buy a motor home and go full time?" The next day they drove to Penticton and bought their RV. (From our 1990 journal)

What makes people decide to become full-timers? Many say they spent more and more time on the road until they finally decided they would save money if they sold their home, stored the possessions they could not part with, and went on the road full time. Sometimes the decision follows an epiphany: they realize their mortality.

Others decide to become full-timers after a crisis such as the death of a friend or family member or a change in their own health or family circumstances. Their decisions are often spontaneous. The following are examples of crisis-motivated full-timing:

> The Couches had a good friend who went to bed one night with a headache and awoke the next morning with a lump on his head. Less than a year later he was dead of brain cancer. One morning after their friend's death Doris said to Urban, "Let's go on the road." They put their belongings in storage, gave up their rented apartment, and left the next day. "And we never looked back," Doris said. (From our 1990 journal)
>
> * * *
>
> Can ennui be a crisis? My stress level at work was near breaking. I was much too old for my job. I was *stuck* in a six-year relationship. Children all on their own and I was a *shop-aholic*. Escapades 84-85 were a lifeline to freedom and renewal. (Comment on a questionnaire)

When they began traveling extensively she worried about whether their home had been broken into in their absence. She also says that when they owned their home they were always cleaning the house *and* the trailer, loading and unloading the trailer with something to clean every time they did it, and trying to catch up on the yard work that accumulated when they were away. Finally he said, "We have to either give up RVing or sell the house."

* * *

She wanted a home that combined mountains with trees, "a trout stream in my backyard and the desert at my feet."

* * *

We woke up one morning and said "What are we doing here? Our lives are almost over and if we are going to do anything we'd better do it now!"

RVing is not for everyone

> Full time isn't for everyone. Pete's brother and his wife were retired and healthy and very envious of us, and so they sold their house and bought a lovely looking motor home and tried it. They really gave it a try but they just aren't cut out for it.
>
> They didn't do their homework before they bought. It has prettier wood than ours and a nicer exterior and sleeker lines, but it is a week-ender's dream, not a home on wheels with easy made bed and easy to get to storage and it isn't built for over-the-road durability. They have a big dog that is dearly loved and makes full timing a big pain sometimes. They are afraid to be without hookups and can't be relaxed unless they are at one of their TWO membership parks — 14 days here and then 14 days there. They wanted to go with us but it would never work. Takes them half a day to get underway. Sometimes we wake up at 4:30 a.m., take off and stop and eat breakfast when the sun gets in our eyes and then

make the bed and wash the dishes. They really missed their "things" and within a year had bought another house so they could be surrounded with their paintings (they both paint) and other hobbies that take up more space than an RV accords. Routine means a lot to them and the same hairdresser, etc.

Full timing is great for those of us who enjoy it — a disaster for those who don't. (From a letter from a full-timer)

Most RVers know someone who tried unsuccessfully to go full-time, and they are quick to agree that serious RVing is not for everyone. Many of them, like the full-timer whose letter is quoted at the beginning of this section, have analyzed the reasons why it sometimes does not work out. They have suggestions about the things a prospective RVer should consider, advice on how to proceed, and opinions about what kind of person is likely to succeed (or fail) at the attempt.

It is important that would-be RVers find satisfaction and meaning in the possibilities offered by a nomadic life style. Otherwise they may find themselves asking "what am I doing here?"

She says after she's been here a while she looks outside and wonders, "What the Hell am I doing here?" Boredom is a serious problem for her as well as for many other people at the Slabs because there is nothing to do here. "How many afghans can you make?" she asks. She says too many people start their happy hour at 3 p.m., have dinner before 5 p.m., and are in bed by 7 p.m. It's dark by 5 p.m. and people don't want to run down their batteries by burning lights. She isn't sure whether boredom causes the drinking or the other way around. (From our 1990 journal)

* * *

I had a conversation with Anne, a fellow dish-washer who asked me how our research was going. She asked if I was aware that full-timing isn't for everybody. It isn't for her. She and her husband have been full-timing for 2 years because he wants to, but she feels "unfulfilled" and as though "I am wasting my talents." She wants to serve others, as The Lord told her, but is only serving her husband. She feels that The Lord will lead them to settle in Florida, near her son and daughter-in-law, so that she will be able to be an influence in the lives of her grandchildren who are being incorrectly raised by the daughter-in-law. In her opinion, people who are content just to travel are "selfish" and "are leading pointless lives." She also thinks they are "running away from something" — specifically family responsibilities. If more grandmothers took an active role in shaping the lives and values of their grandchildren, there would be less trouble with young people. (Discussion while washing up during preparation for Thanksgiving Day dinner at an Escapees Park. From our 1993 journal.)

* * *

She walks, he is in the rock hound club. She says after two or three months she begins to wonder what she's doing that is worthwhile. She spends her time reading, walking, sightseeing, visiting, shopping, and they move around a lot. "Time passes," she says. (Response to our asking "What do you do all day?")

Two issues arise in these comments. One is the need to find meaningful, important activity rather than just to pass time. As we see in Chapter Six, some RVers find satisfaction in travel and meeting new friends. Others find it by working at least part-time or volunteering in their RV community or in the local host community. The second issue that determines whether people are cut out for serious RVing is the issue of separation from family.

Buck thinks that some people are unable to full-time because they are tied to their children and grandchildren. Crystal added, "I don't think they're closer to their family. They're reaching out for something they are lacking." (From our 1993 journal)

* * *

She misses her children and grandchildren. She says that the kids don't like to visit them in their trailer because "it's not home," and their grandchildren don't come and visit in the trailer because there isn't enough room. This worries her because her own children didn't know any of their grandparents well and now the same thing is happening with their grandchildren. (From our 1990 journal)

* * *

I am the granny who visits a week and leaves for far-away places. (Comment on questionnaire)

Frequent and intimate contact with children and grandchildren gives meaning to the lives of many retired people, especially if they live nearby and see them frequently. Most of the RVers in our study are close to their children. When they lived in their former homes, most of them were within an hour's drive of their children and two-thirds still see their children twice a year or more. However, almost 10 per cent (74 per cent of them women) said what they missed most about full-timing was frequent contact with their children and grandchildren. If people are lonely and unhappy because they are separated from their families, serious RVing is probably not for them.

Living in an RV may bring families together. RVers who have children and grandchildren scattered from Maine to California, from British Columbia to New Brunswick, say that RVing enables them regularly to see family members who otherwise would be inaccessible.

> The reason we started being full-timers is that we are a close family, good friends with our three grown kids and their spouses, and the nine grandkids, and one lives in Oregon, one in Washington, and one in Maine. They are all busy and couldn't get home (Southern California) very often so we go see them. Then too, S. Cal is a horrid place to retire, not like it was 40 years ago. Crowded, polluted, crime ridden — so we sold our home, put the money away for a house somewhere else someday and "hit the road." (From a letter by Ruth Dalgleish)

For those people who are reunited with their families through RVing, there is an extra benefit. When they visit they are in their own home where they can go to bed when they choose and make their morning coffee when they decide to get up. Unlike house guests and fish, they do not smell after three days. Some RVers told us that the biggest problem in visiting their families was their hosts getting "huffy" because they preferred to sleep in "that trailer" instead of a "real bed" in the house. Mickey and Phil spoke for many RVers when they explained, "This is our home! We'd rather sleep in our own bed and use our own bathroom." Mickey added, "I don't do mornings, and I don't want to be woke up by the baby crying. I'd rather get up at 9:30, have my coffee, and then go into the house."

For people who are close to their families and who are considering serious RVing, the relevant question seems to be, "Will RVing separate or unite you and your family?"

The difficulties outlined above are expressed in the following letters from people who found they disliked serious RVing. First, disenchanted full-timers speak for themselves in a letter to a columnist in the *Escapees Newsletter*.

You keep preaching about full-timing in your column. You ought to warn your readers it is not for everybody. We tried it for six months and found it wasn't for us.

For one thing, we didn't like the neighbors in the trailer courts.

We missed the grandkids. I missed them more than I expected to, but my wife grieved over them.

Our motor home wasn't a new one and, although it was in good condition when we first started out, eventually the miles added up and we ended up having a lot of expensive problems and repairs. This we had not anticipated in our original budget expectations. Basically, it just wore out.

I didn't miss the bad weather back home or shovelling snow and driving on ice. But I found I missed the good weather. When the season turned, I missed my gardening.

When we sold the house, we left our beloved 10-year-old huge house cat with our son and his wife, and they let her out, and she got run over. We felt so bad. Had we but known how many pets travel perfectly well, we would never have left her, and she would be alive today.

So after six months we quit and bought a condo.

Why don't you tell folks to experiment and try it out for a few months before they burn all their bridges like we did? If we had done that, rented the house instead of selling out, we would have saved ourselves a lot of money.

The bottom line is we enjoy RVing, but only for short periods at a time. We learned the hard way we don't love it enough to give up almost everything we own for it. M. and M.J.[22]

Although the following letters are not from disgruntled full-timers, they do give insight into the reasons some people dislike any style of RVing. Both letters were from retired physicians. The first says:

I am totally convinced that trailering, RVing or camping is only for some people and only if they *love* the experience or have had no experience at all. How anyone could enjoy or justify this inconvenience of surviving in a 10x14 cubicle, which is the kitchen, dining room, living room, and bedroom is beyond comprehension.

These RVers experienced other problems too. They were pulled toward passing 18 wheelers. They had difficulty turning their trailer around. They spent ten days in their trailer in the rain, in a park with closed washroom facilities, and had to walk a half-mile to the toilet because there was none in their rig. Their trailer had no oven. They had to heat their water on the stove, their fridge froze their food "even when it was turned off," and their roof leaked. Because they dreaded pulling the trailer back north during the winter, they phoned friends and invited them to use it free in Florida if they would pull it home. "NO TAKERS." He concludes:

> Considering the initial investment, consumption of fuel, double tolls, equipment failure, hassle of locating suitable accommodations with hookups, it was a disappointment. It is ironic that while the cost of parking per day ranged from $19.00 to $25.00, one could have had a motel efficiency with all conveniences for the same price.... One should rent before investing in any unit and exercise a test run.

The second letter, from a 70-year-old retired obstetrician enumerates the reasons for his disappointment.

> We did try the RV life style soon after my retirement by renting one and heading off to Florida for a month in Feb. I won't say it was total disaster but I can tell you that when we returned home my wife kept the drapes closed against the sight of the obnoxious thing in the drive until we could return it.
>
> Reasons? The major ones (and there were many minor ones) were:
>
> 1. With a RV you must drag your home with you whenever you want to shop, sight-see, or even just get away from the RV site. The answer is perhaps a fifth-wheel trailer or dragging a small car which I note that a lot of RV people do.
>
> 2. We envisaged spending our time at some lovely shaded beach front property. In Florida such properties are occupied either by hotels or condos. The RV parks we found were usually far from water, unshaded, and indeed often concrete jungles in the poorer parts of town. Perhaps given more time we might have discovered nicer places.
>
> 3. We have two dogs. Florida law does not allow dogs to be on a beach, even on a leash. Further it is against Florida law to leave dogs unattended in an RV. So we were unable to go out

for a meal, or an evening, which somewhat destroyed the "raison d'être" for being in Florida. Yes, we could have left the dogs at home, as we must when we go to Europe, but part of the reason for the RV was that we need not leave them.

Even at my age life must offer more than shuffle board, bridge, and waiting for letters from children about grandchildren.

Serious RVers are aware of the sorts of problems these folks experienced and offer advice to potential full-timers that could help them to avoid at least some of the worst difficulties. Their recommendations can be summarized as "Do research and plan before you start." "Try it first." "Consider whether you are the sort of person who would enjoy it, and if you are then do it!" The following are summaries of quotes from and lengthy discussions with full-timers about what "wannabe" RVers should consider.

DO RESEARCH AND PLAN BEFORE YOU START

Many people fail because they start full-timing without doing any research and without trying it first, Cassie said. They hear somebody else talking about it and just decide they'd like to do it too, without having any idea about what is involved. They don't know how to drive big rigs. They don't know how to drain the pipes when the weather gets cold. They don't know where anything is. They don't know you have to shut off the water pump when you travel. "You have to practice this thing," said Cassie. Also, people usually spend most of their time outside the home and with other people and other interests. When they come home from work in the evening they have things to talk about. In contrast, when people are full-timing they are together 24 hours a day in a small space with nothing else to talk about. "They don't know what it is to live in an RV day after day after day. Your whole life is going to change. You'd better prepare first. You must do a tremendous amount of planning." (From our 1993 journal)

TRY IT FIRST

Try trips together before making a commitment. Give up your pets. Caretaking pets is not fair to you or to the pets.

* * *

Don't wait too long, as I did! But try it before disposing of everything.

* * *

Don't cut roots and ties until you see if it's for you and your partner. Be willing to stop and smell the flowers. Live five minutes at a time.

* * *

Keep your house, buy a used RV at modest cost, and give it a try before making a final decision. This is especially true for older people who have never used an RV. (All comments on questionnaires)

CONSIDER IF YOU ARE THE RIGHT KIND OF PERSON

Ask yourself, "Are you gregarious? Ready to greet anyone with a good day? Prepared for anything to break or to change plans?"

* * *

Consider carefully your ability to leave family and friends, home, things, etc. Your comfort in small quarters, especially during bad weather. (Comments on questionnaires)

DO IT

Do it NOW! Don't wait. Your family is just a plane ride away from anywhere. Your children and grandchildren don't need you around all the time.

* * *

Go for it — FAST!

* * *

Capture each day and enjoy. (Comments on questionnaires)

RVing — especially full-timing — is not for everyone. There is wisdom in the advice RVers give those considering the life-style: "Don't burn all your bridges: try it first." Experienced full-time and serious RVers urge beginners to consider the importance of their house, treasured possessions and family. They also encourage those who try the life and like it to keep their options open. If you are not sure, they say, store your things and rent your house. Then, if you do decide to cut your ties to place and possessions, don't look back. No regrets. Your home is now where you park it.

RVing Styles: Planners

Choices between alternative styles of RVing are legion. Among the choices RVers enjoy is whether they carefully plan their itinerary or drift as serendipitous nomads. For committed planners, security is critical and includes knowing where they will be the next night or the next week or the next months. They achieve their security by making reservations in private or membership parks — sometimes months in advance.

The Krings, full-timers whom we first met in 1990 in a failed membership park, are planners and enthusiastic users of the membership park system. They especially value the security provided by the reservation system that enables them to know where they will spend the night before they pull out in the morning. They prefer to know their schedule at least a week ahead, and try to plan for several months at a time. Four years later we met them again in an SKP co-op park where they have a lot. They were helpful with our research, and we continue to correspond.

The Krings

Pat and Newell Kring have been in their current fifth-wheel for the past six years. Newell retired from teaching at age 50 following a heart attack. Pat continued to work as an accountant until she was 62, when their pensions and investments enabled them to go on the road full-time. They are among the few full-timers who described themselves as being "always on vacation." They began serious RVing after Newell's forced retirement because Pat thought he needed to get out of the house, where he had been sitting "watching the walls." Their commitment to RVing is intense. Newell says that RVing is the only reason that he is still alive. The lifestyle keeps him active, enables him to meet new people, and gives him things to do. "If I hadn't had an RV to escape in, I don't know what would have happened," he says.

For the three years following Pat's retirement, the Krings stayed on the road continuously, following their interests in American Revolutionary and Civil War history and tracing their families' genealogies. When they became serious RVers they joined three membership park organizations. They consider these organizations to be ideal for full-timers who move every few days. They argue they got their money's worth from their memberships in the first three years. For example, an 18-month trip made in 1990 cost them an average of only $2.95 a night because they stayed exclusively at membership parks. "They don't owe us a thing if we never use them again," says Newell.

In 1993, the continued deterioration of Newell's health led them to buy into an Escapees co-op. Co-op membership gives them most of the amenities and security that they like but does not require them to be always on the move as they were when they depended on membership parks. Nevertheless, they remain devoted to the membership park idea, insisting that the facilities "are a cut above the average RV park." They have more amenities, planned social activities such as pot-luck dinners and dances where it is easy to meet people and make friends, and "a more congenial class of people with common interests" than do other parks. They assert that people in membership parks have pride in them because they are part owners. They also like the idea that the parks discourage excessive alcohol use and that managers can control repeat trouble-makers by threatening to throw them out of the system.

The Krings are concerned about security, both physical and psychological. They like having reservations so they know where they will spend the night before they leave in the morning. They do not boondock and rarely stay in state parks or national forest campgrounds. They are critical of many privately owned parks whose security precautions they consider to be lax. They like the idea that membership parks provide 24-hour security and locked gates at night. "I would feel safe RVing alone in a membership park," says Pat.

The Krings participate actively in planned recreational activities. They say that many who belong to membership parks plan their routes based on the activities available in particular parks and on who is teaching them. Pat is well known as a line-dancing teacher. She teaches at the same park each summer, and her students come there for two weeks, then go for two weeks to other nearby parks that also feature line-dancing, and then return to her park. Others choose parks for the crafts and teachers for which they are well known. The Krings say that both men and women choose parks and schedules for line-dancing, while women are especially interested in crafts and men look for horseshoes and pool. Sometimes people with special interests move together as teams.

The Krings say their active participation in planned park activities provides them with an ever-increasing network of friends because others follow the same kind of "activity route." So they meet the same people over and over again and friendships develop among those who have common interests.

The Smiths made the decision not to join membership parks because "We don't need the security. We don't need or want time tables or schedules." By security they mean "the security of having to know where we're going to stay tonight. That doesn't interest us," or of knowing where they're going next. They consider the people who stay in membership parks to be homogeneous and say "like attracts like." (From our 1993 journal)

Although RVers like the Krings say that their combination of planning and participation in organized activities provides them with interesting things to do and a supportive network of friends, others argue that following a schedule of reservations and planned activities restricts the freedom that is the hallmark of the RVing lifestyle. Kay Peterson, for example, makes this point in an editorial in the *Escapees Newsletter*.[23] When she received a letter from a Skip saying "Happiness is four consecutive weeks of confirmed reservations," she began to wonder how many Skips never deviate from the security of a circuit of membership parks:

> If you have to have a confirmed reservation *every* night, you have traded one highly organized lifestyle for another that is just as regimented, and I truly believe you are missing one of the greatest joys of RVing.... There is nothing wrong with making reservations unless, when an unexpected opportunity presents itself, you pass it up because it doesn't fit into your reservation itinerary. Any tightly followed schedule keeps you from enjoying the magical experiences of serendipity.

Peterson defines serendipity as "making accidental, wonderful discoveries of places and experiences that are born of a chance encounter." For nomadic seekers of serendipity, it does not matter when they reach their destination.

RVing Styles: Non-planners: Do We Turn Right or Left?

Some people never have a destination. For them, it is the trip, not getting to the end of it, that is important. The road calls them, and they find it hard to stay in one place more than a few days. They revel in the freedom to go where they want, stay as long as they please, and leave when they get the urge. They do not make reservations at RV parks because they refuse to be tied to a schedule. When you ask where they are going, they respond that they don't know. When they get to the next fork in the road, they will have to decide whether to turn right or left. For some people, this stage of RVing lasts only for a time. Then they tire of continuous travel and settle in a park for weeks or months. They may become members of a SKP co-op, buy a lot in an Escapees retreat park, or purchase some other home base. Others seem never to tire. These are the people who have a terminal case of hitch-itch. They continue the nomadic style of RVing for years, for decades, until they are forced by illness or death to "hang up their keys."

The Johnsons

Roy and Mabel Johnson are RVers who follow the nomadic life style. The Johnsons consider themselves nomadic RVers, even though they own a lot in a SKP retreat park. Because of Roy's health problems, they have been forced to spend two or three months at a time at their home base. Both of them get restless after so long in one place. When we met them they had been on their lot for several months while Roy received medical treatment, and they were eagerly looking forward to their next trip. They are fierce non-planners. "We don't know whether we'll turn right or left when we leave this park," Mabel said. She chuckled as she told us that when their daughters haven't heard from them for several weeks, one will call the other and ask, "If you were our mother, where would you be now?"

The Johnsons enjoy the freedom to make spontaneous decisions and contrast themselves with folks who always plan ahead because they must know where they will spend each night. Beverly is an example of the type of RVer Mabel does not want to be. She recounted seeing Beverly come out of a phone booth with joy on her face because she had confirmed her reservation for January in a popular park in Bandera, Texas. Beverly was ecstatic because she had completed all the reservations for her winter's travel. "She knew where she'd be every single night from November until the end of March," said Mable, with a shudder. The Johnsons think that people who refuse to travel without reservations are not free: they are driven by fear and a need for security. There are two kinds of security needs, say the Johnsons. Some people need the security of knowing exactly where they are going to be that evening before they pull out in the morning; others only feel secure when they are protected by a walled park. The Johnsons require neither. They do not carry weapons and have spent maybe six nights in the last year in a regular RV Park, usually only because they couldn't find anywhere else. By preference they are boondockers.

Conclusion

We began this chapter by asking of serious and full-time RVers "Who are they?" As the portraits in this chapter suggest, all kinds of people become RVers, and they follow a variety of styles of RVing. They are partially disabled retired farmers, former business executives, retired teachers, housewives, fishermen, and accountants. Some of them always boondock, some never do. Some spend most of their time in membership parks and others would not consider joining such an organization. Some are just beginning to explore the freedom they sought in becoming RVers while, as we will see in the last chapter, others are sadly contemplating hanging up their keys for the last time. The answer to our question is both simple and complex. They are us.

Notes

1. Clinton 1993:8.

2. Two of the surveys of RVers to which we have access, those by Curtin (1994) and Louis Harris and Associates (1994) were commissioned by the Recreation Vehicle Industry Association (RVIA). These were US nationwide samplings done following rigorous sampling techniques common to the established polling industry, but they were conducted in an effort to get at demographics of *all* RV owners and potential buyers, with particular attention to identifying the characteristics of likely first-time buyers of recreational vehicles for vacation purposes. The survey results do not permit us to readjust the figures to focus on what we have called *serious* RVers.

Data reported by Hartwigsen and Null (1990) were collected by questionnaires and interviews with 100 full-time RVers who were members of a camping organization. Hartwigsen and Null conducted their surveys at camping resorts in Arizona and southern California between February and April 1987. Participation was limited to full-timers who were at least 50 years old or who were married to a spouse aged 50 or above. Because the rules of the camping organization required RVers to move on after two weeks, participants in the study were traveling RVers.

Three other surveys of RVers are based on the membership of particular clubs. One, based on membership of the Family Motor Coach Association, identifies characteristics of those owning particular types of motor homes (Albert 1993). Since the analyses of these data appear to have assumed that only *motor homes* were RVs, the usefulness of the findings to us is limited. Another, by the staff of the Escapees Club, is based on responses to a tear-off questionnaire in the club's newsletter (Kornow 1993). The respondents to this survey were those club members willing to tear it off, fill it out, and pay for a stamp to return it to club headquarters. The third survey was published in an SKP co-op newsletter that was circulated to lot holders in the park (Clinton 1993). This survey reflects the opinions and characteristics of the lot holders who were resident in the park at the time and who were willing to fill it out and return it to the surveyor. While the data collected by these last two surveys are based, as are ours, on the voluntary responses of members of the club, they differ from ours in a number of important respects. First, our data are not limited to, though they are dominated by, members of the Escapees Club. Second, our materials were collected on the road and were overwhelmingly drawn from RVers who were actively traveling. Both the club surveys went to all members receiving the newsletter, whether they continued to be active travelers or not.

3. Almost 50 per cent of our respondents were male, slightly over 50 per cent were female. The SKP park survey organized by Norm Clinton found that 46 per cent of the residents were male, 54 per cent female (Clinton 1993a:7).

Almost half of the full-time and serious RVers who filled out our questionnaire were between the ages of 56 and 65. Most (79 per cent) were retired. Hartwigsen and Null report that the mean age of the full-timers in their study was 63.4 for men, 60.9 for women (Hartwigsen and Null 1990:139). Responses to a questionnaire published in the Escapees club's newsletter, indicate that 93 per cent of the organization's members are over the age of 50 (Kornow 1993:7; Peterson, Kay 1993a:5). Respondents to a survey conducted in 1993 among lot holders at an Escapees co-op park ranged in age from 53 to 80 with an average age of 65.8 (Clinton 1993a:7-8). A study of the membership of the Family Motor Coach Association (FMCA, a club for motor home owners) depicts the "average RV owner" as a retired 63-year-old man or 60-year-old woman with some college education (Albert 1993:16). A study for the Recreation Vehicle Industry Association (RVIA) found that while the typical RV owner in 1993 was 48 years old, the typical motor home owner was 63 years old. The highest ownership rates of RVs in the US population were by people age 55-64, 16 per cent of whom owned RVs. The next highest ownership rates were 12.8 per cent by age 65-74, while the third highest rate was of people age 45-54 with 12.2 per cent owning RVs. Of people age 75 and over, 3.4 per cent owned RVs (Curtin 1994:13, 16).

Although the data collected in these various surveys are not comparable — for instance Hartwigsen and Null were unique in restricting their study to self-defined full-timers over the age of 50, while the RVIA study includes pop-up tent campers and truck campers, items almost exclusively used for vacations and not for living — they strongly suggest that full-timers and serious RVers are likely to be older, retired people.

Clinton's survey of lot holders at one Escapees park found that 65 per cent of respondents had a university undergraduate or graduate degree (Clinton 1993a:7). Of the RVers who completed our questionnaire, more than 77 per cent had some post-secondary education, while 23 per cent had a graduate or professional degree. Albert reports that an FMCA profile of the average RV owner is of a person who has some college education (Albert 1993:16). In a separate survey, Farlow found to his surprise that two-thirds of the respondents to his questionnaire reported having a computer on board their rigs (Farlow 1995:20). In his SKP park survey, Clinton found that occupations before retirement included administrators 24 per cent; educators 15 per cent; homeworkers 11 per cent; finance workers 7 per cent; engineers 5 per cent; workers in electronics, mechanics, construction, real estate, business, and power plants 3 per cent; while 2 per cent were machinists, truckers, telephone workers, nurses, fire fighters, police constables, printers, military, chemical operators, foresters, seamstresses, postal workers, and food service workers (Clinton 1993a:7). Of the respondents to our survey, the most frequent former occupation given was white collar business (17.5 per cent). Next were educators (9.8 per cent) and health services (8.4 per cent). For more details see question 26 in Appendix One.

4. Figures from the Recreation Vehicle Industry Association and from clubs such as the Family Motor Coach Association report an average annual income of between $39,000 and $40,000 US for RVers (Curtin 1994:19-20; Albert 1993:16), but it is unclear whether these are individual or combined family income averages. Further, as averages they obscure the extreme range of incomes that may be included.

More than a quarter (27 per cent) of our respondents said their approximate yearly income *per person* in their rig was between $10,000 and $15,000. Since 84 per cent of those who completed our questionnaire said there were two people traveling in their RV, the combined income for this group was between $20,000 and

$30,000. Almost one in five respondents said their income was more than $25,000 per person in their rig.

5. Thirty-six of the 47 singles who completed our questionnaire were either widowed (16) or divorced (20). In the population of RVers we studied there were three single women for every two single men.

6. Randolph 1995:61.

7. Darby 1986:12.

8. Clinton 1993b:2.

9. The membership ratio of clubs for RVing singles is usually about three women to one man (Curtin 1994:19-20; Albert 1993:16). The exception is Wandering Individuals Network or WIN. WIN was formed March 25, 1988, to help younger singles (those born after 1926) to meet others of similar age and interests. According to Janet Carter, one of the founders of the club, the membership is mostly adventurous men who are aged 60 or younger (personal communication). A cartoon in the club's newsletter *The WINdow* (WIN 1994:4) shows a number of men in line with applications to join WIN. A woman standing at the side is saying to another woman, "At this rate, we'll have to change the club name to WAN (women are needed)." As of 1990 WIN had over 175 members in 31 states and 2 provinces; 41 of these were full-timers. This information and the quote in the text are from Prince 1990:47.

10. Clubs exclusively for women include RVing Women based in Washington state and Women on Wheels (WOW). WOW was started by Lovern King and Zoe Swanagon after they attended the Birds of a Feather (BOF) seminar (for women who travel alone) at the 1989 Escapees Club's Escapade. The organization reportedly got its name when one woman, delighted at finding others like herself, exclaimed, "WOW, and I thought I was the only woman traveling alone!" (Peterson, J. 1991:17)

The quotes stating LoW's policy on cross-gender fraternization are from Ivy (1983:54) and LeDrew (1992:38). LoW's "Statement of Purpose" also emphasizes that it insists on separation of the sexes. It says, "A man and woman traveling as a couple are not eligible for membership. If they appear at LoW gatherings traveling in the same rig, their membership is immediately terminated" (*Loners on Wheels* 1994:2). Although (or perhaps because) the club discourages romance, the club is a source of companionship and support for its members. According to the club's "Statement of Purpose":

"As a group we enjoy campouts, cookouts, pot-luck meals, restaurant meals, campfires, tours, and companionship. Members come from all walks of life, all types of careers and varied economic levels. The main purpose of the club is to give single campers the opportunity to camp with others in the same circumstances."

11. *Loners of America News* 1994:16.

12. Carter, L. 1986:9.

13. LeDrew 1992:38.

14. In February, 1994 Dorothy counted the number of Canadian license plates in BC Flats. Although Canadians were 39 per cent, not 80 per cent of the population, as we had been told, the area is called BC Flats with good reason. The break-down of the 214 rigs in both the long term and short term areas was as follows:

	Long Term Area	Short Term Area	Total
US license plates	119	12	131
Canadian license plates			
Alberta	23	1	
BC	42	5	
Manitoba	3		
Ontario	6 (including us)		
Saskatchewan	3		
Total Canadian Plates:	77	6	83

Canadian RVers seem to be a much smaller percent of the general RVing population. For example, in April 1995 Canadians were only 1 per cent (448 of approximately 37,000) of the membership of Escapees (Clifton and Clifton, personal communication, 1995). Some Americans have the idea that Canadians invade the public and private campgrounds in the southwest. We were told a number of times that "over half" the people in a particular area were Canadians. This was never borne out by our license plate count. The license plates in places that were allegedly "taken over by you Canadians" were usually between 4 and 10 per cent Canadian.

15. Johnson and Johnson 1993:42-43.

16. Goff 1992:A1-A2.

17. Chatfield 1992:7.

18. Members of membership park organizations may sell their memberships at a substantial discount. Although a used membership may not include all the benefits of a new one, many RVers feel that the initial savings is worth the loss of some perks. They also say they can own several different used memberships for the cost of one new one. Many RVing magazines carry advertisements offering used memberships for sale.

19. **How are Canadians Different From Other RVers?**
In 1990 when we were actively seeking out Canadian RVers, almost half (24 of 50) of the interviews we conducted were with Canadians. Of those 24 Canadians, 16 described themselves as full-timers, 8 said they were part-timers. In 1993-94 only 18 out of 296 (6 per cent) respondents were Canadian.

Are they retired? (Q 28)

	18 Canadians		269 Americans	
Retired	13	(72%)	214	(79%)
Semi-retired	3	(16%)	34	(13%)
Not retired	2	(11%)	22	(8%)

How many are full-timers? (Q 37)

	18 Canadians		274 Americans	
Full-timers	7	(39%)	192	(70%)
Serious RVers	4	(22%)	48	(17.5%)
Snow birds	7	(39%)	23	(8%)

Kind of home base (Q39)

Kind	18 Canadians		269 Americans	
House/apartment	6	(33%)	61	(27%)
Mobile home or cottage	5	(28%)	13	(5%)
SKP park lot	1	(5.6%)	85	(31%)
Other RV park lot	0		6	(2%)
Other	1	(5.6%)	21	(8%)
I have no home base	5	(28%)	83	(28%)

How long have they been full-timers? (Q 40)

Time	7 Canadians		203 Americans	
less than 1 year	0		21	(10%)
1-2 years	1	(14%)	22	(11%)
2-3 years	2	(29%)	41	(20%)
3-5 yrs.	2	(29%)	44	(22%)
5-10 yrs.	0		49	(24%)
10-15 yrs.	0		19	(9%)
15 yrs. +	2	(29%)	7	(3%)

Did their decision to start full-timing follow a crisis? (Q 41)

214 answers by full-timers.	7 Canadians		207 Americans	
Yes	2	(29%)	49	(24%)
No	5	(71%)	158	(76%)

What have they done with their home? (Q 44)

Disposition	9 Canadians		234 Americans	
Sold it	4	(44%)	170	(73%)
Renting it	0		10	(4%)
Relatives there	2	(22%)	9	(4%)
Vacant	0		4	(2%)
Still live there	2	(22%)	32	(14%)
Other	1	(11%)	9	(4%)

Have they ever had a medical crisis while RVing? (Q 68)

	18 Canadians		271 Americans	
Yes	2	(11%)	66	(24%)
No	16	(88%)	205	(76%)

Do they have any health problems now? (Q 71)

	18 Canadians		268 Americans	
Yes	5	(28%)	114	(43%)
No	13	(72%)	154	(57%)

How would they describe their health now? (Q 73)

	18 Canadians		273 Americans	
Excellent	4	(22%)	114	(42%)
Good	12	(67%)	137	(50%)
Fair	2	(11%)	20	(7%)
Poor	0		2	(1%)

Do they have private medical insurance? (Q 78)

	17 Canadians		278 Americans	
Yes	10	(59%)	218	(78%)
No	7	(41%)	60	(22%)

Which problem is of greatest concern to them? (Q 97)

Problems	18 Canadians		271 Americans	
Mechanical Breakdown	4	(22%)	96	(35%)
Illness	4	(22%)	64	(24%)
Personal safety	0		27	(10%)
Money	2	(11%)	24	(9%)
Isolation from family	2	(11%)	18	(7%)
Other	1	(5.5%)	9	(3.5%)
Multiple answers	5	(28%)	20	(7%)
No worries	0		13	(5%)

Which problem is of least concern to them? (Q 98)

Problems	18 Canadians		257 Americans	
Mechanical Breakdown	3	(17%)	14	(5%)
Illness	2	(11%)	17	(7%)
Personal safety	2	(11%)	40	(16%)
Money	3	(17%)	57	(22%)
Isolation from family	7	(39%)	113	(44%)
Multiple responses	1	(5.5%)	16	(6%)

Do they carry weapons? (Q 102)

	18 Canadians		272 Americans	
Yes	3	(17%)	141	(51%)
No	15	(84%)	131	(49%)

What do they carry?

Of the three Canadians who said they carry weapons, 1 said a club, 1 said guns (plural), and 1 said a shotgun. Of the 141 Americans who said they carry weapons, 8 (6 per cent) said they carry a gun (generic): 39 (28 per cent) carry guns (plural); 55 (39 per cent) carry a hand gun; 18 (13 per cent) carry a shotgun; 3 (2 per cent) carry a rifle; 5 (4 per cent) carry a gun and some other weapon. The remaining 8 per cent of weapons include mace, clubs, and others such as a crowbar, ice pick, and fire extinguisher.

20. Counts and Counts 1994.

21. Eberhard and Eberhard 1986:11.

22. Carter 1992:17-18.

23. Peterson, K. 1991a:4.

Chapter Six

On the Road Again

The sweetest words of tongue or pen
This morning we will roll again.[1]

When Dorothy asked Buck whether he thought RVing attracted active people or RVing made people active, he responded RVing requires people to be active. "Just the hitching and unhitching requires some physical activity. You do things you wouldn't do if you were just sitting in a house or an apartment."

Buck argues that full-timers must have a hobby to keep their hands busy. Reading is not enough. Crystal agreed and added that she reads less now than she did before they went full-timing. They have improved their lot by building a small shed that serves as a combination living room, game room, and workshop. She likes to play poker, so they host poker parties in their shed several times a week and have converted their card table into a poker table with a round, felt-covered top. Buck makes stained glass windows and hangers in his workshop. He has an eagle window in their trailer door and is making a songbird window to sell. He also makes Indian-type artifacts. Hanging in their shed is a beaded buckskin shirt he made and his mother beaded years ago, some buckskin breeches that he beaded, a "peace pipe," and a drum that he made. (From our 1993 journal)

As we discussed in Chapter Two, a successful retirement requires something interesting to do and friends to do it with. Some RVers, like Buck, say that because of the continuous changes that are part of RVing, the opportunities for new friends and absorbing activities are more readily available to them than they are to sedentary folk.

People who continue to learn and to do new things are more likely to be healthy and long-lived than are those who do not. *Continue* is a key word here. People do not change lifelong habits and attitudes. Indolent people do not suddenly become mentally and physically active after retirement. Jacobs, who did research in the retirement community he calls Fun City, explains why some residents actively participate in social life and some do not:

> It is generally true that the extent of a resident's social life in Fun
> City is directly related to his or her social life prior to retiring.
> Persons with an active social life before coming to Fun City
> continue to be active, while those with inactive life styles prior
> to retirement tend to continue in that mode.[2]

Patterns established during decades of working and family life continue into
old age. For a successful retirement, people should develop habits of activity
that stimulate the mind and body early in life and *continue* them after they
retire. It is, however, *being active* that is important, not the specific activity.
We met one couple, whom we call the Keremons, who had never even
been in an RV before they retired. They said their retirement was successful
because RVing enables them to pursue their dissimilar interests. She enjoys
mixing with people while he prefers to read or work on his computer.
They both love the traveling.

One of the things RVers enjoy most about their lifestyle is the opportunity
to travel. It is an aspect of RVing that many associate with good health — one
encouraged by physicians who advise their patients to "Travel and do what
you want to do. Don't sit around here and have a cardiac arrest." Janet
Carter, a full-time RVer and free-lance writer, says she thinks people stop
the aging process when they start RVing. In her words, "They crystallize
when they start traveling. They don't get any older." RV travel allows some
people to escape from winters their doctors say will kill them. For others,
it is the traveling itself that is beneficial.[3]

> George was diagnosed 10 years ago with a blood disease. His
> physician told him that he would require blood transfusions
> every month and that he must avoid stress and fatigue. Fatigue is
> a symptom of the illness, and George says his physician told him,
> "If I had your blood count I couldn't crawl." In fact, he required
> no blood transfusions at all for the two six-month periods he and
> his wife Betty were in Australia and only once on their trip to
> Newfoundland and Labrador. They think George is in remission
> because he loves to travel and because he relaxes when he is
> driving their rig. Said Betty, "I'm sure that this lifestyle has had a
> lot to do with our well-being and certainly with our happiness.
> We still want to see what's over that next hill."

The perception that travel keeps RVers healthy may have a sound medical
basis. A panel of physicians participating in a symposium in Washington,
DC, reportedly suggested that profound weakness rather than aging itself

is the chief reason seniors lose their independence. Using statistics showing that exercise and the educational opportunities of travel can rejuvenate mind and body, the panel concluded, "Frequent travel can significantly benefit the physical and psychological health of seniors... traveling gives energy and vitality."[4]

Travel seems to be an essential part of successful RVing retirement. Furthermore, travel is the thing many of them would miss most if they had to quit RVing.[5] Why is travel so important in retirement?

People must reorient their lives away from their former work if they are to have a satisfying retirement, according to anthropologist Joel Savishinsky. They shouldn't spend their time sitting in a mall with fellow retirees, reminiscing about the days when they used to work, and waiting to die. One way retirees can put distance (literal as well as figurative) between their past and their new lives, he suggests, is by traveling. Savishinsky was thinking of short-term travel rather than serious RVing when he made his observation. However, his emphasis on the importance of travel as a strategy for reorienting one's life is particularly appropriate in RV retirement.[6]

RVers know change is a necessary part of successful retirement. As the Keremons observed, "When you retire it's a mistake to stay in the same house. You need to put all that behind you. You need a new beginning." Buying an RV and living in the desert for the winter was part of that beginning for them. They had to learn a new set of skills and a new way of life after they retired. This is a challenge facing many new retirees.

RV Retirement: What Do They Do All Day?

> They never have a dull moment, even if they aren't selling in the flea market. Then there are always "house chores" because "something is always wrong with an RV." (From our 1990 journal)

Non-RVers frequently ask us, "What do they *do* all day?" Implied in the question is the assumption that RVers lack something useful to do and must be bored to tears. As we saw in Chapter Five, some RVers complain that they do not have anything important to do and say that life is often boring and meaningless. Others, like the Kents, whose letter follows, are active, busy, and on the go. The need to have interesting and worthwhile things to do is basic.

> Since last December we have covered a lot of territory and are still living in our trusty motor home and loving it. We left the US

for Mexico on the 5th of December 1994 with a group of eight rigs and a guide.... We saw many festivals and local celebrations and witnessed the local life. We spent time at Mazatlan and Guadalajara, where we spent Xmas in a lovely RV park. The park hosted a Xmas and New Year party that was great. We all went to Xmas dinner at a beautiful very old hotel that was superb. We traveled the interior of Mexico then returned to the coast where we stopped at a small RV park at the ocean. This is our favorite. We returned to the US on the 10th of March 1995. We traveled to Quartzsite in Arizona for a few days. We love camping out on the desert there, the evenings are so beautiful.... Then on to Reno to visit Sarah's sister and her husband.... Then to Fresno to the western Escapee RV rally, meeting up with RV friends.

We headed home to BC for the summer.... We visited George's daughter in Pender Harbour where she had moved to be with her boy friend. Then to Vancouver and out to the hills around Merritt where we encountered flowers so thick and tall they turned the hills blue....

August found us headed to North Dakota to the Safari (manufacturer of our RV) rally prior to the FMCA [Family Motor Coach Association, for class A motor homes] rally in Minot, ND. There were 5,200 RVs at the rally, hard to visualize this many RVs parked side by side.... At 5:30 am of the morning following the close of the rally a hail storm struck the area, with hail stones the size of tennis balls. The damage was unbelievable. We had one side of our RV damaged to the extent it had to be replaced. The other side was dented so it required extensive repair, and the hail made a hole in the Fiberglass on the front of our vehicle... We immediately headed for the dealer ... in Oregon and were the first in line to get the repairs done. The repairs took three weeks....

We spent the balance of September and the first part of October back in the hills around Merrit where we spent some wonderful Indian Summer days by the lake in the hills, walking on the forest trails, and watching the leaves turn color. Finally we woke up one morning to find it snowing. We were at 4,000 feet elevation.

Soon we headed south ... to Laughlin where we parked at the Ramada Inn looking out over the valley. The hotel has a miniature train that runs from the casino through the parking lot so that you can get a ride right down to the hotel and casino. Bargain breakfasts and dinners here are designed for those that want to join the ranks of the overweighters quickly. Sarah decided that the food environment at Laughlin was not in the best interest of the two of us, so we took off for Quartzsite where we met a number of old time campers dry-camping in the desert. We socialized several days and visited vendors at the Four Corners Flea Market in Quartzsite. We met one elderly lady who showed us beautiful opals that she and her husband had mined, cut, polished, and collected over the last 40 years....

We are off to Mexico on the 10th of December, delayed a few days by the friend with whom we will travel.... Our mail is forwarded at least monthly and our phone number is still the same. However, it is an answering machine taking messages. We pick up the messages daily when in Vancouver (which is not often) but have the messages forwarded on to us weekly, except when we are in Mexico which will be until the first part of March. (From a letter from George and Sarah Kent, whom we introduced in Chapter Five.)

The lives of retired RVers who do not have interesting and worthwhile things to do lack the challenging and meaningful qualities essential for mental growth and successful retirement. In one sense, this lack is a problem of attitude: the search for meaningful activity is more difficult for some people than for others. Some, like the Kents, find purposeful and interesting things to do in the variety of experiences travel offers. Others need something more.

As we see in the sections below, this search for meaning is one reason why some RVers work and others throw themselves into volunteer activities. It is not a problem for others, even though they no longer travel much: they say they have plenty to keep them busy.

Ruth is active in the local senior's center where she takes ceramics lessons. She spends several days a week working on her crafts and uses their kiln. She makes a variety of things: pots, cups, salt and pepper shakers, night-light holders, nativity figurines with Indians and horses in place of the Magi and their camels. She sells her work at craft shows, rallies, and to park residents and visitors. She also works a couple of months a year at a craft store in town. She paints things for them because people see the results and want to buy the end product rather than make them themselves. She is active in co-op life and plays cards and marbles or Mexican Train dominoes almost every evening.

Ruth is famous among Skips for her friendliness, for greeting newcomers when they enter the park and making them feel welcome. She is also well known for inviting new arrivals to the clubhouse in the evening to play games, and for her innocent smile as she mercilessly trounces her opponents. Everyone who has played games at that park remembers Ruth. (From our 1993 journal)

Some RVers have hobbies such as tying flies

When we asked RVers "What do you do all day?," we received a wide variety of answers. The Kents' letter is a compendium of activities: travel, sight-seeing, attending rallies, solving problems, learning new things, shopping, enjoying nature, spending holidays with other RVers, boondocking, visiting family and friends. Other responses, such as those that follow, emphasize hobbies and crafts, solving problems, work, and travel. Some of these responses are from campground hosts or flea marketers. Some are from boondockers, while others are from residents at resort or Escapees parks. All are full-time or serious RVers. A few people mentioned the excessive use of alcohol. We saw very little heavy drinking during our research. It was not a problem for most of the RVers we met. One survey on RVers and health suggests that the people we met are typical in their moderate use of alcohol.[7]

John and Betty's activities illustrate some of the ways RVers spend their time. John does needlepoint and has for 50 years. He taught some men in the British army who laughed at him at first and then became interested and stopped laughing. He is also learning Spanish from tapes. He and Betty both read a lot. They square-dance and ballroom-dance, and go to swap meets, garage sales, and flea markets to watch the people. They like the Phoenix area because of the cultural activities associated with the nearby university. They have a VCR and TV and rent movies, but watch little TV because "there's just garbage on TV." They miss CBC radio and TV.

Tom and Betty spend their time in other ways. They are campground hosts, so he does maintenance and repair in the campground. She has an electronic keyboard, a sewing machine, and a computer in the motor home.

There are common threads in these accounts of how RVers spend their time. They do some of the same things they would have been doing were they in a house, with new opportunities available in the places they visit. Often they do these things with friends — both old and new. The friendships RVers form and the activities they share underpin RV communities.

One reason the sense of community exists is that people spend a lot of time talking to each other. When members of Escapees or Loners on Wheels meet briefly in a rest area on a highway, they talk. At the Hot Spring, they gather at the spring and talk. In Escapees parks they gather to clean their adopted section of the local highway, or they plant shrubs, or clean the clubhouse, and they talk. In parks with clubhouses, they gather in the evening to play Mexican Train dominoes or cards and marbles, or bridge, poker, or bingo, and they talk. Since their homes are small, they make the outside — under the

"People ask me what I do all winter. Hell, I'm so busy doing nothing that I haven't got time to worry about it." In fact he is continually tinkering and "improving" his rig or his truck. He drinks, starting at dark. He buys whisky in half gallon jugs and he lives alone. (From our 1990 journal)

* * *

He helps other people with mechanical problems and is busy improving his own rig, redesigning his solar generating system, and trying to automate it. He says that his hobbies lend themselves to keeping him interested and busy. There are a lot of people here at the Slabs who don't have hobbies, he says, and they are in trouble. They are the ones who "drink themselves to death."

* * *

He doesn't stay around the campground. They like to go sight-seeing, walk up and down the streets of Tombstone, go shopping, go across to Mexico and haggle-shop, go to museums and see the sights. "There's a lot to do." When they have seen everything of interest they move on. "I don't think I could stay in one place more than a month." They do most of their sight-seeing in the morning. Afternoon is for relaxing and visiting with neighbors in the campground. He says, "I don't drive after noon. I'm retired and I don't have to. Twelve o'clock is beer time."

awning — part of the living area and, especially in boondocking regions, face their doors toward one another. The resulting "circles" encourage neighbors to see a lot of each other — and they talk. RVers talk readily and easily in parks, too. All they need is the suggestion of membership in a joint community. In May 1995, while we were on the road for a month as consultants to the Recreation Vehicle Industry Association, we pulled into a KOA in Alabama. A few hours later, new neighbors moved into the site just behind us. We each spotted the others' Escapees decal simultaneously. We had never met, but before we left the following morning we discovered we had friends in common. We visited each other's rigs and engaged in an impromptu book exchange. Two weeks later we had a note from them saying where they had been after we parted and hoping we would meet again.

Men spend a lot of time talking about their rigs, comparing notes on maintenance and performance. More than one person suggested to David, "If you want to get to know your neighbors, just raise your hood and look under it!" Both men and women discuss ways to modify a rig so it is more

People gather under their awnings to share coffee and to talk

liveable. Women exchange information on craft ideas and on how useful items can do more than one job. One woman, showing Dorothy through her rig, demonstrated how throw pillows for the sofa could serve during the day as storage for pyjamas or infrequently-used down vests. Another illustrated how paper towel tubes provide compact storage space for the inevitable collection of plastic grocery bags. Still another suggested we partially fill our tub with soapy water and toss in our dirty clothes. This would serve as a built-in automatic washer while we were on the road. Walking the dog or doing the laundry are all occasions for conversation.

Much of the work done in private in a fixed house is semi-public activity for RVers. In pleasant weather a woman may take her knitting outside, or a couple may sit under the awning to prepare vegetables for dinner. Neighbors will likely join them with their own tasks or cups of coffee. They will talk. RVers are especially willing to give tips on places to go to neophytes and to talk to them about problems they may encounter.

RV Retirement: Learning the Ropes

It was four o'clock Tuesday afternoon in early February, and the sun was already low in the sky. Outside, a prairie wind had kept the temperature well below freezing all day. Inside, in the clubhouse, 35 or 40 people sat in conversation, most drinking coffee or soft drinks, one or two with a beer. The emcee lifted her microphone as the conversation dropped. There were announcements: coffee and donuts would be available for volunteers who showed up for clubhouse cleaning on the following morning. The park had adopted a family for Easter. Someone had organized a tour of a nearby proposed nuclear waste disposal site that worried people. Pizza night was scheduled for Thursday.

This was a typical happy hour in an Escapees park. Before it was over, residents welcomed new arrivals with hugs and sang farewell to those leaving the next day. The emcee asked for other announcements, jokes, or RV tips. Joan, a slender, attractive woman with some grey brightening her hair, came up and took the microphone. She gave her name and her Skip membership number, and began:

> First, I'd like to thank everybody who came by and gave us hugs when we got in yesterday. I can't think of a time when I've needed them more. Then I'd like to thank all of you who spent this cold morning helping us get the truck unloaded, and the stuff in the shed set up. We're not there yet, but it's coming. I think everyone knows by now I had an accident coming home night before last. I need to talk about that for a minute. I'm OK, and the trailer and the truck both can be repaired, but I want to tell you what I can about what happened and what I learned from it. And I want to tell you what I think everybody here should learn from it. I really don't know whether a gust of wind caught me as I was coming across the pass, or if I had a blowout, or what started it. I do know that without warning the trailer started swaying, and that the truck and the trailer were thrown against one guard rail and then across the road to the other one. I wound up facing the wrong way with all four trailer tires blown. I was only five feet from a schoolbus full of kids. It just managed to stop before it hit me! A lot of you might not know this was the first time I had ever driven while we were towing the trailer, and I had no idea what to do when the trouble started. I'm not hurt. There isn't a bunch of dead children up on the pass. We still have a place to live. That's all due to luck, not to my ability. I don't ever want that to be true again. Before I go back on the road with that trailer — and I will — I mean to know everything there is to know about how to handle it. I want to be able to hitch it and unhitch it. I need to know how to react in an emergency. I'd like to ask someone here to teach me. It can't be Art. I love my husband, but both of us assume too much. I need a teacher who doesn't try to anticipate what I know. The other thing is, there are lots of women in this room who are in

the same boat as me. Get out of it. You may not intend to, but there may be a time when you have to drive that rig. When it comes, you'd better know how.

The people with whom we have been conducting research say that RVing, as a way of life, regularly and consistently demands organized, complex behavior. Joan, speaking to those attending happy hour on that February afternoon, had not been a full-timer for long. She had learned a painful lesson and she intended to profit from it. Being on the road with an RV can be dangerous if a person tries to do it without proper skills and knowledge. Goldy was another woman who started RVing with a lot to learn. She also had resolved to be self-sufficient. When we met her, she was well along toward meeting her goal.

> The site across from ours in the SKP co-op was often covered with tools as Goldy and her friend Sol tried to perfect the solar generating system on her fifth-wheel. Goldy travels alone, and Sol is visiting with his own rig parked nearby. Goldy says when she began RVing in 1990 she knew nothing. She had traveled with her second husband, but he told her to let him take care of things, so she did. After his death, she had a 19-foot motor home and an equally long 4x4 pickup she towed with the motor home. It was a terrible combination, and the first time she tried to drive it she swayed all over the road from Nevada to New Mexico. When she had to drop the truck's drive shaft for the first time, the process took her four hours. She says she wept, cursed, and kicked the tires. But she did it. When she went to ask a dealer about getting a solar charging system, he told her "a woman doesn't need solar panels." She took this as meaning a woman should stay barefoot, pregnant, in the kitchen, and dependent. And in RV parks with hookups. When she met Sol, she insisted he teach her about electrical systems. Now, Sol says, she can figure out things that stump him. She is living proof that motivated people can learn anything they need to.

Getting on the Road

RVers are subject to a disease they call "hitch-itch." The snowbirds who spend the winter in one park may be immune to it, but most of the traveling RVers we met said that after a week or two in one place they begin to feel its symptoms. Once it starts, the only recourse is to hitch up and head down the road. The relief is only temporary. The next time the victim is in one place for a while, he or she will suffer a relapse. At a June 1995 rally of the Ontario chapter of the Escapees club, a participant commented that "hard-core" full-timers (those who proudly announce, "Everything I own is in that rig!") have a terminal case of hitch-itch.

Hitching up, which refers to the process of getting ready for the road, is an integral part of being an RVer. No one who travels for long fails to develop a hitching routine and a set of guidelines. These guidelines are important, for almost every element of the process involves the safety of the traveler. Many people make a checklist to insure they overlook nothing. The list varies, depending on the type of rig. Travel trailers and fifth-wheels are both hitched to a tow vehicle, but the mechanics of attachment are different. Motor homes are not towed. However, they often tow a small vehicle — sometimes called *the toad*, as in "I go where I'm toad to." They must hitch it up too. Many RVers call attaching the towed vehicle "hitching up" and unattaching it "unhitching."

Some procedures are common to all rigs. Most how-to-do-it books for RVers devote considerable space to hitching procedures. For example, in their book *Full Time RVing*, the Moellers devote an entire chapter on "RV procedures." Often people divide preparations for travel into those done inside the rig and those done outside.

Inside preparations include closing windows and vents; turning things off (stoves, air-conditioners, water pumps) and stowing loose items; fastening things down; and locking up. This is the RVing equivalent of battening down the hatches. Outside preparations include raising the steps and the awning; removing wheel chocks, levellers, and stabilizing jacks; checking tires, brakes, wheels, and running lights; attaching the "toad"; and unhooking. Unhooking involves disconnecting the rig from water, sewer, electrical, and TV hookups provided by parks for RV sites. The processes of unhitching and hooking up reverse these procedures. In most respects the order in which things are done is less important than the requirement they all be done. An RVer has to forget only once to connect the trailer electric system to the tow vehicle before becoming a believer in the checklist.

How do they find a good, honest mechanic? "You take your chances and you get screwed more often than not. But what are you going to do? You can't shop around."

RVers are always conscious that, despite all the care they exercise, their homes are not fixed structures designed for years of carefree living. Their homes are vehicles with all the attendant problems that lead to recalls and mechanical breakdown. In a national survey conducted for the recreational vehicle industry, repair and maintenance problems associated with RV ownership were a major concern to fully a quarter of those surveyed.[8] Over one-third of the respondents to our questionnaire said they had experienced a major mechanical problem or complete breakdown during the previous year. An equal number listed mechanical problems as their primary source of worry — many more than expressed a concern about health or safety![9] The difficulty of finding a competent, honest, and inexpensive mechanic exacerbates the frustration of the mechanical breakdown of their homes. At least one of our correspondents eventually gave up RVing altogether because she felt she was being ripped off by dishonest repair shops. This problem is particularly serious for widows who left mechanical responsibility to their husbands.

What problems have you had in the last year?

None. If you take care of your truck and trailer. Fred does this so we haven't had any problems.

A sex-based division of labor often exists in the tasks of driving and maintaining the rig, and in hitching and unhitching, as well. All too often, the Moellers say, the man does the outside work with "the woman making her appearance after everything is done."[10] Men also seem to do most of the rig maintenance and most of the driving. D.J., with her well-used collection of tools and her determination to change her own oil, is an exception, although not among *single* RVing women. Experiences like Joan's and Goldy's lead some women to reconsider the wisdom of a division of labor in which they are ignorant of the technical aspects of RVing. They argue that women must learn the skills that will enable them to be independent and to travel safely. One independent-minded woman is Mabel, profiled in Chapter Five. In Chapter Four, she is the one who claims always to have had "terrible gypsy feet." She is in her 60s.

Mabel and Roy

Mabel grew up tent camping with her family, and she and Roy continued after they were married. She says their daughters still call one another and ask "If I were our mother, where would I be?" Mabel's marriage to Roy has been good, she says, because each of them has had room for their own life. She took their daughters camping for entire summers while Roy was working. He would drive or fly to join them when he had a week's vacation, and then return home. Roy's work was his hobby too, and so the arrangement suited them both.

After Roy had a series of small strokes and learned he had heart problems, he retired, and they became full-timers. His health prevents his either driving their truck or hitching and unhitching their fifth-wheel trailer. So Mabel does that. Their reversal of roles sometimes astonishes other RVers. When they arrive at a camping spot, she unhitches while he readies things inside their rig. Then she takes a nap while he goes for an exploratory walk and builds a campfire if they are in a wilderness area.

Mabel does seminars for Escapees rallies on why women should prepare to be self-sufficient, including being able to hitch, unhitch, and drive their rigs. She has made many converts. She reminds women that a man who has a heart attack in a deserted place might die if his wife were unable either to unhitch a trailer or to drive with it to get help. They would never forgive themselves, she tells them, if their husbands died because they had neglected to learn these skills. (From our 1993 journal)

She does not welcome help in hooking or unhooking her toad, backing up her motor home, hooking up to water or sewer, or in routine maintenance of her rig. She wants people to leave her alone. She thinks that the way to avoid interference and unwelcome volunteers is to "look like you know what you're doing." She says, "Anything you can do I can do. I can do most things a man can do if I have the strength." She airs her own tires, checks her own oil, and washes her own rig. (Interview with a single RVer, from our 1994 journal)

Not all women agree with D.J., Goldy, and Mabel. Some assert they have no intention of learning how to drive or hitch up their rigs. Back at the February afternoon happy hour:

> There was considerable discussion after Joan described her accident and her determination to learn how to manage her rig. Several people commented that a person who had been driving for 30 years could have had an experience like hers. Others noted huge trucks have these problems, too, and all the training in the world cannot prepare you for the gust of wind that catches you. Someone suggested the co-op request that the upcoming Escapade offer lessons for women how to drive rigs. Someone else recommended they get a professional truck-driving instructor to come to the co-op and give lessons to anyone interested. In the midst of apparent consensus, Vivian stood up and said, "I'm sorry, but I have never driven our rig and I don't plan to. If he dies, there will be someone who can help me, and I am too afraid." That ended the discussion.

Although the above exchange focussed on women's lack of training in driving their rigs, inadequate initial preparation is not a gender issue. It may be a problem for many RVers. Our informants frequently criticized RV dealers for not asking potential buyers about their driving skills and background, or whether they know how to ready an RV for the road. Some dealers, our friends tell us, do not even explain to neophytes how to dump their holding tanks or switch their refrigerator from electric power to propane. Our experience of having a dealer's mechanic spend hours with us reviewing safety features and hitching procedures is unusual. It is common for new RV owners who never drove anything larger than a stationwagon to leave the sales lots with a rig of more than 30 feet without instructions. Such inexperience can be dangerous. In October 1993, David had a conversation with a Colorado State Highway Patrol officer who had spent 17 years in a patrol car.

> I described our research project and asked if he thought the increasing number of elderly people on the road with large RVs posed a problem. He didn't bat an eye before replying it was a major problem. There is no training for such drivers. Furthermore, many of them never drove anything larger than a car before taking the wheel of a truck and trailer or a large motor home. This happens, he said, at an age when driving skills are likely deteriorating.
>
> He gave an example of a serious accident involving an elderly couple who had just bought a 35-foot motor home. They had not been on the road long when, needing to use the toilet, the driver engaged the cruise control and walked to the rear of the rig. We could predict the rest, the officer said. The driver survived, and when asked what happened could only respond, "I don't know. I had it on cruise control." (From our 1993 journal)

Variants of the police officer's story are widespread among RVers. It has all of the earmarks of an urban myth — one of those tales with wide circulation that is impossible to pin down or document. Its underlying assumption — that seniors are worse drivers than are younger people[11] — is debatable. Its currency, and the frequency of its retelling, are evidence of the image problem of older RVers.

Backing up her rig is the biggest problem she has driving it. The towed car makes backing up impossible. She has to get herself into situations where she doesn't have to back up. (Interview with a single RVer, from our 1990 journal)

The complexity of getting on and off the road is partly a function of the style of RVing the person chooses. The hitching and unhitching process is the same whether one is boondocking or going from park to park with hookups. However, there are more built-in complications for the boondocker. A boondocker's rig must have self-contained water and waste-disposal tanks. Boondockers must plan for a way to replenish their water and propane supply from time to time and find ways to dispose of sewage. They must also maintain a power supply either with a generator requiring maintenance and feeding or solar charging equipment they must check regularly. Simply finding a spot level enough for the appliances to work and the rig's inhabitants to be comfortable is often a challenge.

Setting up in a park has its own share of complications. Sites are often not level. In a constricted parking space, raising the listing side so things can work properly is not easy. The sites are usually small and require careful placement of the rig to get to the hookups. Many parks lack the RVer's dream feature: the pull-through site. Backing up a travel trailer is (along with dumping the holding tanks) a least favorite task. Some people eventually buy a motor home to avoid it. One frequently mentioned attraction of the fifth-wheel travel trailer is the location of the pivot point of the hitch. The hitch's location above the driving wheels of the tow vehicle simplifies both hitching up (the driver can see the hitch parts!) and backing up.

Getting into a space and setting up is, of course, only the beginning of occupying a new site. All those carefully battened hatches have to be undone, and a rig set for travel mode turned again into living space. Hitching and unhitching, hooking up and unhooking, are not daily events. Unless they are heading to a distant place, RVers do not normally travel every day. Even when they do, they are unlikely to unhitch for an overnight stay if they can avoid it. Nevertheless, these tasks are recurrent and provide opportunity for regular physical activity and planning. They are part of the organizational complexity of life on the road.

Being "On the Road"

Traveling involves more than hitching and unhitching. Driving a tow vehicle-RV combination of 60 feet or longer requires a level of skill and alertness seldom found among ordinary automobile drivers. RVs magnify the difficulty of doing everything. It takes longer to pass or be passed, and the time required for both acceleration and braking increases. Many RVs make only a perfunctory bow to the need for aerodynamic design, so drivers are nervously conscious of wind deflection. The heavy volume of transport truck traffic on North America's controlled-access highways worsens the situation. Being passed by a high-speed transport truck on such a highway may buffet the RV or set a trailer to swaying in ways disconcerting to the most experienced driver. As we saw in Chapter Five, the ordeal of being pulled toward a passing 18-wheeler may contribute to the decision not to RV. Other RVers avoid the major controlled-access routes in their travels. Instead they stay on the "blue highways" — federal, state, or provincial two-lane roads.[12] Some believe that older roads are more interesting as well as safer and more comfortable to travel. "It's possible to go from coast to coast on the interstate highways and see nothing but truck stops and tourist traps!" one disgruntled RVer told us.

Seasoned RVers emphasize that being on the road does not mean using the RV simply as a device to get from point A to point B. They reject the "If it's Tuesday it must be the Grand Canyon" syndrome. Such frenetic travel is acceptable, maybe, for people who must use their RVs for a time-limited vacation. It is not appropriate for serious RVers who are *living* in their rigs. For these folks, time, distance, and destination have a lower order of priority than they have for those who must watch the clock or the calendar. Traveling, instead of being an interlude between events, is in itself an important and enjoyable part of life. Serious RVers are, therefore, likely to go short distances. Most say they seldom travel more than 200 miles a day. Furthermore, they are unlikely to travel even that far day after day. Frequent stops punctuate short traveling days. RVers may pause for a meal, a walk, a nap, or to look at some roadside attraction. The ideal pattern of travel is to move about 200 miles and establish a base camp. From there they explore the surrounding area until they have seen and done everything of interest within a travel distance of an hour or two. Then it is time to move another 200 miles. Some airlines have tried to convince modern travelers that "getting there is half the fun." For the serious RVer who has been at it long enough to be out of vacation mode, this is not just an advertising hook. Traveling really is at least half the fun.

Being There

If getting there is one half of the fun, the other half comes from being there. While RVers may travel at a leisurely pace, they usually have a destination toward which they are moving, however slowly. They may head for a provincial, state or national park or forest, a boondocking spot in the desert or on the beach, or a private park.

Being there: Park living

Question: "What do you do all day?"
Answer: Are you kidding? There are committees, clean-up, and fun at the Ranch, and my new found hobby of woodworking.

* * *

Answer: I have my sewing machine, my crafts, my computer. What else do I need? All membership parks have a book exchange, and both of us like to read. What do you do all day if you're retired and in your house?

There are several kinds of private parks. RV clubs or organizations, such as Escapees or the Wally Byam Club, own or manage some. Many are privately owned RV parks operated as businesses for profit either independently or, like KOA, as part of a franchise operation. Some are membership parks such as Camp Coast-to-Coast or Resort Parks International.

Serious and full-time RVers have a love-hate relationship with membership parks. Many RVers prefer them; others despise them.[13] Having endured the sales pitch of two different organizations (one of which is now defunct), and having read many articles in and letters to RVing magazines either extolling or damning membership organizations, we have reached one conclusion. Anyone wanting to start a heated discussion among a group of serious and full-time RVers can drop the following question into a lull in the conversation: "What do you think of membership parks?" Most RVers are not neutral on the subject. One of our first memorable research experiences was accidentally starting an argument between two full-timers by asking this question. The man had paid $4000 US for a membership in the Coast-to-Coast organization and figured he got his money's worth the first year. The woman thought membership parks were a "ripoff" and could not understand why anybody would buy into one at any price. "Forget it!" she said. "I wouldn't touch them with a 10-foot pole!" We observed. We did not participate.

All private parks have a similar organization and set of protocols. Entering established parks is a formal procedure: the newcomer must stop and register upon entering. Orientation begins then. Most established parks provide a map, a set of rules, and a schedule of events for new registrants. Most also give residents regular chances to get together and newcomers opportunity to integrate into the community. Get-togethers in private or membership parks may take the form of a Saturday morning coffee and donut breakfast or a weekly potluck dinner. In Escapees parks, residents greet newcomers at happy or friendship hour, often a daily affair occurring in the late afternoon.

Parks have rules and formal structure. They have offices, registration desks, and fees. Even if there is no charge, as when a Skip chooses to use the boondock area found in every Escapees park, the traveler must register at the office on entry and show membership in the club. A newcomer often has little choice about where to park because park officials usually assign sites. So, the identity of one's neighbors is arbitrary: they are those who have been assigned to nearby sites.

RV parks are ordered systems. They are bounded, and their space is differentiated into roads, sites for occupancy, and administrative and common areas. Most parks have a full set of amenities: water, electric, and sewer hookups. Some have phone and cable television connections. The installation of these utilities partly determines the layout of the grounds. The utilities are all linked, and the placement of water and sewer lines must allow for efficient flow and drainage. As a result, formal RV parks bear more resemblance to suburban subdivisions than they do to boondocking or rally areas. They have interior streets, and the location of the hookups at each lot usually requires guests to park their RVs in rows situated so the appropriate connectors are accessible. Consequently each RV's door faces the back (street side) of its neighbor.

In parks catering primarily to overnighters there may be only a rudimentary social center, though most parks do have either a games room, a pool, a TV lounge, a playground, or some combination of these. In addition, most have a coin-operated laundry that may serve as a social center (or a place for anthropologists to lurk).

Parks with a returning seasonal clientele usually have a clearly defined social center (such as a clubhouse or assembly room) to ease newcomer orientation. There the new arrival finds a schedule of activities posted on the bulletin board. Horseshoe tournaments, line-dancing, aerobics classes, ice cream socials, and potluck meals are among the leisure activities usually available. Most clubhouses also have paperback exchange libraries, videotape libraries, games, puzzles, and crafts paraphernalia. Residents use the clubhouses for periodic events accounting for much of park social life. The clubhouse is the site for the happy (or friendship, or social) hour in Escapees parks; for potluck dinners, barbecues, holiday get-togethers, meals, and games; and for line-dancing, crafts classes, and meetings of special interest groups (such as computer clubs and book discussion circles).

Social life in established parks is often structured. Parks where most residents rent for a month or more usually employ an activity director. In non-commercial parks, volunteers often hold an equivalent position. The activity director is responsible for organizing activities with wide appeal. Dances, communal meals, parties, trips to local attractions, exercise or other classes are favorites. Bingo and poker nights are also popular, as is dining out in inexpensive local restaurants. Pizza parlors are favorite choices. If there is a pool and a qualified instructor, the activity director schedules regular "swimmercize" classes. An activity director may also arrange special events such as a diesel maintenance seminar, a crafts show and sale, or a seminar where anthropologists discuss their research project. In Escapees parks the activity director or park manager also invites newcomers to help with weekly clean-up chores. Travelers staying for a week or more often become volunteers in the host community's senior center, schools, or other local service facilities.

The clubhouse is the social center where people play games

Given the RVing ethos of freedom and independence, it is vital that all the social activities be consensual and voluntary. There is never overt pressure to join in. However, there is *subtle* pressure. For example, an Escapees park manager will urge visitors to sign up to emcee happy hour. The activity director will ask for help with the weekly cleaning of the clubhouse or invite residents to join a crew planting trees or cleaning trails in the park. In our experience participation levels are high — perhaps because no one is personally pressured or required to join in. The comments of women with whom Dorothy was discussing volunteer work by park residents illustrates the reluctance of RVers to be required to do anything:

> Jean said she was involved in community and school affairs when her children were small, and now she does what she wants to do. If she doesn't want to be involved in community work, she doesn't have to. The woman with seven kids agreed. "I feel like I've put in my time. I've done my bit. Now if I want to volunteer I can. But I don't like organized things." (From our 1994 journal)

The kinds of activities available are partially a function of where a park is in its life cycle (see Chapter Nine for a discussion of the life cycle of parks). Early on, parks tend to cater more to travelers and those who stay for short terms. They are, therefore, more likely to provide opportunities for interaction between newcomers and established residents. Potluck suppers, games, and daily introductory and farewell rituals are common here. Parks late in their life cycle have fewer travelers and more semi-sedentary residents. They are likely to have fewer activities designed to include newcomers and more projects scheduled regularly and on a long-term basis.

Park residents are often involved in the local community. Here Skips from Pair-a-dice park perform for the Pahrump senior center

We belong to a group that builds churches down there (AZ, CA, NV). They are building one this next winter ... the 53rd! Last winter we built a really nice one in Sun City, CA. The church members get the lot and the plan and permits etc. and of course the material and we provide the labor under the supervision of a contractor. Amazing what a group of retired volunteers can do. Snowbirds from all over the country belong and we make some lasting friends. We also belong to Habitat for Humanity. We meet such nice people wherever we stop. We like home made bread so I bake at least 3 loaves a week and many times have shared a loaf with someone at a stop somewhere. (Letter from Ruth and Milton Dalgleish, April 1991)

Residents in these parks are often deeply involved in local community life.

According to one full-timing couple, many people decide to buy a lot because the nearest town has an active senior center with good meals and programs. This couple now spend most of their time at their home base because of declining health. She cooks very little. Instead they usually eat lunch at the senior center in town. It has good, nourishing meals at a reasonable price as well as regular poker and bingo evenings.

Being there: Boondocking

As for overnight accommodation, we try to avoid the full service pay campgrounds, and seek out places where a new road has been put through, and the old road is flat, level and paved, and just over the hill. Also on the list are gravel pits, school yards in the summer, motel parking lots in the winter, churches, police parking lots (the one in Dearborn, Michigan is one block long by four blocks wide), shopping centers, rest areas, etc. (From a letter from a Canadian RVer)

Most RVers boondock at least part of the time.[14] The following comment describes the kinds of places in which they stay:

We usually stay in free places. In the winter, hotel\motel parking lots. In the summer, school yards. Anywhere else that is quiet and that we won't be in anyone's way. Shopping centers, church parking lots (except on Saturday night), and our all-time favorites are old roads that have been straightened. They are often level, drive in and drive out, paved and quiet. Also gravel pits, boat launches, etc. (From a letter from an RVer)

RVers who do this type of boondocking — called "destination boondocking" — want an inexpensive or free place to park while on the way to a destination. If they do not boondock, they might stay in a place catering to overnighters or a membership park associated with an organization of which they are members. Ideally they do not need to unhitch. They spend the night, use whatever facilities are available if they are in a park (showers, laundry, etc.), and resume travel the following day. Other RVers spend long periods dry camping or boondocking in the desert. Long-term boondocking is a particularly demanding style of RVing requiring complex organizational skills, because it means one is "off the grid." By definition, boondockers live without hookups or the clubhouse-type amenities found in parks. They must furnish their own power, conserve and replenish their water supply, find ways to dispose of their waste, provide their own entertainment and arrange their own security. For RVers who consider themselves to be hard-core boondockers, one's style of RVing becomes a statement about character. Sol (whom, ironically, we met while he was visiting an established Escapees co-op) prefers boondocking because he doesn't like rules. To him, "RVing is not hopping from one plug to another." He says that if you go from park to park as people with memberships do, every day and every place is the same. If you are boondocking, you never know whom you will meet or what will happen. You even have to think about whether you will have enough water available to take a shower in the morning. He has never belonged to a membership organization and has little use for people who do, because he feels they are not adventurous. According to Sol, "If I hear somebody say 'I like to boondock' or 'I'm a member of Coast-to-Coast,' then I know something about them as people."

Entering a boondocking area is much less formal than entering any kind of organized park. Often there

Judi and Norm do not stay in private RV parks because the lots are so small they are "like cemetery plots." People who spend six months at a time in RV Resorts "are just waiting to die." (From our 1990 journal)

* * *

They do not stay in Mesa because the retirement places and parks there are full of "the blue rinse bunch," says Betty. A problem with RV parks is that they are full of "old people." Although they are in their 70s they feel that they are younger than most of the people in private, organized parks. (From our 1990 journal)

* * *

What kind of places do you avoid? "RV Parks!" he responded. "When I get so old that I can't boondock, then I'll go into one. They have schedules up on the wall to tell you what you can do and when you can do it. Not me!" His friend, who was listening, chimed in. "Me neither." (From our 1990 journal)

Rig set up for boondocking with solar panels and a TV dish

is no formality at all, as at Slab City. In a government-sponsored area, such as a Long Term Visitor Area (LTVA) in the southwestern desert, the newcomer passes the host's well-signed rig located near the entrance. LTVA hosts are under the authority of the Bureau of Land Management and receive free parking and a small stipend for the work they do. They are responsible for maintaining order and have the authority to evict troublemakers. One of the host's jobs is to check newcomers to be sure they have the sticker showing they have paid either the two-week or seasonal parking fee and to collect the appropriate fee if necessary. After they complete the entrance formalities, LTVA veterans usually ask if friends from earlier years are already there and get directions to the area where they are parked. Even this structure is lacking at the Slabs. Newcomers either drive around until they find a suitable spot or ask residents for advice.

The information center is informal in boondocking areas, but it is sure to be there. At the Hot Spring LTVA, for instance, a bulletin board near the entrance has posted on it the formal rules of the area, news of local events, messages for expected arrivees, and emergency telephone numbers. Under it a cardboard box serves as a paperback book and magazine exchange with posted instructions to "Take one, put one back."

The regulars who return to the Hot Spring each year have created neighborhood circles where they rejoin old friends each fall. These circles may be 100 feet in diameter. Within them, there is often a central common ground around which RVers face their rigs' front doors and awn-

The bulletin board near the entrance to the hot spring LTVA posts the rules, local news, and messages. A cardboard box serves as a book exchange

ings. Established residents tell newcomers where they may park. Should new arrivals attempt to park in a place already "belonging" to a former occupant whose return is expected, someone will tell them the site is already taken and point them to an acceptable, unclaimed space. If they attempt to park in the central social space, residents will direct them elsewhere.

Social centers at LTVAs are informal. In some, people gather in the evening at a large fire pit located near the host's rig to talk, sing, or share food and drink. Other centers are located in impromptu

Social centers at LTVAs are informal

neighborhoods wherever people are parked. There, in the shade of their awnings, people get together to drink coffee, to share tasks such as shelling peanuts, or just to talk. Most neighborhood circles have their own fire pit where evening gatherings, shared meals, and sing-alongs take place. Several horseshoe pitches are scattered among the circles of RVs. The clink of horseshoes hitting the posts forms a nearly continuous background noise during the cool times of the day as neighborhood teams ready for tournament competition.

The southern California LTVA's name, The Hot Spring, derives from its most widely used social center. A hot water tap, a hot pool, a warm pool, and a shower are located at the thermal spring. All these improvements were built cooperatively by local businesses and the winter residents. Local businesses contributed materials, while the residents worked to reroute the spring and build and plumb the pools and shower. Each Monday resident volunteers drain and clean the pools and surrounding area, and they police the area daily for garbage. The spring is a treasured spot to relax. Groups of RVers gather there most of the day and well into the evening, soaking at the spa, chatting, filling water containers, or making plans for other activities.

Boondockers spend much of their time figuring out innovative ways to make life better for themselves and their neighbors. Some, like Sol, focus on technical improvements. Sol is an avid fisherman and spends a lot of his time planning and taking fishing trips. He is also accomplished in the installation and repair of solar-powered charging systems. He even rigged a solar-powered system for the electric motor of his fishing boat. Wherever he is, in a co-op or a boondocking area, he helps his neighbors find ways to improve the efficiency of their charging systems. Other boondockers

The Hot Spring.

develop their social and information networks and use them to help their neighbors as well as themselves. Agatha Komfort spends much of her time finding ways to live economically and, at the same time, affirming and reinforcing her sources of information.

> Agatha walks for an hour each morning with a group of other women at the Hot Spring. As she walks, she scans the roadside for discarded aluminum cans and collects any she sees. She saves them and converts them to small amounts of cash at a local recycling center. At the same time, she and the other women gossip and exchange news about each others' plans and activities. Agatha and Al are at the center of a long-established Hot Spring neighborhood, and her centrality requires her to know where her neighbors are and what they are doing. They are important to the community because they are a fund of information and a source of assistance to many of their neighbors. Over the years they have made friends with many local commercial farmers. Their network of local acquaintances provides them with information about when and where there are fields to glean and local events where they and their Hot Springs neighbors are welcome. Agatha was proud of the fact she had taken a prize in the local "Carrot Festival"[15] with one of her recipes. The Komforts, like others at the Hot Springs,

A lot of activity occurs here in the Imperial Valley: gleaning vegetables after the fields have been harvested, making jam, and canning fruit and vegetables. Alice isn't sure exactly what they do all day, but they always seem to be busy. She can't walk far, but is determined to walk over to the hot spring every day. (From our 1990 journal)

* * *

They pick the harvested farms for vegetables and distribute the surplus — cantaloupes, broccoli, carrots, peanuts. Agatha walks. Al fixes things for other people. Agatha bakes their bread, and from the free food they glean, she cans vegetables and makes jam. Al plays horseshoes. They visit people and circulate constantly. Agatha has taken free courses on computers and household science at local high schools in Holtville and El Centro. (From our 1990 journal)

The main event at Quartzsite, Arizona, where flea marketers gather

work hard to build a community of friends where they have a meaningful life.

The Komforts are a model for serious RVers who are searching for meaningful, challenging things to do. Because their income is limited, they fill their days finding ways to live well on small amounts of money, and they share their discoveries with their friends. Other RVers work at least part time in order to give their lives meaning and to have something interesting to do.

Working on the Road

Their rock and gem selling is an extension of their hobby of 34 years. They used to do it on weekends, but now they do it all year long. They are busier now than they were when they both had jobs eight hours a day. Neither of them can imagine just sitting around with nothing to do. (From our 1990 journal)

* * *

Before they began selling at flea markets they spent a lot of time hiking and backpacking. Now he can't think what they did with their time. He feels he needs to work so he can "know who I am." She feels it is necessary so they can "accomplish something." (From our 1990 journal)

Although they are in the minority, a substantial number of RVers work. Thirteen per cent of the respondents to our questionnaire described themselves as semi-retired. They work part time as campground hosts, flea marketers, or at some other job at least part of the year. Some senior RVers work in order to supplement inadequate pensions. Others work because it gives them something to do. Blanche is a senior who works because she enjoys being busy and in order to replace her capital expenditures.

Blanche

We met Blanche in early March 1998 when she was parked in the site next to ours in the Escapees home park in Livingston, Texas. She was 77-years-old, outspoken, and full of energy. She had been widowed for 36 years. She was small and slender, and had a slight tremor in her hands and upper body. She also had advanced osteoporosis and was in almost constant pain with arthritis in her spine.

Although she had been off the road for five years except for some winter travel when we met her, she had full-timed for five years before that and traveled and worked part-time in a motor home for more than 20 years. In the early 1990s her children convinced her she was too old to be RVing alone. So she sold her motor home and bought an old house in Indianapolis near her children. The house was in terrible shape, and she spent four years renovating it. She tore out the carpet and linoleum, exposing floors which she discovered were oak. She refinished the floors, ripped out panelling and three ceilings, put in subfloors where necessary and a 3/4 inch tongue and groove floor in the kitchen. She put in drywall, plumbing, and electrical wiring, and mounted her kitchen cabinets. She also ripped off the old asbestos siding and put on new siding. She did all the labor except for the new roof which she hired done. Her son-in-law's mother looked at the wreck of an old house and told her she'd bitten off more than she could chew, and she responded, "Maybe so, but I'm going to chew on it." After she completed the renovations, her children moved away.

When we met her she was waiting until it was warm enough to return to Indiana, sell her house, and go back on the road. She planned to do the painting and cosmetic repairs to get her house in Indiana ready to sell and to be her own realtor. Then she intended to resume full-time travel and work. "I can't wait!" she said.

Blanche is a craftswoman of considerable skill and talent. She does woodworking, carpentry, and plumbing, and has designed, made, and sold stuffed bunnies and turtles, purses, wall hangings, and appliqued sweat shirts. When we met her she was making crafts which she planned to sell at a craft fair in Indiana in the summer. She designed "frog things" that weigh a couple of pounds. When heated in a microwave for four minutes they retain their heat for three to four hours. She sells them as bed-warmers. She also makes women's vests with appliques and quilted linings in a variety of styles and sizes as well as exquisite baby quilts. She intended to make 300 frogs and hoped to make $6000 selling them.

She is fast. She can burn the midnight oil and make a complete vest after supper. "I'm a workaholic right now because I've got a goal," she said. She spent $5000 on her motor home and wanted to make enough money to put that amount "back in my nest egg." She expected to have sold her entire stock at the craft sale in less than half a day, as she had done before. Her things sell quickly because she looks for good quality materials, she lines her vests with quilting so they keep their shape, and she's always looking for little extra things (unusual buttons to bring out the theme of a vest) to make her work special.

When we asked what was most difficult about the work she does she said she could think of nothing. "I don't do anything I don't want to do. But after the first 200 frogs it gets tiresome. Then I make some vests or some quilts." When she gets tired of sewing, she takes off for a day or two and drives to all the nearby small towns where she looks through the fabric stores and goes window shopping in the malls (from our 1998 interview notes).

Other RVers, like the flea marketers with whom we began this section, say they work so they can "know who I am," in order to "accomplish something," or because they derive personal satisfaction from being needed. Some of this activity is unpaid, volunteer work. In March 1998 we met Ralph and Marilyn Garneau, retired seniors who were working as volunteers in the CARE[16] facility at the Escapees home park in Livingston Texas.

Ralph and Marilyn

Ralph and Marilyn met in the Royal Canadian Air Force in 1957 and worked for the telephone company for 28 years. They had been retired for four years when Marilyn started volunteering at CARE in October 1996; Ralph began in mid-November that year. Marilyn says that she answered a general request for volunteers. She wanted to get into the volunteer system here and that seemed like a good opportunity. Ralph became involved when the CARE director was looking for somebody to clean and maintain the fish tank. Marilyn told her that Ralph could do that, and that was his entrance into CARE.

Ralph and Marilyn were each committed to volunteer for 20 hours a week at the CARE center. Volunteers take residents into town, pick up meals from the county (CARE is a satellite of the Aging Center in Livingston), do adult baby-sitting so caregivers can have time off, and take participants shopping, to the doctor, to the airport, and to play bingo at the Activity Center. Volunteers enable people to do things they otherwise would be unable to do. Park residents also occasionally drop in and ask if there is anything they can do for a day or for a week. Volunteers receive a free lunch worth $2.00.

Ralph worked at the reception desk greeting visitors and taking calls; gave visitors a tour of the CARE facilities; and did "general functions" such as working on the computer, mail sorting and delivery, and cooking and serving meals on Saturday. Marilyn took lunches to participants who could not leave their rigs. She also worked in the activity room talking to people and helping the activity director.

Ralph said that there is a "learning curve" to volunteering. He had to learn how to present himself. He is a big person (well over six feet tall), and he didn't know that his size intimidated people. "I'm a big person standing in front talking to them in a forceful way." Now he has "mellowed out." Ralph had learned in the military not to volunteer for anything. His experience with CARE had led him to regret that because he thought he would have had a more fulfilling life and would have been a better person if he had begun volunteer work earlier. He had made a good living, but "now I get something out of work without regard for money. I never got fulfilment from my work like I do from this," he said. They work because they receive personal satisfaction from what they do. As Ralph said, "It's always good to be needed. I truly truly enjoy what I do. I'm a better person today because of my volunteering for CARE. It's made a better person of me. We love this place." (from our 1998 interview notes)

Full-time RVers who are too young for pensions are faced with different imperatives than are seniors. Stress forces some younger people to leave their corporate jobs for a simpler life. Rick Chaffee, whose letter we site in Chapter Five, is an example. Others, like Pat and Fred Kennedy, also profiled in Chapter Five, left their jobs because of burn-out and became full-time RVers. These people, too young to have pensions, are pioneers in the new economy of the post-market era when some economists predict that 30 to 80 per cent of current jobs will disappear, resulting in a social economy not based on traditional work.[17] Younger members of the RV community are exploring careers that are compatible with RVing and bitterly resent being forced off the road to work in nine-to-five jobs in order to survive. For them work is not only drudgery that is not fulfilling. it is described as an epithet: it is "the 'w' word."

The variety of work RVers do on the road is stunning. They sell things — milk substitutes, Indian jewellery and artifacts, rocks and gems, balloon sculptures, hotdogs and soft drinks, car and RV parts, solar panels, doll clothes, crocheted covers for fly swatters, and antiques — just to name a few. They have machine shops in their rigs — or towed behind them — where they repair RVs, diesel engines, tow vehicles, TV sets and VCRs, microwave ovens, water heaters, and anything else that might go wrong in or with an RV. Some work seasonally, as hosts in public campgrounds or at private RV parks. Others cash in on skills learned earlier in life. One we met was a musician who played for dances held by what he called "animal clubs" (Moose, Elks, Lions). We met several beauticians. Some teach crafts, aerobics, line- square- or ballroom dancing. Others teach computer or fine-sewing classes in private parks in exchange for free sites with hookups. They are free-lance writers, desk-top publishers, full-timers who house-sit for part-timers who are nervous about leaving their homes unattended, and handy-folk who clean carpets, wash windows, and polish RVs. One retired accountant said she hung up her shingle in March and had enough business in one month doing income tax returns to supplement her pension for the remainder of the year. For a while one enterprising Skip ran a column called "The Working Nomad" in the *Escapees Newsletter* where he suggested money-making schemes. Among his proposals: design and paint storefronts for holidays; photograph shops in small towns and sell color enlargements of those photos to the owners, or trade the pictures for goods or services; make pennant streamers for car sales lots; be an extra in movies or TV commercials where seniors are in short supply; work for American Guide Services selling advertisements on RV park maps to local businesses; tune pianos.

Many RVers work part of the year. In November 1993 Dorothy attended a lunch at Rainbow's End park with 25 other women. Following the meal, an experienced working RVer held a seminar on the topic "Making Money on the Road." About half the women attending were or had been working RVers. Campground host was the most popular occupation. The seminar covered three topics: ways to make money (many of the alternatives above were among those discussed), the reasons employers prefer older people to students for seasonal jobs, and the pros and cons of being a working RVer.

According to the woman giving the seminar, and other experienced working RVers attending it, employers prefer seniors because they can start earlier and stay longer in the season. Their flexibility is important to parks and conces- sionaires. Seniors are also more reliable. They show up when they say they will, do what they say they will do, and have a good work ethic. Park employers also prefer seniors because they can live on low-paying jobs more easily than can students who need travel money to and from the parks and savings to go to university. Most seniors already have pensions and need extra money to pay unexpected expenses (e.g., repairs to a rig)

The RVer from whom we bought our first solar panel in 1990 said he grossed over $190,000 each year just selling solar equipment to other RVers. He took Visa. His business was located in his motor home.

* * *

One enterprising soul had the following sign over his business: "Antiques made here daily."

or for something extra. They ordinarily do not have to work to survive. Furthermore, employers do not have to provide housing for seniors who live in their RVs.

Working has several advantages for seniors. Hosting is desirable work because it usually lasts only two or three months a year ("you can see an end to it"), it is interesting and fun, and "it fills up the time." Other jobs, such as working for private concessions, are also enjoyable. People who plan to work for only one year often return for many years.

The woman giving the seminar and her audience agreed work of all kinds is healthy. For example, park hosts walk a lot. If the park is hilly or mountainous, the exercise builds up their muscles and helps them to lose weight. Work also improves mental health because it can be a learning experience that keeps the mind active. Jobs often require that people learn new skills and put seniors in contact with student employees who are "fascinating and delightful."

Work for seniors is brief in duration, limited in hours, and temporary. Even if an RVer does not enjoy a particular job, the commitment is not long-term. As one woman sharing a table with Dorothy observed, "These aren't careers. They're something to do for a short time." Work experience is especially important for senior women because, as the presenter said, "statistics show that men die first."

If a woman must work after her husband's death, her experience may enable her to get a full-time job. According to a recent poll, half of the people over age 65 surveyed said they want to work but do not because of the difficulty in finding a job.[18] The work most senior RVers do is low-paying or in exchange for free sites or hookups. It is intended to supplement pension income, and is either self-employment or seasonal work. Perhaps more important than the money it brings in, work gives a sense of identity and accomplishment. It can be fun, and it provides elements essential in successful retirement — something interesting and worthwhile to do and stimulating contact with other people.

Conclusion

One of the most common questions asked about the lives of full-time and serious RVers is "What do they do all day?" It is a question that can — and should — be asked about all retirees. Many North Americans find their identity in their work. After they retire they may have difficulty creating a life of meaningful, purposeful activity.

RVers with this problem have several options. One is to stop RVing and do something else that gives their life purpose. Anne, with whom Dorothy shared dish-washing chores, wanted to take this course. Another option is to travel. This is an especially successful strategy if the travel itself has a goal and a purpose. Some, for instance, travel in order to do historical or genealogical research. Others travel to visit museums, historical spots, or national parks and monuments. Some mix travel with volunteer work, as the Dalgleishes do. Others combine travel with compensated work as park hosts, house sitters, or flea marketers. RVers who spend months in a favorite spot or home base do volunteer work in their park or in nearby communities.

It is critical that retired people — including RVers — do something that challenges them and opens them to new experiences. Some RVers find excitement in the constant change provided by travel. Others combine travel with additional activities they find meaningful. Many RVers are familiar with Kay Peterson's book, *Home is Where I Park It*. They would probably agree another phrase could be added to Peterson's title: "I park it wherever I want to be." The freedom RVers have to move — to be where they want, when they want, for as long as they want — is the basis of their ability to find interesting things to do and to control their own lives.

Notes

1. *Escapees Newsletter* 1986a:37.

2. Jacobs 1974:34.

3. The Laniers, for example, began full-timing on the advice of their physician (Lanier and Lanier 1988:39).

4. The report of the physicians' panel is found in Highways (1993:13).

5. Of the people who answered our question, "What do you think makes a person capable of going full-time?," 35 per cent said either a love of travel or an adventurous personality. In answer to the question "What would you miss most about RVing?," 30 per cent said travel while another 20 per cent said travel and meeting new friends.

6. Savishinsky 1995.

7. Amick 1996:59.

8. Curtin 1994:40.

9. We think the difference in percentages between our respondents and those participating in Curtin's survey is explained by the difference in the types of RVer we

were dealing with. Curtin's survey included many respondents who use their vehicles only for limited vacation travel. Ours included mostly serious RVers who are living and traveling in their RVs. For them, mechanical problems are a more serious matter. When their homes break down they must either live in a garage or mechanic's shop or find somewhere else to live until the problem is fixed.

10. Moeller and Moeller 1986:243.

11. A report in *Highways* magazine suggests that a new study has found elderly motorists to be safer than younger ones. The author says, "Researchers compared the driving performance of 20 drivers who were at least 65 years old to groups of drivers in the 18-19 and 25-35 age brackets.... Elderly drivers made fewer errors, obeyed the speed limit and steered more accurately" (Sullaway 1992:16).

12. RVers use the term "blue highways" to describe secondary roads. It is the title of a book by William Least Heat Moon (1982).

13. Of RVers completing our questionnaire, 66 per cent said they belong to a membership park system, 57.5 per cent said they stay in a membership park half the time or more, 41 per cent said they prefer to stay in membership parks, and 40 per cent said they parked in membership or resort parks most of the time during the preceding year.

14. Of those who completed our questionnaire, 16 percent said they usually stay in free overnight spots when traveling from place to place. Almost 53 per cent said they always or often spend the night self-contained (without hook-ups). Slightly over 14 per cent said they prefer to stay in boondocking areas when they are parking for a week or more. Seventeen per cent said they spent most of the last year in boondocking areas.

15. Holtville, California, the town nearest the Hot Spring LTVA, bills itself as the "Carrot Capitol" of the USA. Situated in the Imperial Valley, the town is surrounded by commercial farms providing North America's winter vegetables — especially carrots. Holtville, appropriately, has a Carrot Festival for its annual fair. Agatha's recipe took a prize in the carrot cookery competition and was written up in the local paper.

16. CARE (Continuing Assistance to Retired Escapees) enables Escapees who are prevented by age or infirmity from active travel to continue to live in their RVs and participate in RVing life while receiving the assistance they need. The CARE center includes serviced parking sites that are for lease, in-rig assistance, and a day-care activity center. All are adjacent to the regular RV park in Livingston Texas. The charges for residence at the CARE center are strictly cost-recovery. The availability of volunteers is critical in allowing the Escapees club to keep the cost low.

17. Jeremy Rifkin explores the implications of this phenomenon for the twenty-first century in his book, *The End of Work*.

18. Potter 1993:15.

Chapter Seven

"Home is Where I Park It"

Joe Peterson says that when he passes a place where he has spent the night, he points to it and says "I used to live there." (From our 1994 journal)

"Home is Where You Park It," the title of Kay Peterson's book, is a rallying cry for anyone who has heard the call of the open road. Full-time RVers proclaim her message on the bumper stickers of their rigs. In her book, Peterson encourages people who dream of a nomadic life to "do it *now*." She devotes a chapter to the process of moving out of a traditional home and into the "box on wheels" which will be the nomad's new home. According to Cowgill, the trailerite's rig is more than a home. Whether it is bought or home-made, he says, "the trailerite uniformly attaches his ego to the trailer and takes the 'love me, love my trailer' attitude." But exactly what is a *home*?[1]

What is a Home?

> The house is for sale — never our home, for that is like HAPPINESS and JOY which must be taken with you.[2]
>
> * * *
>
> "We can trust the people in our area because they're like we are.... They try to make their area look homey. They want it to look like home and smell like home." (Mattie, a full-timer at the Slabs)

A home is, as Rawles says, "more than merely a place to 'hang your hat.'"[3] A home is an idea, one that is located in space but not necessarily in a fixed space. It may be a Bedouin's tent or an RVer's rig as well as a villager's house. As Mary Douglas says, "For a home neither the space nor its appurtenances have to be fixed, but there has to be something regular about the appearance and reappearance of its furnishings." The idea of home includes both memory of the past and prediction of the future. For example, people wintering at The Ranch (an Escapees co-op on the high plains of New Mexico) remember previous freezing weather and ice storms and expect more of them in the future. They respond by installing insulation and wrapping their water pipes.

Home is both a space to be occupied and a possession. As such it is a symbol of self and a way of identifying social status, lifestyle, and group membership. Mattie was making this point when she said she identified with others in her area in the Slabs because they — like her — try to make their area "look like home and smell like home." Kay Peterson says "RVers are the ultimate homemakers because they make every place they go home."[4] How do they do it?

How to make a place home

A home is a protective environment, a place where people can withdraw when the outside world becomes too stressful. Many who live in houses see their homes as *inside,* as a place where they are *enclosed*: a separate space from the world *outside*.[5]

Moving from even a small house or apartment into an RV requires a considerable adjustment. Because interior space in a rig is so limited, RVers spend much time living outdoors. Much socializing occurs outside: at the picnic table, or sitting in lawn chairs under the awning, or on the astro turf in front of the rig. For the duration that a rig is parked in a place, these are part of an RVer's home.

The use of outside space as part of the home is not merely instrumental. One way of increasing the usable space in an RV is to include part of the outside — particularly the part under the awning — as living space. But more is going on than just the creation of additional elbow room. The front porch was once part of the North American home. It was a space that invited casual visiting and social contact with passers-by. Visits on the front porch swing encouraged neighborliness and contributed to community. Today the front porch, and the neighborhood-based community it engendered, have almost disappeared from urban and suburban North America, as people searching for privacy withdraw to their TV sets and fenced back yards. These retreats to privacy deprive us of an opportunity to get to know each other well in casual circumstances.[6]

The front porch as a locus for informal social interaction may have disappeared from most North American towns, but its equivalent is alive and well under the awnings in RV parks. The space under the awning, often furnished with astro turf lawn and folding chairs, is an ambiguous area. It is not completely public, as is a park social center, which may be a recreation hall or a fire pit in the middle of a boondocking circle. Neither is it entirely private. It is both. RVers who wish to invite casual visits and conversation sit under their awning and greet passers-by. Their presence signals their willingness to engage in informal social contact and is an invitation to neighbors to bring their coffee — and their own lawn chairs — and visit. The space under the awning and the invitation conveyed when RVers sit there provide anthropologists, too, with opportunity to meet and talk with people. The success of our strategy of walking our Great Pyrenees (we called it "trolling the dog") to meet RVers depended on it. Folks sitting under their awning would call out comments ("Where's his hitch?" "Wouldn't it be cheaper just to buy gas for the truck?") that invited us to stop and talk.

This invitation to casual conversation is non-threatening for both host and visitor. Inviting someone *inside* one's home implies more commitment of time and trust than does chatting with the passer-by and inviting him or her to sit a while. It is easy for both visitor and host to terminate a conversation under the awning without giving offense. Further, the awning area provides people with a venue in which they can explore the possibility of closer friendship without commitment on either side. Park owners understand the importance of this space. Even the most crowded parks usually provide lots big enough to allow RVers to put up their awnings. The absence of this space is conspicuous and conveys a clear message. Annoyed Skips told us about one park where rigs in the free boondocking area were so crowded there was no room for anyone to put out an awning. This practice underlined the park's reputation for unfriendliness. Visitors interpreted it as an unequivocal notice that they were unwelcome.

Areas in an RV community range from public to private. The social center is the most public; a rig's toilet and bedroom are the most private. If the bed is raised into the ceiling on tracks, the bedroom may be invisible to all outsiders, including friends invited into the rig. To the visitor this space does not exist — it provides the rig's owner with the ultimate in privacy.

Like the area under the awning, an RV's living room is both public and private space. Although it is a semi-public area where RVers entertain good friends, it is also private, interior space where RVers may retreat. An RVer wanting to be left alone has only to go inside the rig and shut the door. Some RVers emphasize their desire

Eddie: "Regardless of the weather, when my blinds are open, I'm open for business." (From a 1994 interview)

* * *

George has a way of showing when he is willing to receive company. If the door to his rig is shut and the outside light is on, he is not open to company. If the door is open and the outside light is off, he is open. However, if he is boondocking he doesn't waste power by keeping the outside light on, so the clue is whether the door is open. (From our 1994 journal) for privacy with a bumper sticker warning "If the rig is a-rockin' don't come a-knockin'!" Usually a shut door signals that the residents do not want company. Most RVers understand and respect this signal and are reluctant to knock on a closed door.

Home is a focus of identity

"It's not giving up the things that's hard. It's giving up what has been." (Comment by a full-time RVer.)

As Douglas notes, an essential aspect of home is storage. A home contains needed things and organizes them so they can be found when they are called for.[7] Because it is where people keep precious possessions, home connects them with the past. It is a storehouse of memories: a place where children were born and anniversaries celebrated; the setting of Christmas mornings remembered. "Both the residence itself and the possessions it contains may serve as a museum of life history"; they are "the physical manifestations of a path traversed." As Jean-Paul Sartre said, "The totality of my possessions reflects the totality of my being. I am what I have." Home is a focus of identity.[8]

Elderly people who adopt a new way of life need a home that reflects their idea of who they are. For most elderly full-timers, the decision to make their home in a rig rather than in a house is a dramatic change. Their different style of home sets them apart from other retirees and gives them an opportunity for a new concept of self. RVers such as Mort and Zelda Risch, whose bumper sticker reads "Home is where we park it," explain what makes their rig their home:

> The key word is "home." We are not campers — we have taken what we wanted of our home and put wheels on it. Some scoff at having an RV with washer and dryer, microwave, color TV, tub, freezer, generator, etc. Not us. We enjoy moving our home from one umbilical cord to another. Yes, we do boondock on occasion and enjoy it for short periods, but we like hookups too. What do YOU want as a full-timer? One thing for sure: a happy spouse. So if it takes adding a corn popper, smoker, dehydrator, typewriter, portable organ, or anything else, then do it![9]

As early as 1890, William James observed that our possessions become part of us. Like our home, the possessions in it are linked to social identity and are an important component in our sense of self. Because possessions are so critical to our sense of identity, their unintentional loss lessens our sense of self. However, we gladly rid ourselves of things when they become inconsistent with our self image.[10] Mort and Zelda's advice to would-be full-timers to include the things that each partner requires to be happy (from a corn popper to a portable organ), recognizes the relationship between people and their things. Boschetti eloquently expresses the link between ourselves and our possessions:

> Our past belongs to us. And personal possessions are part of that past. The silver, crystal, fine china, linens ... scrapbooks, photo albums, family portraits, and other random memorabilia of a person's life on earth, which get passed on, are the tangible parts of a person's life.[11]

Deciding which treasures to keep and which to get rid of is a traumatic part of moving into the box on wheels that will be the full-timer's new home. In making the transition, the new RVers must ask "Which reminders of the past are essential to my identity?" Kay Peterson says, "The collector in you will begin to die, but for many of us it is a slow and painful death."[12] The difficulties of deciding to sell the house and dispose of the things in it, and then *doing* it, are favorite topics of discussion by full-time RVers. The decision separates full-timers from other RVers. What leads them to make it?

Some do it because they feel impending death. As one couple replied when we asked why they became full-timers: "We woke up one morning and said 'What are we doing here? Our lives are almost over and if we are going to do anything we'd better do it now!'" Another answered in the following way: "I had two near-death experiences. I saw Christ. I saw the light and everything." Her doctor revived her twice, "so my husband and I decided, 'Why don't we give all our material things to the kids and go out and have a good time?'"

For others, it is a choice between the tangible reminders of their past and the opportunity for a full later life. It is a chance, as one RVers said, "to follow our dreams."[13] Ruth Dalgleish answered our question, "What one thing do you miss the most as a result of full-timing?" as follows:

> I daydream sometimes of again using my Great Grandmother's tables and dishes, but they are safe in storage and will wait for me or my daughters or granddaughters! There is a lot of country out there, and I won't live long enough to see it all.

Similarly, a couple from rural Colorado described the process of selling their house and disposing of their possessions so they could go full-time:

> It took them five years after they sold most of their land in 1972 because they kept backing out of selling their house and the three acres they had kept. They would return in the summer and spend their time pulling weeds and fixing the house, until finally they had enough. Diane said that they only used the house for storage. "It was expensive storage," she said. Finally she distributed keepsakes (a round oak clawfoot table and a piano that were family heirlooms) to relatives and their church and sold the house to a friend of their youngest son. Once it was done, they were relieved. "It's not giving up the things that's hard," she said. "It's giving up what has been." (From our 1990 journal)

The ability to fit essential possessions and the artifacts of memory into a limited space is a requirement for full-time RVing. One full-timer told us, "You do not put anything in here that you do not use or wear." He added that he had only three pairs of trousers: one in the dirty clothes, one he was wearing, and a clean pair. His wife commented that she had reduced her formal wardrobe to one "little blue dress" for funerals and weddings. Although RVers celebrate their ability to minimize, the limited storage space in an RV creates problems. "No matter how large a motorhome you may own, the storage problem is soon upon you," warns Norman Lusk in a letter to *Trailer Life*.[14]

One effect of the storage problem is that RVers must restrict to essentials the artifacts that represent their memories and their histories. There is little room for nostalgia, so the past must be condensed to its essence. This is a familiar experience for nomads, but it may threaten the sense of identity that a home provides. One way RVers solve this problem is by reducing their memories to the pages of a photograph album that they share with others soon after their first meeting. The pictures are usually of their family members and of their RV history and RVing friends. The albums place their owners in a recognizable context. They let other RVers identify with their experiences and share photographs, adventures, and family histories of their own.

Although full-time RVers may succeed in selling their house and disposing of excess things, they often want to control the place where they park and make it their own. This enables RVers — especially nomadic ones — to validate their identity in an unfamiliar setting. Steinfeld observes that moving changes a person from known individual to newcomer. This can be an undesirable change in identity, especially for older people. The ability to personalize home space, and to use it to establish personal identity, may be more important for older people than it is for other members of the population.[15]

Prussin, who worked with the nomadic Gabra of Kenya, says that each time the Gabra arrive at a new site they try to recreate the place they have just left. By repeating spatial patterns, they reconstruct and maintain the *cognitive structure* of their old site. They do this by putting the same kinds of objects in similar places each time. In this way, each time a Gabra woman sets up her house she renews the physical and social form of her existence. When she moves, all that is left behind is a set of stones marking a circle or some hearth stones, with little trace of previous occupation on the landscape. Past living persists only in what people have transported from one site to the next. Constancy and continuity are concentrated in, and bounded by, the moving container.[16]

Like Prussin's Gabra friends, RV nomads carry their cognitive structure with them. They, too, reinvent the past with each stop and setup. RVers reestablish the structure of past sites, assuring that home is where they park it. They repeat the rituals of unhitching and setting up their external space. They open their awnings, roll out mats or outdoor carpet, arrange lawn chairs and maybe a table or hanging plants. Some even plant gardens and leave them for the next resident. "Leaving a garden when moving on is a way to mark the fact that we were there."[17]

Boondockers who return to the same site year after year may stake out a considerable area for themselves. Their sites are typically larger than either those allowed residents of private parks or the campsites in many public campgrounds. In the Slabs, for instance, we saw a "No Trespassing" sign blocking off a dirt track leading down into a shallow ravine where a trailer was parked. When we asked our neighbors whether individuals did own land in the Slabs, they confirmed that the sign had no legitimacy. As one said, "We're all trespassers here." Nevertheless, the resident's territorial claim was respected; no one attempted to join the trailer at the end of the dirt road.

A group that winters at Slab City is called the Looney Birds. The following excerpt from our 1990 journal illustrates the way in which Slab City groups claim territory and exclude outsiders:

> We found a large cluster that includes several people from British Columbia and Alberta in a group calling themselves the Looney Birds. Their area is cordoned off with tape, is flying

Canadian and US flags, and has a sign giving their name and the names of their members. There is also a sign that says "Don't Even Think About Parking Here." Their cars and RVs are drawn in a circle with a campfire pit in the middle.

They are a group of friends who originally met here and come back every winter to camp together in the same place. About half of them are Canadians from British Columbia and Alberta, while the rest are from the US.

The name was given the group by a Minnesotan who said that the group should be named

The site claimed by the Looney Birds at the Slabs

after the state bird. Now that Canada has put the loon on its dollar coin, the Canadians are planning to make badges out of loonies and have the name of each member of the group engraved on the badge.

Personalizing space

People who want to go full-time have a set of problems. The first is letting go of their house. You can't have a nest. You must strip your belongings down to the bare essentials and get rid of the rest. You can't take a lot of things with you. Too many people try to hang onto their house and rent it out. Renters tear the place up and they lose their shirts. I tell them, "Give it up and sell." Second, you must give up your notion of territory. People have a lot of trouble realizing that they don't own the land where they are parked. You can't put a fence around the place where you park. (Mary Roach, full-time RVer)

While it is true, as Mary Roach says, that nomads cannot put a fence around the place where they park, many RVers do try to "make it like home." When RVers personalize their sites they may be leaving a part of themselves that will lead others to think of them each time they pass by. Or they may be staking a symbolic claim to a place they know they can never own and that they will soon leave. Even if they plan to be in a place only a few days, many

Some decorate their sites with plaster coyotes, cactus, colored rocks, and figurines

Some RVers decorate their sites with Christmas trees

people attempt to personalize their outside space. They brush it clean and hang bird feeders and baskets of plants.

They fly flags identifying them by nationality (US, Canadian), affiliation (RV club), or ideology (Christian cross, the Jolly Roger, the Confederate Stars and Bars). They bound it with stones, bits of broken glass, small white picket fencing, or strings of colored lanterns. They plant flowers, cactus, or vegetables. They put down an astro turf lawn. They decorate it with pink flamingos, fountains, plaster coyotes, colored rocks, cow skulls, figurines, and Christmas trees. They build patios, campfire circles, and barbecue pits.

One resident has decorated the rock at the entrance to Slab City where he lives to reflect his sentiments and make it his home

Some, like the long-time resident who lives near the entrance to Slab City on the right-hand side of the road, go to extraordinary lengths to mark their territory. The resident is an artist who lives in a trailer at the base of a large (perhaps 30-foot high) rock called "Salvation Mountain" which he has colorfully decorated with religious sentiments.

Some, like the Looney Birds, erect *No Trespassing* signs, flags, and signs naming their area and listing the names of the people who live there. One boondocker observed, "When you get situated in one group it's like a family, but we don't have a name yet!" In short you may find anything in the area outside an RV that you might find outside a suburban home to identify it as the personal space of the occupant.

Such practices place the unique signature of the new residents on the site, legitimizing their claim to it. This happens both in established parks where people may lease or own their lots and in boondocking areas. After an RVer has parked his rig in the same boondocking spot for three or four years, and personalized that space, it "belongs" to him or her. We have heard of fights occurring between a newcomer who confiscated a claimed and decorated site and the "owner." People told us that neighbors always support the original residents whose personalization of the site has established use rights over it for as long as they wish to claim it.

The notion that one's home includes the out-of-doors is well known cross-culturally. In his definitive work on dwellings, Oliver observes that they do not require permanent structures:

> To dwell is to ... live in, or at, or on, or about a place. For
> some this implies a permanent structure, for others a temporary
> accommodation, for still others it is where they live, even if
> there is little evidence of building.... It is this double significance
> of dwelling — dwelling as the activity of living or residing,
> and dwelling as the place or structure which is the focus
> of residence — which encompasses the manifold cultural and
> material aspects of domestic habitation.[18]

As well as being part of an RVer's home, the outside is important anywhere
RVers gather. It is the location of the shared social space where people meet
one another, where many social activities occur, and in which everyone
involved has rights.

Social space may be formally structured and organized, as in serviced
parks where water mains, sewage lines, and electric connections dictate that
RVs must line up in rows. In these parks people socialize on their pads
where their vehicles are parked. Pads and the areas around them are usually
only a few feet wide. People also meet in public areas such as recreation
halls, golf courses, or swimming pools. In public parks such as national
parks, individual sites are usually a bit larger than in private parks. Public
space in these parks includes campfire areas where campground hosts
deliver educational talks, recreation areas such as playgrounds or swimming
beaches, and picnic areas.

Home is where you are in control

Whether it is a house full of possessions and memories or an RV, your
home is the place where you are in control. It is your personal castle.
This is especially important to older people whose opportunities to control
events in the outside world become increasingly circumscribed. The ability
to control their environment, to make choices, is an essential aspect of the
meaning of home for many elderly people. It was an important aspect of
the vitality and "adventurous spirit" Betty Friedan found in a mobile home
community of seniors. Her description of this community, which she calls
Trailer Estates, could have been written about an Escapees park:

> A community ... like this seems to create the greatest camara-
> derie of the aged. They are gregarious, they take care of each
> other, they get very involved in the community. They feel
> adventurous. Although most of their homes are set in concrete

now, they keep the feeling that they could always pull up stakes and leave.[19]

This ability to leave whenever they choose is the source of freedom for RVers. Cowgill called attention to this over 50 years ago: "He [the trailerite] is able to get away from unpleasant environments to go in search of health, beauty, comfortable climate, freedom or whatever it is he desires."[20] Being able to leave when they wish gives RVers the power to choose and allows them to control their physical and social environment. "If I don't like the neighbors, all I have to do is turn the key" is a statement of freedom and control. Their ability to "turn the key" permits RVers to escape strife, crowds, and rules that restrict freedom. An RVer from New Hampshire whom Dorothy met in a laundromat in Quartzsite, Arizona, succinctly articulated his right to make his own choices, even if they seem peculiar to others. The man complained there were too many people and too many rules in Quartzsite for his liking. "I think I'll go to Bouse," he said. Bouse, Arizona, is a desolate-looking crossroads in the desert, so she asked, "Why? What's in Bouse?" "Nothing," he responded. "That's the point!"

Solving Problems

Living in a home that moves with the turn of a key gives people control. It also presents them with problems to solve. The problem of limited space or, as Kay Peterson puts it, "learning how to live in a sardine can," is especially trying when there are two people in the can.

Living in a sardine can: Traveling with a partner

Advice to those considering full-timing: Don't try it if you don't like being confined with your spouse. Some don't get along that good. Both have to like RVing.

* * *

Be sure you want to spend 24 hours a day, 7 days a week with your spouse. Be sure you both want to do it.

* * *

What kind of people are best suited to full-timing? Those who do not feel confined in an RV. Those who have lost a mate. Those without close family.

* * *

Both partners have to love to travel and they must get along. They must be able to communicate. If you can't communicate, you don't belong in an RV.

RVers are well aware of the tensions that develop between people who share restricted space. An experienced full-timer told us there is a high rate of divorce among full-timers.[21] He thinks the problem is that married couples do not know each other, even after years of marriage and several children. He says most married people meet for "dinner and a little sex" during their working years. When they retire they are together 24 hours a day. If you add to this the confined space of an RV and separation from children, church. and friends, you have trouble.

> According to Buck, with whom we spoke in 1993, "You've got to like your partner." Crystal added that RVing hadn't hurt their personal lives at all. Instead they have become closer. Buck laughed and said that the RV is so small that every time he goes past her he can pat her bum. He could not do that in their house. If people are not compatible their choice is either to get a divorce or stop RVing. They know of three divorces in this park during the past three years and of others who stopped RVing rather than divorce. Their advice to those who are interested in RVing: "Try it for a year before you sell your house because if you don't like it your equity in your home is gone." (From our 1993 journal)

Early in our research we had a dramatic lesson in the stress level that can develop between incompatible RV partners. As we were ending our research in December 1990, we briefly met another RVing couple who were also heading north rather than south on I-5. When we cheerfully remarked that they and we were going the wrong direction, the man responded by warning us never to sell our home and buy an RV. They had done this and had purchased expensive memberships in two park organizations during the past summer. Now, only six months later, they were going home to get divorced. He said he had been financially ruined by the investment and "by that piece of shit back there," pointing toward the RV. The rig was a new and expensive one, so we asked "What's wrong with it?"

You'd better like yourself and your mate. It's a small space. (Comment on the back of a questionnaire)

"I'm not talking about the rig," he snarled. "I'm talking about the woman in it."

When we told this story to RVers in 1993-94, several responded that they knew the couple. None of them identified the same people.

The "three Ms": Money, mail, and medicine

When we asked which problems concerned RVers most, one full-timing couple replied that the first things that all RVers must deal with are the "three Ms": money, mail, and medicine. We will consider these in turn.

MONEY

What problems have you had in the last year? "Too much month at the end of the money!"

Non-RVers commonly ask "How do you get money on the road?" "How do you pay your bills?" These are problems easily solved. Plastic cards — credit, debit, charge, and ATM cards — enable RVers to travel without carrying large amounts of money. Serious RVers pay their bills in one of several ways. Some put a trusted family member on their bank account or give them access to a credit card, and the family member pays the bills. Others take advantage of bill-payment services offered by their local bank. Or they use a mail-forwarding service and take care of it themselves. How-to-do-it books have at least one chapter on the economics of RVing. These cover topics such as "How much does it (the rig, campground fees, travel) cost?," "Are membership parks an economical investment?," and "How does an RVer make money on the road?" We briefly discussed the options for working RVers in Chapter Six and suggest resources that new RVers can consult for information in Appendix Five. For details consult those resources and specialists such as the Petersons, the Moellers, the Hofmeisters, and the Townsends.[22] In this chapter we ask how RVers compare the cost of living in their rig with the cost of living in a house. How much money does a person need to be a full-time RVer?

1. It is an inexpensive way of life

Why did they start full-timing? It was the only way they could afford to live on his disability pension. Full-timing allows them to live in the mountains on a lake in the summer, to grow their own vegetables and freeze them, and to go to the desert in the winter where expenses are minimal and food is cheap.

Some RVers spend a good deal of time thinking about the economics of RV living and argue that it is an inexpensive way of life. Janet Carter, a single full-time RVer and widely published freelance writer, is convinced of it. After an RVer pays for the rig and sells the house, costs decrease dramatically because there are no property taxes, no house maintenance, and no mortgage. People who could not live well in a fixed house can have a good, full life as RVers, she says. For example, many LoWs at the Slabs are elderly women living on Social Security pensions. For them RVing is the only way they can live, and they are living a *good* life [her emphasis]. They have few expenses, are among a supportive group of friends, and have a good social network. If they were not RVing, Janet says, they would have virtually no life at all.

When Dorothy said she thought, on balance, RVing and fixed house living cost about the same Janet responded, "No Way!" Her reasoning:

1. Traveling is inexpensive. It costs her 15 cents a mile.
2. Even if full-timers stay in a park that charges $29.00 a night, they usually stay for only a day or two. Most full-timers who regularly stay in expensive parks belong to membership parks and pay $1.00, not $20.00, a night.
3. Even RVers who use their rig up usually get something when they sell it. Meanwhile, they get their money's worth out of it. She admits that buying an RV is not the investment a house is supposed to be. However, houses depreciate too, she says.
4. The life style is less expensive for several reasons. First, entertainment is less expensive. When full-timers have guests the numbers are small, guests bring their own food and drink, and preparations are simple. Most RVers entertain under their awnings. Second, clothing expenses are minimal. When she started as a working RVer, she did not even own a dress. When she buys something new, she has to get rid of something old. Lack of space prevents an RVer from spending much money on clothing. Third, space restrictions limit consumption. RVers do not have space to put a lot of things, so they do not spend money on them.

Most of the RVers we talked to or who completed our questionnaire agree with Janet that RVing is less costly than living in a house. Anne, who has been a full-timer for several years explained how her life became simpler:

> An advantage of RVing is that it is cheaper to travel in an RV than it is to live in a home. If you own a home you have fixed expenses: taxes, maintenance, utilities, etc. On the other hand, when RVing you can decide how much you want to travel. The cost of gasoline is the expensive part of RVing, she says. If cash

gets tight, you stay in one spot for a month or two. RVers can avoid the expensive entertaining, and clothes are casual. Anne sold or gave away most of her wardrobe of fine, expensive clothing. Although other RVers acknowledge Anne to be the most elegantly dressed person in the park, she says that she's just wearing her older things. She didn't even own a pair of tennis shoes before she started RVing, and wore high heels to shop at the grocery store. Now she seldom wears heels because most RVers wear jeans and running shoes. (From our 1993 journal)

Some people say that RVing is the only way they could retire early and travel. It is the only way others say they can afford to have a decent life. Mary, a Canadian full-timer, says that many people build their dream homes only to find that property taxes or heating costs are so high they cannot afford to live in them. She and her husband live less expensively in their rig than they could in a house. Others say that RVing is the only way they can have a life with quality.

Because of a serious accident several years ago, Al is unable to work their farm. So, their budget is Al's disability payment and whatever money Agatha can earn on their farm or working in the nearby town during the summer. She saves the money she earns in the summer to pay for their winters here in the LTVA. She calculates the cost of everything to the penny. They spend $500 for gas traveling between Alberta and southern California, and rising fuel prices require them to scrimp elsewhere. Agatha is saving cans to refund and has carefully calculated her profits. She discusses the advantages of taking a lower price per pound (seven and a half cents) in El Centro versus the additional cost of gas to take them to Yuma where she can get eight cents a pound. She hopes to have 100 pounds of cans before Christmas to receive a free turkey plus the money for the cans. Agatha says that when she spends money it has to count. They do not buy pop or beer or any junk food. The custom here at the LTVA of residents sharing food they glean from the fields helps them get through the winter. She searches out things that are free, everything from places to stay when they travel to free university classes in town, and does their laundry by hand. People back home tell them they cannot live like this. "They say we're going to lose our farm. We haven't lost it yet and we're getting by." Al says that living in their trailer down here is the reason he is still alive. His illness and adversity have made him treasure his life. "It sure does make it seem like every morning is beautiful," he says. (From our 1990 journal)

Others full-time because they cannot afford to do anything else.

Goldy is full-timing because after her husband's death from cancer, she discovered his medical insurance had covered only half of the cost of his illness. Two of the bills not covered by insurance were for $72,000 and $42,000. She filed for bankruptcy and lost three homes and an airplane. Now she lives on $500 a month, but she doesn't go hungry, she says. She considers herself to be fortunate because she has a roof over her head and friends who will help when she needs them.

2. What does it cost?

Gail Hartwigsen and Roberta Null wrote in 1989 that full-timing is likely to be less expensive than living in a conventional home. They estimated a full-timing couple could live comfortably on $1,300 a month. This sum included both necessities and luxuries such as dining out and travel. Our informants would probably agree. In 1994, 22 per cent of people answering our questionnaire said they spend between $1500 and $1999 a month, with the most expensive items in their budgets being food and fuel. The majority (60 per cent) of respondents said they spend between $700 and $1999 in a normal month.[23]

In 1988 the Escapees club asked full-timers to send in sample budgets so they could answer the question prospective full-timers often ask: "How much does it cost?" Responses ranged from about $326.00 to $2,000 a month. Some, like the Wiersmas, in their 50s and ineligible for Social Security, said they spent more than they could afford. Velma Wiersma asks:

Does anyone *really live on a thousand a month* — that is, counting ALL expenses? It doesn't seem possible. At the moment we are very depressed about the whole F/T experience. The only thing we do for entertainment is bird watch. Seems a lot of people manage to play golf, do crafts, take bus tours, go to concerts, ball games, etc — a lot of things we couldn't even think of doing.[24]

Canadian RVers Frank and Iris Grieg reported their average monthly budget is $1,486 Canadian. This includes out-of-Canada medical insurance and the cost of exchanging Canadian money for American funds.[25]

At the other end of the scale are Naomi Smith and Orrill Darby. Darby is a single woman with a monthly income of $700 US, an annual income of $8400. She considers herself to be a snowbird because she moves between three sites. She spends spring and fall in a mountain cabin her children own. In the summer she stays in free forest campgrounds in northern California. She winters at the Slabs. She boondocks exclusively because there is no money in her budget for camping fees. The most expensive item in her monthly budget is health insurance at $259. The second most expensive item, at $275, is the category Darby calls "controllables." It includes food, clothing, dues, laundry, pet food and vet bills, postage, subscriptions, and eating out. Other items in her budget are gasoline $40, vehicle insurance $40, propane $15, repairs $50, vehicle registration/license $20.[26]

Smith is also a single woman with the lowest budget for which we have details: $326 US a month or $3921 a year. She spends the summer in New Mexico state parks which charge less than $1 a day. During the winter she lives free at the Slabs. She does not use a refrigerator and so keeps her propane costs to about $2 a month. She spends $766 a year on gasoline.

> There is no room in my budget for long distance calls, beauty shops, magazines, cigarettes. Occasionally, I go to a museum or to church, but my entertainment is usually public libraries with an occasional splurge at McDonald's. Medical cost was a bottle of aspirin. I have *no* medical insurance. The small difference between my $326 a month expenses, and slightly larger income, goes to future vehicle or medical emergencies.[27]

RVers frequently responded to our questions about cost by pointing out the flexibility of RV living. You can spend a lot of money if you travel almost every day, stay in expensive private parks, and eat out in restaurants. Or you can live on very little. Our informants told us there is a minimum income needed to be a full-time RVers, but the amount varies. Boondockers can limit their expenses to $600 a month or less for food, fuel, and incidentals, as the two preceding budgets show. People who want full hookups, eat in restaurants, and smoke and drink spend much more. It is up to the individual. "The important thing," one RVer wrote on the questionnaire, is to "budget and have faith your money will be enough."

MAIL OR "KEEPING IN TOUCH"

Money isn't everything, but it helps you keep in touch with the children.[28]

As we saw in Chapter Five, a major concern that prevents many people from becoming serious or full-time RVers is their attachment to their families, especially children and grandchildren. Are those who do decide to leave home to go on the road estranged from their families? If not, how do they keep in touch?

One of our informants asserted that many full-timers do not miss their families. They are, in fact, running away from them, he says. We would be surprised, he said, if people in the park talked frankly about their relationship with their families. Many seldom see their children and want nothing to do with them. Although some RVers are alienated from their families — about 4 per cent of the people who answered our questionnaire said they seldom or never see their children — most are not. Almost 66 per cent of our respondents said they see their children at least twice a year, and almost 73 per cent said their families either thought their going on the road was a good idea or accepted their decision. For the others, the relationship of full-timers with their children can be marred by tension and failure to understand the other's point of view.

Jan says, "We hope to be able to see more of our kids now. They're busy people and we don't want to be in the way." She says they can visit the cities where they live, see the sights and not be underfoot.

She says that the family joke is that when the kids find out where they are and call them, they move on. She said it jokingly, but there was an undercurrent of ambivalence. (From our 1990 journal)

* * *

She and her husband bought their motorhome about three months before his death. After he died in May, she stayed around until October and then decided to take off and travel. Her kids (all 7 of them) were horrified and said, "How can you do that?" She says she replied, "All I have to do is turn the key — watch me!" (Response to questionnaire)

* * *

When she heard about their purchase of the fifth-wheel, their 13-year-old granddaughter said, "When do we leave?" Her mother is a single parent, and the girl is like one of their own and has been everywhere with them. (From our 1990 journal)

Their kids have had a hard time with their full-timing and want them to settle down. They call their three kids in turn, once a month. The last time they called their younger daughter, she announced that she had just bought a five-bedroom home on seven acres and invited them to live with her. Eve told her that they love her but that they would never live with her. Their daughter replied, "Well, you can find some place on the seven acres to park your rig and settle down, can't you?" Eve told her "We don't want to settle down. Leave us alone!" Now, Eve says, "Our kids have decided that Mom and Dad have flipped." (From our 1993 journal)

Some people say that becoming serious RVers was one of the best things they did for their children. "Now that we're gone, our kids have to depend on each other. It's brought them together and made them grow up. It's the best thing we ever did for them," one woman declared. Another said, "You have to let your kids live their own lives. You have to be able to love your family, but you've graduated from taking care of them. Now live your life your way." Kay Peterson agrees:

> Somewhere along the way, our family relationship changes. Once we had to let go of our children so they could grow and become their own "I." Now is their turn to let go of us. When children and other loved ones are deep-rooted, they may have trouble understanding that our needs are not the same as theirs. But if you are really as close to your family as you think you are, you should be able to communicate your desire to move on to a new phase of life and gain your freedom with their blessing.[29]

Once they have made the decision to go on the road, most RVers choose a mail-forwarding or voice-mail service to keep in touch with their families. We tried a cell phone. It was an expensive source of frustration. Others like Mabel Johnson, whom we profiled in Chapter Five, have more original solutions:

> After their daughters moved out and before Roy retired, Mabel continued to camp alone. She was in the Rapid City area one summer when there were floods and avalanches, and many vacationers were hurt or killed. She was doing her own thing, without TV and not listening to the radio and didn't have any idea there was a problem. Meanwhile, her family was frantic because they didn't know if she was dead or alive. Now they paint a large ID number on the top of their trailer. If their family needs to find them, they can be identified from the air. She says she can't imagine any situation in which it would be necessary, but it makes their kids feel better, and so they do it. They also let their daughters know in what general direction they're heading. They do not have a cell phone because they are expensive, but they do have CBs in the truck and the fifth-wheel for emergencies. (From our 1993 journal)

HEALTH AND SECURITY

People should be free from fear in their own home. Unfortunately this is sometimes not the case in modern North America. Elderly people worry about illness and fear random violence, and most people lock their doors. Prospective RVers wonder what they could do were they to get sick away from their family doctor. They worry about robbery and violence while they are in an RV. The following letter to the Escapees newsletter and an exchange in an Escapees park illustrates these concerns and the response of experienced RVers to them.

> Margaret having radiation therapy for lymphoma cancer... in stage 1 so is curable but curtails our travels for now. Glad we kept our home base. Flew her home, but what do F-T'ers do in cases like this? Where do they go? (Editor's response: Go to the closest big treatment center. When you full-time you *are* home. Many hospitals have room to park an RV.)[30]
>
> * * *
>
> During a discussion of why people hesitate to become full-timers, one woman said the thing she was most afraid of when they began was not being able to find a good physician if they became ill. She asked other full-timers what they did, and they assured her that if they needed medical care they could find it. Several people commented that most physicians are now specialists, so if you have a medical emergency your family physician may not be able to deal with it any better than the physician in an emergency ward in a local hospital. Another person said that people ask him, "Aren't you afraid of being robbed or worse?" A man from New York commented that he had a hard time keeping a straight face when people from big cities ask him a question like that. He turns the question around and asks them, "How many people living in a city *aren't* afraid?" There were general nods of agreement. (From our 1993 journal)

We address the concerns of health and security in turn.

MEDICINE: RVERS AND HEALTH

On July 1st, Bob's back was hurting so Gene Goehrung #651 stopped by and repaired the electric step. (Refused money.) Next day, pain was worse so Gene took him to the hospital in Bend, Oregon, and waited with us until 1 a.m. for the test results. On July 3rd he picked Bob up and brought him home. We had never met Gene until July 1st! That's what SKP "caring" is about![31]

* * *

Last winter I was hospitalized in Phoenix, AZ. While I was there, I was sustained by a stream of letters, phone calls, and cards of encouragement from the SKPs at North Ranch. On my return to North Ranch for recuperation, SKPs took my rig out of storage, set it up, and proceeded to take care of this old loner without fuss or fanfare. I hope I have the opportunity to pass on the love shown to me.[32]

The solution to finding a good doctor or dentist is simple, RVers say. Ask other RVers who know the area. Ask the park manager or the campground host. They will either recommend someone or help you find someone who can. Emergency evacuation programs, such as Sky Med, are also available for ill RVers who want to go home. And, as the above letters illustrate, other RVers — even strangers — will step forward to help in an emergency.

Because most serious RVers are retired seniors, outsiders may assume that illness is a problem for them. Instead, most RVers say they feel young and healthy. As Tonia Thorson said in her letter, quoted in Chapter Two, "people stay young on the road." Not only do most RVers claim to enjoy good health, many argue it has changed for the better since they began RVing. This is, they say, primarily because they are under less stress. Many are passionate about the improvement in their health and are determined to preserve their feeling of well-being. As Mrs. Thorson said, RVers do not play much "organ music."

We know of only one study of the health of RVers, a health questionnaire that surveyed 723 Escapees in 1996. Their health profile was promising in that they reported only moderate use of alcohol and virtual abstinence from the use of tobacco. However, there was a problem with weight. The physician who analyzed the results advised members of the club, "At least half of you are significantly overweight to the extent that, statistically, your survival may be impaired."[33]

We think that self-selection combined with determination and a positive attitude are largely responsible for the physical well-being that RVers report. Many people stop RVing when they become ill. Others, however, continue to travel even when they have serious health problems. Many of them downplay their physical difficulties.[34]

Les, whom we estimate to be 71 years old, has been full-timing for eight years, having retired early to become an RVer. He has a spreading prostate cancer. On his questionnaire he described himself as being in excellent physical condition for his age and said "Except for my cancer, I feel great."

* * *

In a letter to the *Escapees Newsletter*, Ed Spoerl says: "After a divorce, prostate and back surgeries, then quadruple bypass, I was going blind. I had a miraculous recovery and can again drive my RV! I've already been across the country, seeing new places and square dancing. It's great to be alive!"[35]

* * *

They decided to go full-time when her husband was diagnosed with bone cancer and was given 2 years to live. That was 9 years ago. "We're still going" she says.

* * *

Norm, who is over 75, has been RVing since 1944. He started full-timing in 1992. He has glaucoma, cataracts, and "residual problems from 1993 colon cancer, bladder cancer, and prostate cancer surgery." Nevertheless on his questionnaire he described his health as good compared to other people his age, and said it is the same as when he began full-timing.

Most RVers say that health is not their first worry, and many carry little or no health insurance.[36] Over half of the respondents to our questionnaire (most of them Americans) said they were not covered by a public medicare plan. Twelve per cent had no medical insurance coverage of any kind. Although most Americans do not seem to worry much about the cost of health care, most Canadians do. As we observed in Chapter Five, they are especially troubled by the potential cost of uninsured hospitalization in the US. The horror story (perhaps an urban myth) told by Canadian RVers is of an inadequately insured Canadian who became ill and was financially ruined by hospitalization in the States. A favorite topic of conversation among Canadian RVers is the relative coverage and cost of private health insurance plans that provide protection in the US. Many said that when they could no longer afford private insurance they would stop traveling outside of Canada. Those few Canadians we met who carried no health insurance explained their decision in one of two ways. Some, like the Frenches whom we profiled in Chapter Five, did not meet any province's residence requirements and thus were ineligible for provincial health care. Private plans supplement provincial health insurance and so were of little value to them. Instead they trusted a combination of religious faith, healthy living, and good luck to keep them well. Because provincial health plans cover only a fraction of the cost of hospital care in the US, and private plans do not cover the pre-existing medical problems that were their chief risk, others are fatalistic. One Canadian does not have any insurance because he "read the fine print" on all the policies available and found that they would not cover his pre-existing heart condition. If he gets sick, he says, he'll either die quickly or get on an airplane to Canada. Anything else would just be a waste of money. If he does die, "It costs the same to cremate you in the States as it does in Canada. They can ship you home in a coffee can," he said.

These RVers would agree with another philosophical Canadian who does not fret about medical costs in the United States. "If you're going to worry a lot about that kind of thing you might as well just stay home and not travel," he said.

SECURITY AND PERSONAL SAFETY

I wouldn't be down here without weapons. There are some really bad people out there. (Michigander in Arizona explaining why he carried handguns when camping)

* * *

You should never camp alone or be the first to pull off into a rest area. We all know that Canadians don't carry weapons. There are a lot of crazies down here where it's hot. (Warning from an American full-timer about where we should not camp on our way home to Canada, from our 1990 journal)

* * *

I would not be without a gun close at hand. There are too many creeps out there in the world. There are nice people, but you can find good food in a garbage can and a stopped clock is right twice a day. (American full-timer, from our 1990 journal)

* * *

Their dog guards their home. They see no reason to carry a gun. There are more problems with "riff-raff" now. That's why they stay in this [county] park and why they no longer boondock. (From a conversation with a full-time American couple in their 80s in our 1990 journal)

Just as the Canadian's nightmare is the $2000 hospital bill for removing a splinter, Americans fear random violence by "the crazies out there" who seem to consist primarily of roving gangs of drug addicts.[37] The reality is not so frightening. Only 10 per cent of our respondents said they had ever felt threatened by someone while they were RVing. Only 2 per cent of those carrying weapons had ever had to use them. We talked with only one RVer who had actually experienced a threat to her personal safety so serious that she had fired a gun in self defense. The night after she had sold her house in an American city, Karen was sleeping in her motorhome in the alley behind the house when several men surrounded her motorhome and began to rock it. She opened her door and fired her pistol into the ground. The men ran away. American RVers disagree about which places are safe and which are potentially a danger. One RVer who lived in a camper on the back of his truck said he felt perfectly safe in rural state parks. He pointed out that others in the park left possessions, including a TV set, sitting outside on their picnic table without a problem. However, he avoids campgrounds near cities and private RV parks with guards to patrol. "They'd be as likely as anyone to steal while you weren't around," he said. Another returned to the topic of guns several times in his discussions with us. In many states it is illegal to carry a hand gun in your tow vehicle, but it is all right in your motorhome because it is your house, he assured us. He thinks their RV is safer than staying in a motel because they are in their own bed every night and so don't have to worry about theft. His wife remarked that their experiences so far have been that a bouquet of roses would be a more useful thing to carry than a gun. "We've met wonderful people," she said, adding "I hate guns."

Although personal safety is normally a concern for single women, RVing women seem to have few problems and approach potential danger with both caution and humor. In an article on women RVers in *Ms.* magazine, Marilyn Murphy says that RVing is both the safest and most enjoyable way for women to travel. RVing women are well equipped to take care of themselves, as Murphy discovered at a safety workshop for RVers. "Many women have CB radios, cellular phones, alarms, baseball bats, tire irons, mace, their dogs, stun guns, and even regular guns with them for protection." They knew of no women who had experienced any "male violence" trouble, but several women had left a remote campground in a hurry because the behavior of a man "disquieted" them.[38] Arden Powell argues that the only safe way for a woman to be on the road alone is in a motorhome that allows "fast getaways." She recommends getting one with a floor-plan that allows the driver to see straight through to the rear window of the coach. She also suggests adding a wide-angle plastic lens low on the rear window because it enables the driver "to see who's tailing you while you are maneuvering in the driver's seat." She has an alarm system that responds to peripheral rocking of her motorhome. When "suspicious-looking people" approach her RV she sets it off. "The fright effect is wonderful."[39]

William Anderson discovered a less serious approach to safety when he met a group of women he calls "the merry widows":

While I was losing my shirt, I discovered they were four widows who had bought a travel trailer and were following the sun. Instead of molding at home and being a problem to their kids, they were fishing, gossiping, hunting husbands, and developing a deadly poker game. And there was no moss on these golden girls. As I left the game with a flat wallet, I noticed a pair of size 14 boots on the trailer step. Asking about this, I was informed they were for protection. "Would you break into a trailer," asked Agnes, eyes atwinkle, "if you thought there might be a guy inside who wore size 14 boots?"[40]

Mabel Johnson spends little time worrying about her personal safety. Although she either camped alone or with her daughters for many summers, she had only one uncomfortable experience with which she quickly dealt. She had parked for the night with her two teenagers when a biker gang pulled in and made obscene comments about her. They did not see the girls, and she instructed them to keep down. She grasped her steel bar so they would think twice about bothering her, cranked down the pop-up camper, unlocked her truck, and pulled out leaving her levelling blocks behind.

Roy and Mabel do not carry weapons. They do not "do dumb things" such as stay in urban areas. They also do not worry about violence. Roy has a cousin who keeps her short wave-radio tuned to a police radio so all she hears are reports of murder and mayhem. Consequently she lives in fear. People do not talk about all the times they park safely in rest areas. They do focus on the one story — usually heard third-hand — about somebody being attacked in a rest area, he says. Roy suggests that RVers who are worried about intruders get a big dog bowl and chain (used) and attach them to the front of their rig. Mabel recounted hearing a widow say that she kept a pair of old work boots, setting them outside the door of her trailer when she parked (echoes of the merry widows).

CANADIAN RVERS AND VIOLENCE

When we've camped in the wild all we had was a can of Easy-Off and a crowbar. (From a 1990 interview with a Canadian full-timer)

* * *

We've never had an uncomfortable feeling in all the years we've been traveling. If you feel so unsafe that you have to carry a gun, you might as well stay home. (Canadian RVers, from our 1990 journal)

Most Canadian RVers with whom we talked are a bit bemused by their American counterparts' preoccupation with security. When we asked about security precautions, Canadians usually responded that common sense and reasonable caution are the best defense against potential violence. Some observed that the combination of fear and guns were the source of greatest danger for RVers. One Canadian, in response to a question about security precautions described how fear can be dangerous:

> This is one area where the American attitude is frightening. I can recall at least three instances. (1) We spent a weekend with American friends in Ghost Town Terlingua (West Texas) for the Chili Cookoff. About 11 p.m. several young lads pulled revolvers and started shooting at street signs. Our friend immediately grabbed his rifle and was ready to blast away if a stray bullet should come our way. (2) A garage owner in Florida confessed to me that he had almost shot a customer who drove across his lawn after having been previously warned. (3) In Cape Breton, an American invited me to visit. Must have forgotten and threatened to shoot if I came closer.

Another Canadian wrote:

> We have never had a problem with violence, although we do know of some specific cases where there has been a problem. We once were circled by a gang of motorcycles late at night just off a highway near Boston. We remained cool, hoped for the best, and eventually they tired of buzzing us and left. Another time in an open field in Saskatchewan, a drunk cowboy drove around and around my trailer, cursing "the rich bastards from Central Canada." He too got tired and went home. It would have been comical had there not been the possibility of a problem. We do not keep guns of any kind. If there was an occasion to use one, the advantage would be entirely with the other guy(s). I was once bugged by a very persistent panhandler in Portland Ore. but it was on a main street during the day and people began to turn their heads as I told him in an increasingly loud voice to buzz off. He did. Don't they tell women who think they are about to be raped, to take a very strong and positive approach, but authoritative, etc., on the basis that it's better than being submissive. Again, I would think judgement comes into play.

The Bards, whom we met in an Arizona park in 1990, are typically Canadian in their refusal to carry guns. They also refuse to worry about security. They destination-boondock (see Glossary) in rest areas on interstates and K-Mart parking lots (where permitted). They also carry the *Truck Stop Locator and Services Directory* because many truck stops will permit RVers to spend the night free. They say that they like having an old RV because no one would break into it. "An expensive one may be mortgaged to the hilt, but they'd still pick it to break into and not ours." They like having a motorhome because "If rowdies are around, all we have to do is pull the curtains open, start the engine and we are gone."

Some experienced American RVers also advocate the advantage of discretion over deadly weapons. In a discussion about whether RVers need guns, Maurice Johnson rejected the idea that the proper preparation for the possibility of violent crime is a gun:

> I feel better protected with a wrench or a club in my hand than I do with a gun.... I do carry the moral conviction that *if* someone bent on violent crime approaches me or my RV it is very possible — even likely — that he possesses a gun. If he suspects I have a gun he might very logically shoot me; but if he believes I do not, then he probably will not.... I do not want to kill someone over an emotional or property problem. However, I would not hesitate to strike someone with a club who threatened me or violated my property. Thus I arrive at the conclusion that if I hear someone invading my RV, both he and I are going to be safer if I attempt to repel his invasion with a club.

He and his wife Jean have been full-timing for 10 years, traveling in the US, Canada, Mexico, Europe, Australia, and New Zealand "but have never been harmed or threatened with violence."

> I am personally critical of any person's opinions or attitudes suggesting that he needs a gun to protect himself from violence in Canada. (Remember — it is their law and we are the visitors.) The Canadian record of domestic tranquility is far superior to our own in the US by *any* yardstick you choose. They do not feel *they* need guns to protect their homesteads. Surely we have no right to impose our fears upon them.[41]

Recalling that, like Johnson, few of our informants had experienced either crime or violence while they were RVing, we give the final word on the subject to the Petersons and their article entitled, "Is boondocking safe?" They maintain that fear of boondocking is usually fear of the unknown. Those who say it is unsafe usually have never boondocked, while RVers who boondock are not afraid. Although there are many rumors about boondockers who were robbed or murdered, they have only heard of three incidents from the victims. Two involved the burglary of an unattended RV, and the third was someone robbed in a rest area where there were no other RVs. They quote an unnamed statistician who, using figures from the US Crime Council, says "The actual chance of an RV being robbed is one in a million, and the chance of anyone getting murdered in an RV in this country [the USA] is one in 30 million." The Petersons add, "Compared to the number of robberies and murders that occur in conventional homes, it seems strange that people who sleep soundly in a house are afraid to spend a night in the RV when it is parked in a highway rest area."[42]

Conclusion

When nomads — whether they are the Gabra of Kenya or the RVers of North America — arrive at a new place they try to recreate physically the mental idea of home. RVers do this by placing artifacts (a picnic table, lawn chairs, potted plants, name signs) in similar places each time, thus reconstructing a memory of home. Each time RVers unhitch and set up their homes they renew both the physical and social aspects of their existence. In her discussion of the Gabra of Kenya, Prussin comments that the repetition of fixed spatial patterns reinforces the cognitive structure of their interior space. We take this further and argue that when RV nomads set up at a new site, their repetition of spatial patterns reinvents and reinforces their cognitive structure of home, society, and community. Although RVers carry with them the form of social structure, the form is empty. Because they share no history with their RV neighbors, there is no one to fill the position of friend or family. The ideal content of these forms is shared knowledge. Therefore, when a newcomer pulls in, the strangers who are now neighbors immediately begin to perform the roles of friend and family by sharing substance and labor, by building shared history, however short. They help the newcomer set up, bring food, give advice, and exchange information and personal history. This sharing allows RVers who do not have a common past to recreate the structure of history from one place to another and to surround themselves with familiar social structure. Like the Gabra, their reconstruction of history and society enables them to insulate themselves against a hostile environment — the "Crazies" out there. They transform the stranger who will "rip you off" into the friend who will look after you in your time of need. This, indeed, is the essence of home.

Notes

1. Cowgill 1941:53.

2. Edington and Edington 1983-84:25.

3. Cowgill 1941:53; Rawles 1987:336.

4. The notion of the idea of home as both a space and a possession is from Steinfeld 1981:202. Also see Peterson, K. 1995c:2.

5. See Rawles 1987:340.

6. Bellah *et al.* 1985:135.

7. Douglas 1991:296.

8. The analogy of the home as a museum of life history is from Rawles 1987:341. Also see Sartre 1956:754.

9. Risch and Risch 1984-85:12.

10. Russell Belk (1988) has written a fascinating essay on the relationship between possessions and the extension of self.

11. Boschetti 1984:39, quoted in Rawles 1987:341.

12. K. Peterson 1982:8. Almost 75 per cent of the respondents to our questionnaire said they had sold their homes and either gotten rid of or stored their possessions; 19 per cent of respondents to our questionnaire said that the hardest thing about making the decision to go full-time was getting rid of things.

13. Carlson 1995:63.

14. Lusk 1991:19.

15. Steinfeld 1981:202, 206, 209.

16. Prussin 1989:154-155.

17. Peterson, K. 1995c:2.

18. Oliver 1987:7.

19. Friedan 1993:357, 364.

20. Cowgill 1941:45.

21. We are unable to confirm his statement.

22. Peterson and Peterson 1997; Moeller and Moeller 1986 and 1998; Hofmeister and Hofmeister 1992 and 1999; Townsend and Townsend 1991.

23. Hartwigsen and Null 1989:320. For information on our respondents, see responses to question 90 in Appendix One.

24. Wiersma 1989:8-9. Their reported six month budget is $11,347.09. Average monthly budget is $1,891.18. Figures are as follows (p. 8)

Item	6 month total	1 month average
Insurance (health, life)	$1172.57	195.43
Taxes	346.30	57.72
Medical (incl RX)	653.02	108.84
Rent for sites	882.91	147.15
Electricity	11.05	1.84
Propane	61.56	10.26
Groceries	1354.92	225.82
Eat out	1427.24	237.87
Wearing apparel	316.54	52.76
Laundry	115.35	19.23
Household purchases	801.68	133.61
Gasoline	1027.78	171.30
Toll road fees	6.80	1.13
Auto expenses	600.04	100.01
Battery charges	6.00	1.00
Telephone	467.91	77.98
Newspapers	33.23	5.54
Mail & Message SKP service	192.00	32.00
Charity/Church	9.29	1.55
Beauty care	166.12	27.68
Entertainment	135.51	22.59
Cigarettes	813.93	135.66
Dues & Subscriptions	19.00	3.17
Gifts (Christmas)	609.58	101.60
Lawyer	50.00	8.33
Dog	65.76	10.96
Misc.	1.00	.17

25. Grieg and Grieg 1989:11. Their budget:

Camp (rent)	$216.71
Fuel (truck)	161.07

Propane	3.34
Food (incl. paper products, soap etc)	240.51
Maintenance: Truck	88.63
Trailer	189.54
Insurance (vehicles, contents, health)	108.29
Cost of currency exchange	150.94
Misc. (clothes, entertainment, gifts phone, postage, taxes)	326.95

26. Darby 1988:6.

27. Smith, Naomi 1990:8.

28. *Escapees Newsletter* 1986a:37.

29. Peterson, K. 1983:2.

30. Julkowski and Julkowski 1985:25.

31. Gobar and Gobar 1988:39.

32. Graham 1993:50.

33. Amick 1996:59.

34. Eighty-eight per cent of the people responding to Clinton's survey (1993a:7) reported their health to be excellent (41 percent) or good (47 per cent). Ninety-three per cent of the people we surveyed described their health as being either good (54 per cent) or excellent (39 per cent). When we asked if their health had changed since they began RVing, 67 per cent replied that it was about the same, 25 per cent said their health had changed for the better. Seventy-three per cent of these attributed the improvement to less stress in their lives.

Almost 8 per cent said their health had worsened since they started RVing. Most of these attributed their decline to getting older, while almost 30 per cent said it was due to lack of exercise and a poor diet. Fifty-seven per cent of the people answering our questionnaire said they had no health problems bothering them at the time; 43 per cent reported current physical problems. Almost 18 per cent of people with a bothersome physical condition said they had multiple difficulties. Among the problems reported were arthritis (14.4 per cent), diabetes (8.5 per cent), heart disease and high blood pressure (7.6 per cent each), and back problems (6.8 per cent).

35. Spoerl 1988:43.

36. Over 86 per cent of those who answered our questionnaire said they had not had a serious illness or health problem while they were on the road during the past year. Less than one-quarter of our respondents said that health is the greatest concern they have as RVers. Over half said they were not covered by medicare or a provincial health plan, and almost one-quarter of those also carried no private medical insurance. Canadians were much more concerned about health insurance, a finding consistent with

our impression from talking with them about the subject both in 1990 and in 1993-94. Eighty-nine per cent were covered by a provincial health plan, 55 per cent carried private medical insurance, and half had both.

37. This concern was expressed in many conversations but is not reflected in questionnaire responses. Only 9 per cent of respondents said that personal safety was their greatest concern, while 15 per cent said it was their least concern. Perhaps this is because 95 per cent of our respondents who said they carry weapons said they carry a gun or guns.

38. Murphy 1992:44.

39. Powell, A.G. 1993:61, 64, 66.

40. Anderson, W. 1991:73, 77.

41. Johnson 1989:22.

42. Peterson and Peterson 1995:16-17.

Chapter 8

"They're My Family Now"

One Saturday afternoon we went to a large used-to-be Army WWII base where thousands of RVers spend the winter. Milt stayed in the car and said, "Go find someone to talk to." In about five minutes, I came back and got him and introduced him to 6 campers who were sitting in their folding chairs under someone's awning and we had a great 2 hours learning all kinds of things about winter and/or full time living in an RV of one kind and another. Campers are for the most part kind, helpful, friendly, considerate pioneer type people. Rich or poor, Christian or Atheist, Republican or Democrat, fat or thin, doesn't matter out there. You are all living the same kind of life, depending on your batteries and the capacity of your propane tank, and sometimes, each other. (Excerpt from a letter by Ruth Dalgleish)

RVers and Community

In the quote that opens this chapter, Ruth Dalgleish describes the time when she and Milton were trying to decide whether to become serious RVers. Embodied in their experience are several elements that explain what RVers mean when they say they have found community on the road. Other RVers are friendly and helpful, even to strangers, and they embrace the ideal of equality. These are the mores of the pioneer. Throughout this book we have discussed the ways in which RVers relate to community: the communities that were theirs before they became RVers, the local communities that are hosts to RV parks, and communities of RVers themselves. In this chapter we focus on how RVers create and maintain their own communities.

RVing ... is about a way of life that has revolutionized recreation for a vast number of people ... it has taken senior citizens out of their rocking chairs and created a travelling community with a camaraderie that can't be matched. (Edwards 1991:55)

The term "community" conjures up neighborhoods and small towns — fixed places where people share interest in a common territory — and on the relationships and activities built there over years of familiarity and interdependence. In this model, one's community is a series of circles containing family,

The old gang here at the Ranch were all campers. They all know what it was like to camp in the rain with kids and to get back of nowhere and run out of supplies. They still have the same feeling about each other. (From an interview with a retired university professor in our 1993 journal)

friends, neighbors, and fellow townspeople, with the most intimate relationships at the center. However, as North American society has become more mobile, social interaction based on shared, fixed territory has become less important. Today, as sociologist Thomas Bender observes, identifying community with a fixed place confuses form with substance and excludes those who should be included.

> A preoccupation with territory ... ultimately confuses our understanding of community.... A community involves a limited number of people in a somewhat restricted *social* space or network held together by shared understandings and a sense of obligation (emphasis added). Relationships are close, often intimate, and usually face to face. Individuals are bound together by affective or emotional ties rather than by a perception of individual self-interest. There is a "we-ness" in a community. One is a member.[1]

Escapees self-consciously try to build community among the members of their organization. The following column, by Cathie Carr, the Petersons' daughter and the Club's Administrator, offers a definition of community that recognizes some key characteristics: the idea that the group is special, the use of symbols to allow members to recognize one another, and a sense of inclusion:

> As an RVer it is essential to develop the art of inclusion. Escapees are generally masters of this because we have the tools to make people want to include us. One of those tools is our badge. The house-in-a-wagon logo gives us a sort of license to start a conversation. If someone doesn't notice it, you can always say, "You can see by my badge that I am an Escapee." Who could resist a response?
>
> Being an RVer makes us special. It gives us the opportunity to be unique in a world full of house-livers. We are the evidence that there is more to life than a rocking chair on a porch....
>
> I believe if you want to enter a circle, you can just erase the lines. It is up to you to make the first move. It is up to you to become a part of the community.
>
> The term "community" is loosely defined as a group of people living in the same locality. It can be a town, an RV park, or a rally location. In every case, the best way to break the ice is to volunteer to help. Inclusion is a guaranteed result.[2]

Because nomadic RVers share neither common territory nor common history, they have developed ways to create instant community. These include the use of space and symbols to identify and define themselves and create a sense of "we-ness" that quickly brings newcomers into the circle. They also include an insistence on reciprocity. As Carr suggests, serious

He says Escapees is really a community — a family. His evidence is that if you need help, whether from illness or ignorance of how some system in the RV works or should be repaired, there is always someone who is both knowledgeable and willing to share that knowledge. While other parks may not be as friendly (with bell rings and hugs) as this park, all of them they have visited have been friendly if you make the first effort, and all of them have the same willingness to share and be helpful. (From our 1993 journal)

RVers expect both to provide and receive help and support from other RVers in time of crisis. They share food, volunteer service, and cooperate to insure mutual security of person and property. These reciprocal relationships reinforce the equality that RVers value. They put into action the idea that people are "all the same here." Reciprocity and equality are two principles that underlie the creation of community among serious RVers.

The feeling of community is well illustrated in an article entitled "Campgrounds are Communities!" by Paula and Peter Porter:

> It didn't take us long to realize that the RV parks along our favorite north-south and east-west routes were the friendliest places we had ever stayed on vacation. Everywhere we travelled, people were open and helpful, sometimes insisting on setting up our awning for us, or helping Pete level the trailer. On a couple of occasions, when we forgot the technique for setting something up, we knew that there was always a neighbor ready to lend a hand. It was like joining a club … every RV couple we met wanted to drop by and say "welcome to the campground."[3]

During a discussion about why people become full-time RVers Dwayne — a full-timer and a part-time manager of a resort park — explained that people live in a subdivision in southern California for 20 years and do not know the name of the people next door. "Here, and in RV parks generally," he observed, "you get a real sense of community and people becoming friends and helping each other. It is as if people see others living like themselves and feel they can trust them."

Another RV resort owner-manager, in response to our observation that people in the park were friendly and all seemed to know each other, said "That's what they come here for. They have it here and they don't have it back home. They get back home and they miss it. That's why they keep coming back. Most of our people come back here every year. When they come back here they're coming home."

When we asked Vanessa, a full-timer, why she and her husband returned to the Slabs year after year she explained, "It's like coming home. They're your family. Everybody watches out for everybody else. Everybody's so eager to help. When you get situated in one group it's like a family, but we don't have a name yet."

Upon what do RVers base their sense of community? In modern, mobile, North American society shared territory and history are increasingly rare qualities on which to create community. As Bender observes, "Community, then, can be defined better as an experience than a place. As simply as possible, community is where community happens."[4] What makes it happen for RVers?

Creation of Community Among RVers

"Let me ask you a question. How many of you who lived in a city or a suburb knew as many of your neighbors to talk to there as you do here in this park?" The response was laughter and general agreement that they talked to few people when they lived in a house, but they know many people here in this park. (Question asked by a full-timer in an Escapees clubhouse at happy hour; from our 1993 journal)

* * *

"Each time we pull into a new spot some one will knock and ask where in Ontario we are from. We meet more people from Ontario on the road than ever we have met in Ontario." (From a letter from a Canadian RVer)

Though they prize their mobility and the freedom to "turn on the key" and leave behind incompatible neighbors or an uncomfortable situation, RVers quickly establish good relationships with people they can trust. As we have seen in earlier chapters, they do this by helping newcomers park and set up; by exchanging stories and photographs that establish personal history and, perhaps, illustrate common experiences or friends; and by sharing food, information, and assistance. These new friends become part of the community circle. Indeed, some people *become* RVers because they find among their fellows a sense of community lacking in the suburbs where they lived for decades.

Getting to know each other: Greetings and hugs

Happy trails to you until we meet again.
Happy trails to you, keep smilin' until then.
Who cares about the clouds when we're together?
Just sing a song and bring the sunny weather.
Happy trails to you till we meet again.[5]

Because RVers must quickly initiate friendly relations with their neighbors if they are to enjoy the security and companionship of community, their first contacts should be welcoming and supportive. Recall Al Komfort's strategy. He helped newcomers park and got to know them so they would look after his things, not rip him off. An ideal greeting is the welcome RVers receive when they arrive at the home park of Escapees. An RVer describes this welcome in an article in *Trailer Life*:

> Your first act at Rainbow's End is to pull the rope on the big ol' bell. As the tones ring over the grounds, people with smiles as big as Texas appear, and they're there for one reason: to welcome you. Hugs all around. Handshakes and introductions. Invitations to happy hour, dinner, a trip into town. Offers to help find a spot, hookup, settle in. Oh, boy, your tired bodies say gratefully, this feels like home! And that's exactly the intent.[6]

This is the ideal Escapees greeting ritual: residents welcome new arrivals and offer them help. We saw another example of ideal Happy Hour greeting and departure rituals in 1993:

> Happy Hour has nothing to do with alcohol. It is a time when all residents get together to greet new arrivals and sing "Happy Trails to You" to departing residents, and to hear announcements. The ritual greeting/parting includes statements by arriving visitors that the greetings here are the friendliest in the SKP system. Departing visitors affirm that this is the friendliest park they have visited. People often say the warm reception led them to stay longer than they had intended, and that they plan to come back again. (From our 1993 journal)

As the following letter from Helen Peters attests, new RVers who experience these rituals do, indeed, feel themselves included in a community. Peters describes the fears and mistakes experienced by herself and her husband when they left home for the first time. They headed for Rainbow's End, Escapee's home park and "the place where real live SKPs would be." There they would learn whether "Escapees were like what we'd been led to believe, there really was a bell you rang, SKPs did come to welcome you, they really hugged, and this organization was truly a network of support and help, warmth and friendship, as the Newsletter articles always inferred." When they arrived it was a December night, and it was starting to rain. Peters describes their welcome:

We climbed out of the truck. We found the bell. In silence, in darkness, in a beginning drizzle, in a world alien to us, we tugged at the rope. We rang the bell at Rainbow's End.

And then — out of the night came people: tall people, short people, people with hats on, people without hats, people in bathrobes, people in cowboy vests. SKPs. Men and women, all smiling, all welcoming us, all hugging, all *real* SKPs, *really* there, at Rainbow's End.

Skips asked if they needed help hooking up. They did. They were shown where to park, given hoses and lines and everything else they needed.

The words in the Newsletter had always rung with encouragement and spirit. But the words were just words, no matter how much we wanted to believe in them — until that night at Rainbow's End. That night we learned that SKPs are, indeed, a network of people giving each other support, help, warmth, and friendship, as we all travel down the road, Children of the Rainbow.[7]

Skips do not limit their greetings to parks. They should greet one another wherever and whenever they meet, especially on the road. The preferred greeting is a hug, a gesture that some Skips readily embrace, but about which others feel diffidence. As one couple of new RVers said: "It may take us awhile to get used to hugging — in New York when somebody puts their arms around you they're after your wallet."[8]

Steve Smith expresses the importance of the greeting ritual to the Escapees' sense of community in the following letter. It originally was a response to complaints about the organization's dues. People suggested that he write it up as a letter, and he did. The letter became a classic and has been reprinted several times. Now, when someone does something nice for a person, the recipient of the favor often says, "I just got my $40 back." Sometimes the *favor giver* says it. Judy Stringer, who was director of CARE when we met her in 1993, told us about this letter and found a copy of it for us. Her eyes got moist as she talked about it. Steve is dead now, and Judy said that she wept and wept when she heard of his death.

Each year we pay dues but what do they buy? They buy the Newsletter and that's all, except:
  • In 1984 we came to Rainbow's End to see the lot we had bought. There were six rigs there. We had electricity, but no

water or sewer. We spent the days laying water and electric lines for the campground. We spent the evenings in fellowship. After five days, we had to return to California and work. In those five days I got my forty dollars back.

• In 1986 I was at Rainbow's End clearing my lot. Verna was still in Calif. One day I came back to the motor home tired, dirty, and hungry. There on the table was a big piece of chocolate cake. One of the ladies had baked a cake and left a piece for me. She gave me my forty dollars back.

• That summer we were at Acadia NP in Maine. As we returned from a walk someone shouted "Hey, SKPs, it is happy hour!" The time spent with those three SKP couples, caravanning to Canada, gave us our forty dollars back.

• On a trip west we stopped at the Ranch in Lakewood, NM for a couple of days. Verna ended up in the hospital for three days. Our "couple of days" turned into ten days. Every day for ten days I got my forty dollars back.

• A couple of weeks before Thanksgiving I was at the clubhouse and Mirth Banta shouted my name. She gave me a big smile, a big hello, a big hug, and my forty dollars back.

• A few nights ago after happy hour someone said "Hey, Steve" and a woman gave me a hug. While I was wondering "who is this?" her husband came up. It was Tom and Lois Yingling, giving me my forty dollars back.

• Again last night at happy hour Harley and Phyllis Jackson gave me my forty dollars back.

• Your dues don't put food on the table, fuel in your tank, or money in your pocket. Those dues buy you the privilege of being with the greatest group of people in the world. Next time you see an Escapee, give him or her a big smile and a big hug, and you'll give them their forty dollars back. And you'll get your forty dollars back, too.[9]

In a lighter vein, another Skip recommends hugging as economically practical, environmentally friendly, and healthy.[10]

Hugging is practically perfect: No movable parts, no batteries to wear out, no periodic checkups, low energy consumption, high energy yield, inflation-proof, non-fattening, no monthly payments, no insurance requirements, theft proof, non-taxable, non-polluting, and, of course, fully returnable. Hugging is

Hugging is economically practical, environmentally friendly, and healthy

healthy: it relieves tension, combats depression, reduces stress, improves blood circulation, it is invigorating, it is rejuvenating, it elevates self-esteem, it generates good will, it has no unpleasant side effects, and it is nothing less than a miracle drug!

Although for some Escapees, hugging is "practically perfect," others are uncomfortable with it. In an editorial Kay Peterson recognizes their discomfort, observing that people are different and do not respond the same to the practice of hugging. In explaining how the practice began, Peterson gives the history of hugging using the metaphor of family. She then offers practical advice for those who do not wish to hug.

The practice of "hugging" began at our first Escapade when 23 families who were total strangers met for a 4-day rally. By the end of the rally we were close friends. It was natural to hug as we promised to "see you next year."

When we met again at the next Escapade, we hugged each other. But new faces greeted us too. It wasn't planned — it was just a natural extension of that joy of reunion that made us turn to the new SKPs and include them in the hugging.

After all, one usually hugs new relatives even when meeting for the first time. We believed that we were part of a "family" — the SKP family. New SKPs or those who have had no prior exposure to the "family feeling" that develops between SKPs at rallies and through communal living (at Co-Ops and Retreats) may not understand that.

Some people only hug blood relatives and special friends and feel that hugging strangers is phony, she continues. It detracts from the specialness of hugging to treat everybody the same, they say. Some people don't like it, are embarrassed to say so, and therefore avoid rallies. What, then, are Skips to do? "It comes back to the SKP philosophy: *Never impose your personal preference on another*," she says. Reluctant people can avoid hugs by staying in their rig when they meet people and offering to shake hands instead. They can step back when somebody tries to hug them while extending their hand. Or they can get a badge addition that says "I'm not a hugger." Finally, "When in doubt, don't hug."[11]

In response to the editorial, Louise Pike wrote that she was sorry Kay felt that she had to write it because the hug is unique. She continues:

> I've always felt the SKP Club was built on LOVE and CARING and the greeting was a *smile* and a big *HUG*. Now I find myself saying "Can I hug you?"
>
> SKPs are my family now. I need and care about them. I hope the hugging custom never stops. That's what makes us different from ALL other clubs. Let's keep this spirit going. Don't let a few spoil these things for the majority of us.

As the club has grown, the reluctance of Escapees to hug strangers has also grown. Some Skips told us of knocking on a rig displaying the Escapees logo expecting to give and receive hugs only to be rudely turned away. Sometimes the rig owner had bought the vehicle with the logo in place without knowing its significance. Others had joined the club solely to take advantage of its inexpensive parks. We were rebuffed by a couple who did not hug. They informed us that the organization membership was in the tens of thousands and they had no intention of trying to hug them all. The Gibbs had a similar experience. They write as follows:

> Many times this past winter in Florida, we have seen SKP stickers and gone to the door to meet "our family" only to get a negative response. (No hug.) One SKP told me he didn't have "junk mail" forwarded so he hadn't seen an Escapee newsletter. Why are they joining the Club if they don't want to enter into the fellowship of our caring family? Is it only to belong to a Co-Op so they can get cheap rent? Maybe if some of them stay in long enough, real SKPs can melt their reserves — if we don't get tired of trying![12]

Rebuffs have led some Escapees to question the organization's policy of actively recruiting new members. These disgruntled members want to discontinue the inclusive policy of the organization. We discuss the issue later in this chapter.

Metaphors of community: They're my family now

> Skips is family. If your husband gets ill, people will come right away to give support. That's family. (A full-timer, from our 1993 journal)
>
> * * *
>
> The SKP family is best thought of as siblings — not parents or children. What's at issue is that people help and care for each other. (A full-timer, from our 1993 journal)
>
> * * *
>
> What a wonderful world this is with our SKP friends. We call them our new family.[13]

In the above comments and throughout earlier chapters, RVers frequently use the metaphor of family to describe their feeling of community. To describe the "family feeling," they use words such as "friendship," "love," "trust," and "caring" and recount times when other RVers helped and supported them in crisis. Some, like Polly Neuhaus, use sibling terms to describe their relationship with other RVers. A fellow Skip helped her when she was in hospital. She says of her friend, "I could not have received better or more loving care from my family and take her as my 'chosen' sister." Judy Parrack, who was widowed in 1988, describes a similar experience. Her letter is an eloquent testament to the community feeling among Escapees. She says: "Family was with me for a week after Ernie died, but it is the continuing support of my SKP Family who write and drop by to visit that keeps me going. I don't think I'd have made it without SKPS! You'll never know now grateful I am."[14]

The founders of Escapees self-consciously used the metaphor of family to describe and shape the relationships they hoped to foster among members of the club. Kay Peterson says:

> Our main goal has always been to unite SKPs into an RV "family" that cares about each other. Chapters, Co-Ops, and BOF groups provide a close "family feeling" in the same way that it works with any large family. The family unit consisting of parents and children is closer than the extended family that includes aunts,

uncles, and cousins. Yet when the small units come together, they are all part of the larger family unit.[15]

Escapees achieve the "family feeling" through the act of sharing. The Petersons explicitly encourage club members to share with one another *in order to* become like family. They say:

> *Sharing* is the key to all phases of the Escapees Parks from SKP Co-Ops to Retreats to the new combination concept. Therefore, it isn't surprising to find the members also share rides to town for doing laundry, going shopping, and for social events. They are [a] tight-knit group who think of themselves as *"family."* Because of this, those who are in the park keep a watchful eye over a travelling member's property.
>
> Even more important than the feeling of security for *things* is the knowledge that there is someone there to help you when you need it. There is, for example, special concern shown if someone fails to appear at an expected time. A neighbor will knock on the door to make sure everything is all right. Having neighbors who know and care about you, and who will be there to help you if you are sick, is reminiscent of the old village life that in most places has been replaced with a mind-your-own-business attitude.[16]

There is no doubt that RVers are sincere when they say, "they're my family," to describe their feelings toward their fellows. What do they mean by these words? What *exactly* are they saying when they assert that an organization of RVers is their family now?

Their comments may reflect the North American ideal of family and friendship. As Stephanie Coontz argues in *The Way We Never Were*, the ideals exemplified by Beaver Cleaver's family never were reality. They were not the typical American family. However, people were raised with this myth and want to believe that sometime in the past this ideal existed, even though it was not part of their experience. Coontz argues that the family ideal has become the metaphor for evaluating relationships, including relationships of responsibility for others. The family has become a model for public life:

> When family relations become "our only model for defining what emotionally 'real' relationships are like," we can empathize and interact only with people whom we can imagine as potential

lovers or family members. The choice becomes either a personal relationship or none, a familial intimacy or complete alienation.[17]

Consequently there is no language for speaking of public responsibility. Instead "community" refers to our identification with others like ourselves rather than an association of a variety of people. Rather than bringing together people with different motives to achieve common goals, we have "lifestyle enclaves" of people who construct personal (not public) relationships based on leisure and consumption. People who are different are suspect and there is an effort to exclude them from "the family circle." Using family as a model for public life results in a definition of community that is unrealistic, possibly even destructive, because people want to share family-type, personal feelings inappropriately.

The use of the metaphor of family to describe their relationships with other RVers does not reflect wide-spread isolation from family members. Recall that in Chapter Five we reported that two-thirds of the RVers in our study said they see their children twice a year or more. Further, only 9 per cent said the thing they missed most when they were full-timing was frequent contact with their children and grandchildren. Most RVers seem to be satisfied with the connection they maintain with their relatives. Similarly, their words do not necessarily signal that they were isolated from their families before they became RVers, or that their relationships are shallow. Rather, if Coontz and Bellah and his associates are correct, their words suggest that they look for in strangers the warm, supportive bonds symbolized by the family. The relationships that nomadic RVers create may seem to be more ideal than the reality ever was *because* they are short term and focused on mutual help in crisis rather than on tedious, day-to-day problems. Escapees may especially have ideal expectations because of their emphasis on mutual help and their ethos of sharing and caring.

Community and reciprocity

Marshall Sahlins, in exploring the idea of reciprocity as social exchange, distinguishes what he calls "generalized reciprocity" from other kinds of interchange. Generalized reciprocity exists between persons who have a close personal relationship (family, for instance) and keep no accounting of the favors they bestow on each other. They assume that eventually the person they have helped will reciprocate — or that someone else will do it in their place. There is no *quid pro quo* — no bargaining, no "if you do this for me, I'll do that for you" — between those linked by generalized reciprocity.[18] It

RVers create community by sharing food: Thanksgiving dinner at Rainbow's End

is found in the Good Sam Club's call to be a "good Samaritan." It is implicit when Skips say they regard their fellows as "extended family." However it is communicated, helping one another because the need is there is a key value for RVers. Ruth Dalgleish makes that point in the quote at the beginning of this chapter.

Kay Peterson compares the emphasis on mutual aid promoted by Escapees to the way people in remote areas, whose lives may depend on reciprocity, give help when it is needed. In the Australian outback or on the Alaska highway, people follow the unwritten rule of indirect reciprocity.

> You don't drive past someone who looks as if they need help....
> I must help you today because tomorrow I may need someone's help.... Maybe it is something as simple as bringing a bowl of soup to a sick neighbor. Maybe it's taking care of a dog while it's [sic] owner attends to some emergency. And maybe it's towing a widow's trailer a thousand miles. SKPs do whatever has to be done.[19]

The ethos of reciprocal help is especially important when RVers gather in a place like the Slabs where there are few amenities and life is hard. In spite of the hardships RVers endure there — or perhaps *because* of them — many people return year after year for the sense of community they experience.

> "The Slabs" is the annual winter nesting grounds for RVers....
> RVers started parking there and soon they'd turned it into
> a beautiful community. Beautiful because the people live in
> harmony with nature and with each other. There are no frills.
> No electricity except what you make yourself from the sun or
> with your generator. No water except what the people carry in
> themselves. And no trash — because the people carry that out
> with them. Beautiful because the people have both a hands off
> and a hands on understanding. The "hands off" is that everyone
> minds their own business; the "hands on" is that if your neighbor
> needs help, you drop everything and turn to. Next time it may
> be *you* who needs help.[20]

Reciprocity between equals is a key value for RVers.[21] They become
aroused if someone violates the principle in a way that suggests they are
inferior. They accept with gratitude help given in time of crisis, but they
are also enriched by the opportunity to help. As Myerhoff notes among the
people of the Aliyah Senior Citizens' Center, it is necessary to one's sense of
self respect to be a giver as well as a taker.[22] Reciprocity is pervasive among
RVers and is expressed in many different contexts: when RVers give and
receive food, goods, and help; when they exchange information; when they
provide help to others expecting that someone will help them someday; and
when they assist anthropologists with their research.

The Good Sam Club, the largest and most influential RV club in North
America, was founded on the assumption that an RVer in trouble can safely
call on other RVers for help. The organization was begun by people who
agreed to carry a sticker on their car or RV. The sticker identifies the bearers
as club members who are willing to stop and help others and to accept the
help of others also carrying the decal. Today most of the RVs we see on the
road carry the emblem, which portrays a smiling face with a halo. Joens
says, "We are not ashamed to ask for or to give help to a fellow trailerist,
camper or what-have-you, because of a predicament he or we may be in....
[I]n my years of trailering, I have yet to find an unfriendly trailering family."[23]
Trust and reciprocity are essential to the success of the enterprise. In spite
of the pervasive fear of violence from strangers, from "the crazies out there,"
Good Sam members assume that they can trust and expect reciprocity rather
than violence from one another. Other RVers make the same assumption.
Our informants repeatedly advised us to seek out other RVers in rest areas
and truck stops for mutual security. They warned us that in isolated areas
we should park beside other RVers so that we could look out for each other.
RVers create trust and reciprocity in a number of ways.

Shared food and reciprocity

> Food is life-giving, urgent, ordinarily symbolic of hearth and home.... Food dealings are ... a ritual statement ... of social relations, and food is thus employed instrumentally as a starting, a sustaining, or a destroying mechanism of sociability.... About the only sociable thing to do with food is to give it away, and the commensurably sociable return ... is the return of hospitality or assistance.... Food has too much social value ... to have exchange value.[24]

If Marshall Sahlins had known about RVers when he wrote those words, he might have added, "The least important thing an RVer can do with food is to eat it alone." He might also point out that Karen, Annemarie, and Karl (see sidebars) recognize that food sharing involves more than just eating a meal together. It is a sacred act that fundamentally changes the relationship between the participants. In other cultures shared food becomes part of the recipient's *person*, establishing ties of shared substance as well as sociality. Feeding someone is often a way of becoming kin to them. People who share food are, by the very act of sharing, establishing and expressing a relationship of trust and mutual aid. This was the case among the Lusi-Kaliai with whom we did research in Papua New Guinea. Kaliai *never* accept food from untrustworthy persons or from those they do not know well.[25] Karen, Annemarie, and Karl suggest that the same thing happens among RVers. People who share food share essence and thus become family.

"Eating together is a sacred thing," Annemarie said, "like the Last Supper." (From our 1993 journal)

* * *

Karen said that people offer food when you come into a park because "it becomes part of you; it becomes part of yourself." (From our 1993 journal)

* * *

Karl said, "I'm not big on eating stuff made by people I don't know, but it doesn't take long to get to know these people and then it's ok." (From our 1990 journal)

It is the little gifts, given spontaneously for no special reason, that touch our hearts the most. We have two friends who mix up an extra batch of dough when they bake bread so they can give the extra loaf to someone as a way of saying, "I am your friend." (Kay Peterson 1995 [November/December]:2)

RVers exchange and share food both formally — during food-sharing rituals such as pot luck dinners — and informally. Eating together is an integral and ubiquitous part of RV life, as the description of happy hour announcements from our 1993 journal illustrates.

> First there was a set of announcements, most having to do with food: finger foods after Happy Hour; Thanksgiving dinner arrangements; a fund raising multi-ethnic dinner (Lasagna, Greek salad, French bread) for CARE on Thursday night instead of the usual group dining out at a local restaurant; a pot luck on Saturday because the CARE dinner will cost money, and

folks who can't afford to buy a meal should not lose out on the opportunity to eat together. We introduced ourselves and talked about our project and we were warmly received. The emcee told us that SKPs love to work their jaw muscles, either talking or eating. If you see a bunch of SKPs together they'll be doing one or the other, and maybe both, he said. He also noted that most of the announcements focused on events of eating together.

The most common food-sharing ritual among RVers is the pot-luck dinner. Pot-luck dinners are a regular event at RV resort parks, at many state parks during the winter, in boondocking areas, and at RV parks of all sorts at Thanksgiving and Christmas. RVers who are away from their families during the holidays may pool their funds to buy a turkey and share a holiday meal. Some RVers travel year after year to the same park where they meet friends to share Christmas or Thanksgiving dinner. Finally, any important celebration — such as a wedding — includes a pot-luck dinner.

Ice cream social at the ranch

Newcomers join the community by participating in ritual food-sharing. Among boondockers especially, food sharing permits the redistribution of an essential resource without challenging the egalitarian ideal that "We're all the same here."

Our introduction into the community through food-sharing in December of 1990 is a good example of how the system works. We pulled into an LTVA boondocking area only two hours before a wedding was to be held. Before we had unhooked our trailer, residents invited us to take part in the festivities. Because we had just arrived they did not expect us to prepare anything elaborate. "Just bring something if you can," they said.

We put on a breakfast every other Saturday. We have either a pancake-and-sausage breakfast or biscuits and gravy. Our frequent Sunday afternoon ice cream socials also draw good crowds. Most of us here believe that, if the Lord had meant all of us to be skinny, He wouldn't have made skin that stretches! (Description of KOFA Co-op, *Escapees Directory* 1994a:36)

We made a small salad and took photographs of the ceremony. We gave copies of the wedding pictures as our gift to the bride and groom. The following day our neighbors began to include us in other LTVA activities. They invited us to join campfire song fests, to help clean the hot spring where people bathed and relaxed, to join walks, and to go on a weekend trip to Las Vegas. Our neighbors also gave us gifts of fruits and vegetables they brought back from gleaning expeditions to large farms. Our participation in the wedding brought us into the community circle. Membership in the community was not short-lived, either. Though we spent only a little over a week there in 1990, when we returned to the same area in 1993, people we had met three years earlier greeted us (and Kynon) with hugs. They directed us where to park, included us in the distributions of gleaned food, and looked after Kynon and our trailer while we went to anthropology meetings in San Diego. It was as though no time had passed. The feeling of community was so strong that we trusted them to do precisely what they said they would do: care for our trailer, our field notes, and our dog.

Wedding at the Hot Spring.

RVers also create community by sharing activities — work as well as play. They play games of all kinds — from bridge to bingo to washer toss. People gather to learn line dancing and square dancing. They meet to share knowledge — how to use computers, how to do crafts. They volunteer to build and maintain their parks, organize holiday feasts, and clean park trails and buildings. Volunteers show up at the LTVA's Hot Spring each Monday morning through the winter to clean and disinfect it. Those same volunteers built the LTVA's pools and shower. Escapees particularly emphasize volunteer participation as a way of keeping costs down and, more important, of bringing potential strangers into the community. Recall Cathie Carr's promise, "The best way to break the ice is to volunteer to help. Inclusion is a guaranteed result." Volunteers are assured that they will have fun, enjoy camaraderie, and make lasting friendships as well.[26]

Whether they join a park-based community or a community of boondockers, RVers usually enter a clearly visible society with its structure in place. They participate for as long as they remain, but when they move on the community continues to exist. Sometimes, however, RVers create a contingent society which disappears when they do. An example of a contingent community is the rally.

Johnny Golby, who looked after our trailer, our field notes, and our dog

Rvers create community by working together. Volunteers build Escapee parks

Contingent Community: The Rally

When newcomers join a park-based community, park officials formally tell them the rules and customs. A boondocker community socializes the new entrant in a more informal way, but in both cases a community structure already exists. In contrast, the structure of a rally pre-exists only in the minds of the organizers. As the name implies, the purpose of a rally is to revitalize the spirit of the group that comes together. Rallies are organized according to some common principle. For example, rally members may all own the same brand of RV, or the same type of RV. They may belong to a club such as Escapees or Loners on Wheels. Most RV organizations have rallies occasionally. The scale of such gatherings varies widely. They may be small and informal: five or six Escapee rigs meeting in the desert for the Thanksgiving weekend. They may be large: an international rally of the Good Sam Club or the Family Motor Coach Association where thousands gather for several days of activities. Rally communities are unique in several ways. First, the participants have some common interest. Second, organizers choose the place for the rally for that purpose alone. Third, except for the organizers, everyone arrives at the same predetermined time, so all are equally newcomers. Therefore, participants must create a rally community on the spot. As with traditional nomads, the rally participants (especially the sponsors) carry a template of organization with them and reconstruct it each time they gather.

Rallies are never completely spontaneous. Even a small one must be announced, and notice of its date and location passed along an information network to potential participants. An announcement may be as simple

The covered area where ralliers played games and shared meals

as a couple writing in their club newsletter that they will be in Why, Arizona, on a particular date and will act as rally hosts. A later newsletter informs members who was there, what they did, and why others should have come.

Rally recruitment may be entirely informal. For instance, in mid-February 1994, David went into Holtville, California, near the Hot Spring LTVA to fill our water containers. While he was at the public dump station and water tap, a rig with an Escapees sticker pulled in. David acknowledged our common membership in SKPs with a wave. The woman of the couple immediately came over, gave him a hug, introduced herself, and asked if we were going to the rally. "What rally?" David asked. After chiding him for not reading his club handbook, she said that the Yuma chapter of the club was having a three-day rally nearby in the desert, starting that afternoon. David went back to the LTVA, and we hitched up and went rallying.

About half of the 35 rigs attending belonged to members of the Yuma chapter. Others learned of it through the newsletter or by being at a dump station at the right time. The setting was on US government land on a flat stretch of desert on the border between California and Arizona. The organizers, who arrived first, set up the covered area

At about 10 a.m. people collected under the shelter made by drawing three rigs in a U, opening their awnings, and putting up a tarp over the open space. Rugs and astro-turf on the ground make a floor. Women were stringing beads to make boot bracelets and hat bands and comparing notes on ways to braid or knot the strings. One woman showed me a bag of 1000 beads that she bought for $2.50. Others had several bags of beads, and were swapping them to complete patterns they had started. One woman had a large tackle box full of beads, conchos, and leather or other strings. There were about a dozen women either making things, giving instructions, showing the bands/bracelets/necklaces that they had made and used to display SKP badges, or just watching. Other people were playing games. There were two tables of rummy going, and people played Mexican Train until almost midnight last night. (From our 1994 journal)

Yuma rally washer toss

where ralliers would play games and share meals. Participants brought their own chairs there or to the campfire circle where people gathered around the fire for evening sing-alongs or conversation. The atmosphere was relaxed, but usually some organized activity was going on: a car rodeo, a "washer toss" elimination tournament, or musical performance. While none of the games engaged all the participants, almost everyone was either a participant or a cheering spectator. No one took the competition seriously.

Some of the rally's participants were lease holders at the nearby Escapees co-op where they had a winter home base. These folks said they were "on vacation" from their normal life routine. They had gone camping. They also were enjoying "time out" from the tensions the close living and cooperative self-government of their park generated.

After three days of games and fellowship, the rally ended with a "hitch-up pancake breakfast" on the morning of the fourth day. Travelers went their different ways while the co-op members turned their camping rigs back into their homes. The rally had provided an opportunity for people enmeshed in tensions created by semi-permanent RV living to put aside their differences, and for strangers to become friends. For example, we first met the Kents at this rally. We later met them again at another, much larger, rally. There we arranged to meet them months later to spend several days at their favorite boondocking spot in British Columbia.

One of the lot holders commented that he'd been at the park a long time and that it had not turned out like the founders had hoped. There is a lot of "bickering and squabbling" among the lot holders, but all that stops when they get out here. People who never talk to each other at the co-op are singing, dancing, and playing games together. But, they'll be back at it when they get back to the park, he said. (From our 1994 journal)

The conversion of strangers into friends is an important and ongoing part of being on the road.

Rallying provides this opportunity, but with added intensity because so many are strangers together. Also, like other nomads' camps, it is a transitory phenomenon. In an established area where RVers come and go, there is a continuous renewal of community and less urgency to form relationships quickly. The rally opens only a small window, and when it closes, the opportunity is gone. When the Yuma rally was over, nothing remained but ashes in the firepit and tire tracks the first strong wind would erase.

Notes

1. Bender 1978:8.

2. Carr 1993a:5.

3. Porter and Porter 1991:13.

4. Bender 1978:6.

5. *Happy Trails*, words and music by Dale Evans, Copyright 1951 and 1952 by Paramount-Roy Rogers Music Company, Inc. (quoted by permission).

6. Courtney 1991:76.

7. Peters 1986:15.

8. Peeples and Peeples 1989:42.

9. Smith 1991:19.

10. Morton 1986:37.

11. Peterson, K. 1985:2. Pike's letter in response is on page 12 of the same issue of the *Newsletter*.

12. Gibb and Gibb 1987:31.

13. Henley and Henley 1987:32.

14. Citations are from Neuhaus 1986:26 and Parrack 1988:41.

15. Peterson, K. 1986a:3.

16. Peterson and Peterson 1991:56-57.

17. Coontz 1992:115. The term "lifestyle enclaves" in the next paragraph was used by sociologist Robert Bellah and his collaborators in *Habits of the Heart*.

18. Sahlins 1972a.

19. Peterson, K. 1989 (March/April):3.

20. *Escapees Newsletter* 1987:44.

21. For a discussion of the principle of reciprocity, see Sahlins 1972. Our discussion of key principles is based on Ortner's analysis of the characteristics of key symbols. See Ortner 1973:1339.

22. Myerhoff 1978:141.

23. Joens 1991:4.

24. Sahlins 1972a:215, 217-218.

25. In Lusi-Kaliai society prospective adoptive parents give foods that nurture the fetus to a pregnant woman whose child they plan to adopt. After the child's birth they give the mother foods that will produce milk. As soon as the child can eat solid foods they are responsible for its feeding. To give food is to share substance. Those who garden, fish, hunt, and cook spend body essence (sweat) to produce food that becomes part of the child. In this way, adoptive parents create *biological* kinship with their child. See Counts and Counts 1983.

26. *Escapees Newsletter* 1991:6.

Chapter Nine

Hanging Up the Keys

To every thing there is a season, and a time to every purpose under the heaven.
(Ecclesiastes 3:1)

In Chapter Eight we investigated the ways in which nomadic RVers create and maintain community. In this chapter we examine how they and the communities they create change as they move through the life cycle. We also see how RV communities include RVers who are no longer traveling and allow them to preserve their freedom and independence. There are many options for RVers who hang up their keys. We concentrate on the Escapees Care center, but there are others that also permit RVers who cannot travel to stay in the RVing community. Many do not stay, however. Some leave altogether. They throw their keys away and may, like Tonia Thorson, regret their choice. Others never leave. They take their keys with them, or at least engrave their identity as RVers on their headstones.

The RVing Life Cycle

As our account of the Yuma rally suggests, RVing communities may experience destructive discord and controversy. Illa Alfredson described the problem this way:

> Community is certainly a word that applies to the SKP Co-Ops. Sometimes a community is made up of all one race, or all one occupation, or all one belief, but SKP Co-Op members come in all sizes. We arrive from everywhere, having retired (mostly) from a great variety of jobs, and having all had very individualistic life experiences.

Usually, when we buy into a SKP Co-Op, we have a feeling we want to live *there* with *those* people in *that* community, but those feelings do not always last.

Why?

Well, I think we get disillusioned and, sometimes, bitter. Not all of us want to blend in a community in spite of the "sharing/caring" words we have avowed. Many of us are still "rulers," and we think we know best (about most anything). We are not ready for a peaceful co-existence.... Couldn't we approach living in a SKP Co-Op with understanding and appreciation of our differences? Couldn't we approach this with a sense of community?... When we live in a SKP Co-Op, we are part of something bigger than ourselves. We need to think about that sense of community. We need to realize that ours is a new, different lifestyle. We need to apply new understandings to it so it will last.[1]

Alfredson describes a phenomenon that often occurs when serious RVers enter the second, less nomadic stage of the RVing life cycle. When they find a home base they may become part of a park community that is bedeviled by strife as well as being blessed by mutual support and friendship. We will briefly discuss the first, nomadic stage of the RVing life cycle. Then we look at the problems and benefits associated with the second stage, when RVers settle into a home base.

The first stage: Being on the road

The first stage of the life cycle, the years when people are on the road, is a time of intensive travel and discovery. The activities the Kents describe in their letter quoted in Chapter Six are typical for serious RVers early in their life cycle. They spent the winter caravanning to Mexico. In the spring they boondocked in the desert, visited relatives, toured, and attended an Escapade. During the summer and fall they returned to their home province where they toured and visited friends and children. They made brief trips out of province to attend rallies, and spent time solving problems caused by storm damage to their rig. When it started to snow they headed to the US southwest with plans to return to Mexico in December. The motto of these years might be "Home is where I turn off my key." People in the nomadic stage of their life cycle rarely get involved in bitter controversy. When things become unpleasant they turn on the key and are gone. The Kents' travels, while not random — they must plan to attend the rallies — are flexible. Others start out with a clear goal and plan their travel accordingly. Some trace their genealogy; others intend to visit all the US states and Canadian provinces. Still others are history buffs and develop their schedule around research or visits to Civil or Revolutionary War sites. Pat and Newell Kring's tour is an example of a planned itinerary with a goal:

> Pat retires in February. In April they will start a two-year trek across North America. They will leave California with friends and spend two months reaching Washington, DC. There they will spend two months in membership parks around the Washington area. They have reservations at each park for one or two weeks. They are going there for the national Samboree and to do research at the Smithsonian Institute, Newell on Civil and Revolutionary War history, Pat on family genealogies. Newell also wants to visit all the museums, art galleries, memorials, and other things of interest in the area. Then they will go to New York where they both will do research. They also plan to visit Civil War and Revolutionary War battlefields and cemeteries where members of their families are buried. (From our 1990 journal)

The second stage: Finding a home base

As RVers age and become less capable or desirous of continual travel they enter the second stage in the RVing life cycle. They spend more time in one spot, perhaps moving seasonally between a home in the north and a mobile home in the sun belt. Others buy or lease a park lot for a home base.

RV parks meet the need of aging RVers for a home base in a variety of ways. In the process, RV parks also move through a life cycle. Although some are established to accommodate people who spend little time traveling, others enter this stage as they age with their clientele. They respond to the needs of their visitors who return year after year and stay longer and longer. These parks start by giving residents favorable seasonal rates for longer stays. Then they allow residents to lease a lot by the year and leave their rig there, skirted in. Although these parks may reserve sites for travelers, they are characterized by permanently skirted-in rigs, attached sheds and decks, landscaped lots with permanent structures, and park-model trailers.

Apache Junction Park was well along in its life cycle when we spent a week there in 1990. While the park's owner was still accepting some

Home base in an Escapees park

overnight and short-term guests, many of the rigs were skirted in. While the residents may once have been RVers, they could have resumed a traveling life only with difficulty. Most of the residents were seasonal occupants, winter visitors who no longer towed their rigs. Some had park model trailers on lots they leased on an annual basis. Many residents had added permanent awnings to cover their concrete patios. Others had built storage sheds or had covered up their hitches and used the covering for a platform for rock gardens or other decorative effects. Some owners occupied their rigs year-round.

Skirted in and with an attached, screened-in porch, this trailer will never go on the road again

According to one manager, the park was becoming more like a mobile home park or a settled neighborhood. As this occurs, he said, the club house will become less important as a focus for activities, and people will go to it less for interaction. In 10 years no one will use it, he said. This manager was the first to alert us to an RVing cycle in which people are on the move as full-timers only for a year or two. Then they spend several months in one place, and finally they skirt-in.

In contrast, Murray, the owner of Point of Rocks Park in Prescott, Arizona, said that when he first took over the park many people were permanent residents. Because they were ill or disabled, they could no longer pull their rigs, and they had nowhere else to go. Although he did not want his to be a park with permanent residents, he did not have the heart to turn them out. So he let them stay. One by one, they grew older and entered nursing homes or catered-care facilities. He did not allow others to replace those who left. Consequently his park was in the process of reversing the typical park life cycle and becoming one that catered only to traveling RVers.

The Escapees club began its co-op parks so it could meet the needs of members who wanted a home base and still provide inexpensive parking for traveling members. Because Skips are committed to travel, the Petersons assumed that lot-holders would occupy their spaces for only a few months each year. The rest of the time the lots would go into a rental pool and become available for short-term rent to traveling Skips.

Although the idea was to meet both needs by having a rental pool made up of lots whose owners were on the road, the same thing that happened to the Apache Junction Park has affected the co-op parks. Over time, co-op members use their home bases for longer periods. Some want to travel less, while others put park models on their lots and travel in smaller RVs. The result is that fewer lots are available in the rental pool for nomadic members, who are frustrated because the system does not meet their need for inexpensive places to stay. While we visited only one co-op that was far advanced into the change from travelers' park to park for semi-sedentary residents, we could see the process underway at all the co-ops where we stayed.

In response to life cycle changes, Escapees Club officers decided to move from sponsoring more co-ops to creating Rainbow Retreat parks. These parks reserve a core of rental and boondocking sites for nomads. They also permit members wanting a home base to buy a lot where they can build a roofed shelter over their RV. The advantage to less mobile members is two-fold. First, when they want to travel they have only to drive their rig out from under the shelter. This gives them "both mobility and permanence

In some SKP parks, members can build a roofed shelter over their RV

without having to own both an RV and a house." Second, their property is secure while they are gone. As the Petersons put it:

> When they leave their home base behind, they know that their neighbors are going to watch over it for them because this is a mutual exchange. And when the day comes that they have to hang up their keys, they have an established and comfortable place to settle down among good friends made over the years.[2]

The Petersons highlight a problem that all serious and full-time RVers must eventually face. What do they do when they can no longer travel? Escapees co-op and retreat parks provide one set of options. About one-third of our questionnaire respondents said that they would move into an Escapees or other RV park when they had to leave the road. People choose this option for several reasons. For example, Bill and Brenda, who began full-timing less than a year before we met them in 1994, have their names on two co-op waiting lists. They say it may take years before their number comes up, but "it doesn't cost much to put your name on the list." They have applied now, even though they are still traveling, because they want to have a home base where they can store her dining-room set and his boat. When will they quit RVing? Brenda says "I want to do it forever. I have everything I want that I can live with. I have my crafts, I have my computer (she has a notebook with a color screen), I'm happy with what I have." She would like a mobile home on a home base someday. Her mother, sisters, daughter, and grandchildren could visit her there.

Others, like Joy, join a co-op for its feeling of community. The contrast between life on the road and life in a co-op, Joy says, is that the park is "more like a village." The longer she stays in the park the more involved in community life she becomes. She and her husband stopped full-timing to help build the park where they live. Now she is on the board of directors and her responsibilities do not allow them to take long trips, even if they could afford to. They are no longer "heavy travelers" because gas is too expensive and their truck is too old to pull their rig over the passes.

Most Escapees looking for a home base choose between a co-op and a retreat (see the Glossary for an explanation of the difference between SKP retreat parks and co-ops). However, some Skips own lots in both and travel between them. People choose to buy into an Escapees park for many reasons: they are joining friends there; they want a place where they can safely store heirlooms; the park gives them an inexpensive site in an area where they want to spend several months at a time; or they are preparing for the time when health or age prohibits extensive travel. This is the situation of Buck and Crystal Alder, who are in their 70s. We met them briefly in Chapters Five, Six, and Seven. They have been full-timers for years. By 1993 he had suffered several strokes so they spend most of their time at their home base in a co-op park.

Buck and Crystal Alder

The Alders had been full-timers for nearly nine years when we met them in November of 1993. Though they describe themselves as full-timers, that is true now only in a limited sense. They have had their lot in the co-op since 1985 and say that their experience there is typical. They came in planning to stay three or four days, "fell in love with the people," and stayed a month. When they left they had their names down for a lot. They are socially active. On the day we interviewed them, they took their neighbor out to find Pecos diamonds — crystal formations — in the nearby hills, and they had ten visitors, including some who stayed for lunch. Buck considers the people here to be "like my brothers and sisters." He added "If you don't have family around, you have to have friends." When they lived in Denver, they knew few of their neighbors. "Here we know doggone near everybody."

They began RVing because they knew too many people who retired and were dead in a few months. Before they began full-timing in 1985 they were collectors of heirloom furniture and antiques. They stored their treasures with friends for four years. Finally they decided that they'd never move back into a house. So they rented a utility trailer, loaded their furniture in it, went the rounds of their kids' houses telling them to take what they wanted, and sold the rest. When they finished, the trailer was empty. "One of the hardest things was giving up our antiques," said Crystal. Buck added, "Now that they're out of our lives, it doesn't bother me." Crystal agreed, "Yes the kids have them, so it's ok." Buck said that after they had sold everything "I looked in the rear-view mirror and thought, 'Everything I own I'm pulling behind me.' It scared me to death."

The attraction of full-timing for Crystal is "Less housework." With eight kids they had huge houses, and she spent too much of her life cleaning them. She doesn't have to do that now. Buck's response: "We can live comfortably within our means." They could not have afforded the taxes and maintenance costs on their house in Denver on their retirement income. "This is the only lifestyle we could afford and be happy in," he said. He added that in RV parks that are run for profit, "We're out of our class, socially and economically." Crystal agreed: "They do things we couldn't afford to do. In this organization it doesn't matter if you have a lot of money. Some people here are comfortably well off, but it doesn't matter because everybody lives the same way here."

Buck restricts his RVing to short trips now because of the after-effects of his stroke. They cannot bear to give up their association with other RVers and their involvement in the way of life. Buck is convinced "the RV lifestyle extends your life because you have something to do." His stroke has led them to think about the possibility that someday they will be unable to live in their trailer, just as they are now unable to travel as they did. Crystal says that they would probably do what some friends in a similar situation are doing: buy a lot in a nearby town and put a mobile home on it. Buck added, "I'm not looking forward to that time. I'm afraid of it." He said this several times.

The "wrong kind of people"

Not all Skips have a "children of the rainbow" experience like the one described by Helen Peters in Chapter Eight. Instead, they arrive at an Escapees park, and nobody rings the bell or gives them a hug. When this happens Skips are disappointed, for "this is not the SKP way." They feel cheated, angry, and unwelcome and write indignant letters to the club's newsletter. Why does this happen? Why do some parks fail to welcome their guests as they are supposed to? Skips offer several explanations. One is that, as the club advertises and gets new members, people who join for the "wrong reasons" do not behave like proper Skips. The Hazzards explain the problem as follows:

It is easy to encourage people to join us for the wrong reasons — i.e., "Join SKPs and you can buy a lot in a Co-Op cheaper than you can rent or purchase elsewhere." Better to get members who want to join because we are a group of helpful, sincere camping enthusiasts. Yes — there is room for everyone — we just make the circle bigger. But in widening it, we must keep the feeling of "family" and not let growth destroy the positive goals our founders believe in.[3]

Another explanation is that some parks do not want visitors. Most of their occupants are non-mobile lot-holders who resent transients using their facilities. Or, because they are concerned about growth, some parks pass by-laws excluding categories of people from membership. By extension, they do not welcome these people as visitors. A fellow visitor at one park pointed out to Dorothy that one of the first things people ask newcomers is "Are you a member?" If you are not, she says, they dismiss you.

We heard several discussions about fears that the "wrong kind of people" were joining Escapees. They include children, young people, transients, renters (as opposed to lot owners), and singles. People who seek to exclude others unlike themselves may be in the process gerontologists call disengagement.[4] Or they may be withdrawing from mainstream society in an effort to create a lifestyle enclave composed only of people like themselves. Other RVers are incensed by exclusionary rules and behavior because they violate the family ethos promoted by the organization. The Freeses express this point of view:

> Over the years we've heard time and again, "SKPs are all one big Family." No "associate" memberships for those not yet able to full-time; no separate group for singles. How ironic, then, that rumor has it the Co-Ops are quietly trying to put in the bylaws a rule forbidding children. Doesn't FAMILY include children — as well as cranky grandparents, frazzled parents, single aunts and uncles who are set in their ways.... Is this the true family way?[5]

Concerned about the divisiveness of the issue, Kay Peterson addressed it in an editorial:

> Some of you fear the "wrong kind of people" are joining. "That danger," you remind us, "is increased proportionately with the numbers."

Should we lock the door, keeping all newcomers out to prevent a few undesirables from slipping in amongst them? Our 15-year history shows the term "wrong kind of people" is hard to define. Some people simply have personalities that clash when they are together, but each is a good person and a friend of many other members.

As for those who do not share our caring-and-sharing philosophy, either they will adapt or will feel so out of place they will drop out.[6]

Although there is dissension in home-base parks, many RVers say that the sense of family and the feeling of community are positive aspects of co-op living that outweigh the disadvantages. The important thing, they say, is to be inclusive. In this vein, Magda Green, an under-55-year-old boomer, explains why she joined a co-op:

We liked the location and the climate, we weren't welcome at "55 and over" parks, the waiting list was too long, etc. But most of all, because we found friendship, courtesy, smiles, hugs, and generosity of spirit, along with plenty of sunshine, awesome sunrises, and breathtaking sunsets. We liked the looks of the park, the expressions of individuality, and the taste in shed styles. We noticed the dedication of the board of directors and the managers and the lack of too many rules....

Yes, we did notice a few whiners and what's-in-it-for-me types. Caring and sharing is not (probably never has been) their lifestyle. To them, being a SKP means nothing more than a cheap place to roost.... Some of these roosters find nothing else to do but snoop, gossip, nit-pick, and lie in wait for someone to break a rule. But whatever happened to courtesy, compassion, respect, tolerance, Christian love, and the live-and-let-live attitude? Does one forget these values when one lives a certain number of years?

More than ever, we *need* to widen our circle of friendships, not form cliques. We *need* to accept and welcome RVers of multiple generations and all walks of life. We *need* to replenish the pool of volunteers, lease buyers, quality managers, and impartial boards of directors.

We *need* each other!

We need to *rekindle, practice, and pass on* the Escapees philosophy of *caring and sharing* to all RVers, full-time or part-time, young or old.

We must not let a few create divisions and distrust. We must continue to nurture the qualities that make all parks a very special place to call "home," and a group of once strangers "family."[7]

"Everybody here enjoys a good fight"

As some of the quotes above suggest, dissension is common in home-base parks. In every place we visited where people spend months at a time, boondocking area as well as formal park, the residents squabbled. Quarrels and contention were usually over issues of control. "Who has the right to control my life and make decisions that affect me?" "Who has the right to control the property I think is mine?" "How are these decisions to be made?" People quarrel about whether park rules should be inclusive — permitting anyone who wishes to rent or buy a lot — or exclusive. The inclusively inclined often accuse the others of being "a bunch of snobs." They argue about the proper treatment of feral cats. Should they be killed or fed? They squabble over whether and how much lot-holders should be compensated for improvements to their lot; about whether they should leave lots in a "natural setting" or plant them with nursery flowers and foliage; and over who has the right to make that decision. They disagree about whether the park should levy a fee on all members to install a TV dish; over whether people should be allowed to use soap in the hot spring bathing area; about the procedures used by the park's board of directors ("little Hitlers" in one person's judgement) to pass rules. They have heated meetings about whether they should permit park-model trailers in the park; over whether there is a need for drapes in the clubhouse; about whether they should use a clubhouse room for crafts or a pool table.

The dissent that divides harmonious communities often surprises RVers. For example, Fred and Susan, who were LTVA hosts in 1994, were shocked by the dissension and dissatisfaction that focused on them. They had been winter visitors at the LTVA for years and had so many friends they thought the job of host would be a snap. "We thought it was just one big happy family," Fred said. Instead, people complained constantly to and about him. "Everything is *my* fault," Fred said. It was his fault that the six-month camping fee went from $25 to $50. It was his fault that LTVA officials no longer permitted residents to use soap in the showers. It was his fault that the military flew jets over the area. It was his fault that short-term visitors had to go to the back instead of being able to park where they chose. People were angry when he told them they must register when they came in. He was often cursed and verbally abused. When he'd had enough of it, Fred called the ranger, who expelled the abusers. Fred and Susan said they will never again be hosts.

Why does the dissension occur?

THE NEED FOR AN EXIT OPTION

RV communities are real. Their members have true friendships and participate in genuine reciprocity, but the reality is linked to the ability of RVers to hitch up and pull out at any time. Things change when people live at a home base much of the year. Because they spend most of their time in one place, they have a stake in how it is run and what decisions are made. If they are responsible for deciding on park issues and policies, they must be *there*, not on the road. So, people who treasure their freedom to say, "If I don't like the neighbors all I have to do is turn on the key," can no longer use their ignition switch to avoid problems. Furthermore, RVers are not as insulated from their neighbors as are most suburbanites. In the suburbs there are no front porches and few sidewalks, and people spend most of their outdoor time in fenced back yards. In a park, the cramped space in an RV catches up with people, and they move outdoors. Because so much RV living takes place under the awning and in clubhouses and other public places, people must deal with each other daily. Differences in philosophy, attitude, and priorities become exaggerated. People whose key values are freedom and independence struggle to maintain their autonomy while trying to impose their will on others. The result is tension and confrontation. So, people feel that the community they valued has been destroyed.

The following letter eloquently expresses the frustrations residents in home-base parks have with authority, and their worry about the fragility of community:

> Do we need people constantly telling us what we can plant, what we can put on our sites, how we can decorate, and then peering over our fences and behind our rigs to see if we are doing something they don't approve of? I know of many instances in this park where someone has been told they can or can not do something when there was no legal or valid reason for that restriction. Why?

Are we being carried away by nit-picking, superfluous rules and regulations? Are we so bogged down in restrictions, cans, and can'ts that we are dividing and antagonizing the members? Are the over-zealous piling rules upon regulations upon restrictions to the point that they are going around looking for infractions?

The members as a whole own this park. We bought our sites to have a "Home Base." That "home base" is sacred and special to each of us. We MUST remember that each of us is different, in what we want to plant or not plant, in what we want to have in our yards or not have, in how we want to beautify our sites or leave as is. Whatever happened to Civil Rights, or members' rights, if you will?...

Let's not bind ourselves up in a restrictive web that makes us afraid to move for fear of "Big Brother" coming down on us. Let's give members the freedom to do their own thing as long as it isn't harmful. Let's not have any jealousy because someone is rich and can do beautiful things with their site that others can't afford. Let's not point fingers, nor judge each other, nor feel its [sic.] our "duty" to run the park. Let's each of us try to honor differences, not to manage each other, and to search diligently for "How Much Is Enough" before we do more harm than good.[8]

As the above letter suggests, the experience of Fred and Susan, the LTVA hosts, is not unique. People in authority in RVing communities have a hard time. Park board members may either resign as a group or be expelled from office over contentious issues. Board members in several parks sadly told us that, although they had many friends before they accepted a term of office, now they had none.

THEY NEED SOMETHING TO DO

The conflict may not be entirely a bad thing. We say this for several reasons. First, as we discussed in Chapter Five, boredom is a problem for those who lack something interesting and productive to do. RVers who do not find purposeful activity eventually wonder, "What am I doing here?" Many people play games, go to flea markets, and do crafts because "It helps to pass the time." One of the attractions of the Imperial Dam LTVA is the availability of the military base facilities. As several people told us, "There's lots to do over there." A cause that is worth fighting about is by definition important, and the disputants have something meaningful to do and an interesting way to pass time. We are reminded of the advice of a veterinarian: "If you are going to leave them alone all day it's better to leave two cats that hate each other than one cat by itself. It's better for the cats. It gives them something to do." Although the animal models are chickens rather than cats, the following letter makes the same point: people need many people to interact with and something useful to do.

> If you have been on a farm where chickens are kept in a coop, you know if one chicken gets a small bloody spot, the other birds will immediately peck it to death. How like a Co-Op (or other long-term park) where a member can be shredded by gossip. Some people's main source of entertainment seems to be gossiping about each other.
>
> At the fall Escapade, I heard Kay Peterson's talk "How to Live in a Sardine Can." It dawned on me that we can apply the same strategies for two people living in harmony in a small space to a group of people living harmoniously in an RV park.
>
> The answer then, is to encourage SKPs to seek activities and friends *outside* the Escapees Park.... There are a zillion fascinating things to do. Get away from the "coop" and you'll come back refreshed by new experiences and new friends. The park problems that seemed so monumental will have shrunk to their proper proportion.
>
> If you want to keep your Co-Op (or any park) from being a coop, don't put all your eggs in that one basket. If you *must* have a fence around it, at least put in a gate!
>
> Footnote: In studying the history of the Amish/Shaker and Mennonite communities, I learned the only communities that survived were the few who reached out to the world around them. The ones that did not survive were the ones that became ingrown.[9]

IT'S WORSE TO BE IGNORED THAN TO BE HATED

In her study of the Center—a community of elderly Jews—Barbara Myerhoff focuses on the advantages of social engagement over isolation rather than on the benefits of meaningful activity over boredom. Nevertheless, her analysis of the reasons for dissension between members of the Center also applies to sedentary RVers. In a chapter entitled "We Fight to Keep Warm," Myerhoff explains that the people at the Center quarrel because it is worse to be ignored than to be hated:

Anger is a powerful indication of engagement between people, the very opposite of indifference. It may be regarded as the most dramatic proof of responsiveness and caring.... It is a basic form of remaining attached. And among people who are not inevitably bound together, anger may become a refutation of the possibility of separation. Anger is a form of social cohesion, and a strong and reliable one. To fight with each other, people must share norms, rules, vocabulary, and knowledge. Fighting is a partnership, requiring cooperation. A boundary-maintaining mechanism — for strangers cannot participate fully — it is also above all a profoundly sociable activity.[10]

Two RVers, discussing why their park has its unique personality and why its residents fight, suggested a variation on this theme. The following is from our 1993 journal:

"We live life on the edge. People who live here are people who have an independent personality. We're not a patty-cake park," Bill told us. At their twice-yearly meetings, people break loose and fight. "It's just like a marriage," says Margy. Bill added, "We don't have climate going for us. It's hot in summer and nippy in the winter. There aren't any forests or lakes or swimming pools. We're off the beaten track. We're here because we want to be. This place is not for sissies. We're tough because we have to be to live here. There's a type of person who can come here and say 'That's for me,' and stick it out." They admit there are some "prickly personalities" here. "You've gotta be," said Bill. Margy added, "Everybody here enjoys a good fight."

Some RVers go questing. Others work to supplement their pensions or to finance their travels. Some settle into a home base and become deeply involved in the local community or in building their park. Others keep warm by fighting with each other. Some live in formal parks, while others band together to make the desert home. Whichever options they choose, RVers create communities which become substitute families for many of them. Eventually, however, their pace slows, some of the parts begin to show wear, and even the most intrepid begin to slow down. Inevitably their health begins to fail, and the traveling they love becomes a burden and a chore. Then serious RVers must face hanging up the keys.

Hanging Up the Keys

"I hope to God I'm never captive back in a house." (Adelle Clifton, full-time RVer)

Buck Alder and Adelle Clifton are not alone in fearing the time when they can no longer live in their rigs. Over one-third of the respondents to our questionnaire had made no plans for that time. When we asked them how long they expected to continue RVing, they gave replies like "Forever!" "Nothing but death, terminal illness or old age would make me quit." "I don't want to think about that yet." "You can die in a trailer just as well as in a house." Some, when asked about plans for when they could no longer travel, said things such as "We can't imagine doing that." These folks may be a bit like Ian and Joan, long-time full-timers in their 80s, whom we met in 1990.

Ian and Joan

We met Joan at a water pump in the campground at Lost Dutchman State Park where she was filling a water bottle. Ian, who finished washing the breakfast dishes, joined us later. She was 84, he was 86 years old. They both were curious about us and our research. She spoke repeatedly of how wonderful the area was, how they had enjoyed hiking the trails around the mountain, and how much they loved the outdoors.

Joan thinks that she and Ian are atypical of both older persons and RVers because they have been active, outdoor people all their lives. They met in a mountain climbing club, and she has climbed Mount Ranier and all of the other mountains in Washington and Oregon. They also hiked, canoed, and skied. "You name it, we did it," she said. They continue to hike, fish, and explore the area wherever they park. They spent the summer of 1990 in Yellowstone Park because he likes to fly-fish. She commented that to get to his favorite fishing spot, Ian had to walk through several miles of the 1988 burn. That was depressing. Both believe their active lives keep them healthy. Although Ian is crippled with arthritis, they were planning to hike up the Superstition Mountain trail when we met them. Looking up, Ian commented, "We should be up on that mountain right now."

They no longer avoid formal campgrounds. Now they prefer public parks, although they have stayed for brief times in private parks with pools and other facilities. Joan quivered with distaste and exclaimed "Yekkk" when we asked what she thought about parks with spas and organized social activities. They have spent some time in a private park near the Salton Sea because the hot springs relieve Ian's arthritis symptoms. They don't stay long because "I have to have mountains," she said.

Their mobile life started when they bought their first boat in 1941. They fished commercially out of Seattle for many years, going up the Inside Passage to Alaska 18 times. They retired from fishing in 1959 because too many of their friends were lost at sea. "It's a big ocean out there," Joan commented. They couldn't stand inactivity, so they got jobs as firefighter/firetower watchers on the Mogollon Rim. They worked there for seven summers until Ian had to retire in 1962 because he was too old to fight fires any longer.

They have not lived in a house for 48 years. They lived on a boat for 20 years and have lived in travel trailers and motor homes for 30 years. "People have too much stuff," Joan said, and then added that they have collected "too much junk" in their motor home. She intends to clean out the cupboards and take what they don't need to the Salvation Army.

Ian's arthritis and failing eyesight make it more difficult for them to travel. Moving between Arizona in the winter and the northern mountains in the summer is becoming a chore. Their driver's licenses both expire in two years, and they aren't sure they will be able pass the test. Then they will have to find permanent quarters. "We've been looking for a place to settle for 50 years and haven't found one yet," Joan joked. They have had several offers of places to stay, including one on San Juan Island where they could work as caretakers for a large property. It tempts them because it is beautiful, with a view of Vancouver Island, and because they could stay there free. They are determined not to go into a nursing home. They worry about friends who are in one in California because "everything is done for them and they do nothing but sit all day."

Thinking of their friends reminded them of their plans for the morning, and they set off up the trail to Superstition Mountain. (From our 1990 journal)

What will serious RVers miss most when they have to hang up their keys?

To be independent while traveling, to be independent while visiting others. Freedom to look over the next hill or see around the next curve in the road.

* * *

"Friends and activities and all of the hugs I get daily — they keep my personal batteries charged up."

* * *

Going, moving, traveling, a different view out my front "window" all the time, AND ALL THE FRIENDLY PEOPLE.

* * *

The freedom to go where we please.

CARE: The Escapees alternative

Ian and Joan are remarkable people who, like many other RVers, dread the day when they can no longer travel. When it is time to "hang up the keys," many RVers fear they must give up the friends, freedom, and independence that they cherish. Consequently, some people may not quit even when their physical problems create a danger for them and others on the road. Hartwigsen and Null addressed the unwillingness of full-timers to quit when they wrote, "No one knows how long full-timers remain on the road: it is too recent a phenomena (sic). There is some feeling, however, that failing health, including visual impairment, does not cause these road warriors to cease their travel." While there is no evidence that Hartwigsen and Null were aware of the Escapees club or of their CARE program, their analysis of the problem and suggestions for solution are blueprints for CARE.

> One way to satisfy full-timers' interest in remaining with the lifestyle while being in a stationary environment, providing safety and, if needed, health care security, is to provide RV resorts that resemble those that are visited during the traveling years. While some traditional trailer courts are available now, they tend to be located in undesirable areas, away from the services older people need most: shopping, post offices, bands, libraries, senior centers, entertainment and medical facilities. Others, located in desirable retirement areas, are too expensive for many full-timers.... A realization of the long-term care prospects of this lifestyle needs to be made. It's not for everybody, but what type of housing is? Consider the possibility as suggested by our 81-year old widowed respondent: an RV park with small lots for rent; a large, centrally located facility for recreation, dining and laundry; management staff including a recreation director, a visiting nurse, and aide (to help with such tasks as getting items down from high shelves); and a mainte-nance man, all specializing in the needs of the older generation. In addition, a meals-on-wheels program could be made available for those needing help with food preparation. By placing such a park in a location convenient to the aforementioned community needs and providing a van for transportation, life could be quite convenient and affordable. And, it would be provided with little or no public financial support.[11]

Many full-timers would agree with Hartwigsen and Null. They want an option that does not require them to give up friends, freedom, and independence when they can no longer travel. After all, "Who wants to live in a nursing home when all that is really needed is a little help with bathing, dressing, or getting around? When your home is an RV, how can anyone expect you to give up the freedom of your RV life-style just because you need a little help due to an accident, a sickness, or plain old age?"[12]

Personal independence requires that one not be a burden on others. Kay Peterson discusses the points made by Norman Crook in a seminar held at the spring 1992 Escapade, entitled "What do you do when you have to hang up your keys permanently?" As an answer, Crook said he and his wife bought a lot in an SKP lot. There they have wonderful neighbors who practice caring and sharing. When the Crooks could no longer drive, those neighbors would "pick up groceries for us when they go to town, and if we have to go to the doctor, they will drive us there, wait for us, and then bring us back to the park. That's the kind of people SKPs are." Then, after a pause, Norm asked, "But is that fair to our friends? Do we have the right to ask that of our neighbors? For a short time, everyone is willing to help — but *for the rest of our lives?* We are all in this lifestyle because we want to travel. Will our friends feel guilty when they are ready to leave on a trip, and will they resent us for making them feel as if they've abandoned us?" What options are there? Go home to their families? Is it their responsibility? Go into a nursing home and let the government take care of them? Peterson replies:

> Neither answer seems right to me. We encourage people to sell their old homestead and enjoy their golden years as free-spirited RV travelers. "Home is where you park it," we tell them. But what happens when no one wants you to park your home next to them because your disabling illness is hard to deal with? You become too much trouble, too much of a worry, too much of a burden.[13]

As our earlier discussion of the age profile of the Escapees Club suggests, these questions have become increasingly important to its members. The club's solution is the CARE program. It is a non-profit retirement center providing care for American Escapees who can no longer travel because of disability or age. The center — located at Escapees headquarters in Livingston, Texas — allows people to remain in their RVs and maintain their independence.[14] There is no equivalent of CARE in Canada. Retired Canadian RVers buy a home-base lot in a park that is open year around (weather restricts these locations to British Columbia); move into a mobile home, house, apartment, or retirement home; or become dependent on their family. Barbara Case poignantly expresses the need for a solution such as CARE:

I'm glad there will be a CARE facility. We are all going to need something sometime. I want to be a part of helping it to happen. My mother is 97, and, until recently, she took care of herself. Now she isn't next door to friends, no kids to watch from her window. I hope CARE will be a homey place.[15]

There are two components to CARE: assisted living and adult day care. Except for park lot owners and participants from town, participants in either component live in their rigs on a leased RV site with full hookups, a storage shed, and a patio. Participants in assisted living may take part in daily activities in the CARE center, while participants in adult day care come to the center each morning and remain there until their caregivers pick them up in the evening.[16] The assisted living component of CARE began in 1992.[17] By 1996, the club had set aside a section of their home park in Livingston where participants could lease an RV site with full hookups and a shed and patio, and they had built the CARE center. The center building was expanded in 1998. This is where residents are served lunch for a small donation, seminars and classes are conducted, and social activities including pet therapy are held. Registered nurse volunteers are available, and a home health agency has an office in the center. CARE also provides residents with security checks, transportation to local services, weekly RV cleaning and laundry service, and a recreation and exercise program. These services are an alternative to nursing home placement for retired RVers who want to continue to live in their rigs. The cost in 2000 was $490 a month for assisted living participants, $600 monthly for adult day care participants who live in their rigs, and $28 a day for area residents who belong to the adult day care program.[18]

Costs are kept low by the extensive assistance of volunteers like Ralph and Marilyn Garneau, who are profiled in Chapter 6. Some volunteers, like the Garneaus, commit 20 hours a week for several months. Others who are just traveling through the park offer their help for a few days or weeks. Some of the most consistent and dependable volunteers are caregivers whose spouses are CARE residents and CARE participants themselves. Volunteers take tours through the center, provide transportation for doctor's appointments and grocery shopping, answer telephones, help feed participants who cannot feed themselves, help with laundry, play games with participants whose mobility is limited, fold linens, help in the kitchen, and — like participant Pete Gates — regularly write columns about CARE in the Escapees magazine.[19]

Another CARE participant who was also a volunteer was D.J. Jackson, whose story began in Chapter Two. In the summer of 1995 D.J. left

Pete Gates and her dog "Monkey" on her lot at the CARE center

the center to travel to western Canada and Alaska with her 17-year-old grand-daughter. After her trip she helped at the CARE booth at the fall 1995 Escapade in Ohio and then drove to Texas to resume her residence at the CARE center. She conducted daily tours of the facility for visitors for several years and is featured in the video *On the Road* distributed by Bullfrog Films.[20]

CARE residents receive the on-going help they require and more besides. In an article entitled "What CARE Taught Me," Pete Gates explains why she decided not to leave the program and move into an RV park near cousins to whom she is close. She made the decision to stay in CARE for several reasons. First, as her health deteriorates she does not want to be dependent on or disrupt the lives of her family. She insists, "I must not saddle them with my old age." Second, to her surprise she discovered that in the CARE environment she can love and help others, as well as receive help and love from them. And, finally, she found that old people are interesting, vital, and share their infirmities with good humor. She says:

> I was surprised to realize that there are persons at CARE who need me. They need, and can accept, compassion and understanding, sympathy and assistance from me without ego or emotional cost, and I can accept these from them.... I was even more surprised to realize that the people at CARE love me — and that I love them. It is no simple matter to allow oneself to need and be needed, to love and be loved.[21]

Although there is widespread recognition among Skips of the need for CARE, the desire for and admiration of independence is strong. D.J.'s feisty self-sufficiency was widely respected, as is the spunk of an elderly woman we learned about at a SKP park in 1994. During happy hour a new club member asked how people coped when they lost a spouse or were unable to continue RVing because of infirmity. Several people told her about the CARE center. Then someone told the story of an 86-year-old woman traveling alone who had applied for a CARE lot. By the time her application was approved, she had written the club's office that she had found a new partner and was back on the road, so they should forget it! There was general laughter and applause.

Over the Last Hill

Although many serious RVers tenaciously maintain their freedom and independence, the community is an elderly one. Death is a familiar presence to most of them. During the meeting of a book-study club at an Escapees park, one participant asked the others if they knew the name of a poem by Emily Dickinson that deals with death. She recited a few lines of it, and though nobody could identify the poem, the discussion turned to death. Death happens so often in the park that people get inured to it. "I have a different reaction to it now," one woman said. "Death becomes another part of life. It's just a part of the scheme. It's really no big deal. All relationships end in one way or the other. Nothing endures." Everyone in the study group knew someone outside the RVing community who was still grieving the death of a spouse years after it had happened. "People outside are immobilized by death." In contrast, the group agreed that their community, and the close ties maintained by members of the club, helped survivors to adjust to their grief. One member talked quietly about the death of his wife three weeks before. She had a series of strokes, the last one leaving her para-lysed. She had said she wanted to die at home, so he modified the kitchen of their fifth-wheel to take her bed and all the necessary equipment — oxygen, feeding tubes, etc. She required 24-hour-a-day care, and he had no family to help as both of their children had died years before. A nurse and doctor came several times a week to check her, but the rest of the help he needed was provided by Skips. "If this had happened anywhere else, I don't know what I'd have done" he said.

The headstone of an escapee: Photograph by Ann Dawson

For some RVers, the attachment to their way of life transcends death. In a letter to Road Roamer News, Ann Dawson gave notice of the death of her husband. They were full-timers for 10 years and spent most of their time boondocking in the southwestern desert. Ann writes, "His headstone has an

8th Air Force emblem on one side and the SKP wagon logo on the other, the first SKP logo known to be on a headstone."[22] When we read the notice we wrote to Ann asking if she would send us a photograph of it. We also asked her about their lives as RVers and about her plans. The following is from her letter of March 24, 1996:

> Shortly after John and I were married (both working) we started weekend camping with friends. Sleeping bags on the ground, food, etc. in pasteboard boxes. Much fun. Then a canopy for the pickup — much better. Longer trips on our vacations. A nice big bonus and we ordered a camper built. Portapotty, ice box, four burner range and an *oven*, seating for four to six, closet, storage, a good bed. Such luxury! Of course it cost a whopping big $1500. Over time John added holding tanks, gas refrigerator, water pump, shelves in the "bathroom," etc. Then we traveled: CA to 8th Air Force reunion, Seattle, Missouri, Wisconsin, Kansas, Minnesota, Montana, Canada. Every trip a joy.
>
> 1980 and retirement A brand new fifth-wheel, more places to see, and people to meet. South in winter, Fruitland area in summer. Now that's the way to live! 1989 first cancer surgery, so we rented a nice old house (my sister) and unloaded our long-stored furniture, tools, and junk. Then more winters south and summer traveling. John slowing down so we stayed home two winters.... The world stopped in '94. Only happy memories left.
>
> So here I'll stay in this ragged old house until carried kicking and screaming away. Much to do — large yard, garden, flowers, trees, sewing quilts and dragarounds in winter. Lots of family and company. I can sleep 14 more or less comfortably. I think the kids come for my homemade venison mincemeat!
>
> I kept an old pickup with pop-up camper. Good for weekends. Went to Montana last summer. Getting old. Eyesight not the best, but I surely had a great time while it lasted.

Escapees are not the only RVers who want to go with the keys in their pocket. In 1994 a colleague of David's told him about a small cemetery in Chatsworth, Ontario. "There's a grave there you have to see," he said. "There's a picture of an RV on it." We drove to Chatsworth and took photographs of the headstone. When we located the widow, Isabelle King Bates, in April 1996, it was a busy time — both sad and happy — for her. She graciously agreed to talk with us the day after her sister's funeral and just a week before her wedding. She is a small, vibrant woman with dark eyes and hair. Her mobile home has a for-sale sign in front. She was packing to move to her new home the next week.

She and John started camping in a home-made trailer when their children were small. In 1986 they bought a small van, and they and two of their daughters traveled in it to the World's Fair at the Canadian Exposition in Vancouver. It was crowded, but John loved it. He had never wanted to leave their home, which had a lovely view out the back onto a ravine and creek. He would ask, "Why would we want to go anywhere? We have everything we want right here." After the trip in the van his dream was to live in an RV and travel. They went to RV shows and visited RV lots, and in 1987 bought their 27-foot motor home. They took trips in it every chance they got, and in 1989 sold their house and moved into it. John loved it, Isabelle said. "He wanted to be *in* that motor home." Their plans were to spend the winter in Florida in 1991, after he retired in 1990, and to go to California and drive up the west coast the next year. They left for Florida in January 1991. Six weeks later he had a fatal heart attack. The next months were difficult ones for Isabelle, but she is grateful they had that time together in their motor home. "It was the best six weeks of our lives."

After John died, she kept the motor home for a year, rented it out, and drove it twice herself. The last time she and a friend took it to Michigan, and it stalled in the middle of I-94 in Detroit. She finally got it started again, but decided she could not cope with traveling in it by herself and sold it.

She remembers with fondness the years they lived in their motor home. When we asked her what she missed most about it, she replied emphatically, "Being in the motor home. There is a different kind of freedom in it. There's no life like it. I have super good memories." Although the space was small, she thinks that living in it brought her and John closer together. They would sometimes just drive it a few miles and park where they could look out on a lake. "You don't have to go far," she said. "You just leave all the worries behind. The freedom is in your head." She also found freedom in getting rid of "all that stuff" when they sold their house. "What are possessions? I didn't miss them. I didn't need to worry about all that stuff."

Why did she engrave John's headstone with the picture of a motor home? It was their children's idea because they knew how much their father enjoyed it. Their artist son-in-law made the drawing for the engraving. It is the exact picture of their rig. "That was his life," Isabelle said. "He just loved that motor home."

Like everyone else, RVers must cross over the last hill, but some continue to try to scratch their hitch-itch even in the grave. This book is about a group of people whose itch to expand their horizons, to make new friends, and to discover new forms of freedom adds zest to their third age. These folks provide a role model for other seniors who do not want their final years to be characterized as a "plight." We can hardly do better than to recall Tonia Thorson's words: "People stay young on the road, and I wish I was back in my motor home."

He wanted to be *in* that motor home

Notes

1. Alfredson 1994:24.

2. Peterson and Peterson 1991:55.

3. Hazzard and Hazzard 1987:22.

4. Cummings and Henry 1961.

5. Freese and Freese 1986:18.

6. Peterson, K. 1993b:4.

7. Green 1993:26-27.

8. Briseno 1993:8.

9. Cannain 1993:40.

10. Myerhoff 1978:184.

11. Hartwigsen and Null 1990:144. Hartwigsen and Null found that 86 per cent of their respondents said they planned to continue full-timing indefinitely, 82 per cent said they would stop RVing for illness, while 7 per cent said their reason would be their own

death (Hartwigsen and Null 1990:143-145). The responses we received did not indicate as strong a dedication to continued full-timing no matter what. In earlier versions of our questionnaire and in follow-up interviews, we asked the following questions: **"How long do you think that you will continue RVing?"** Over 55 per cent said they will continue RVing as long as they can or until they die. **"What would lead you to resume sedentary life?"** Sixty per cent said ill health, 7.5 per cent said nothing or "can't imagine," 12.5 per cent said finances, and death was the reply of 5 per cent. **"Do you have plans to do this?"** Half said they have made no plans and/or they "don't want to think about it." The Hartwigsen and Null quote in which they propose a long-term health care facility for RVers who can no longer travel is from page 145.

12. *Escapees Newsletter* 1994:7. Although Kay Peterson's name is not on the byline of this article, the style and message is hers.

13. Peterson, K. 1992:4.

14. Peterson, K. 1992:4-6.

15. Case 1993:49.

16. Lacy 2000:78.

17. Peterson, K. 1999:31.

18. Lacy 2000:78.

19. Gates, Davida (Pete): 1999:9.

20. Peterson, K. 1996a:7. In *On the Road* made in 1996, D.J. guides a tour through the CARE center and serves less mobile CARE participants. By 1998 her health had deteriorated and she was no longer able to take tours. She has since passed away.

21. Gates, Davida (Pete) 2000:48.

22. Dawson 1995:59.

Appendix One

RV Living Survey

We appreciate your helping us in our research on RVing as a retirement alternative by completing the following questionnaire. If you have comments about any of the questions, or wish to expand on the answer, please write on the back of the last page of the questionnaire. Your identity, comments, and answers will be completely confidential.

Please return the completed questionnaire in the box provided.

Thanks very much for your help with our research on RV living.

Site: _____

1, 2, 3, _____ (office use only)

How many respondants are SKPS? 274 of 296 — 93%

Personal History

The following questions are about your personal history and background. They are designed to help us discover what people who are serious RVers have in common.

4. How old are you? (294 responses)
1. under 40	(1)	(0.36%)
2. 41-55	(37)	(12.58%)
3. 56-65	(146)	(49.60%)
4. 66-75	(93)	(31.60%)
5. over 75	(17)	(5.78%)

5. What is your citizenship? (296 responses)
1. American	(278)	(94.00%)
2. Canadian	(18)	(6.00%)

6. What is your sex? (295 responses)
1. Male	(145)	(49.20%)
2. Female	(150)	(50.80%)

7. How much formal education did you complete? (292 responses)

1. no high school	(4)	(1.37%)
2. some high school	(15)	(5.14%)
3. high school diploma	(47)	(16.10%)
4. some post-secondary	(96)	(32.88%)
5. post-secondary degree/diploma	(63)	(21.57%)
6. graduate/professional degree	(67)	(23.00%)

Note: 77.45% have some post-secondary education or better.

8. Before you began RVing, did you tent camp or back pack on vacations? (293 responses)

1. yes	(225)	(76.8%)
2. no	(68)	(23.2%)

9. Current marital status (295 responses)

1. never married	(7)	(2.3%)
2. member of unmarried couple	(4)	(1.3%)
3. married	(248)	(85.3%)
4. divorced	(20)	(6.8%)
5. widowed	(16)	(5.4%)

10. Do you have children? (295 responses)

1. yes	(280)	(95.0%)
2. no	(15)	(5.0%)

11. Do any of your children live within an hour's drive of your home or former home? (294 responses)

1. yes	(155)	(53.7%)
2. no	(125)	(42.5%)
3. I have no children	(14)	(4.7%)

12. Do you have grandchildren? (294 responses)

1. yes	(255)	(86.7%)
2. no	(39)	(13.3%)

13. How often do you see your children or grandchildren? (292 responses)

1. twice a year or more	(192)	(66.0%)
2. about once a year	(59)	(20.3%)
3. every couple of years	(16)	(5.5%)
4. infrequently	(9)	(3.1%)
5. never	(3)	(1.0%)
6. no children	(13)	(4.5%)

14. Which of the following most accurately describes your children's reaction to your decision to become serious RVers?[1] (289 responses)

1. thought I was crazy	(19)	(6.6%)
2. were worried or concerned about it	(31)	(10.7%)
3. expressed no opinion	(15)	(5.2%)
4. accepted it	(81)	(28.0%)
5. thought it was a great idea	(129)	(44.6%)
6. no children	(14)	(4.5%)

15. How often do you travel with children/grandchildren? (291 responses)

1. frequently	(4)	(1.4%)
2. occasionally	(62)	(21.3%)
3. seldom	(100)	(34.4%)
4. never	(112)	(38.5%)
5. no children	(13)	(4.5%)

16. Do you travel with a pet? (294 responses)

1. yes	(104)	(35.4%)
2. no	(190)	(64.6%)

Home Community

The following questions are about your involvement in the community where you live now, or where you last lived if you are a full-time RVer.

17. How long have you lived (did you live) in your last home? (285 responses)

1. 0-5 yrs.	(51)	(17.6%)	5. 21-25 yrs.	(40)	(13.8%)
2. 6-10 yrs.	(68)	(23.4%)	6. 26-30 yrs.	(17)	(5.8%)
3. 11-15 yrs.	(45)	(15.5%)	7. 31-40 yrs.	(15)	(5.2%)
4. 16-20 yrs.	(44)	(15.2%)	8. 41 yrs. +	(5)	(1.7%)

18. How well would you say you know (knew) your neighbors? (293 responses)

1. Very well. Some are good friends	(114)	(39.0%)
2. Well. I visited with them occasionally	(89)	(30.4%)
3. Casually. I know their names to speak to them	(68)	(23.2%)
4. Not well	(16)	(5.5%)
5. I didn't know them at all	(6)	(2.1%)

Are/were you active in any of the following in your home community?

19. Church (292 responses)

1. yes	(126)	(43.2%)
2. no	(166)	(56.8%)

20. Civic/social service organizations such as Lions, Rotary, Masons, Knights of Columbus, Shriners (293 responses)

1. yes	(83)	(28.3%)
2. no	(210)	(71.7%)

21. Social clubs such as garden clubs, bowling leagues, seniors groups. (292 responses)

1. yes	(108)	(37.0%)
2. no	(184)	(63.0%)

22. Business organizations such as the Chamber of Commerce, merchant's associations (285 responses)

1. yes	(42)	(14.7%)
2. no	(243)	(85.3%)

23. Local politics or political organizations (290 responses)

1.yes	(39)	(13.4%)
2.no	(251)	(86.6%)

24. Volunteer work or volunteer organizations (294 responses)

1. yes	(137)	(46.4%)
2. no	(157)	(53.4%)

25. Totals of community involvement (out of 295 responses)

0 involvement	(63)	(21.4%)
1 organization or club	(74)	(25.1%)
2 organizations or clubs	(74)	(25.1%)
3 organizations or clubs	(46)	(15.6%)
4 organizations or clubs	(22)	(7.5%)
5 organizations or clubs	(12)	(4.1%)
6 organizations or clubs	(4)	(1.4%)

Note: 28.7% involved in 3 or more organizations.

Employment History

The following questions assume that all adults spend many years being employed in some way. Some people are employed outside the home for wages. Some farm, manage households and rear children, or do other work at home, sometimes for pay and sometimes not.

26. What is (was) your occupation? (286 responses)

1. business – white collar	(50)	(17.5%)
2. business – blue collar	(19)	(6.6%)
3. civil service	(8)	(2.8%)
4. clergy	(1)	(0.3%)
5. educator	(28)	(9.8%)
6. farm/ranch	(6)	(2.1%)
7. health services	(24)	(8.4%)
8. homemaker	(17)	(6.0%)
9. laborer	(0)	
10. management (banking, CEO)	(17)	(5.9%)
11. mechanic	(5)	(1.7%)
12. military	(10)	(3.5%)
13. police, fire, prison guard	(9)	(3.1%)
14. professional	(16)	(5.6%)
15. resources	(4)	(1.4%)
16. sales	(16)	(5.6%)
17. service	(7)	(2.4%)
18. small business	(8)	(2.8%)
19. transportation	(5)	(1.7%)
20. construction	(5)	(1.7%)
21. other (jockey, self-employed)	(12)	(4.2%)
22. none	(1)	(0.3%)

| 23. engineer | (16) | (5.6%) |
| 24. multiple | (2) | (0.7%) |

27. How much does (did) your job require you to travel? (285 responses)

1. constantly, for example truck driver	(13)	(4.5%)
2. frequently (once or twice a month)	(32)	(11.2%)
3. occasionally (several times a year)	(67)	(23.5%)
4. seldom (once a year or less)	(62)	(21.8%)
5. never	(110)	(38.6%)
6. multiple answers	(1)	(0.3%)

28. Are you retired now? (287 responses)

1. yes	(226)	(79.3%)
2. semi-retired; I work part-time	(16)	(5.7%)
3. semi-retired; I sometimes work as a campground host, sell in flea markets, etc	(21)	(7.3%)
4. no, I am not retired	(24)	(8.4%)

29. If retired from full-time employment, at what age did you retire? (245 responses)

1. < 45	(20)	(8.2%)	4. 56-60	(71)	(29.0%)
2. 46-50	(27)	(11.0%)	5. 61-65	(66)	(27.0%)
3. 51-55	(54)	(22.0%)	6. 66-70	(7)	(2.9%)

30. Did you retire from your last full-time position (283 responses)

1. early by choice	(168)	(59.4%)
2. early, not by choice	(36)	(12.7%)
3. at the "normal" age	(55)	(19.4%)
4. I am not retired	(24)	(8.5%)

31. Did you retire in order to RV? (287 responses, 263 retired)

1. yes	(133)	(50.6% of retired)
2. no	(130)	(49.4% of retired)
3. I am not retired	(24)	

The RV Life Style

32. When did you start RVing? (294 responses as of 1995)

1. before 1955 (40yrs +)	(10)	(3.5%)
2. 1955-1959 (35-39yrs)	(10)	(3.5%)
3. 1960-1964 (30-34 yrs)	(18)	(6.4%)
4. 1965-1969 (25-29 yrs)	(33)	(11.7%)
5. 1970-1974 (20-24 yrs)	(35)	(12.4%)
Note: 45.7% have been RVing for 20 years or more.		
6. 1975-1979 (15-19 yrs)	(35)	(12.4%)
7. 1980-1984 (10-14 yrs)	(35)	(12.4%)
8. 1985-1990 (5-9 yrs)	(71)	(25.2%)
9. 1990-1994 (0-4 yrs)	(47)	(16.7%)

33. Do you travel (292 responses)

1. alone	(35)	(12.1%)
2. with a partner	(229)	(79.2%)
3. with my family	(28)	(9.7%)

34. How many RVs have you owned? (286 responses)

1	(36)	(13.6%)	7	(12)	(4.2%)
2	(61)	(21.3%)	8	(8)	(2.8%)
3	(54)	(18.9%)	9	(6)	(2.1%)
4	(47)	(16.4%)	10	(7)	(2.5%)
5	(24)	(8.4%)	11	(1)	(0.33%)
6	(29)	(10.1%)	18	(1)	(0.33%)

35. What type do you own now (292 responses)

1. travel trailer	(36)	(12.3%)
2. 5th wheel	(110)	(37.7%)
3. Class A motor home	(98)	(33.6%)
4. Class C motor home	(17)	(5.8%)
5. van conversion	(4)	(1.4%)
6. other	(7)	(2.4%)
7. multiple answers	(20)	(6.8%)

36. My rig is (294 responses)

1. fully equipped for long term boondocking	(177)	(60.2%)
2. equipped for short term or overnight boondocking	(108)	(36.7%)
3. equipped to use standard hookups only	(9)	(3.1%)

37. I am a (292 responses)

1. full-timer. My RV is my home	(199)	(68.2%)
2. serious part-timer; I spend six months or more in my rig each year	(52)	(17.8%)
3. snow bird who spends less than six months in my RV each year	(30)	(10.3%)
4. vacation user of my RV	(11)	(3.8%)

38. How many months did you spend in your RV in the last year? (290 responses)

1	(5)	(1.7%)	7	(13)	(4.5%)
2	(12)	(4.1%)	8	(13)	(4.5%)
3	(9)	(3.1%	9	(5)	(1.7%)
4	(11)	(3.8%)	10	(17)	(5.7%)
5	(15)	(5.2%)	11	(7)	(2.4%)
6	(20)	(6.9%)	12	(163)	(56.2%)

39. What kind of home base, other than a mailing address, do you have? (293 responses)

1. house/apartment	(63)	(22.3%)
2. mobile home or cottage	(18)	(6.4%)
3. SKP co-op or rainbow park lot	(86)	(30.4%)
4. a lot in another type of RV park	(6)	(2.1%)
5. other (child's home, lot with hookups)	(23)	(8.1%)
6. I have no home base	(97)	(34.3%)

Full-Timing

40. If you are a full-timer, how long have you been one? (210 responses)

1. < 1 year	(21)	(10.0%)	5. 5-10 yrs.	(49)	(23.3%)
2. 1 yr +	(23)	(11.0%)	6. 10-15 yrs.	(19)	(9.0%)
3. 2 yrs +	(43)	(20.5%)	7. 15 yrs +	(9)	(4.3%)
4. 3-5 yrs.	(46)	(21.9%)			

41. If you are a full-timer, did your decision to start follow some important change or crisis in your life (unexpected retirement, death of a close relative or friend, divorce, illness, etc.)? (244 responses, 214 full-timers)

1. yes	(51)	(23.8% of full-timers)
2. no	(163)	(76.2% of full-timers)
3. not a full-timer	(30)	

42. If yes, please describe. (55 responses)

1. bankruptcy	(1)	(1.8%)
2. burn-out, stress	(2)	(5.5%)
3. death – family member	(6)	(10.9%)
4. death – spouse	(4)	(7.3%)
5. divorce	(2)	(3.6%)
6. marriage/remarriage	(3)	(5.5%)
7. illness – self	(2)	(3.6%)
8. illness – other	(3)	(5.5%)
9. loss of job	(5)	(9.1%)
10. retirement	(3)	(7.3%)
11. other	(21)	(34.6%)
12. multiple answers	(3)	(5.5%)

43. Did/Do you own your home? (258 responses)

1. yes	(241)	(93.4%)
2. no	(17)	(6.6%)

44. If you owned your home, what have you done with it? (243 responses)

1. sold it/it is listed for sale	(174)	(74.7%)
2. renting it through an agency	(10)	(4.3%
3. relatives are living in it	(11)	(4.7%)
4. it is vacant	(4)	(1.7%)
5. I still live there part time	(34)	(14.6%)
6. other	(10)	(4.3%)

45. If you are full-time and have sold your home, when did you do that? (220 responses)

1. immediately after/when I went full-time	(130)	(59.1%)
2. after a trial period of full-timing	(26)	(11.8%)
3. after a lengthy period (please specify)	(12)	(5.5%)
4. not applicable, I still have my home	(50)	(22.7%)
5. other	(2)	(0.9%)

46. What have you done with your possessions? (229 responses)

1. I still have them in my home	(30)	(13.0%)
2. I have things stored with family, in a storage facility, etc.	(65)	(28.1%)
3. I have things stored at a home base (RV lot shed, etc).	(51)	(22.1%)
4. I sold or disposed of everything that is not in my RV.	(74)	(32.0%)
5. other	(9)	(3.9%)

47. What was the hardest thing about making the decision to go full-time? (218 responses)

1. leaving children	(9)	(4.8%)
2. leaving family (unspecified)	(11)	(5.9%)
3. staying in touch with family	(1)	(0.5%)
4. finances	(14)	(7.5%)
5. leaving friends	(8)	(4.3%)
6. leaving grandchildren	(2)	(1.1%)
7. leaving home, garden, familiar areas	(10)	(5.3%)
8. leaving house and associated activities	(9)	(4.8%)
9. leaving neighborhood community	(3)	(1.6%)
10. no problems	(64)	(34.2%)
11. possessions, getting rid of, storing	(36)	(19.3%)
12. lack of space, living together in confined space	(6)	(3.2%)
13. technical problems	(2)	(1.1%)
14. multiple answers	(12)	(6.4%)
15. other	(31)	(16.6%)

48. What one thing do you miss the most as a full-timer? (214 responses)

1. communication ease: telephone, mail	(13)	(6.1%)
2. conveniences	(28)	(13.1%)
3. family: seeing children, grandchildren	(19)	(8.9%)
4. friends from home	(20)	(9.3%)
5. home and garden	(18)	(8.4%)
6. home community: church, clubs, volunteer work	(11)	(5.1%)
7. money	(15)	(7.0%)
8. nothing	(44)	(20.6%)
9. space	(15)	(7.0%)
10. storage	(3)	(1.4%)
11. possessions	(5)	(2.3%)
12. other	(13)	(6.1%)
13. multiple answers	(10)	(4.7%)

Full-timing is not for everyone. Your answers to the next questions will help us to understand what full-timers have in common.

49. What do you think makes a person capable of going full-time? (226 responses)

1. economic circumstances, a good pension.	(6)	(2.7%)
2. capable of change, flexible, adaptable.	(31)	(13.7%)
3. couple has a good relationship	(11)	(4.9%)
4. able to let go of family	(9)	(4.0%)
5. independent, self-reliant	(19)	(8.4%)

6. adventurous	(56)	(24.8%)
7. ability to live simple life	(18)	(8.0%)
8. social qualities	(10)	(4.4%)
9. travel: love to, always been a gypsy	(25)	(11.1%)
10. attitude	(8)	(3.5%)
11. self confidence	(6)	(2.7%)
12. multiple answers	(6)	(2.7%)
13. other	(21)	(9.3%)

50. What kind of people are best suited to full-timing? (214 responses)

1. independent	(8)	(8.0%)
2. both partners want to	(15)	(7.0%)
3. self-confidence	(17)	(7.9%)
4. not tied to family, family obligations	(7)	(3.3%)
5. healthy, active, have the right skills	(6)	(2.8%)
6. flexible, capable of change, adaptable	(26)	(12.1%)
7. adventurous	(49)	(22.9%)
8. friendly, gregarious, outgoing	(37)	(17.3%)
9. not attached to things, house, garden	(9)	(4.2%)
10. happy, fun-loving, optimistic, easy going	(10)	(4.7%)
11. wants to travel, has itchy feet, a gypsy	(12)	(5.6%)
12. don't know	(3)	(1.4%)
13. multiple	(2)	(0.9%)
14. all kinds, everyone, anybody, all campers	(7)	(3.3%)
15. has no roots; doesn't like anchors	(4)	(1.9%)
16. retired people	(2)	(0.9%)

51. What kind of people are not suited to full-timing? (220 responses)

1. bad relationship between travelling partners	(9)	(4.1%)
2. economic reasons.	(2)	(0.9%)
3. can't give up family, children, grandchildren	(33)	(15.0%)
4. poor health.	(2)	(0.9%)
5. home bodies	(39)	(17.6%)
6. insecure	(34)	(15.5%)
7. beatnicks; complainers; grouches	(19)	(8.6%)
8. dependent	(6)	(2.7%)
9. materialistic	(23)	(10.5%)
10. need lots of space	(4)	(1.8%)
11. inflexible	(21)	(9.5%)
12. other: is up to the individual, no one	(9)	(4.1%)
13. multiple answers	(2)	(0.9%)
14. people with deep roots	(17)	(7.7%)

52. What changes in attitudes and habits does successful full-timing require? (189 responses)

1. flexibility	(66)	(37.0%)
2. travelling partners be considerate of each other; respect other's need for space	(17)	(9.6%)
3. budget and have faith money will be enough	(1)	(0.6%)
4. independence from family	(6)	(3.4%)

5. freedom from possessions	(17)	(9.6%)
6. self-confident, self-sufficient	(4)	(2.2%)
7. social skills	(14)	(7.9%)
8. have a sense of humour; stop worrying; relax	(13)	(7.3%)
9. be able to live in small spaces; think small	(12)	(6.7%)
10. be adventurous; have the pioneer spirit	(7)	(3.9%)
11. multiple answers	(1)	(0.6%)
12. none	(12)	(6.7%)
13. don't know	(4)	(2.2%)
14. don't look back; learn that this is a life-style, not a vacation	(10)	(5.6%)
15. get exercise; eat healthy	(5)	(2.8%)

53. What advice would you give to someone who is considering full-timing? (224 responses)

1. couple must be able to get along in small space; if both don't want to, don't do it	(11)	(4.9%)
2. do it: don't wait too long; go for it *fast*	(43)	(19.2%)
3. try it first	(99)	(44.2%)
4. if you have to ask about gas mileage, an RV is not for you	(1)	(0.4%)
5. plan to give up things	(3)	(1.3%)
6. plan diet carefully; have regular checkups	(2)	(0.9%)
7. capture every day and enjoy; have hobbies, especially those requiring littlespace; keep RV uncluttered	(3)	(1.3%)
8. meet, talk to other RVers	(8)	(3.6%)
9. are you gregarious, flexible? how important are home, community, family and friends; if you like gardens, routines forget it	(9)	(4.0%)
10. inventory belongings and keep list somewhere other than RV; buy a well-insulated RV; RV insurance must carry the serial number of your rig	(4)	(1.8%)
11. research the lifestyle	(12)	(5.4%)
12. research rigs before buying	(1)	(0.4%)
13. other: have a home base of some sort; mix with others and give of self; enjoy yourself	(8)	(3.6%)
14. multiple advice	(8)	(3.6%)
15. join Escapees	(5)	(2.2%)

Places

54. In which of the following do you usually stay when travelling from place to place? (294 responses)

1. free overnight spots	(11)	(4.9%)
2. public parks with partial or no hookups	(21)	(7.1%)
3. membership parks	(87)	(29.6%)
4. private parks with hookups	(42)	(14.2%)
5. private parks with hookups, resort facilities	(5)	(1.7%)
6. multiple responses	(92)	(31.3%)

Note: Of the 47 whose answer was #1, 44 answered question 86 about income. Of those,

    3 (6.8%) have yearly income of less than $5000 per person in rig
    5 (11.4%) have yearly income between 5–10K per person in rig
    17 (38.6%) have yearly income between 10–15K per person in rig
    3 (6.8%) have yearly income between 15–20K per person in rig
    9 (20.4%) have yearly income between 20–25K per person in rig
    7 (16%) have yearly income over 25K per person in rig

55. How often do you spend the night self-contained (without hookups)? (288 responses)

1. always	(22)	(7.6%)
2. often	(130)	(45.1%)
3. seldom	(126)	(43.8%)
4. never	(10)	(3.5%)

Note: Of 22 answering 1, 17 answered question 86 about income. Responses as follows:

    1 (5.9%) has yearly income less than $5000 per person in rig
    6 (35.3%) have yearly income between $5–10K per person in rig
    7 (41.2%) have yearly income between $10–15K per person in rig
    0 have yearly income between $15–20K
    2 (11.7%) have yearly income between $20–25K per person in rig
    1 (5.9%) has yearly income over $25000 per person in rig.

Of 130 answering 2, 125 answered question 86 about income. Responses as follows:

    4 (3.2%) have yearly income less than $5000 per person in rig
    21 (16.8%) have income between $5–10K per person in rig
    32 (25.6%) have income between $10–15K per person in rig
    21 (16.8%) have income between $15–20K per person in rig
    22 (17.6%) have income between $20–25K per person in rig
    25 (20%) have income over $25K per person in rig

56. When you are parking for a week or more, where do you prefer to stay? (284 responses)

1. boondocking areas: (BLM land, the Slabs, Quartzsite)	(41)	(14.4%)
2. public (county/state/national/forest) parks	(30)	(10.6%)
3. membership parks, eg. Coast to Coast, RPI, TT/NACO	(117)	(41.2%)
4. private parks with hookups	(38)	(13.4%)
5. private resort parks	(8)	(2.8%)
6. driveway or yard of friends or relatives	(5)	(1.8%)
7. multiple responses	(45)	(15.8%)

Note: of 41 answering 1, 37 replied to question 86 about income. Responses as follows:

    1 (2.7%) has yearly income less than $5000 per person in rig

8 (21.6%) have yearly income between $5-10K per person in rig
10 (27%) have yearly income between $10-15K per person in rig
8 (21.6%) have yearly income between $15-20K per person in rig
5 (13.5%) have yearly income between $20-25K per person in rig
5 (13.5%) have yearly income over $25K per person in rig.

57. Where did you park most of the time during the last year? (250 responses)

1. boondocking areas	(42)	(16.8%)
2. public parks	(19)	(7.6%)
3. private parks	(71)	(28.4%)
4. membership or resort parks	(97)	(38.8%)
5. driveway or yard of friends or relatives	(16)	(6.4%)
6. multiple answers	(5)	(2.0%)

Note: of 42 answering 1, 34 replied to question 86 about income. Responses as follows:

2 (5.9%) have yearly income less than $5000 per person in rig.
7 (20.6%) have yearly income between $5–10K per person in rig.
9 (26.5%) have yearly income between $10–15K per person in rig.
6 (17.6%) have yearly income between $15–20K per person in rig.
7 (20.6%) have yearly income between $20–25K per person in rig.
3 (8.8%) have yearly income over $25K per person in rig.

58. What is it that you especially like about the place(s) where you spend the most time? (272 responses)

1. hookups; golf course; planned activities	(23)	(8.5%)
2. appearance: attractive, beautiful.	(1)	(0.4%)
3. cleanliness of park/air/restrooms	(5)	(1.8%)
4. inexpensive; paid for it already	(10)	(3.7%)
5. warm climate; rockhounding, fishing; views of sunrise and sunsets; mountains; wildlife	(63)	(23.2%)
6. friendly people; people we meet	(53)	(19.5%)
7. lack of imposed rules	(4)	(1.5%)
8. location	(15)	(5.5%)
9. privacy; space; away from herd	(12)	(4.4%)
10. activities, lots of things to do	(8)	(2.9%)
11. other; it's home base; it is like coming home and I can stay as long as I like; it (SKP park) belongs to is; is a SKP park; full-timers congregate there; Overnighters Welcome signs	(26)	(9.6%)
12. multiple answers	(47)	(17.3%)
13. security	(5)	(1.8%)

59. How often do you go to the same location in the summer? (295 responses)

1. Always	(26)	(8.8%)
2. Often	(133)	(45.1%)
3. Seldom	(117)	(39.7%)
4. Never	(17)	(5.8%)
5. Write-in answers	(2)	(0.7%)

60. How often do you go to the same location in the winter? (284 responses)

1. always	(33)	(11.6%)
2. often	(148)	(52.1%)
3. seldom	(90)	(31.7%)
4. never	(12)	(4.2%)
5. multiple answer	(1)	(0.4%)

61. Do you belong to a membership park such as CCC system, TT/NACO, RPI? (288 responses)

1. yes	(190)	(66.0%)
2. no	(98)	(34.0%)

62. How much do you use your membership(s)? (272 responses, 200 members; percentages are calculated out of 200)

1. I never stay anywhere else if I can help it.	(55)	(27.5%)
2. I stay there about half the time.	(60)	(30.0%)
3. I stay there less than half the time.	(50)	(25.0%)
4. I almost never stay there	(35)	(17.5%)
5. I am not a member of a membership park system	(72)	

63. If you stay less than half the time or almost never use your membership, why is that? (112 responses)

1. advance planning required	(2)	(1.8%)
2. difficulty getting in	(11)	(9.8%)
3. economic reasons	(1)	(0.9%)
4. inconvenient location	(39)	(34.8%)
5. lifestyle in park: too structured, too crowded	(2)	(1.8%)
6. prefer other activities/parks	(44)	(39.2%)
7. other: only cheap, emergency backup, joined to be with friends and they're dead	(9)	(8.0%)
8. multiple reasons	(4)	(3.6%)

64. What is the best thing about membership parks? (206 responses)

1. activities planned	(5)	(2.4%)
2. good campgrounds; full hookups	(18)	(9.8%)
3. more control by managers	(1)	(0.9%)
4. low cost	(47)	(22.8%)
5. location of park	(3)	(1.5%)
6. high quality of park; well maintained	(5)	(2.4%)
7. security	(24)	(11.7%)
8. better class of people; full-timer focused; residents have pride in park	(19)	(9.2%)
9. nothing	(10)	(4.9%)
10. have to take you in; you can always get in	(14)	(6.8%)
11. multiple answers	(36)	(17.5%)
12. other	(24)	(11.7%)

65. What is the thing you like least about membership parks? (174 responses)

1. advance planning/research required.	(7)	(4.0%)
2. difficulty getting in, overbooking, reservations required	(48)	(27.6%)
3. park likely to go belly-up; expensive	(25)	(14.4%)

4. inconvenient location	(20)	(11.5%)
5. cliquish; unfriendly; don't know anyone	(14)	(8.0%)
6. pressure to join, to update membership, to pay more money	(6)	(3.4%)
7. park crowded, dirty, no full hookups	(17)	(9.8%)
8. time stay limited	(13)	(7.5%)
9. multiple answers	(13)	(7.5%)
10. none, I love them	(11)	(6.3%)

66. Which of the following is most important in selecting a place to stay overnight? (290 responses)

1. size of parking space	(41)	(14.1%)
2. cost	(93)	(32.0%)
3. hookups	(33)	(11.3%)
4. security	(69)	(23.8%)
5. resort facilities	(2)	(0.7%)
6. multiple answers	(41)	(14.1%)
7. location	(9)	(3.1%)
8. convenience	(2)	(0.7%)

67. Which of the following is most important in selecting a place to stay for a week or more? (289 responses)

1. size of parking space	(41)	(14.2%)
2. cost	(78)	(27.0%)
3. hookups	(51)	(17.6%)
4. security	(26)	(9.0%)
5. resort facilities	(17)	(5.9%)
6. multiple answers	(59)	(20.4%)
7. location	(13)	(4.5%)
8. friends are there	(1)	(0.3%)
9. environmental factors	(3)	(1.0%)

Quality of LIfe

Health concerns

Health problems affect the lives of many older people. We are interested in knowing whether RVers are a healthy lot, and how they cope with health problems when they occur.

68. Have you ever had a serious medical crisis while you were RVing? (289 responses)

1. yes	(68)	(23.5%)
2. no	(221)	(76.5%)

69. If yes, please describe the incident and how you coped with it. (78 responses)

1. accident	(11)	(14.1%)
2. acute illness	(39)	(50.0%)
3. chronic problem	(4)	(5.1%)

4. emergency	(3)	(3.8%)
5. surgery	(14)	(17.9%)
6. death of spouse	(3)	(3.8%)
7. multiple problems	(2)	(2.6%)

70. Have you seen a physician or been hospitalized in the last year? (289 responses)

1. yes	(79)	(27.3%)
2. no	(210)	(72.7%)

71. Is there any physical condition, illness, or health problem that bothers you now? (286 responses)

1. yes	(119)	(42.8%)
2. no	(167)	(57.2%)

72. If yes, please describe it. (118 responses)

1. accident related problems	(3)	(2.5%)
2. acute illness	(1)	(0.8%)
3. allergies	(4)	(3.4%)
4. arthritis	(17)	(14.4%)
5. cancer	(4)	(3.4%)
6. circulatory problems, high cholesterol	(4)	(3.4%)
7. diabetes	(10)	(8.5%)
8. digestive tract	(2)	(1.7%)
9. hearing problem	(2)	(1.7%)
10. heart disease	(9)	(7.6%)
11. high blood pressure	(9)	(7.6%)
12. neurological problems	(3)	(2.5%)
13. respiratory problems	(4)	(3.4%)
14. sight problem	(1)	(0.8%)
15. uro-genital tract	(2)	(1.7%)
16. back trouble	(8)	(6.8%)
17. joint problems, hip replacement	(7)	(1.7%)
18. other; shingles; carpel-tunnel syndrome; old age; skin; dental; pinched nerve in hip; dizziness	(7)	(1.7%)
19. multiple problems	(21)	(17.8%)

73. How would you describe your health as compared to other people your age? (291 responses)

1. excellent	(118)	(40.5%)
2. good	(149)	(51.2%)
3. fair	(22)	(7.6%)
4. poor	(2)	(0.7%)

74. Has your health changed since you began RVing? (291 responses)

1. yes, for the better	(73)	(25.0%)
2. no, it is about the same	(195)	(67.0%)
3. yes, it is worse	(23)	(7.9%)

75. If your health has changed, why do you think it happened?
Of 70 responses, health is for the better:

1. age, getting older	(1)	(1.4%)
2. climate, lower altitude	(4)	(5.7%)
3. less stress, fewer worries; more relaxed	(52)	(74.3%)
4. more exercise, better diet	(6)	(8.6%)
5. access to better doctors, hospitals	(2)	(2.9%)
9. other: RVing has kept me feeling as well as I am — I know more about caring for myself; we don't sit around	(2)	(2.9%)
10. multiple: answers 2+3; 3+4	(2)	(2.9%)
12. friends and support network	(1)	(1.4%)

Of 21 responses health is worse:

1. age, getting older	(12)	(57.1%)
6. new illness	(1)	(4.8%)
7. progression of pre-existing medical problem	(1)	(4.8%)
10. multiple answer (1+11)	(1)	(4.8%)
11. not enough exercise, more sedentary, poor diet	(6)	(28.6%)

76. During the last two weeks have there been days when you could not carry on your usual activities because you were ill? (296 responses)
1. no	(278)	(93.9%)
2. yes	(18)	(6.1%)

77. Are you now eligible for U.S. or Canadian medicare coverage? (296 responses)
1. yes	(146)	(49.3%)
2. no	(150)	(50.7%)

78. Are you now enroled in a private medical care insurance plan? (295 responses)
1. yes	(228)	(77.3%)
2. no	(67)	(22.7%)

Of those 150 not covered by medicare (see Q.77) 36 (24%) have no private coverage either. 12.2% of 295 have no medical insurance of any kind.

Before leaving on your current RV travel did you do any of the following?

79. Visit your physician for a thorough checkup? (295 responses)
1. yes	(160)	(54.2%)
2. no	(135)	(45.8%)

80. Make arrangements for routinely required prescription drugs? (293 responses
1. yes	(169)	(57.7%)
2. no	(45)	(15.4%)
3. no, I take no drugs routinely	(79)	(27.0%)

81. Take out special health insurance? (284 responses)

1. yes	(35)	(12.3%)
2. no	(249)	(87.7%)

Note: Americans Skips consider Sky Med to be special health insurance. Sky Med is an emergency medical evacuation plan recommended by the Escapees club.

82. Make arrangements to return home in case of a medical emergency? (288 responses)

1. yes	(69)	(24.0%)
2. no	(219)	(76.0%)

83. Leave instructions with relatives in case of a medical emergency? (285 responses)

1. yes	(113)	(39.6%)
2. no	(172)	(60.4%)

84. Obtain copies of your medical records to carry with you? (286 responses)

1. yes	(117)	(40.9%)
2. no	(169)	(59.1%)

Finances

Finances are a major issue for most retired people and may determine whether a person becomes an RVer. The following questions will help us to find out what sort of financial resources are necessary for successful RV living.

85. How many people travel in your rig? (283 responses}

1	(33)	(11.7%)
2	(238)	(84.1%)
3	(3)	(1.0%)
4	(1)	(0.4%)
4 +	(8)	(2.8%)

Note: of 33 people giving answer #1 (1 person in the rig), all answered question 86 below. 1 reported an income of less than $5,000, 4 said their income was between $5-10K; 10 reported an income of $10-15K, 6 said their income was $15-20K, 8 reported an income of over $25K.

86. What is the approximate yearly income per person in your rig? (278 responses)

1. less than $5,000	(10)	(3.6%)
2. between $5,000 and $10,000	(42)	(15.1%)
3. between $10,000 and $15,000	(75)	(27.0%)
4. between $15,000 and $20,000	(52)	(18.7%)
5. between $20,000 and $25,000	(47)	(16.9%)
6. over $25,000.	(52)	(18.7%)

87. In my experience, the RVing life style (276 responses)

1. is an expensive way of life	(14)	(5.1%)
2. costs about the same as a sedentary way of life	(94)	(34.0%)
3. is an inexpensive way of life	(168)	(60.9%)

88. What is the largest item in your budget? (278 responses)

1. dues, campground fees	(10)	(3.6%)
2. food, restaurant meals	(83)	(29.9%)
3. fuel, gasoline	(69)	(24.8%)
4. health costs (not medical insurance)	(3)	(1.1%)
5. insurance (unspecified)	(22)	(7.9%)
6. medical insurance	(9)	(3.2%)
7. payments: house, vehicle, rig	(33)	(11.9%)
8. vehicle/rig expenses, maintenance	(32)	(11.5%)
9. other: living expenses, paying off credit cards, teephone calls, house maintenance even though not living in it	(6)	(2.2%)
10. multiple answers	(11)	(4.0%)

89. What do you estimate that you spend on this item? (268 responses)

1. < $300 month	(43)
2. $300-499 month	(66)
3. $500-699 month	(22)
4. $700-999 month	(9)
5. $1000-1190 month	(9)
6. $1200-1499 month	(1)
7. $1500-1999 month	(1)
8. $2000-2499 month	(1)
9. $2500 + month	(0)
10. < $500 season/yr	(1)
11. $500-699 season/yr	(2)
12. $700-999 season/yr	(2)
13. $1000-1199 season/yr	(1)
14. $1200-1499 season/yr	(4)
15. $1500-1699 season/yr	(8)
16. $1700-1999 season/yr	(2)
17. $2000-2499 season/yr	(14)
18. $2500-2999 season/yr	(0)
19. $3000-3999 season/yr	(8)
20. $4000-4999 season/yr	(6)
21. $5000 + season/yr	(22)
22. don't know	(11)
23. wide range, varies with circumstances	(23)
24. other (too much, lots, 1/3 of our income)	(12)

90. What do you spend during a normal month (either a specific figure or a range)? (244 responses, percentages calculated out of 230 responses specifying amounts. Note: 60.2% spend between $700 and $1999 per month.)

1. < $300 month	(9)	(3.9%)
2. $300-499 month	(3)	(1.3%)
3. $500-699 month	(19)	(8.3%)
4. $700-999 month	(31)	(13.5%)
5. $1000-1199 month	(30)	(13.0%)
6. $1500-1999 month	(50)	(21.7%)
7. $2000-2499 month	(27)	(11.7%)

9. $2500-2999 month	(22)	(9.6%)
10. $3000 + month	(11)	(4.8%)
11. don't know	(7)	(2.9%)
12. wide range, varies with circumstances	(2)	(0.8%)
13. other: too much, whatever it takes	(5)	(2.0%)

Problems and RVing

Some problems are either particularly worrisome to RVers or affect RVers more than other people. For each of the following commonly expressed concerns, please indicate whether you have experienced the problem in the past year.

**91. Major mechanical problem or breakdown of RV or tow vehicle.
(292 responses)**

1. yes	(105)	(36.0%)
2. no	(187)	(64.0%)

92. Serious illness or health problem while on the road. (289 responses)

1. yes	(39)	(13.5%)
2. no	(250)	(86.5%)

93. Threat to personal safety. (286 responses)

1. yes	(9)	(3.1%)
2. no	(277)	(96.9%)

94. Running out of money. (295 responses)

1. yes	(26)	(8.8%)
2. no	(269)	(91.2%)

95. Losing touch with family members. (289 responses)

1. yes	(24)	(8.3%)
2. no	(265)	(91.7%)

97. Which is normally of the *greatest* concern to you? (289 responses)

1. mechanical breakdown	(100)	(34.7%)
2. illness	(68)	(23.5%)
3. personal safety	(27)	(9.3%)
4. money	(26)	(9.0%)
5. isolation from family	(20)	(6.9%)
6. other (please specify)	(10)	(3.5%)
7. multiple answers	(25)	(8.7%)
8. no concerns	(13)	(4.5%)

98. Which of these problems normally concerns you the *least*? (277 responses)

1. mechanical breakdown	(17)	(6.1%)
2. illness	(19)	(6.9%)
3. personal safety	(42)	(15.2%)
4. money	(60)	(21.7%)
5. isolation from family	(120)	(43.4%)
6. multiple answers	(17)	(6.1%)
7. no concerns	(2)	(0.7%)

99. What security precautions do you take? (271 responses)

1. avoid potentially threatening situations (1) (.4%)
2. behavior: be alert; use common sense; depend on others; check in with others at regular time; ask truckers for help; don't display valuables; don't look for trouble; appear harmless; mind my own business; get acquainted with neighbors (18) (6.6%)
3. communication devices: CB radio, cell phone (4) (1.5%)
4. dog (9) (3.3%)
5. locks, alarms (49) (18.1%)
6. don't drive down unlit roads after dark, don't stay in national forests, wilderness areas, don't stay in roadside rest areas [in the US; in CA], don't stay in public parks, scout parking area for potential problems, don't park in out-of-the way places, don't park alone, don't boondock, park in well-lit areas, stay in campgrounds with security, stay in rural state parks: (33) (12.2%)
7. drive motor home (don't have to get out to leave), drive old vehicle that doesn't look expensive; keep tow vehicle in good working order so can get out fast: (7) (2.6%)
8. weapon (gun) (20) (7.4%)
9. weapon (other than gun): (7) (2.6%)
   examples: (including responses from earlier version of questionnaire) baseball bat, can of Easy Off and a crowbar, stick, flare gun, golf club and salmon bonker, hammer just inside door
10. other: mace, pepper spray, fire extinguisher (8) (2.3%)
11. multiple (10) (3.7%)
12. none (7) (2.6%)
13. locks + parking and driving precautions (52) (19.2%)
14. guns + other methods (46) (17.0%)
15. weapon other than gun + other method (5) (1.9%)

100. Have you ever felt threatened by other persons while you were RVing? (285 responses)

1. yes (28) (9.8%)
2. no (257) (90.2%)

101. If yes, please describe the incident and how you handled it. (40 responses)

1. forced entry into vehicle (4) (10.0%)
2. harassment (2) (5.0%)
3. robbery (4) (10.0%)
4. suspicious behaviour (22) (55.0%)
5. threats (1) (2.5%)
6. unwarranted fear (2) (5.0%)
7. other (5) (12.5%)

102. Do you carry weapons? (290 responses)

1. yes	(144)	(49.7%)
2. no	(146)	(50.3%)

Note: 141 (51%) of Americans responding to this question said they carry weapons. Of these 8 (6%) said they carry a gun (generic); 39 (28%) carry guns (plural); 55 (39%) carry a hand gun; 18 (13%) carry a shotgun; 3 (2%) carry a rifle; 5 (4%) carry a gun and some other weapon. The remaining 8% of weapons include mace, clubs, and other such as crowbars, ice picks, fire extinguishers.

103. If yes, what kind? (140 responses)

1. club	(1)	(0.7%)
2. gun (generic)	(8)	(5.7%)
3. guns (plural)	(40)	(28.6%)
4. hand gun	(55)	(39.3%)
5. shot gun	(19)	(13.6%)
6. rifle	(3)	(2.1%)
7. mace	(1)	(0.7%)
8. other	(5)	(3.6%)
9. gun + other	(8)	(5.7%)

104. If you carry weapons, have you ever had to use them? (168 responses)

1. yes	(3)	(1.8%)
2. no	(165)	(98.2%)

105. If yes, please describe the incident. (3 responses)

1. attempted forced entry	(1)	(33.3%)
2. harassment	(1)	(33.3%)
3. target practice	(1)	(33.3%)

Leaving the RV Life Style

106. When health or finances force you to stop active RVing what will you do? (285 answers)

1. retire to the Escapee CARE center	(15)	(5.3%)
2. retire to an RV, park model, or mobile home in an RV park	(85)	(29.8%)
3. move into a house or apartment	(40)	(14.0%)
4. go into a retirement home or community	(18)	(6.3%)
5. move in with family members	(3)	(1.1%)
6. I have made no plans	(97)	(34.0%)
7. other (please specify)	(24)	(8.4%)
8. an SKP park, co-op	(3)	(1.1%)

107. What would you miss most about RVing? (267 responses)

1. new experiences, interesting life, the excitement of change, adventure	(18)	(6.7%)
2. freedom	(45)	(18.0%)
3. independence	(4)	(1.5%)
4. swapping information about RVing, living outdoors	(7)	(2.6%)

5. social interaction	(32)	(12.0%)
6. travel	(80)	(30.0%)
7. other: having choices, security, good weather, being able to escape bad neighbors, playing poker	(9)	(3.4%)
8. everything	(8)	(3.0%)
9. multiple answers	(7)	(2.6%)
10. nothing	(0)	
11. travel & friends/ new places & new people	(54)	(20.2%)

108. Is there anything that you look forward to about leaving RVing? (273 responses)

1. yes	(37)	(13.6%)
2. no	(236)	(86.4%)

109. If yes, what is it? (37 responses)

1. ease of communication including telephone, mail	(1)	(2.7%)
2. conveniences: dishwasher, home laundry, bathtub	(1)	(2.7%)
3. family: being near children, grandchildren	(2)	(5.4%)
4. having a workshop, garden	(7)	(18.9%)
5. home community: church, old friends	(3)	(8.1%)
6. space, personal and space to do things	(5)	(13.5%)
7. no more vehicle/rig problems, flat tires	(2)	(5.4%)
8. other: staying in one place long enough to study crafts, read books, smell roses, take classes; private room in boarding house with no cooking, housekeeping problems; going on cruises; settling down; being home if ill; stability; morning paper; less hassle; I'm looking for a place to settle down	(14)	(37.8%)
9. multiple answers	(2)	(5.4%)

If you are willing to talk about your RVing experiences, or if you have questions, please sign your name and give your site number or information on how to locate you.

NAME: _____

SITE or LOCATION: _____

Thank you very much for helping us in our research on the RV community.

Appendix Two

Research Method

Participant observation has been a strength of anthropology since Malinowski's work in the Trobriand Islands during World War I. As Bloch says, the continuous and intimate contact with the people we study requires us to learn at least some of the skills they use to cope with the problems of daily life. The informal and implicit co-operation between anthropologists and the people they study forms the basis of anthropological knowledge at a visceral as well as an intellectual level.[1]

In an earlier publication we discussed our concerns about questionnaires and our unsuccessful attempt in 1990 to use them.[2] In her discussion of research method, Kaufman says that the use of a questionnaire forces people to structure their discussions and answers "according to the researcher's priorities rather than their own."[3]

These concerns, are not new. In 1941 Cowgill found it was impossible to get a figure on the number of trailerites or to describe the trailer population with any accuracy. Therefore, it was also impossible to get a representative statistical sample of RVers. Any population of RVers he studied would omit others. So, he decided to supplement his limited statistical data with an "insider's description of the life of a trailerite," collected through participant observation. This method enabled him to interpret his survey data more accurately because "in the lack of such interpretation by one who knows the inside of the situation, the outsider may be led to many erroneous conclusions."[4] When Cowgill analyzed his data he found people were more frank about the disagreeable aspects of trailer living when they talked with him in person than when they completed his questionnaires. "The personal contact was able to overcome a barrier that the questionnaire could not." Cowgill concluded:

> The author's personal conviction after this experience is all in favor of the interview method. It allows a flexibility that, while somewhat difficult to handle in an exact statistical way, obviates the possibility of the student missing completely the

really significant points because he is unable to get outside of predetermined categories.[5]

Our data for this study, collected during 1990 and 1993-1994, and by correspondence between field studies, include responses to 369 question-naires (three versions). We analyzed 296 of the responses by computer using the database program in Microsoft Works. Our data also includes 105 interviews. Each interview lasted a minimum of two hours. We also use letters and columns from 16 years (1984-2000) of the *Escapees Newsletter*.

Our various questionnaires have produced useful information, some of which we could not have obtained in any other way. Nevertheless we continue to have reservations about questionnaire-based research — reservations reinforced by problems with our data. One source of difficulty with the questionnaire as a research tool for our project lies in the dynamic nature of the RV life-style. Because they are always on the move, meeting new people and having new experiences, RVers say they are constantly changing. Some said their answers this year were different from those they would have given the previous year. Others thought the answers they gave when they were actively traveling would not have been the same had they been settled for a lengthy period in a park. Their lives, values, and patterns of interaction change dramatically under different circumstances, they said, and so would their answers. This problem will likely arise with other research methods too. However, interviews and conversations allow people to discuss the ways in which their answers might change and to modify their statements. Questionnaires used alone do not permit such qualification.

Other problems arose from our inability to list all options from which people might choose and from the questionnaire structure that required people to choose between answers they found equally valid. People often rejected the range of choices we offered, adding one or more numbers and writing in their own answers. For example, in two questions (numbers 66 and 67) we asked which of five things — size of parking space, cost, hookups, security, resort facilities — is most important in selecting a place to stay overnight (66) or for a week or more (67). Many people added a number 6 and wrote in "location." In our analysis we added location as an option, but it is under-represented. If it had been a choice on the questionnaire we think more people would have selected it.

People often marked two or more of the possible answers, despite verbal instructions to choose only one. For example, many people checked all the options for questions 66 and 67. Some wrote on the form that all the choices were valid depending on where they were and what they wanted to do at the time. We added a handwritten request on the questionnaires to "mark only one answer please, or rank your answers." Nevertheless, many people continued to mark several without ranking them. As one couple explained in apology, "We couldn't make a choice because all the things we checked are important to us." Another couple checked both yes and no to question 31, "Did you retire in order to RV?" In explanation they said both answers were right for them. They retired for other reasons, but with the intention of RVing full-time. If we could start our research anew, we would revise our questionnaire again.

On the positive side, the questionnaire was useful as the starting point for an interview. On the form we gave respondents the option of either remaining anonymous or of signing their name and indicating their willingness to talk with us. When we could, we scheduled a follow-up interview with all who signed their questionnaires.

The flaws of questionnaires in general, and of ours in particular notwithstanding, we think it was a useful research tool. People who chose to talk with us were usually helpful and cooperative and often had suggestions that aided us in our research. While it was not always true, for the most part the follow-up interviews permitted us to enrich the material contained on the written form. It allowed us, for example, to ask respondents why they did not answer a particular question, or to invite them to elaborate on sometimes cryptic answers. We also found we had sometimes misunderstood what people had meant by their answers. Only the follow-up discussion allows for correction of such error.

Our questionnaire did not reach a random sample of serious RVers. It was not intended to. First, our sample is from people we met (mostly members of Escapees) who were willing to complete our questionnaire. We suspect that people who are willing to fill out a questionnaire constructed by academics are better educated — and therefore possibly more affluent–than the RVing population would appear to be in a random sample. Second, there is no agreement on what constitutes a "serious RVer" or a "full-time RVer," or on how many of them there are, however they are defined. It is not possible to define an unbiased sample of a population whose demographic shape is unknowable.

There are other surveys of RVers, but it is difficult to compare our findings with theirs. Given the methods and assumptions used in each case, the lack of comparability is no surprise. Two of the surveys of RVers to which we have access, those by Curtin (1994) and Louis Harris and Associates (1994), were commissioned by the Recreation Vehicle Industry Association. These were US nationwide surveys done following rigorous sampling techniques common to the established polling industry. They were conducted in an effort to get at demographics of *all* RV owners and potential buyers, with particular attention to identifying the characteristics of likely first-time buyers of recreational vehicles for vacation purposes. The survey results do not permit us to readjust the figures to focus on those we have called *serious* RVers.

Two other surveys of RVers are based on the membership of particular clubs. One, based on the membership of the Family Motor Coach Association, identifies characteristics of those owning particular types of motor homes.[6] Since the analyzer of these data appears to have assumed that only *motor homes* were RVs, the use of the findings is limited. The other, by the staff of the Escapees Club, is based on responses to a tear-off questionnaire in the club's newsletter.[7] Their data are based, as are ours, on the voluntary responses of members of the club: strictly speaking, those willing to tear it off, fill it out, and pay for a stamp to return it to club headquarters. It differs from ours in a number of respects. First, our data are not limited to, though they are dominated by, members of the Escapees Club. Second, our materials were collected on the road and were overwhelmingly drawn from RVers who were actively traveling. The club's survey went to all members receiving the newsletter, whether they continued to be active travelers or not. We suspect that some of the discrepancy in the data from our survey and that of the club may be attributed to a higher proportion of non-traveling club members reporting in Kornow's survey. When they begin serious RVing, people travel most of the year and spend only short times in one place. After a year or more, most RVers look for a home base where they park for several months at a time. While some RVers actively travel all their life, most spend more time at their home base as they age.

Although the figures we derive from the analysis of our data represent only the ideas and preferences of those who responded, our questionnaire permitted us to collect more comparable data than we could otherwise have done.

Notes

1. Bloch 1991:193-195.

2. Counts and Counts 1992b.

3. Kaufman 1986:22.

4. Cowgill 1941:15.

5. Cowgill 1941:16.

6. Albert 1993.

7. Kornow 1993.

Appendix Three

Canadian Federal and Provincial Rules Regarding Residence Requirements for Eligibility for Provincial Health Care

Canadian Federal Definitions

A "dwelling-house" is defined in the Criminal Code of Canada as follows:

"dwelling-house" means the whole or any part of a building or structure that is kept or occupied as a permanent or temporary residence, and includes

(a) a building within the curtilage of a dwelling-house that is connected to it by a doorway or by a covered and enclosed passage-way, and

(b) a unit that is designed to be mobile and to be used as a permanent or temporary residence and that is being used as such a residence;

"Resident" means, in relation to a province, a person lawfully entitled to be or to remain in Canada who makes his home and is ordinarily present in the province, but does not include a tourist, a transient or a visitor to the province.

Services out-of-country are to be paid, as a minimum, on the basis of the amount that would have been paid by the home province for similar services rendered in-province (Canada 1993:Health Act Overview:6).

The following information was submitted to Health Canada by the provinces. Under the provisions of the *Canada Health Act*, each province and territory must provide information on the operation of their health care plans as they relate to the criteria and conditions of the *Act*. Accordingly, the material which follows describes the operation of the provincial health care insurance plans for the period April 1, 1998 through March 31, 1999.[1] The material has been edited to include only sections relevant to Canadian RVers.

Alberta

All residents of Alberta, with the exception of members of the Canadian Forces, members of the Royal Canadian Mounted Police, and inmates of federal penitentiaries, are entitled to coverage under the Hospitalization Benefits Plan, provided they are registered with the Minister. Seniors are required to pay premiums at the same rate as non-seniors.

Minimum residence
The minimum residence period for coverage under the Alberta Hospitalization and Medical Benefits Plans does not exceed three months. A resident who is temporarily absent from the province for vacation, visit or business engagement reasons must maintain benefits for a minimum of 12 consecutive months.... A resident who routinely spends periods away from Alberta must live in Alberta for the major portion of each year in order to maintain coverage. Premiums must continue to be paid during a temporary absence (premium assistance programs apply as for in-province coverage).

Regardless of the reason for temporary absence, residents are required to notify Alberta Health as soon as it appears likely that treatment for a single accident or illness will continue for more than three months.

Payment arrangements outside Canada
Hospitalization benefits are payable only when services are provided in active treatment general hospitals that provide standard services such as ICU or emergency ward or auxiliary hospitals that provide standard acute care services to long-term or chronically ill patients. If services are not insured in the province, they are not insured when provided outside the country.

The maximum amount payable for out-of-country in-patient hospital services is $100 per day (not including day of discharge). The maximum out-patient per visit rate is $50. Some specialists' out-patient services, such as CAT scans, are paid at higher rates. Benefits for out-of-country practitioner services are payable according to the fee charged or the Alberta rate, whichever is the lesser.

Full coverage of treatment costs outside Canada may be provided under the following two programs: the Out-of-Country Health Services Program, which may apply where the required service is not available in Canada; and the Emergency Financial Assistance Program, which may apply where the treatment expense could not have been guarded against.

British Columbia

All residents, excluding members of the Canadian Forces and the Royal Canadian Mounted Police, inmates of federal penitentiaries and those eligible for compensation from another source, are entitled to hospital and medical care insurance coverage. As of April 1, 1998, residents must be enrolled in the Medical Services Plan to receive insured hospital services. There are no additional premiums.

There are no premiums for insured hospital services. However, there is a daily charge for extended-care hospital services for patients over the age of 19. The client rate, representing the cost of accommodation and meals, is established once a year. At the end of 1998-99, the maximum non-subsidized rate was $50 a day. Residents of limited means are eligible for assistance, on a sliding scale, being 85 per cent of the Old Age Security and Guaranteed Income Supplement. In certain circumstances there is a provision to waive a portion of the $25.30 fee. Client rates of less than $50 per day are reviewed quarterly and patients are advised one month before any changes.

Enrolment in the Medical Services Plan is mandatory, and payment of premiums is ordinarily a requirement for coverage. However, failure to pay premiums is not a barrier to coverage for those who meet the basic enrolment eligibility criteria. Residents of limited means may be eligible for premium assistance. There are five levels, ranging from 20 per cent to 100 per cent of the full premium.

Minimum residence
The minimum residence requirement for hospital insurance and medical care coverage is a waiting period ending at midnight on the last day of the second month following the month in which the individual becomes a resident.

Individuals who leave the province temporarily on extended vacations or for temporary employment may be covered for up to 12 months. Effective January 1, 1998, approval is limited to once in five years for such absences exceeding six months in a calendar year. Residents may take annual vacations of up to six months, provided they are physically present in Canada for six months each calendar year.

Payment arrangements outside Canada

With prior authorization, coverage is provided for hospital service not available in Canada at the hospital's usual and customary rate. In other circumstances, with prior authorization, in-patient coverage is at the established standard ward rate. Renal dialysis day care is available at the interprovincial and interterritorial Canadian rate. In all other cases, including emergency or sudden illness during temporary absences from the province, in-patient hospital care is paid up to $75 Canadian per day for adults and children, and $41 Canadian per day for newborns.

Out-of-country medical services are covered for emergency or sudden illness during temporary absences from the province. These are paid up to the same fee payable for that service, had it been performed in British Columbia. Cases pre-authorized because of extenuating circumstances, however, are paid at the rate applicable where the service is rendered. With prior authorization, payment for non-emergency medical services outside the country may be made at usual and customary rates, when the appropriate treatment is not available in the province or elsewhere in Canada.

The attending specialist must request prior consent from the Ministry of Health. Consent may be given based on the merit of each request, even though the service is available in the province or elsewhere in Canada.

Elective services are provided only with prior authorization by both the Medical Services Plan of British Columbia and the Regional Programs.

Persons moving permanently outside Canada are entitled to coverage to the end of the month of departure.

Manitoba

Minimum residence

Persons temporarily absent from the province may continue as insured persons for up to 12 months, or up to 24 months if they are taking full-time employment outside Canada under a written contract of employment.... A person must be physically present in the province for at least six months of each calendar year to qualify as a resident.

Payment arrangements outside Canada

Hospital services received outside Canada due to an accident or sudden illness, while temporarily absent, are paid as follows:

in-patient; the lesser of the actual hospital charges for the insured services provided and the per diem rate established by regulation, according to hospital bed size; and out-patient; the lesser of the actual hospital charges for the insured services provided and the flat rate per visit established by regulation. When hospital services are recommended by an appropriate Manitoba specialist and approved by the Minister, but are not available or cannot be adequately provided in Manitoba or elsewhere in Canada, the Plan pays the following fees:

> in-patient; the greater of 75 per cent of the actual hospital charges for the insured services provided and a per diem rate established by regulation, according to hospital bed size; and

> out-patient; the greater of 75 per cent of the actual hospital charges for insured services provided and a $100 fee per visit established by regulation. Payment for hospital services is made in US funds. For physician services received outside Canada in an emergency or upon referral by an appropriate specialist and approved by the Minister, payment is made according to the current Manitoba Physicians' Manual in Canadian funds.

New Brunswick

Universality

All insured persons in the province are entitled to coverage. Not entitled are regular members of the Canadian Forces; members of the Royal Canadian Mounted Police; persons serving a prison term in a federal penitentiary, and people from another province or territory who are in New Brunswick for educational purposes, and who are eligible for coverage under their provincial or territorial plans.

In order to be entitled to insured health services, beneficiaries and their dependants must register. Upon registration, eligible persons are issued a New Brunswick Medicare card bearing the resident's name, date of birth, Medicare number and expiry date. This card must be produced when requesting services from a medical practitioner or a hospital. No premiums are levied.

Minimum residence

A person is eligible to become a beneficiary under the health plan on the first day of the third month following the month of arrival in the province, when entering from another province or territory.... Coverage is provided to people from outside Canada who are in the province on work permits for periods of 12 months or longer. Effective January 1, 1993, New Brunswick increased its minimum residence requirement to 183 days, in order to bring it in line with other jurisdictions.

An eligible person may be temporarily absent from the province for the purpose of vacation, visits or business arrangements; however, this absence must not exceed 182 days in a 12-month period, unless approved by the Director of Medicare.

Payment arrangements outside Canada

Effective April 1, 1997, only emergency services are covered and are paid in Canadian funds. Hospital in-patient services are paid at a daily maximum of $100, while out-patient services are paid at a maximum of $50. Physicians' fees associated with these services are paid at New Brunswick rates. If a service is not available in Canada, Medicare will negotiate a rate with US providers, if the service has received prior approval.

Newfoundland

Universality

All insured residents of the province are entitled to coverage, with the exception of regular members of the Canadian Forces, members of the Royal Canadian Mounted Police and persons serving a prison term in a federal penitentiary. No premium payment exists. Registration under the Medical Care Plan and possession of a valid Medical Care Plan card are required in order to have access to insured services.

Minimum residence

Insured persons moving to Newfoundland from other provinces or ter-ritories are entitled to coverage as of the first day of the third month following the month of arrival, whereas persons arriving from outside Canada to establish residence are entitled to coverage as of the day of arrival, as are discharged members of the Canadian Forces and the Royal Canadian Mounted Police, and released inmates of federal penitentiaries. For coverage to be effective, however, registration is required under the Medical Care Plan. Immediate coverage is provided to persons from outside Canada who are authorized to work in the province for one year or more. Persons must reside within the province for a minimum of four months each year in order to qualify for coverage. However, persons temporarily absent from the province may be granted an extension of 12 months' coverage, providing satisfactory evidence is given that they intend to return.

Payment arrangements outside Canada

Out-of-country hospital in-patient and out-patient services are covered for emergency or sudden illness at established rates. Elective hospital services are also insured when services are not available in the province or in the country. The maximum amount payable by the government's hospitalization plan for out-of-country in-patient hospital care is $350 per day if the insured services are provided by a community or regional hospital. Where insured services are provided by a tertiary care hospital — a highly specialized facility — the approved rate is $465 per day. The approved rate for out-patient services is $62 per visit and haemodialysis is $220 per treatment. The approved rates are paid in Canadian funds.

Physician services are covered for emergency or sudden illness, and are also insured for elective services, when they are not available in the province or in the country. They are paid at the same rate as would be paid in Newfoundland for the same service. If the services are not available in Newfoundland, they are usually paid at Ontario rates, or at rates that apply in a province in which they are available.

Northwest Territories

Universality

The Northwest Territories Plans entitle all residents of the Northwest Territories, excluding members of the Canadian Forces and the Royal Canadian Mounted Police, and inmates of federal penitentiaries, to be registered. Residence requirements are in accordance with the interprovincial Agreement on Eligibility and Portability and Northwest Territories Eligibility Guidelines. No premiums are levied.

Minimum residence

The minimum residence period does not exceed three months, though the Plan reserves the right to apply specific guidelines to determine whether an individual has taken up residence.... Individuals who are temporarily absent from the Northwest Territories are covered for up to 12 months, provided prior notice is given.

Payment arrangements outside Canada

The Northwest Territories Health Care Plan covers insured hospital services provided out of the country up to Northwest Territories rates, paid in Canadian funds to residents. The Plan covers insured medical services provided out of the country, up to Northwest Territories rates. If service is not available within the Northwest Territories, the Department of Health and Social Services uses the rates set by an appropriate location within Canada.

Nova Scotia

Universality

The legislation provides that all residents of the province … are entitled to receive insured hospital services. In addition, Nova Scotians are insured for emergency services outside the country, for insured residents, to the limits of the Nova Scotia fee schedule.… This provision ensures coverage for all residents of the province. A resident is defined as "a person who is legally entitled to remain in Canada and who makes his/her home and is ordinarily present in Nova Scotia, but does not include a tourist, a transient or a visitor to Nova Scotia."

Minimum residence

Those temporarily absent from the province may be granted an extension of coverage to a maximum of 12 months.

Payment arrangements outside Canada

Out-of-country in-patient hospitalization as the result of an accident or sudden illness while temporarily absent from Canada is covered in Canadian funds. Hospital services are paid for at the lesser of two rates: a rate calculated on the basis of the average per diem of the Halifax metro hospitals at the time services are rendered, or at the per diem of the hospital providing the service. Unapproved non-emergency or elective treatment, unreferred hospital services received in a psychiatric hospital or addiction centre outside Canada, and hospital out-patient services are excluded from out-of-country coverage. Out-of-country physician services, as the result of an accident or sudden illness during a temporary absence from Canada, are covered in Canadian funds at Nova Scotia rates.

Ontario

Universality
All residents of Ontario are eligible for coverage, subject to a three-month waiting period.... Every resident of Ontario is required to register. All insured hospital, medical, and dental services to which federal contributions are related are available to Ontario residents on uniform terms and conditions.

Minimum residence
Subject to certain exceptions, new or returning residents who apply to become insured persons are subject to a three-month waiting period before they are eligible for or entitled to insured health services.... Each resident must make a permanent and principal home in Ontario for a minimum of 153 days in any 12-month period.

In accordance with the Interprovincial Agreement on Eligibility and Portability, it is possible for residents to maintain continuous coverage while temporarily working or studying in another Canadian province. To avoid a lapse in coverage, the person should notify the Ministry of Health about an intended absence.

An insured person can also maintain continuous coverage while temporarily out of the country for reasons such as work or study. However, the individual must notify the Ministry prior to leaving and receive confirmation of eligibility. Restrictions apply to the nature and duration of out-of-country absences.

Payment arrangements outside Canada
Effective September 1, 1995, out-of-country emergency hospital costs are reimbursed at Ontario fixed per diem rates of

- a maximum $400 Canadian for in-patient services,
- a maximum $50 Canadian for out-patient services, and
- a maximum $210 Canadian per dialysis treatment.

Medically necessary out-of-country physician and other eligible practitioner services (chiropractors, dentists, optometrists, podiatrists, and osteopaths) as well as laboratory tests required on an emergency basis, are reimbursed at the rates listed in the Ontario Ministry of Health's Schedule of Benefits or the amount billed, whichever is less.

Prince Edward Island

Universality
Every person permanently residing in Prince Edward Island, with the exception of members of the Canadian Forces (regular), the Royal Canadian Mounted Police, or persons on student visas, who has registered under the Plans and provided the Department with all information required, is eligible for insured services. Eligibility is based on permanent residence and full compliance with the Interprovincial Agreement on Eligibility and Portability. No premiums are levied.

Minimum residence
Every person registering for insured services under the Plan becomes eligible on the first day of the third month following the date of establishing residence. Provided registration requirements as set out in the Regulations are complied with, landed immigrants, repatriated Canadians, returning Canadians, returning landed immigrants, Canadian citizens or spouses of Canadian citizens assuming residence in Canada for the first time, persons living in the province under the authority of a work permit issued under the Immigration Act (Canada), discharged members of the Canadian Forces and Royal Canadian Mounted Police, and discharged inmates of federal penitentiaries are entitled to benefits, once the date of residence is established.

Regular annual absences of fewer than six months per year are allowed, provided permanent residence does not change. Persons temporarily absent from the province may be granted an extension of up to six months' coverage, provided the Department is notified in writing.

Payment arrangements outside Canada
Hospital in-patient insured services received under emergency or sudden illness circumstances are paid in Canadian funds at a rate not exceeding the per diem rate of the Queen Elizabeth Hospital in Charlottetown. Hospital in-patient elective services not available in Canada are paid, with prior approval of the Department, at a rate not to exceed the total amount payable for in-patient services at the hospital, including room and board and medically necessary hospital services, and are payable in appropriate funds, depending on the country of origin.

Hospital out-patient services received under emergency or sudden illness circumstances are paid in Canadian funds at PEI rates, or appropriate Canadian rates where applicable.

Quebec

Universality

Registration with the hospital insurance plan is not required. Registration with the Régie de l'assurance-maladie or proof of residence is sufficient to establish eligibility. All residents or deemed residents of Quebec must be registered with the Régie de l'assurance-maladie to be eligible for the health insurance programs…. No premium payment exists.

Minimum residence

If outside Quebec for 183 days or more, students and full-time unpaid trainees, can retain their status as a resident of Quebec in the first case for four consecutive calendar years at most, and in the second case for two consecutive calendar years at most. Quebec government civil servants, employees of non-profit organizations with head offices in Canada and employed abroad in assistance or cooperation programs recognized by the Minister of Health and Social Services, and the spouses and dependants of all such persons maintain their resident status, provided the Régie is notified of their absence…. Resident status is also maintained by those persons who remain outside the province for 183 days or more, but fewer than 12 months within a calendar year, provided such an absence occurs only once every seven years and is reported to the Régie.

Provincial Rules of Residency as Applied to Health Care Plans

In June 1995 we sent a letter to all provincial departments of health asking for clarification of their residence rules as they apply to eligibility for covered by the provincial health care plan. The following is a sample of that letter:

We are anthropologists who have been conducting research with retired North Americans who sell their homes and live full-time in their recreation vehicles. We are currently writing a book on this topic. Canadian RVers say it is extremely difficult for a Canadian to become a full-time RVer because of provincial legislation requiring residence within a province in order to be eligible for provincial health care. Most Canadian RVers we have talked to are unsure what the residency rules are in their province and there is much conflicting information and confusion.

We are writing for information about the residency rules of your province so that we may include this information in our book. We would appreciate knowing how residence is defined in your province and how a legal residence is defined for the purpose of eligibility for provincial health care. It would be especially helpful if you could either send us a copy of the pertinent legislation or give us a citation to it so that we may find it in our university library.

We would also appreciate having definitions of the terms used in defining legal residence for the purpose of eligibility for provincial health care. Some of the questions raised by our RVer friends about this are quite complex. On the following page are some examples of the types of questions RVers have asked us.

We very much appreciate any help that you can give us in trying to understand and clarify this matter.

1. John and Mary have sold their home and live full-time in their RV. They rent a room in their daughter's basement for insurance purposes and in order to store some treasures there. Their daughter answers their mail for them, and they use her address for vehicle registration and on their provincial income tax return. When they are in the province they do not stay in this room, although they may park their trailer in their daughter's driveway. They have no other home than this room and their trailer. Could the province challenge their claim that this is their legal residence and cancel their health insurance?

1a) Can a person claim a single room, without a separate entrance, bath, or kitchen as a legal residence?

2a) Does a person have to be physically present, actually live, in their claimed residence in order for it to be a legal residence?

2. Bob and Betty have sold their home and live full-time in their RV. They have an un-winterized summer cottage in the northern part of the province where they spend the months of June, July, August, and September. They leave the province during the winter, but always return within the time limit and are physically present in the province for the number of days required to establish residence. Some of this time they visit family and friends because their cottage is uninhabitable during cold weather. Their cottage is their address for the purpose of vehicle registration and their income tax return. When they are not staying there they use a mail forwarding service. They have no other residence or home except their cottage and RV. Could the province challenge their claim that their cottage is their legal residence and cancel their health insurance?

3. Tom and Nancy have sold their home and live full-time in their RV. They lease a lot in an RV park which stays open only five months a year. They stay in province enough time to meet residence requirements, but because their park is closed they stay in other parks or park in the driveways of friends and family. They use a child's address for the purpose of vehicle registration and income tax return and a mail forwarding service when their park is closed. They have no other residence or home. They pay provincial income tax, and their pension funds originate in the province. Could the government challenge their claim that they are legal residents of the province and cancel their health insurance?

4. Mike and Penny have sold their home and live full-time in their RV. Their son rents them a room in his house where they store treasures, and they use his address for vehicle registration and income tax purposes. While they remain in Canada for more than six months a year, they spend much of that six months traveling between British Columbia and New Brunswick to visit their other children and grandchildren. They have no other residence than their recreational vehicle and the room in their son's home. They pay provincial income tax, register their vehicle in the province, and carry provincial driver's licenses. Could the province deny that they are provincial residents and cancel their health insurance?

We realize how complicated a problem this is and that there are no simple answers, but the answers to these questions are of great importance to many elderly Canadians. Great numbers of them fear the loss of their health care. They feel that they are, and they wish to be, within the law in planning for their retirement years, but they do not wish either to be hemmed in or to be thought to be taking a free ride.

We very much appreciate any help that you can give us in trying to understand and clarify this matter.

Only some provincial health ministers replied. Their responses are as follows:

British Columbia

In order to qualify for BC provincial health care a person must be a resident of BC under the definition of the Medical and Health Care Services Act. Requirement that a person (a) be a citizen or lawfully admitted permanent resident of Canada (b) who makes his/her home in BC and (c)is physically present in BC at least six months, need not be consecutive, of calendar year. The minister says (Mochrie 1995:2):

Individuals who routinely travel outside British Columbia should advise the Medical Services Plan (MSP), on an annual basis, of their expected dates of departure and return for the upcoming year. They should also indicate the reason for their absences and provide a British Columbia mailing address through which they can be reached while travelling. Those who travel outside Canada are strongly recommended to purchase additional insurance, through a private carrier, to supplement their provincial health care benefits....

This Ministry employs investigators to review the residency of individuals who are believed to be participating in our provincial health care system while ineligible to do so. The investigators look at such factors as the individuals' immigration status in Canada, their immigration status in the United States if that is a factor, where any homes they own or rent are located, whether they can substantiate the amount of time spent in British Columbia, where they are licensed to drive, and where their vehicles are registered. Those with itinerant lifestyles should consider keeping a diary of their absences from the Province and retaining any receipts that verify time spent in British Columbia.

With respect to the scenarios outlined in your letter, the first couple is eligible for benefits if they meet paragraphs (a) and (b) of the definition of resident and spend at least six months per calendar year in British Columbia. There is no purpose, from the perspective of eligibility for provincial health care benefits, for them to rent a room in British Columbia that is not lived in.

The second and third couples are also eligible for coverage, assuming that they meet (a) and (b) of the definition of resident. There is no requirement for them to remain in one location in British Columbia, as long as six months per calendar year are spent in the Province.

The fourth couple is not eligible for benefits because they are not meeting the six month residency requirement. This may, however, change in the future. It is anticipated that when proposed revisions to the *Medical and Health Care Services Act* Regulations come into force, provision will be made to accommodate most travellers who spend six months per calendar year *in Canada*, assuming they meet conditions a) and b) of the definition of resident.

Mochrie recommends travelling BC residents contact the Medical Services Plan client services at 386-7171 (Victoria), 683-7151 (Lower Mainland), and 1-800-663-7100 (elsewhere in British Columbia). They can also write to Medical Services Plan, PO Box 1600, Victoria, BC. V8W 2X9.

Manitoba

The Health Services Insurance Act was amended at the 1986 session of the Legislature to clarify that a person must be physically present in the province for at least six months in a calendar year to qualify as a resident.... I am sure you will appreciate that without eligibility criteria based on residence, the province would be expected to provide insured status to many former residents who, for example, return on vacation or on business....

Manitoba makes provision for persons who wish to take extended trips from time to time and, in this regard, the Plan would provide up to twelve months' coverage, providing absences of this length are not on a recurring basis....

Eligibility for health coverage is based entirely on physical presence in the province, regardless of whether the person resides in a home or Recreational Vehicle.

The persons as identified by the four examples in your letter would only qualify for coverage if they were physically present in the province a minimum of six months in a calendar year.

You may be interested to know that the Federal Government will be developing an interpretation of the term "resident," and how such a definition affects persons who live six months of the year out of the country and who, during the remaining six months, may live in more than one province. Until such time as the Federal Government comes up with a new definition of "resident" that is acceptable to all provinces, we must abide by our current legislation.

New Brunswick

The provision of our *Medical Services Payment Act* defines a "resident" as follows: a person lawfully entitled to be or to remain in Canada, who makes his home and is ordinarily present in New Brunswick, but does not include a tourist, transient or visitor to the province [sic].

Maintaining a dwelling or the ownership or property in the Province[,] the payment of property or income tax or the fact that a person is a Canadian citizen and/or former resident of any Canadian province does not by itself constitute grounds for eligibility. A person must be physically present in the Province on a permanent basis to qualify as a resident for Medicare purposes.

The relevant act restricts to 182 days in a twelve-month period the days a person can be temporarily absent from the province. The Director of Health and Community Services can increase this time under extenuating circumstances.

It is difficult to generalize about who is or who is not a resident. The department has policies to assist in determination of residency for the purpose of the Act, and in some cases must examine a wide range of other facts to determine the intention of the individual.

Only the couple who spend over six months a year in Canada but not necessarily in NB would be ineligible for NB Medicare.

Provided the residency criteria is met and the legislated amount of time is spent residing in New Brunswick, it would be difficult to dispute that a person does not live in New Brunswick based on the fact that one's home is not a stationary dwelling.

This is badly phrased. Mr. Finn probably means it would be difficult to dispute a person's claim that they live in New Brunswick on the basis that their home is not a stationary dwelling.

Ontario

Each province is responsible for determining its own eligibility and residence requirements in accordance with the broad provisions of the Canada Health Act. Residency is the sole determinant of eligibility.

Ontario health benefits are extended to residents of Ontario only. Under the Health Insurance Act, in order to be a *"resident"* and be entitled to be enrolled for health coverage, a person must meet *two tests.*

The first test is that the person must provide the appropriate Citizenship/ Immigration documentation....

The second test is that the person must be *"'ordinarily resident'* in Ontario." This means that the person makes their *"permanent and principle home"* in Ontario and be constructively present in Ontario for at least 183 days in any 12 month period....

Eligibility for health coverage in Ontario depends on a person's status as a resident, as defined by the Health Insurance Act. Payment of Provincial Income tax, automobile registration and receipt of provincial pension funds have no bearing on eligibility for health insurance (Segal 1995).

Addresses for Inquiries Concerning Provincial Health Plans

Alberta
Deputy Minister of Health
10025 Jasper Ave.
PO Box 2222
Edmonton, AB T5J 2P4

British Columbia
BC Ministry of Health
Deputy Minister's Office
1515 Blanshard St.
Victoria, BC V8W 3C8

Medical Services Commission, same address as above.

Canadian Federal Departmental Legal Services Unit
Health Canada
Brooke Claxton Bldg.
Ottawa ON K1A 0K9

Manitoba
Administrative Officer
Deputy Minister of Health
308 Legislative Bldg.
Winnipeg, MN R3C 0V8

New Brunswick
Deputy Minister of Health
Carleton Place
P.O. Box 5100
Fredericton, NB E3B 5G8

Newfoundland
Minister of Health
Confederation Bldg., W. Blk.
PO Box 8700
St. John's, NFLD A1B 4J6

Northwest Territories
Assistant Deputy Minister
Department of Health
Ste. 500, 4920-52nd St.
PO Box 1320
Yellowknife, NWT X1A 2L9

Nova Scotia
Legal Council, Deputy Minister's Office
Department of Health
Joseph Howe Bldg., 12 Floor
1690 Hollis St.
PO Box 488
Halifax, NS B3J 2R8

Ontario
Assistant Deputy Minister for OHIP
80 Grosvener St., 10th Flr.
Toronto, ON M7A 1R3

Prince Edward Island
Deputy Minister's Office
Department of Health and Social Services
16 Fitzroy St., 2nd Floor
PO Box 2000
Charlottetown, PEI C1A 7N8

Quebec
Ministre de la Santé et des Services sociaux
Roger Prudhomme, Coordonnateur
6161, rue St-Denis
Montreal, Quebec H2S 2R5

Saskatchewan
Director, Health Insurance Registraton
Department of Health
T.C. Douglas Bldg.
3475 Albert St.
Regina, SK S4S 6X6

Yukon Territory
Director, Health Care Insurance Services
Department of Health and Social Services
P.O. Box 2703
Whitehorse YK Y1A 2C6

Notes

1. The sources of information regarding provincial health plans are provided by the provincial Ministries of Health. They were taken in September, 2000 from the Health Canada website *www.hc-sc.gc.ca / medicare / plans.htm*

Appendix Four

Glossary

BOF or Birds of a Feather Subgroups within Escapees of people who share common interests: e.g., singles, computers, metaphysics, boondockers. Usually these groups just get together at Escapades but some meet more often and have a newsletter. Boomers are an example of an active BOF.

Boomerang A get-together of members of the Escapees BOF, Boomers.

Boomers are a Birds of a Feather of the Escapees Club. As their name suggests, their organizing principle is that they are primarily younger members of the club, part of the "baby boomer" generation. Though most of them were born after 1940 they, like other SKPs, are inclusive and declare that if you *feel* like a boomer, you are welcome to join their BOF. They have some youthful-acting members in their late 60s.

Boondocking The term "boondocking" comes from parking (docking) "out in the boonies" where one does not have full hookups, heated swimming pools, and other luxuries. RVers have extended the meaning to include parking their RV anywhere without hookups and free of charge. By SECURITY they mean "the security of having to know where we're going to stay tonight; that doesn't interest us," or of knowing where you're going next. They consider the people who stay in membership parks to be homogeneous and say "like attracts like." They say that because these people are dependent on schedules, they aren't able to go to see what's interesting.[1] There are at least two types of boondocking, "destination boondocking" — spending the night in free areas such as parking lots, truckstops, and roadside rest areas while en route to a destination — and "long term boondocking" — parking for days or longer in free or inexpensive areas. In order to boondock, a rig must have self-contained water and waste disposal tanks and a 12-volt electrical system which, for long-term boondockers, is powered by either solar panels or a generator.

CARE (Continuing Assistance to Retired Escapees) is located at Rainbow's End park in Livingston, Texas, the site of the headquarters of the Escapees RV Club. The CARE center allows Escapees who are no longer able to travel actively to continue to live in their RVs and be part of the way of life while receiving the assistance they need. The CARE center includes serviced parking sites that can be leased, in-rig assistance, and a day care/activity center, all in the park.

Co-op (SKP) "Each Co-Op is a separate *non-profit* corporation jointly owned by 120 SKP members who have an assigned full-hookup lot on which to park, put up a storage shed, etc. That lot belongs to them *for their lifetime* with the option of selling it back to the Co-Op. Co-Op members pay an equal share of the expenses and elect a Board of Directors to run their Co-Op park. Each Co-Op has a *retreat area* where any SKP may park free (no hookups). SKPs using it have full club house privileges and use of dump station and water. These Retreat Areas are under the management of the Co-Op on whose ground they are located and have a liberal time limit."[2]

Coyote camps "The romantic name full-timers use for the many temporary communities where they congregate each winter."[3]

Destination boondocking Boondocking overnight while traveling to a destination. Term used by Eddie Stinson in his seminar at Escapade, April 26, 1994.

Down-agers cited by Escapees speaker on activities. From the *Popcorn Report*: defined by the speaker as "people who act a decade younger than the age stereotype created by earlier generations."

> This refusal to be bound by traditional age limitations is the trend we are calling Down-Aging: redefining *down* what appropriate age-behavior is for your age....
>
> The first aspect of Down-Aging has to do with redefining-down the idea of age: 40 now is what used to be 30, 50 is now what used to be 40, 65 now is the beginning of the second half of life, not the beginning of the end.... Down Aging is how you explain Dr. Seuss on the best-seller list, *three* movies in one season in which a kid and an adult switch bodies ... and all that advertising that tell you how Snickers and Oreos and Frosted Flakes and Kool-Aid connect you back to the kid you have inside.... We are turning, as often as we can, into big goofy kids. And oh, the release it affords us.[4]

Dump One of the parts of living in an RV that no one enjoys is the periodic need to "dump." Most RVs are self-contained, meaning that they have holding tanks for the "grey water" (bath and dish water, etc.) and for the "black water" (sewage). These must be "dumped" by attaching a flexible hose to the outlet on the underside of the vehicle and opening a sliding valve to permit the contents to flow into a "dump station" opening. In addition to being a smelly job, it takes some strength to open and close the valves.

Escapade The major rally of the Escapees club held twice a year. Fall Escapades are held in the mid-west, and Spring Escapades are held in the west.

Escapees is the non-commercial club for serious and full-time RVers with whom we conducted most of our research in 1993-94. The club's headquarters is located at its home park, Rainbow's End, in Livingston, Texas.

Established parks By established parks we mean bounded areas with formally designated sites for RVs or tents. They may be public or private, and most have user fees. They will also have some sort of authority — a host, manager, owner — and a set of rules enforced by that authority.

Gerontophobia The irrational fear and/or hatred of old age and the elderly both by society and by old people themselves. This fear exists in spite of the fact that most people age comfortably and in good health.[5]

Glory hole or gopher hole Some boondockers, especially in Slab City, dispose of their sewage by simply digging a hole in the desert, putting their drain pipe into it, and covering it over. This solution to having to drain one's holding tanks is called using a glory hole. Glory holes are most often used to dispose of grey water.

Good Sam Club The Good Sam Club began in the mid-1960s as a way to provide RVers with a way to know each other. The assumption was that if RVers of good will could somehow recognize each other they could safely offer help to (and accept it from) other club members. By 1991 it had a membership of nearly 800,000. Today the Good Sam Club is part of TL (Trailer Life) Enterprises, North America's largest commercial, profit-making operation catering to RVers. Club members are sometimes known as **Good Samers**. Their large rallies are called **Samborees**.

Happy hour or friendship hour The regularly scheduled get-together of Escapees park residents to share news, make announcements, greet newcomers, and say farewell to those leaving the next day. Ideally it is held every afternoon at 4:00 p.m., but in some parks it occurs less often. The name Happy Hour refers to the ideal mood of Skips when they get together and not to alcohol consumption. The frequent misunderstanding of the source of the happiness by new Skips has caused some parks to rename their meeting "friendship hour."

Hitch-itch A disease suffered by serious RVers. After a week or two in one place, they begin to feel its symptoms — restlessness and dissatisfaction. Once it starts, the only recourse is to hitch up the rig and head down the road. The relief is only temporary. The next time the sufferer is in one place for a while, he or she will suffer a relapse.

Holding tanks   are tanks carried under a rig for the storage of fresh water, grey water, and sewage. Holding tanks are essential for self-containment and for RVers who wish to park without hookups.

KOA   is the acronym for Kampgrounds of America, a widespread franchise chain of RV parks. Many KOA parks cater to vacationers and overnighters. Others have permanent residents and are used as a home base by full-time RVers.

Long-term Visitor Areas (LTVAs)   Areas in the United States, especially in Arizona and California, that are administered by the Bureau of Land Management of the Department of the Interior. RVers with self-contained rigs (holding tanks for water and sewage are the main criteria) may camp in these areas free or for a small charge for a short time (two weeks or less) or, in 2000, for as long as six months for a fee of $100.

LoW   stands for Loners on Wheels, one of the first and largest organizations for single RVers.

Membership Parks   Membership park organizations are profit-making associations of affiliated RV parks which provide their members with inexpensive camping sites in exchange for hefty membership fees (most are thousands of dollars) and annual dues or maintenance charges of several hundred dollars. The most well-known membership park organizations are Camp Coast-to-Coast (CCC), Thousand Trails/NACO, and Resort Parks International (RPI). Although the details differ between membership organizations, and may change over time in a single organization as it copes with financial difficulties, the following is generally true. Membership park organizations operate like time-share condos. There are many more members of an organization than there are spaces for them at any given time. Purchasers of an organization membership may be affiliated with a "home park." If they are, this is where they buy their membership and pay annual dues or maintenance fees. In return, members have the right to stay in their home park free of charge for a limited time (generally about 30 days) each year. They also obtain the right to park for a limited period (ordinarily one or two weeks) for a minimal cost (usually at least $4.00 a night) at other parks affiliated with the membership park system. If the organization does not use the "home park" system, members have access to all parks in that system for a nominal fee. Camping fees are generally set below the recovery costs for the campground. Therefore, in order to remain solvent, an affiliated park or membership organization must continue to sell new memberships. They are not required to continue adding spaces reserved for the use of their members. Some organizations guarantee all members a parking spot for at least one night, even if the member shows up without reservations. Others require reservations.

Mini-rang   A small **Boomerang**. An impromptu get-together of a group of **Boomers** who happen to be in a park or some other event/place at the same time.

Mobile home   A mobile home is essentially a moveable house — often 10 or 12 feet in width — and can only be moved by a proper tractor; not to be confused with a motor home (see **RV** for the definition of a motor home).

Park trailers or park-model trailers   A "park-model" trailer is not quite a recreational vehicle, nor is it quite a "mobile home." A *real* RV must be capable of being towed by the owner's private vehicle at will. A "park-model" is no more than eight and one-half feet [2.6 metres] wide and 40 feet [12 metres] long, within the size and towability limits for a recreation vehicle. It may, therefore, be parked in an RV park. People who order park-models from the factory have the option of regular appliances and fixtures (an electric-only refrigerator instead of a two-way gas-and-electric refrigerator, a flush toilet rather than a marine-type toilet, free-standing furniture rather than built-ins) in place of those designed for movable recreational vehicles. If it does not have holding tanks, it is not self-contained. A park that allows residents to set up park-model trailers is well along in the second stage of its life cycle.

Pull-through sites or pull-throughs   Pull-through parking spaces are designed so that the driver can approach from the rear, pull through the space, and hook up. A departing driver simply pulls ahead into a departure lane. While drivers — especially of trailers — prefer them, they are rare in parks where space is at a premium. They require twice as much road space as do sites that must be backed into.

Quartzsite   Quartzsite, Arizona, is located in the desert about 50 miles north of Yuma. The population of this small town of a few hundred permanent residents swells through the winter, peaking in February at figures estimated to exceed one million. While there are a few established parks in Quartzsite, most of the winter visitors boondock on land belonging to the US government and designated as a Long Term Visitor Area.

RV   a recreational vehicle, most commonly either a towed travel trailer, a fifth-wheel trailer or a motor home. The term refers to products such as motor homes, fifth-wheel travel trailers, travel trailers, folding camping trailers, truck campers, and conversion vehicles.

The spellings of motor home (motorhome) and fifth-wheel (fifth wheel) are in free variation among RVers. We use motor home and fifth-wheel, following Recreation Vehicle Industry Association (RVIA) publica-

RVs and Conversion Vehicles

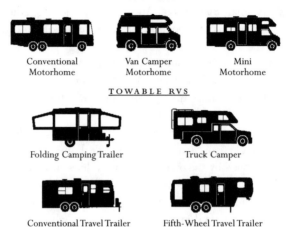

MOTORIZED RVS

Conventional Motorhome

Van Camper Motorhome

Mini Motorhome

TOWABLE RVS

Folding Camping Trailer

Truck Camper

Conventional Travel Trailer

Fifth-Wheel Travel Trailer

CONVERSION VEHICLES

Van Conversion

Truck Conversion

Sport-Utility Conversion

tions. The RVIA defines an RV as "a motorized or towable vehicle that combines transportation and temporary living quarters for travel, recreation and camping. RVs do not include mobile homes, off-road vehicles or snowmobiles." The RVIA describes a towable RV:

> An RV designed to be towed by a motorized vehicle (auto, van, or pickup truck) and of such size and weight as not to require a special highway movement permit. It is designed to provide temporary living quarters for recreational, camping or travel use and does not require permanent on-site hook-up.

The RVIA describes a motorized RV:

> A recreational camping and travel vehicle built on or as an integral part of a self-propelled motor vehicle chassis. It may provide kitchen, sleeping, and bathroom facilities and be equipped with the ability to store and carry fresh water and sewage.[6]

RVIA Recreation Vehicle Industry Association. This organization represents RV manufacturers and plans their marketing strategy.

Retreats (SKP) a type of park owned by the Escapees Club. Any SKP member may stay at a retreat park for a small charge for hookups. The charge for boondocking is minimal. "No time-use limit will be set unless length of stay is abused. No matter how long an SKP stays at one of these Retreats, he/she is a 'guest' and should not expect any 'ownership' rights."[7]

Skips The Escapees RV Club has adopted the letters **SKP** as its acronym. SKP stands for a variety of values, and goals espoused by the club's members: "Sharing, Karing People"; "Special Kind of People"; etc. In everyday use among the members of the club, the acronym itself has been condensed to "Skip." Club members often call themselves Skips. To be a "real Skip" one should embrace the values and traditions of the organization.

Skirted in A rig is skirted in when its wheels are covered to prevent weather damage due to long immobility. Owners of skirted-in rigs often put plywood or other shielding material around the bottom of their RV to protect the bottom from weather and vermin and to make the area under the rig available for storage. A rig that is skirted in does not travel much; many are permanently placed on their sites.

Snowbirds people who move seasonally, following good weather, to spend months at a time in one spot. Although the term implies leaving the snowbelt for the sunbelt in the winter, some RVers who leave southern or desert heat for cooler northern weather in the summer also refer to themselves as snowbirds. Sometimes they stay on sites they own or lease and where they leave RVs which have been "skirted in." Some snowbirds have park-model trailers or "double-wides" on their lots.

Toad a small vehicle towed behind a motor home, also known as *The Toad*, as in "I go where I'm toad to."

Notes

1. See Peterson, K. 1991b.

2. *Escapees Newsletter* 1984:16.

3. Peterson, K. 1983-84:12-13.

4. Popcorn 1991:57, 59.

5. Berezin 1978:542.

6. RVIA n.d.b.

7. *Escapees Newsletter* 1984a:16.

Appendix Five

What Now?

If you'd like to try full-time or serious RVing, you may be wondering "What do I do now?". The following information will help you to get started.

Learn From the Experts

If you have never done any RVing you should first learn as much as you can from the experts — serious and fulltime RVers. Then try it before you commit yourself. Start by going to an RV park near you. Ask the manager if any full-timers live there, and knock on doors. Or walk around the park and start conversations. Explain that you are thinking about full-timing and are wondering how other people like it. Ask people about their rigs: "Do you like your fifth-wheel?" "Is your trailer easy to tow?" "What gas mileage do you get?" Or ask them how long they've been RVing. Most RVers love to talk about what they're doing and will be happy to recount their experiences, discuss the pros and cons of rigs they have owned, and answer your questions. Talk to as many people as you can. Then sift through the information you receive and apply it to your own situation.

If you have a computer and enjoy doing research on the net, you will have fun exploring the RVing Websites. The Recreation Vehicle Industry Association Website (*www.rvia.com*) will provide you with an overview of the industry and some of the resources available. Then look at RVers On Line at www.rversonline.org. This site is based on the principle of RVers helping RVers and provides non-commercial RV-related information and help. There is no advertising, and nobody can buy a spot on their site. Two of their useful services are Links for RVers and Full-Timers Corner. They have a Bookshelf that includes reviews of books on RVing listed in alphabetical order and information on how to order. They also link to RV products and services, RV clubs and organizations, travel and destinations, general interest RV sites, commercial sites of interest, RV manufacturers, RV park and campground directors, and a mailbox for RVers.

The RV Club is another on-line resource. While this club costs $10 to join, you don't have to pay to visit their Website address at *www.rvclub.com*. The site offers answers to RVing FAQs (Frequently Asked Questions), provides reviews of campgrounds by club members, and links to topics for new RVers such as: Is RVing for you?; how to become an RVer; pitfalls of life on the road; do your homework before buying; tips and ideas if you wonder what kind of RV is best for you; advice to a new RVer with kids; RV check lists so you won't forget anything; tips from veteran RVers; and recommended reading.

RV Clubs

Excellent sources of information are the RV clubs that exist for people with all sorts of needs and interests. The following is only a small representative sample.

The original club for full-time and serious RVers is

> The Escapees RV Club
> 100 Rainbow Drive
> Livingston, TX USA 77351-9300

If you use the internet, visit their home page at www.escapees.com. It will keep you busy for hours. The page includes a "knowledge section" that will either answer most of your "how-to" questions or suggest where you can find the answers; a section of Web and internet resources for RVers; a chat and discussion room; a list of publications by the club; Web links to books on RVing through Amazon.com; information about free camping in the western US; and a link to RV Corner — a helpful resource that links to other relevant sites. If one of the chapters is holding a rally near you, go to it and talk to people. If you live within easy distance of one of their semi-annual rallies called Escapades, go to it. You will be overwhelmed by friendly people, seminars on practical problems (how to back up a large rig, the advantages of a solar power system), special interest groups for single RVers, young working RVers, and folks with all sorts of hobbies and special interests and needs (are you a bird watcher, do you have three large dogs, is your hobby hiking or quilting or surfing the net?), and lots of fun.

If you are Canadian you may want to join either the

> Wayfarer Explorer RV Club
> 1235 Bay Street, Suite 1000,

Toronto, Ontario, Canada M5R 3K4 (1-800-999-0819)
Website address: explorer-rvclub.com

or the

Federation Quebecoise de Camping et de Caravanning, Inc.
4545 avenue Pierre-de-Coubertin, CP1000 succ. M
Montreal, Quebec, Canada H1V 3R2, (514-252-3003).

The largest commercial organization for RVers is the Good Sam Club, whose parent organization, TL Enterprises, publishes *Trailer Life* and *Motor Home* magazines. Members of Good Sam receive *Highways* magazine as part of their membership. Here is its address:

Good Sam Club
2575 Vista Del Mar Drive
Ventura, CA USA 93001
E-mail: goodsam@goodsamclub.com
Website address: www.goodsamclub.com

There are several RV clubs for people who travel alone. Some of these are:

Loners of America (LOA),
P.O. Box 3314 IN
Napa, CA USA 94558-0331.
 e-mail address: loainfo@napanet.net
Website address: www.napanet.net/~mbost/

This club has chapters in many states. In the winter months members of the club live at The Slabs near Niland, California. The organization is a member-run club for adult RVers who travel as singles. If you marry or adopt that life style the club terminates your membership. Another club for singles is

Loners on Wheels (LoW),
P.O. Box 1355 -WB
Popular Bluff, MO USA 63902
e-mail address: lowbunch@onelist.com
Website address: www.lonersonwheels.com

This organization is an international club of single RVers who enjoy traveling, camping, and RV caravanning. A singles club specifically for female RVers is:

RVing Women
P.O. Box 1940
Apache Junction, AZ USA 85217
Phone number: 1-888-55RVING.
e-mail address: RvingWomen@juno.com
Website address: www.rvingwomen.com

You also may visit this club for single women RVers at 1000 W. Apache Trail, #103, Apache Junction, AZ.

Escapees also has a special interest group for singles called SOLOs. For additional information send a self addressed stamped envelope to:

Myra Johnson
14 High Court
Shelter Cove CA 95589-9081
e-mail address: highct@saber.net
Website address: www.escapees.com/bof/solo

A club for single RVers under the age of 70 is:

Wandering Individuals' Network (WIN)
Dept. H, PO Box 2010
Sparks NV 89432-2012

A popular RV organization for families is the Family Camping and RVers club (FCRV). It is a member-owned, family-oriented organization with activities and programs for youth, teens, adults, and retirees. It has programs in a number of areas including conservation, wildlife, self-propelled camping, and disaster awareness training. Their mailing address is

4804 Transit Rd Bld #2
Depew, NY 14043
e-mail address: FCRV-nat@pce.net
Website address: www.fcrv.org

The Family Motor Coach Association (FMCA) is for RVers with motor homes. They define a motor coach as a self-propelled, completely self-contained vehicle which contains cooking, sleeping, and permanent sanitary facilities and in which the drivers' seat is accessible in a walking position from the living quarters. If your rig meets these criteria you may want to investigate the club as it offers members a number of benefits at reasonable rates. These include mail forwarding and message service, a discount telephone calling card, group rates on an emergency road service program, and a variety of insurance coverage including accidental death, travel accident/medical insurance reimbursements, and motor coach insurance. You may write to them at:

Family Motor Coach Association
8291 Clough Pike
Cincinnati, OH 45244-2796
Website address: www.fmca.com

There are many other RV clubs for people with special things in common. For example, NAARVA (National African American RVers Association) is a club dedicated to the Black experience. Its Website address is *www.naarva.com*. Another special interest club is S*M*A*R*T (Special Military Active Retired Travel), for retired career military personnel. The organization organizes low cost caravans and maintains up-to-date information on military campgrounds at military installations. Those who are eligible include retired and active duty personnel, widows and widowers of qualified persons, Medal of Honor recipients, former POWs, and veterans who are 100 per cent disabled. Their mailing address is:

SMART
600 University Ofc Blvd. #1A
Pensacola, FL. USA 32504
Phone: 1-800-354-7681
email address: Rvsmarttrvl@cs.com
Website address: www.smartrvclub.org

If you want to work, or need to work in order to RV full-time, an organization to look into is Workers on Wheels. From them you can can find information for working RVers that includes help for people with particular kinds of problems, information for Canadian RVers, and articles and information for the single RVer. Their publication is *Workers on Wheels*, and their mailing address is:

Workers on Wheels
4012 S Rainbow Blvd Ste K94

Las Vegas, NV 89103.
Website address: www.workersonwheels.com

You may also want to ask for a sample issue of *Workamper News*, a publication specifically for working RVers. Write to

Workamper News
201 Hiram Road
Heber Springs, AR 72543-8747
Phone: 501-377-1563.

Many RVers prefer to boondock or dry camp in order to save money. Others enjoy boondocking because of the freedom from rules and schedules imposed by park management. If you think you'd like to try it look at the Website at: *http://clubs.yahoo.com/clubs/boondocking* or *www.boondockingguide.com*.

Books and Websites

Books and Websites by full-timers are also excellent resources. Kay and Joe Peterson's publications include *Home is Where You Park It, Survival of the RV Snowbirds, Travel While You Work*, and *Encyclopedia for RVers II. Home is Where You Park It* covers both the practical and psychological aspects of family living and traveling in a recreational vehicle. *Survival of the Snowbirds* focuses on retirees and gives practical advice on how people on a limited income can make full-time RVing work in spite of inflation, rising gasoline prices, and ever-increasing campground fees. *Travel While You Work: Earning Money as You RV* describes how the Petersons began full-timing while they still had dependent children and explains how people can travel full-time, raise children, and have paid employment. *Encyclopedia for RVers II*, published in 1999, is a comprehensive reference book that covers the Three M's (mail, money, and medicine) as well as RV maintenance, legal information for American RVers, and tips on a variety of subjects such as travel safety, how to travel with pets, and the many uses of a hair dryer or baking soda. Instructions on ordering the Peterson's books are found on the club's Web page, or you can call 1-888-757-2582.

Other excellent how-to books for new RVers include:

Full-time RVing by Bill and Jan Moeller and *Move'n On* by Ron and Barb Hofmeister are both written by full-timers. They discuss issues of concern to serious RVers including finances, selecting and customizing a rig, and how to make the best use of your RV's space and facilities.

Take Back Your Life! Travel Full-Time in an RV by Stephanie Bernhagen Bernham-Collins. This book is both informative to those who are experienced RVers and valuable for people who are new at RVing or who are planning to try it. The book is unusual in that it covers topics of interest to full-timers with children. This book can be ordered from the author's email address *stephanie@escapees.com* or found at her Website: *www. rvhometown.com.*

Woodall's *RV Owner's Handbook* and J.D. Gallant's *The RV Rating Book* and *How to Select, Inspect and Buy an RV* are sources of practical information for potential purchasers. The RV Consumer's Group offers consumer oriented suggestions for selecting an RV. Their mailing address is:

> 250 Fish Hatchery Road
> P.O. Box 520. Quilcene WA 98376
> Phone: 360 765 3846
> Website address: www.rv.org

Spirit of the Open Road, by Canadian full-time RVer Peggi McDonald, was published in 1996 and is especially helpful to Canadian RVers. The McDonalds also have a Website at *www.rvliving.net* where you can find information, a bulletin board, and a guest book.

An excellent resource for younger RVers with families still at home is Shelley Zoelleck's Website Families on the Road *www.familiesontheroad.com.* This site includes a newsletter, a section on what's new, a bookstore with reviews of books on RVing, a section on products and services, and a bulletin board and e-mail list for people who want to exchange ideas.

Things Experienced RVers Say That Newcomers Should Know

Try it first

Living in an RV for months or years at a time is not for everybody. If you've never driven a rig or traveled in an RV, you have no way to judge whether you will enjoy full-timing. Before you sell your home in order to buy an RV you should try temporary RV living. Rent an RV for your first experience. U-Haul and other rental businesses often have RVs available. Most RV lots carry used rigs, some on consignment, and many will be happy to rent one, perhaps on a rent-to-buy arrangement. We rented or first RV — a travel trailer — this way, but most lots that specialize in RV rental will have only motorhomes available. Pulling a travel trailer or fifth-wheel will require modifications to your truck or car, and these can be expensive. Check the classified ads for private rentals, and look on the internet for information about rental agencies.

Several Websites provide general information for people who want to rent an RV. Woodalls's site, found at *www.woodalls.com/camp101/camp101.html*, discusses where to rent, the types of RVs available, and the costs of renting an RV. Another informative site is *www.familiesontheroad.com/rentbuy.html*. It provides links to several sites specifically concerned with RV rentals. The RV rental network is found at *www.rvrent.com*. This group of independent and corporate RV rental businesses say they will help you find a motorhome or other RV to rent almost anywhere and will have the rental rates sent to you if they are not on line. Finally, on *www.rv-rentals.net* you will find discussion of topics such as where to travel, where to spend the night, features to look for in a rental unit, driver's licenses, Canadian and US customs, how to operate an RV safely, and campground etiquette and jargon.

To find a list of Canadian and US businesses who specialize in RV rentals go to *www.rvamerica.com/rentals/*. Here you can search a data base by company name or by city and state, select a state from their list, or click the place on a map of the US or Canada where you would like to pick up your rental RV. The search provides you with a city-by-city list of RV rental agencies complete with address, phone number including toll-free or fax numbers, and email or Website addresses for the agencies that have them.

One of the largest RV rental resources is Cruise America. Their home page, *www.cruiseamerica.com*, lists the names and addresses of some 150 rental agencies in the US and Canada as well as other information for new RVers.

Some sites that provide the names and addresses of Canadian RV rental agencies are *www.rvnetlinx.com/rentals.htm*, *www.rvamerica.com/rentals/canada.htm*, and *www.vellner.com*. The Canadian Motorhome and RV rentals home page is *www.candan.com*.

If you decide to rent, try to do so for two or three months so you can get a feel for living in an RV. Ask your rental source to show you how to hitch and unhitch your rig, where your holding tanks and hot-water heater are located, and how to use/start/empty and/or fill them. Be sure you understand when and how to use a two-way refrigerator. Practice hitching, unhitching, and backing up in an empty parking lot before you go on the road or pull into a park.

Try as many varieties of RV living as you can

There are many different kinds of places to spend the night or to camp. Try all of them. Stay in commercial parks where you'll have full hook-ups and probably a pool and a club house with organized activities. Spend some time in forest service, state, and provincial campgrounds where you will learn about conserving water and become aware of the capacity of your holding tanks. Try destination boondocking overnight in a truck stop or a parking lot; dry camp for a few days by a stream or a lake or in a casino parking lot, or for weeks on the desert. Most serious and full-time RVers do all of these and enjoy some more than others. When it's time to go home are you relieved that it's over, or do you feel like you could do this forever? If you are a couple, do you agree? Was it a dream for one of you and a nightmare for the other? Once you know what kind of RVing is the most fun for you, you'll have a better idea of what kind of rig you want to buy and the kind of facilities you will need. If you love to boondock you will want to investigate solar panels. They are quiet and efficient, the energy source is free, and they seem to last forever. Ours survived a major hail storm without a dent or crack. If you prefer to spend most of your time in parks that offer full hook-ups, an alternative energy source will not be so important for you.

Try different types of RVs

Did you like the kind of rig you rented — fifth-wheel, travel trailer, or motorhome? It's a personal choice, and any decision involves a tradeoff. Travel trailers can be less stable and more difficult to tow and to back up than are other types of RVs, but all the room in your tow vehicle is available for storage. A fifth-wheel trailer is easier to tow and is more stable than is a travel trailer of the same size, but you must have a truck to tow it, and you give up most of the storage room in the bed of your pickup. A motor-home doesn't require towing, but if you want to go sight-seeing in town you must either take your rig along, carry bikes or motorcycles, or tow a car. If it breaks down you will have to live in a garage or factory while it is being repaired or stay in a motel. When the motor wears out you may need to buy a new rig. Before making a final choice, learn all you can about each type and perhaps rent all three types. Whatever you choose, go for the smallest rig you think you can live with. Small rigs are more versatile, are easier to park, and are usually more economical. On the other hand, be sure that the rig is big enough that you can spend the time you have allotted in it without feeling claustrophobic: think about three days of rain and whether you and your partner and the rest of the family (dog? cat? children?) will be able to give each other room to breathe. The first RV you buy will be an investment whose cost you want to amortise over a period of years, so do a "worst-case-scenario" study. If the rig you buy is too large you may feel restricted in what you can do and where you can go; if it is too small, you may quickly get an attack of what RVers call "two-foot-itis" (if this rig were only two feet longer we'd be able to ...). In either case you may want to trade your rig for another; RVs are not like houses — they depreciate.

If you are going to buy a new RV you may want to ask RV Consumer group about your intended purchase. RV Consumer Group is a nonprofit consumer advocate organization that rates all brands, models, and types of RVs. You can contact this group by writing

RV Consumer Group
PO Box 520
Quilcene, WA USA 98376
Phone 360-765-3846
Fax 360-765-3233
Website address: www.rv.org

Questions New RVers Ask

Can I afford to be a full-timer?

Most of the people we talked to said that you don't have to be rich to be a full-timer. Indeed they argued that RVing is less expensive than living in a house. If you sell your house you eliminate many of your on-going expenses such as property taxes, house insurance, utilities, and property maintenance. Your clothing costs will probably go down too. Most RVers dress casually, and many people said that they had only one dress outfit that they reserved for church, weddings, and funerals. Dry cleaning will probably be a thing of the past too, as washable casual clothing is the fashion statement for RV living. Some expenses will stay the same. If you enjoy expensive hobbies you will want to budget for those, but many parks and boondocking communities help RVers stretch their budgets with free activities such as sing-along campfires, movie nights, pot-luck dinners, games, and hikes. Your food costs will probably remain constant, although you may find that you are so busy exploring and meeting new friends that you eat less and snack less often than you did when you lived a sedentary life. You will also save money on meals when you are traveling in an RV. Rather than pay for a restaurant meal or be a victim of a fast food joint along the interstate highways, you can pull off into a rest area or city park and prepare your own meal in the comfort of your home.

You will have to budget for RV payments if you did not buy your rig outright, and in some jurisdictions recreational vehicles are taxed as real property. In addition, insurance and license fees, gasoline, and camping charges are unavoidable. Check out the state or province where you live to find out how these taxes and fees will apply to you. On the positive side, you can control the cost of gas and campgrounds by spending several weeks in one place while you relax and explore the area. Many city or county campgrounds are free or very reasonable in cost and will allow you to stay for two weeks or more. If you have a generator in your rig or have invested in a solar power system and like to boondock, your camping expenses will be negligible. Four information about low-cost or free camping in western Canada, look at Kathy and Craig Copeland's *Camp Free in BC* published by Voice in the Wilderness Press, Inc., Vancouver, British Columbia. Although BC forest campgrounds are no longer free, they are still a bargain. Some other sites are still free and are RV accessible if your rig is small. You can also camp for a nominal fee or free at many campgrounds in the US run by the National Forest service, the Corps of Engineers, and the Bureau of Land Management. For information on free and/or inexpensive campsites in the US look for Michael Hodgson's guide to BLM western wild lands, *America's Secret Recreation Areas* published by Foghorn Press. Don Wright's *Guide to Free Campgrounds*, published by Cottage Publications, is also an excellent resource.

Will I like full-timing?

The people we interviewed agreed that while almost anybody *can* be a full-timer, some people will enjoy it more than others. It doesn't matter whether you're a zen RVer (you decide whether to go right or left only when you get to a fork in the road) or a planner (you like to know where you are spending each night at least a week in advance). You may prefer commercial parks with all the amenities and structured activities, or you may love to boondock in the desert where you can live as a minimalist and do your own thing for months at a time. If you have a partner both of you must want to do it and agree on camping style. Otherwise you are inviting disaster.

If you are agreed that it is what you want to do, you then have to decide what you will do with your stationary home and your possessions, and you must choose what to take with you. Think minimalist. You will not need enough dishes to give a dinner party. RVers expect to bring their own place setting when they go to a pot-luck dinner or get together at someone's rig. Leave behind those things that you rarely use. Argue with yourself and make a case for anything — clothing, tools, linens — that doesn't have at least two functions. If you like to go tent camping, your sleeping bags can double as your bed cover. Use your down vest as stuffing for a throw pillow. Restrict your wardrobe to those things that you wear often. On the other hand, the idea is to enjoy yourself, so don't deprive yourself of something that you really will miss. We've met RVers who are creative in finding a place for things they treasure: a collection of Hopi katchina dolls, a keyboard, a model train set, a sewing machine or quilting hoop, a garden of house plants, a string bass (!). Use your ingenuity and enjoy!

References and Internet Resources

References

Albert, Fred. 1993. Heaven on Wheels. *Pacific: The Seattle Times*. 12 August: 13-20.

Alfredson, Illa. 1994. Different Viewpoints: About Community. *Escapees Newsletter* 15(4): 24.

Amick, A.F. 1996. Good Health and Long Life: Survey Results. *Escapees for the Serious RVer* 17(5): 58-59.

Anderson, William C. 1991. More Fun Than Plucking Ducks. *Highways* 25(10): 32, 73, 77, 81.

Apple, Judy. 1987. If We Can't Pay — We Won't Go! *Escapees Newsletter* 8(5): 19.

Baltes, Paul B. 1993. The Aging Mind: Potential and Limits. *The Gerontologist* 33(5): 580-94.

Bartko, John J. and Robert D. Patterson. 1971. Survival Among Healthy Old Men: A Multivariate Analysis. In *Human Aging II: An Eleven-Year Biomedical and Behavioral Study*, Samuel Granick and Robert D. Patterson, eds. US Public Health Service Monograph. Washington, DC: US Government Printing Office. 105-19.

Belk, Russell W. 1988. Possessions and the Extended Self. *Journal of Consumer Research* 15: 139-68.

Bellah, Robert N. *et al.* 1985. *Habits of the Heart: Individualism and Commitment in American Life*. Berkeley: University of California Press.

Bender, Thomas. 1978. *Community and Social Change in America*. Baltimore: Johns Hopkins University Press.

Berezin, Martin A. 1978. The Elderly Person. In *The Harvard Guide to Modern Psychiatry*, A.M. Nicholi, Jr., ed. Cambridge, MA: The Belknap Press of Harvard University Press. 541-49.

———. 1980. Isolation in the Aged: Individual Dynamics, Community and Family Involvement: Intrapsychic Isolation in the Elderly. *Journal of Geriatric Psychiatry* 13(1): 5-18.

Berezin, Martin A., Benjamin Liptzin, and Carl Salzman. 1988. The Elderly Person. In *The New Harvard Guide to Psychiatry*, Armand M. Nicholi, Jr., ed. Cambridge, MA: The Belknap Press of Harvard University Press. 665-80.

Bloch, Maurice. 1991. Language, Anthropology and Cognitive Science. *Man* 26(2): 183-98.

Boschetti, M.A. 1984. *The Older Person's Emotional Attachment to the Physical Environment of the Residential Setting*. Ph.D. dissertation. University of Michigan, Ann Arbor.

Bonis, Karen and Scott Bonis. 1993. Reality. *Escapees Newsletter* 14(4): 22.

Born, T.L. 1976. Elderly RV Campers Along the Lower Colorado River: A Preliminary Typology. *Journal of Leisure Research* 8: 256-62.

Briseno, Fran. 1993 (October). Letters to the Editor: How Much is Enough? *Speak E-Z*. Park of the Sierra, Coarsegold, CA: 8.

Brown, Lana. 1988. Following the Dream. *Escapees Newsletter* 10(2): 17.

Browning, Christine. 1988. Different Viewpoints: Thanks SKPs! *Escapees Newsletter* 9(6): 20.

Bryson, Bill. 1989. *The Lost Continent: Travels in Small-town America*. Harper Perennial: New York.

Butler, Robert. 1980. Ageism: a Foreword. *The Journal of Social Issues* 36(2): 8-11.

Canada, Government. 1985a. *Criminal Code of Canada. Revised Statutes of Canada*. Vol 3. Ottawa: Queen's Printer for Canada. Chapter C-46, s.2.

———. 1985b. *Revised Statutes of Canada 1985*. Vol 1. Ottawa: Queen's Printer for Canada. Chapter C-6, s.2.

———. 1993. *Canada Health Act Annual Report 1992-93*. Health and Welfare Canada Cat. H1-4/1993. Ottawa: Minister of Supply and Services.

Cannain, Mo. 1993. Co-op or Coop? *Escapees Newsletter* 14(4): 40.

Carlson, Fran. 1995. Letter to Road Roamer News. *Escapees for the Serious RVer* 17(3): 63.

Carr, Cathie. 1993a. Thoughts for the Road: It's Up to You. *Escapees Newsletter* 14(5): 5.

———. 1993b. Club news. *Escapees Newsletter*. 14(6): 6-7.

Carter, Janet. 1992. Two Sides to the Full-timing Question. *Escapees Newsletter* 13(6): 17-18.

Carter, Lea. 1986. Life in the Slow Lane: New Corporate Status for LoWs. *Escapees Newsletter* 7(6): 9.

Case, Barbara. 1993. Note to Road Roamer News. *Escapees Newsletter* 4(6): 49.

Chappell, Neena L. 1990. *The Aging of the Canadian Population. About Canada/Canadian Studies Directorate*. Ottawa: Department of the Secretary of State of Canada.

Chappell, Neena L., Laurel A. Strain and Audrey A. Blandford. 1986. *Aging and Health Care: A Social Perspective*. Toronto: Holt, Rinehart and Winston.

Chatfield, R. 1992. The Editors Corner. *RV Traveller for the Canadian Camper* 16(2): 6-7, 19.

Clinton, Norm. 1993a (May). Statistical Kind of People: Results of Questionnaire. *Speak E-Z*. (Park of the Sierra, Coarsegold, CA): 7-8.

———. 1993b (August). On the Road With Meathead. *Speak E-Z* (Park of the Sierra, Coarsegold, CA): 1-2.

Coontz, Stephanie. 1992. *The Way We Never Were: American Families and the Nostalgia Trap*. New York: Basic Books.

Cooper, Matthew, and Margaret Critchlow Rodman. 1992. *New Neighbours: A Case Study of Cooperative Housing*. Toronto: University of Toronto Press.

Counts, David, and Dorothy Ayers Counts. 1996. Quests, Pilgrimages and Home Bases: Life cycle movement for RV nomads. Paper delivered to session on Secular Pilgrimage in North America, American Anthropological Association.

———. 1995. TV Interview, DC Morning News, Fox. Subject: research on RVing.(November 17, 1995).

———. 1994. What's Driving the RV Movement? *Escapees Magazine* 15(6): 16-17.

Counts, Dorothy Ayers, and David R. Counts. 1983. Father's Water Equals Mother's Milk: The Conception of Parentage in Kaliai, West New Britain. *Mankind* 14(1): 46-56.

———. 1992a. I'm Not Dead Yet! Aging and Death, Process and Experience in Kaliai. In *Aging and Its Transformations.* Dorothy Ayers Counts and David R. Counts, eds. ASAO Monograph No. 10. Pittsburgh, PA: University of Pittsburgh Press. Reissued. Originally published 1985, Lanham, Md.: University Press of America. 131-56.

———. 1992b. "They're My Family Now": The Creation of Community Among RVers. *Anthropologica* 34(2): 153-82.

Courtney, Myrna. 1991. Great Escape Artists. *Trailer Life* 51 (6): 76,78-79.

Cowgill, Donald O. 1941. *Mobile Homes: A Study of Trailer Life.* Ph.D. dissertation. University of Pennsylvania.

Cummings, Elaine, and William Henry. 1961. *Growing Old: The Process of Disengagement.* New York: Basic Books.

Curtin, Richard. 1994. *The RV Consumer: A Demographic Profile.* Reston, VA: Recreational Vehicle Industry Association.

Darby, Orrill. 1986. Different Viewpoints: Thoughts on Full-time RV'ing. *Escapees Newsletter* 7(5): 12.

———. 1988. SKPs Compare Budgets: Boondocker's Budget. *Escapees Newsletter* 10(1): 6.

Davis, Richard H., and James A. Davis. 1985. *TV's Image of the Elderly: A Practical Guide for Change.* Lexington, MA: D.C. Heath and Company.

Dawson, Ann. 1995. Letter to Road Roamer News. *Escapees Magazine for Serious Rvers* 16(4): 59.

Diamond, Marian Cleves. 1988. *Enriching Heredity: The Impact of the Environment on the Anatomy of the Brain.* New York: The Free Press.

Douglas, Mary. 1991. The Idea of Home: A Kind of Space. *Social Research* 58 (1): 287-307.

Drury, Margaret. 1972. *Mobile Homes: The Unrecognized Revolution in American Housing.* New York: Praeger.

Eberhard, Eldon, and Ramona Eberhard. 1986. Different Viewpoints: Applauding Our Lifestyle. *Escapees Newsletter* 7(4): 11.

Edington, Mutt, and Dottie Edington. 1983-84. Letter to Road Roamer News *Escapees Newsletter* 5(3): 23-31.

Edwards, Beverly. 1991. It Was a Very Good Year. *Highways* 25 (4): 14,52-55.

Errington, Frederick. 1990. The Rock Creek Rodeo: Excess and Constraint in Men's Lives. *American Ethnologist* 17(4): 628-45.

Editor, *Canadian Social Trends.* 1992. Preface comment to Well-being of Older Canadians, by Julie Keith and Laura Landry. *Canadian Social Trends* No. 25: 16-17.

Escapees, Inc. 1994a. KOFA Ko-Op: Yuma, Arizona. *Parking Directory and Organizer.* Livingston, Texas: RoVing Press. 36

———. 1994b. Overnight Parking for SKP's With SKP's. *Parking Directory and Organizer.* Livingston, Texas: RoVing Press. 103-25.

Escapees Newsletter. 1983. SKP Retreat Report. *Escapees Newsletter* 5(2): 17.

———. 1984a. SKP Report 5(4): 16.

———. 1984b. Cartoon. *Escapees Newsletter* 6(1): 21.

———. 1986a. On the Light Side. *Escapees Newsletter* 8(1): 37.

———. 1986b. Special Contest. *Escapees Newsletter* 8(3): 3.

———. 1987. News Flash!! The Slabs Goes On. *Escapees Newsletter* 9(3): 44.

———. 1991. Rainbow Builders. *Escapees Newsletter* 12(4): 6.

———. 1994. Declare your Independence with TLC. *Escapees Newsletter* 15 (4): 7.

Escapees Website, July 28, 2000. *www.escapees.com/website/how.htm*

Evans, Bergen (ed.) 1978. *Dictionary of Quotations.* New York: Avenel.

Farlow, Bill. 1995 Summary of RV Features Survey at Spring Escapade 1994. *Escapees Magazine for RVers* 17(2): 20-21.

Farris, Ken. 1995. A "Cool" Custom Battery Box. *Trailer Life* 55(5): 91-94.

Fernandez, James W. 1971. Persuasions and Performances: Of the Beast in Every Body ... and the Metaphors of Everyman. In *Myth, Symbol and Culture*, Clifford Geertz, ed. New York: W.W. Norton. 39-60.

Financial Post. 1954 (April 10). New Trailer Coach Association Champion for "Trailerites." *Financial Post* 48: 36.

Finn, Jean-Guy. Deputy Minister, Health and Comunity Services, Province of New Brunswick. 1995, July 19. Personal correspondence.

Freese, Al, and Trudy Freese. 1986. Different Viewpoints: Are SKP's Really a Family? *Escapees Newsletter* 8(2): 18-19.

Friedan, Betty. 1993. *The Fountain of Age* (Special Reader's Edition). New York: Simon and Schuster.

Fries, James F. 1990. Medical Perspectives Upon Successful Aging. In *Successful Aging: Perspectives from the Behavioral Sciences.* Paul B. Baltes and Margret M. Baltes, eds. Cambridge: Cambridge University Press. 35-49.

Gates, Davida (Pete). 1999. We Try to Help, Too! *Escapees for the Serious RVer* 20(6): 9.

———. 2000 What CARE Taught Me. *Escapees for the Serious RVer* 22(2): 48.

Gibb, Ron, and Moira Gibb. 1987. Letter to Road Roamer News. *Escapees Newsletter* 8 (5): 29-37.

Gifford, C.G. 1990. *Canada's Fighting Seniors.* Toronto: James Lorimer.

Giltrow, Janet. 1995. Introduction to "They're My Family Now": The Creation of Community Among RVers. In *Academic Reading.* Janet Giltrow, ed. Peterborough, ON: Broadview. 49-51.

Gobar, Bob, and Jinny Gobar. 1988. Letter to Road Roamer News. *Escapees Newsletter* 10(2): 39.

Goddard, Lucille. 1983. Russell's Story. *Escapees Newsletter* 4(5): 4.

Goff, Kristin. 1992 (April 14). Snowbirds Put on Residency Alert: Could Lose OHIP Coverage. *The Spectator.* 14 April: A1-A2. Story originated in *The Ottawa Citizen* April 14, 1992 under the title Time out: Ontario "Snowbirds" Fly Afoul of OHIP's Tougher Residency Rules.

Graham, Ed. 1993. Note in Road Roamer News. *Escapees Newsletter* 14(6): 48-54.

Granick, Samuel, and Robert D. Patterson. 1971. *Human Aging II: An Eleven-Year Biomedical and Behavioral Study.* US Public Health Service Monograph. Washington, DC: US Government Printing Office.

Green, Magda. 1993. A View From the Boomer's Site. *Escapees Newsletter* 14(6): 26-27.

Grieg, Frank, and Iris Grieg. 1989. Canadian's Budget. *Escapees Newsletter* 11(1): 11.

Gropper, Rena C. 1975. *Gypsies in the City: Culture Patterns and Survival.* Princeton, NJ: The Darwin Press.

Guinn, Robert. 1980. Elderly Recreational Vehicle Tourists: Life Satisfaction Correlates of Leisure Satisfaction. *Journal of Leisure Research* 10: 198-204.

Harris, Louis and Associates. 1994. *Consumer Perceptions of Recreation Vehicles: A Communications Planning Study Based on Surveys of Prospective and Current Owners*. Conducted for the Recreation Vehicle Industry Association. NY: Louis Harris and Associates, Inc.

Hartwigsen, Gail, and Roberta Null. 1989. Full-timing: A Housing Alternative For Older People. *International Journal of Aging and Human Development* 29: 317-28.

———. 1990. Full-timers: Who Are These Older People Living in Their RVs? *Journal of Housing for The Elderly* 7(1): 133-47.

Harvey, R. H. Executive Director, Insured Benefits Branch, Department of Health, Province of Manitoba. 1995, July 20. Personal correspondence.

Hazzard, Bill, and Jeannie Hazzard. 1987. Different Viewpoints: Spreading the word on Escapees. *Escapees Newsletter* 9(1): 22.

Health and Welfare Canada. 1982. *Suicide Among the Aged in Canada*. Ottawa: Policy and Information Branch.

———. 1993 *Canada Health Act Annual Report 1992-93*. Cat. H1-4/1993. Ottawa: Minister of Supply and Services, Ottawa.

Henley, Archie, and Sylvia Henley. 1987. Letter to Road Roamer News. *Escapees Newsletter* 8(6): 29-37.

Highways. 1991. Mr. Good Sam: A Conversation With Art Rouse. *Highways* 25(4): 18, 55+.

———. 1993. Newsline: Medical Panel Reports Health Benefits in Travel. *Highways* 27(9): 13.

———. 1994 (November). Marathon XLV/Prevost Bus. *Highways*.

Hofmeister, Ron, and Barb Hofmeister. 1992. *An Alternative Lifestyle*. Livingston, TX: R and B Publications.

———. 1999. *Move'n On: Living and Traveling Full-Time in a Recreatonal Vehicle*. 3rd ed. Livingston, TX: R and B Publications.

Hogan, Timothy. 1987. Determinants of the Seasonal Migration of the Elderly to Sunbelt States. *Research on Aging* 9(1): 115-33.

Hoyt, G.C. 1954. The Life of the Retired in a Trailer Park. *American Journal of Sociology* 19: 361- 370.

Institute of Medicine (US) Division of Health Promotion and Disease Prevention. 1990. *The Second Fifty Years: Promoting Health and Preventing Disability*. Washington, DC: National Academy Press.

Ivy, Carol. 1983. Loners on Wheels. *Modern Maturity* February-March: 54-55.

Jacobs, Jerry. 1974. *Fun City: An Ethnography of a Retirement Community*. New York: Holt Rinehart and Winston.

Joens, Ray D. 1991. Good Samaritan Decal. *Highways* 25(4): 4 (originally published June 1966 in *Trail-R-News*).

Johnson, H. Maurice. 1989. Rebuttal to Self-protection for RVers: Are RV Guns NECESSARY? *Escapees Newsletter* 10 (6): 22.

Johnson, Jim, and Joyce Johnson. 1993. Full-time RVing for Canadians. *Escapees Newsletter* 14(6): 42-43.

Julkowski, Ev, and Margaret Julkowski. 1985. Editorial. *Escapees Newsletter* 6 (4): 25.

Jury, Florence. 1930. Camping With a Car: Practical Suggestions for the Holidays. *The Chatelaine* 3(5): 52-53.

Just, Susan. 1995. Pioneering bloodlines. *Escapees Magazine for RVers* 17(1): 20-21.

Kaplan, M.S., M.E. Adamek, and S. Johnson. 1994. Trends in Firearm Suicide Among Older American Males: 1979-1988. *The Gerontologist* 34(1): 59-65.

Kaufman, Sharon R. 1986. *The Ageless Self: Sources of Meaning in Later Life*. Madison: University of Wisconsin Press.

Keating, Bern. 1988 (March). Recreational Vehicles: Ode to the Road. *50 Plus*: 26-29, 82-83.

Keith, Julia, and Laura Landry. 1992. Well-being of Older Canadians. *Canadian Social Trends* No. 25: 16-17.

Kornow, Susie. 1993. Results of 1992 Survey (Based on 6,055 responses). *Escapees Newsletter* 15(2): 7.

Kuhl, Julius. 1986. Aging and Models of Control: The Hidden Costs of Wisdom. In *The Psychology of Control and Aging*. Margaret M. Baltes and Paul B. Baltes, eds. Hillsdale, NJ: Lawrence Erlbaum Associates. 1-34.

Labouvie-Vief, Gisela. 1985. Intelligence and Cognition. In *Handbook of the Psychology of Aging*. 2nd ed. J.E. Birren and K.W. Schaie, eds. New York: Van Nostrand Reinhold. 500-30.

Lachman, Margie E. 1986. Personal Control in Later Life: Stability, Change, and Cognitive Correlates. In *The Psychology of Control and Aging*. Margaret M. Baltes and Paul B. Baltes, eds. Hillsdale, NJ: Lawrence Erlbaum Associates. 207-36.

Lacy, Gene. 2000 CARE, a Unique Facility. *Escapees for the Serious RVer* 22(1): 78.

Lamarche, Robert, and Jacques Langlois. 1987. Earning Money. *Trailer Life* 47:60-61: 144-54.

Langer, Ellen J. *et al.* 1990. Nonsequential Development and Agency In *Higher Stages of Human Development*. Charles N. Alexander and Ellen J. Langer, eds. New York: Oxford University Press. 114-36.

Lanier, Bob, and Mary Lanier. 1988. Letter to Road Roamer News. *Escapees Newsletter* 9(5): 33-45.

LeDrew, Marjorie. 1992. Alone But No Longer Lonely. *RV Traveller for the Canadian Camper* 16(2): 38,42.

Lepowsky, Maria. 1994a. Writing for Many Audiences. *Anthropology Newsletter* 35(8): 48.

———. 1994b. An Anthropologist in Media Land. *Anthropology Newsletter* 35(9): 27.

———. 1994c *Fruit of the Motherland: Gender in an Egalitarian Society*. New York: Columbia University Press.

———. 1995. Getting the Word Out. *Anthropology Newsletter* 36(1): 37,47.

Loners of America News. 1994. What Loners of America is About. *Loners of America News* 7(1): 16.

Loners on Wheels. 1994. Statement of Purpose. *Loners on Wheels* 24(3): 2.

Lusk, Norman M. 1991. Letter to Mail Box. *Trailer Life* 51 (6): 19.

Maclean, John P. 1956. Be it Ever So Mobile This is Luxury Home. *Financial Post* June 23: 31.

Maclean's Magazine. 1958 (January 4). The Brave New World of Trailer Living. *Maclean's Magazine* 71: 10-11, 30-31.

Marcus, George E., and Michael M.J. Fischer. 1986. *Anthropology as Cultural Critique: An Experimental Moment in the Human Sciences*. Chicago: The University of Chicago Press.

Marple, Al. 1990. Letter to the Editor, *Sierra Star*, March 15, 1990. Reprinted in *A Dream Come True: A History of the SKP Park of the Sierra, Coarsegold, California. October 1984 to November 1991*. Lois Collins ed. Mountain View, CA: The Printing Club, 1992. 9.

McDonald, P. Lynn, and Richard A. Wanner. 1990. *Retirement in Canada*. Toronto: Butterworths.

McIntosh, John L. 1992. Epidemiology of Suicide in the Elderly. In *Suicide and the Older Adult*, Antoon A. Leenaars, Ronald Maris, John L. McIntosh and Joseph Richman, eds. New York: The Guilford Press. 15-35.

McKie, Craig. 1993 (Summer). Population Aging: Baby Boomers Into the 21st Century. *Canadian Social Trends* No. 29: 2-6.

Minkler, Meredith. 1981. Research on the Health Effects of Retirement: An Uncertain Legacy. *Journal of Health and Social Behavior* 22: 117-30.

Mochrie, John A. Chair, Medical Services Commission, Province of British Columbia. 1995, July 25. Personal correspondence.

Moeller, Bill, and Jan Moeller. 1986. *Full Time RVing: A Complete Guide to Life on the Open Road*. Agoura, CA: Trailer Life Books.

———. 1998. *Full Time Rving*. Agoura, CA: Trailer Life Books

Moon, William Least Heat. 1982. *Blue Highways: A Journey into America*. Boston: Little Brown.

Morris, William, ed. 1982. *The Houghton Mifflin Canadian Dictionary of the English Language*. Markham, ON: Houghton Mifflin.

Morton, Paul. 1986. On the Light Side. *Escapees Newsletter* 8(1): 37.

Muncy, Archer. 1987. Letter in Special Birthday Letters. *Escapees Newsletter* 9(1): 26-29.

Murphy, Marilyn. 1992. Roam Sweet Home. *Ms.* May/June: 42-45.

Myerhoff, Barbara. 1978. *Number Our Days*. New York: Simon and Schuster Touchstone Books.

Nash, C.E. 1937. *Trailer Ahoy*. Lancaster, PA: Intelligencer Printing Co.

National Advisory Council on Aging (NACA). 1990. *Understanding Seniors' Independence. Report No. 2: Coping Strategies*. Ottawa: Government of Canada.

Neuhaus, Polly. 1986. Letter to Road Roamer News. *Escapees Newsletter* 7(5): 26.

Newman, Peter C. 1954 (August 14). Rolling Bungalow: Today's Prairie Schooner. *Financial Post* 48: 13.

Oliver, Paul. 1987. *Dwellings: The House Across the World*. Oxford: Phaidon Press.

Ontario, Government. 1991a. English Index. *Revised Statutes of Ontario 1990*. Toronto: Queen's Printer for Ontario.

———. 1991b *Revised Statutes of Ontario 1990*.Vol 5. Chapter H.6 s.1 Toronto: Queen's Printer for Ontario.

Orlean, Susan. 1995. Popular Chronicles: We Just Up and Left. *New Yorker* 12 June: 48-51, 63-65.

Ortner, Sherry B. 1973. On Key Symbols. *American Anthropologist* 75: 1338-46.

Parrack, Judy. 1988. Letter to Road Roamer news. *Escapees Newsletter* 10(1): 41.

Patterson, Robert D., Leo C. Freeman, and Robert N. Butler. 1971. Psychiatric Aspects of Adaptation, Survival, and Death. In *Human Aging II: An Eleven-Year Biomedical and Behavioral Study*. Samuel Granick and Robert D. Patterson, eds. US Public Health Service Monograph. Washington, DC: US Government Printing Office. 63-94.

Pease, Mary Agnes. 1930 (July). Gypsying With a Caravan. *The Chatelaine* 3: 12, 53.

Peeples, Bill, and Susan Peeples. 1989. Letter in Road Roamer News. *Escapees Newsletter* 10 (6): 35-46.

Peters, Helen. 1986. Shifting Gears: "Children of the Rainbow." *Escapees Newsletter* 8(3): 15.

Peterson, Joe. 1991. Other Clubs: WOW. *Escapees Newsletter* 12(5): 17.

———. 1994. Answering Your Questions. *Escapees Newsletter* 15(4): 8.

———. 1995. Alliance Between Escapees, Inc. of the USA and International Caravanning Association (ICA). *Escapees Magazine for RVers* 16(6): 56.

Peterson, Joe, and Kay Peterson. 1991. *Survival of the Snowbirds* (New Revised Edition). Livingston, TX: RoVers Publications.

———. 1995. Is Boondocking Safe? *Escapees Magazine for RVers* 16(4): 16-17.

———. 1997 *The New Survival of the RV Snowbirds*. Livingston, TX: RoVers Publications.

Peterson, Kay. 1982. *Home is Where You Park It* (New Revised Edition). Livingston, TX: RoVers Publications. First edition published 1977 by Follet Publishing Company, Chicago.

———. 1983. Editorial *Escapees Newsletter* 5(2): 2.

———. 1984. History of Escapees. *Escapees Newsletter* 6(1): 7.

———. 1985. Editorial. *Escapees Newsletter* 6 (4): 2.

———. 1986a Answering Your Questions. *Escapees Newsletter* 8(1): 3.

———. 1986b. Editorial. *Escapees Newsletter* 8(1): 2.

———. 1987a. When Dreams Collide. *Escapees Newsletter* 8(4): 16-17.

———. 1987b. Looking Back. *Escapees Newsletter* 9(1): 24.

———. 1989. Editorial *Escapees Newsletter* 10(5): 3.

———. 1990. *Home is Where You Park It*. Livingston, TX: RoVers Publications.

———. 1991a Editorial. *Escapees Newsletter* 12(6): 4.

———. 1991b. Overnight Boondocking. *Escapees Newsletter* 12(6): 10.

———. 1992. Escapees Celebrates 14th Birthday. *Escapees Newsletter* 14(1): 4-6.

———. 1993a. Looking Back. *Escapees Newsletter* 15 (1): 5.

———. 1993b. Editorial *Escapees Newsletter* 15(1): 4.

———. 1995a. Escapees History in Brief. *Escapees Magazine for RVers* 17(1): 14.

———. 1995b. From Auto Gypsies to Modern RVers. *Escapees Magazine for RVers* 17(1): 8-9.

———. 1995c. Thoughts For the Road: RVers Make Every Place They Go Home. *Escapees for the Serious RVer* 17(3): 2.

———. 1996a. CARE Program Moves Forward. *Escapees for the Serious RVer* 17 (4): 7.

———. 1996b. CARE Report. *Escapees for the Serious RVer* 17 (6): 4-5.

———. 1999. CARE Report. *Escapees for the Serious RVer* 21(1): 30-31.

Peterson, Kay, and Todd Paddock. 1998. *History of the Escapees Club in Prose and Pictures*. Livingston, TX: RoVers Publications.

Petit, Charles. 1996 (November 12). Happy Campers. *San Francisco Chronicle* A1, A12.

Pike, Louise. 1985 (May/June). Different Viewpoints: To Hug or Not to Hug? *Escapees Newsletter* 6 (5): 12.

Pilisuk, Marc, and Meredith Minkler. 1980. Supportive Networks: Life Ties for the Elderly. *The Journal of Social Issues* 36(2): 95-116.

Phillips, Ray. 1992. Letter to Good Sam Grapevine. *Highways* 26(3): 8.

Polk County Chamber of Commerce. n.d. (obtained November, 1993). *Polk County Chamber of Commerce Membership Directory*. Livingston, Texas.

Popcorn, Faith. 1991. *The Popcorn Report*. New York: Doubleday Currency.

Porter, Paula, and Peter Porter. 1991. We Said Yes to the RV Lifestyle. *RV Buyers Guide* 19(7): 8-10, 13, 16.

Potter, Bill. 1993. Working on the Road. *Escapees Newsletter* 14(4): 15.

Powell, Arden Giampaolo. 1993. Getting Started. *Trailer Life* 53(7): 61-66.

Priest, Gordon E. 1993. Seniors 75+: Living Arrangements. *Canadian Social Trends* No. 30: 24-25.

Prince, Dorothy. 1990. Other RV Groups. *Escapees Newsletter* 11(4): 47.

Prussin, Labell. 1989. The Architecture of Nomadism: Gabra Placemaking and Culture. In *Housing, Culture and Design*. Setha M. Low and Erve Chambers, eds. Philadelphia: University of Pennsylvania Press. 141-64.

Randolph, Pauline. 1995. Letter to Road Roamer News. *Escapees Magazine for RVers* 16 (4): 61.

Rawles, Graham. 1987. A Place to Call Home. In *Handbook of Clinical Gerontology*. Laura L. Carstensen and Barry A. Edelstein, eds. New York: Pergamon Press. 335-53.

Recreation Vehicle Industry Association (RVIA). n.d.a *Research-based Talking Points for Industry Spokespeople*. Reston, VA: RVIA.

———. n.d.b RV *Types and Terms* (1 page).

———. 1992. News.

———. 1994. *Information Sources: Camping and the RV Lifestyle*. PO Box 2999, Reston VA.

Reed, Dee. 1996 (February). Never Too Old to Learn. *Highways*: 25-27, 64.

Reimer, Marie. 1992, September. Letters to the Editor. *Speak E-Z*. Sierra Oaks, CA: Park of the Sierra.

Rensen, Jerry. 1988. Reminiscin' with Rensen. *Escapees Newsletter* 10(1): 2.

Rifkin, Jeremy. 1995. *The End of Work*. New York: G.P. Putnam's Sons.

Risch, Mort, and Zela Risch. 1984-85. Different Strokes. *Escapees Newsletter* 6(3): 12.

Rod and Gun in Canada. 1960. New Look in Travel. *Rod and Gun in Canada*. 61(8): 14.

Rodin, Judith, and Ellen Langer. 1977. Long-term Effects of a Control-relevant Intervention With the Institutionalized Aged. *Journal of Personality and Social Psychology* 35(12): 897-902.

———. 1980. Aging Labels: The Decline of Control and the Fall of Self-esteem. *Journal of Social Issues* 36(2): 12-29.

Rowe, John W., and Robert L. Kahn. 1987. Human Aging: Usual and Successful. *Science* 237(48II): 143-49.

Ruth, Harold C. 1984. Different Viewpoints: Are You a Cheapskate? *Escapees Newsletter* 5(6): 19.

Sahlins, Marshall. 1972a. On the Sociology of Primitive Exchange. *Stone Age Economics*. Chicago: Aldine. 185-275.

———. 1972b. The Original Affluent Society. *In Stone Age Economics*. Chicago: Aldine. 1-40.

Sartre, Jean-Paul. 1956. *Being and Nothingness*. Hazel Barnes, trans. New York: Washington Square Press.

Savishinsky, Joel. 1995. The Unbearable Lightness of Retirement: Ritual and Support in a Modern Life Passage. *Research on Aging* 17 (3): 243-59.

Schulz, Richard. 1976. Effects of Control and Predictability on the Physical and Psychological Well-being of the Institutionalized Aged. *Journal of Personality and Social Psychology* 33(5): 563-73.

Segal, Donna A. Director, Ministry of Health, Province of Ontario. 1995, August 4. Personal correspondence.

Smith, Naomi. 1990. Bare Bones Budget: Living on $326 per Month. *Escapees Newsletter* 12(2): 8.

Smith, Steve. 1991. What Do My SKP Dues Buy? *Escapees Newsletter* 12(4): 19.

Spoerl, Ed. 1988. Letter to Road Roamer News *Escapees Newsletter* 10(1): 43.

Statistics Canada. 1993a. *Population Ageing and the Elderly: Current Demographic Analysis.* Cat. 91-533E Occasional. Ottawa: Statistics Canada, Demographic Division.

———. 1993b. Seniors 75+: Living Arrangements and Lifestyles. *Canadian Social Trends* No. 30:23.

Stehlik, Dick, and Pat Stehlik. 1984. Road Roamer News. *Escapees Newsletter* 5(6): 29.

Steinfeld, Edward. 1981. The Place of Old Age: The Meaning of Housing for Old People. In *Housing and Identity: Cross-cultural Perspectives.* James S. Duncan, ed. London: Croom Helm. 198-246.

Sullaway, John, ed. 1992. Newsline: Study Debunks Senior Driving Myth. *Highways* 26(10): 16.

Sutherland, Anne. 1975. *Gypsies: The Hidden Americans.* London: Tavistock.

Sway, Marleney. 1988. *Familiar Strangers: Gypsy Life in America.* Urbana and Chicago: University of Illinois Press.

Taylor, Peter Shawn. 1995. Grandma! Grandpa! Back to Work. *Saturday Night* 110(5): 18-23, 96.

Tinseth, phred [sic.]. 1984. Don't Call it Boondocking. *Escapees Newsletter* 5(5): 6-7.

Thornburg, David. 1991. *Galloping Bungalows: The Rise and Demise of the American House Trailer.* Camden, CT: Archon Books: Shoestring Press.

Toronto *Globe and Mail.* 1940. Trailerites Are Told to Vacate or Face City Prosecution. 2 May 1940: 4.

———. 1941. You'd Like Forest Hill Better, Township Tells Trailer Group. 14 November 1941: 25.

———. 1945a. Woman, 62, and Her Caravan Part of Cargo for Alaska. 3 October 1945: 3.

———. 1945b. Board of Control Orders Removal of Trailer Camp. 31 October 1945: 4.

———. 1947. "Trailerites May Get New Site Next Week" 31 October 1947: 5.

Townsend, Harold E., and Deanne M. Townsend. 1991. *The Whaddaya-mean Leave-home-and-travel For-the rest-of-my-life!* Book. Fowlerville, MI: Wilderness Adventure Books.

Trailer Life. 1988. The View From the Driver's Seat. *Trailer Life* 48(11): 7, 165, 169.

———. 1991 Special Section. *Trailer Life* 51(7): 27-71.

Van Note, Robert. 1990. Letter to Mail Box: Whippersnappers' Complaint. *Trailer Life* 50(11): 144.

Wallis, Allan D. 1991. *Wheel Estate.* New York and Oxford: Oxford University Press.

Weston, Dave. 1986. Different Viewpoints: SKP Co-Op Concept. *Escapees Newsletter* 8(1): 13.

Wiersma, Velma. 1989. Six-Month Budget. *Escapees Newsletter* 19(5): 8-9.

Wolf, Christine. 1992. Full-timers Not Old-timers. Cincinnati: *Cincinnati Enquirer* 13 August. C-1, C-5.

Wright, Don. 1990. *Don Wright's Guide to Free Campgrounds.* 6th ed. Elkhart, IN: Cottage Publications.

Youmans, E. Grant, and Marian Yarrow: 1971 Aging and Social Adaptation: A Longitudinal Study of Healthy Old Men. In *Human Aging II: An Eleven-Year Biomedical and Behavioral Study.* Samuel Granick and Robert D. Patterson, eds. US Public Health Service Monograph. Washington, DC: US Government Printing Office. 95-104.

WIN. 1994. Cartoon. *The WINdow* 6(6): 4.

Internet Resources

Websites and webpages

Boondockers http://clubs.yahoo.com/clubs/boondocking
www.boondockingguide.com

Escapes RV club www.escapees.com

Families on the Road www.familiesontheroad.com

Family Camping and RVers club (FCRV) www.fcrv.org

Family Motor Coach Association www.fmca.com

Good Sam Club www.goodsamclub.com

Health Canada www.hc-sc.gc.ca/medicare/plans.htm

Loners of America (LOA) www.napanet.net/~mbost/

Loners on Wheels (LoW) www.lonersonwheels.com

National African American RVers Association (NAARVA) www.naarva.com

Recreation Vehicle Industry Association www.rvia.com

RV Club www.rvclub.com

RV Consumer's Group www.rversonline.org

RVing Women www.rvingwomen.com

Special Military Active Retired Travel (S*M*A*R*T) www.smartrvclub.org

Wayfarer Explorer RV club (for Canadians www.explorer-rvclub.com

West New Britain http://arts.uwaterloo.ca/ANTHRO/WNB/WestNewBritain.html

Woodalls www.woodalls.com/camp101/camp101.html

Workers On Wheels www.workersonwheels.com

RV rentals — several webpages

www.rvamerica.com/rentals

www.rvrent.com

www.rv-rentals.net

Canadian Motorhome and RV rentals home page www.candan.com

Cruise America www.cruiseamerica.com

www.rvnetlinx.com/rentals.htm

www.rvamerica.com/rentals/canada.htm

www.vellner.com

Index